"Brilliantly researched, revealing new material and interviews, and grippingly written with insight and understanding, this searing biography of a complex individual should be compulsory reading."
—ANNE SEBBA, *New York Times* bestselling author of *Les Parisiennes*

"A distinctive contribution to Holocaust studies, Eischeid's significant biography of Maria Mandl will offer page-turning insight about the Holocaust and humanity."
—JOHN K. ROTH, author of *Sources of Holocaust Insight*

"Susan Eischeid's new biography of the chief female guard of the Women's Camp at Auschwitz-Birkenau affords the reader a glimpse of how the Nazi female perpetrators participated in that 'terror state.'"
—DANIEL PATRICK BROWN, author of *The Camp Women: Female Auxiliaries Who Assisted the SS in Running the Nazi Concentration Camp System*

"Eischeid's book will make you a stronger parent, teacher, friend, and social justice advocate. It will move you closer to being your best self."
—SARA LAMBERT BLOOM, oboist, educator, recording artist, author of *The Robert Bloom Collection*

"Fascinating and unflinching, *Mistress of Life and Death* draws on powerful sources and original research to scrutinize the complexities of a notorious Nazi criminal. An important addition to the growing body of work about female perpetrators in the Third Reich."
—LUCY ADLINGTON, author of *The Dressmakers of Auschwitz: The True Story of the Women Who Sewed to Survive*

"A masterful, deeply researched, and painstaking account of Maria Mandl's life, her rise as head overseer of the women's camp at Auschwitz-Birkenau, and her eventual descent as a war criminal. Eischeid has drawn an indelible and detailed portrait of a terrifying enigma, giving us a timely biography at a moment when modern history threatens to repeat itself."

> —GINA ROITMAN, author of *Don't Ask;* subject and co-producer of the award-winning documentary film *My Mother, the Nazi Midwife, and Me*

"These staggering pages, the culmination of more than two decades' work, include research avenues beyond standard expectations. This is not only a book for students of the Holocaust and its lessons, but one every denier should read."

> —ALISON OWINGS, author of *Frauen: German Women Recall the Third Reich*

"Eischeid reveals in impressive breadth and detail the story of one of the most horrific female SS overseers that existed during the Nazi era. The book is brilliantly and accurately researched. Do we need to know all this? Yes, we must, because we must NEVER forget what happened."

> —STEFAN HEUCKE, composer of the opera *Das Frauenorchester von Auschwitz*

"In this revealing and riveting story of Maria Mandl, we are captivated and intrigued by a woman who was responsible for some of the greatest war crimes in our recent history."

> —FRANCINE ZUCKERMAN, producer/director, Z Films

"Maria Mandl's actions as a concentration camp guard are a stark reminder of the brutality and inhumanity of the Holocaust and serve as a testament to the importance of remembering and studying this dark period in human history."

> —PHILIPPE KAHN, inventor, scientist, and creator of the first camera-phone

Mistress of Life and Death

THE DARK JOURNEY OF MARIA MANDL, HEAD OVERSEER OF THE WOMEN'S CAMP AT AUSCHWITZ-BIRKENAU

Susan J. Eischeid

CITADEL PRESS
Kensington Publishing Corp.
www.kensingtonbooks.com

CITADEL PRESS BOOKS are published by

Kensington Publishing Corp.
119 West 40th Street
New York, NY 10018

All Kensington titles, imprints, and distributed lines are available at special quantity discounts for bulk purchases for sales promotions, premiums, fund-raising, educational, or institutional use. Special book excerpts or customized printings can also be created to fit specific needs. For details, write or phone the office of the Kensington sales manager: Kensington Publishing Corp., 119 West 40th Street, New York, NY 10018, attn: Sales Department; phone 1-800-221-2647.

CITADEL PRESS and the Citadel logo are Reg. U.S. Pat. & TM Off.

ISBN: 978-0-8065-4285-0

First printing: January 2024

10 9 8 7 6 5 4 3 2 1

Printed in the United States of America

Library of Congress Control Number: 2023944251

First electronic edition: January 2024

ISBN: 978-0-8065-4287-4

For those who had the courage to speak
And for all who suffered

Map of Europe, showing present-day borders and the towns and camps where Maria Mandl lived and worked. ILLUSTRATION BY NICKY BARNEBY.

Contents

PART FOUR

Author's Note

HER NAME WAS MARIA MANDL; her face—which later became as familiar to me as my own—was largely unknown. Her story, then and now, is couched in clichés and assumptions about good and evil.

Later, when I knew most everything about her, the effort of telling her story became even more daunting. How *does* one tell the tale of a murderer? Is it wrong to try to understand her actions from some previously assumed mantle of empathy? And how does one tell Maria's story with compassion without negating the very real suffering of her victims?

In *Mistress of Life and Death* the fabric of Maria's life is woven together, utilizing dozens of interviews with survivors, perpetrators, witnesses, and family members, and culminating in the hangman's noose.

By training and credentials I am a classical oboist who has always nurtured a strong interest in music and musicians of the Holocaust. When I first began to perform these compositions, I was awed by their power and grateful for my ability to return a voice to so many who had their own voices so cruelly and prematurely silenced. I was drawn to Mandl's story when I discovered her connections to the Auschwitz-Birkenau women's orchestra. It was my great pleasure and privilege to speak with several of the musicians from that orchestra, many of whom became very dear friends. Although most have now died, my life has been infinitely enriched by knowing them. I am honored that they trusted me with their memories.

What factors led Maria Mandl to follow the path into atrocity and evil? This larger question soon took precedence and became the strongest impetus behind *Mistress of Life and Death*. Maria was not *intrinsically* evil, but for her—and so many others—the path toward evil was a slippery slope of frightening ease.

Thanks to the work of scholars such as James Waller and Christopher Browning, we now recognize many of the factors that can cause an erosion of morality and culpability. Nonetheless, there have always been people who act ethically despite external negative influences of community, government, and family. Why do some turn to evil while others do not? By focusing on this *one* life and fully exploring Mandl's transformation, I have sought to provide a greater understanding of what is, perhaps, an unanswerable conundrum.

Ultimately, Maria's life journey encompasses the eternal questions of right versus wrong, good versus evil, and the paradox of how cruelty and compassion can exist in the same person. It reveals how easily even the most unlikely person among us can be influenced toward evil in a climate of hate and fear.

This book is the result of a mutual journey of discovery, hers and mine. I trust and hope I have done it justice.

If only there were evil people somewhere insidiously committing evil deeds, and it were necessary only to separate them from the rest of us and destroy them. But the line dividing good and evil cuts through the heart of every human being. And who is willing to destroy a piece of his own heart?

—ALEKSANDR SOLZHENITSYN,
THE GULAG ARCHIPELAGO

Maria
September 1946

"NAZI WHORES! MURDERERS! KILL THEM!" The roars of the crowd out-side the train were like crazed beasts; insensate, rabid. Fists pounded on the passenger car where the terrified prisoners huddled. American guards laughed at their agitation, mocking and encouraging the horde outside. Several threatened to throw the female overseers to the wolves, as surely as those very overseers had thrown other women into crematory ovens—some with their own hands, others by their order.

The air was thick with fear and sullied by the smell of acrid perspiration. The car swayed slightly as the enraged crowd sought entry, emboldened and strengthened by their hate. Suddenly a contorted face thudded into the window, savage, bestial, inhuman. A piercing howl accompanied its appearance as it fell back to the ground.

One of the prisoners, Maria Mandl, began to hyperventilate and suddenly fumbled her way into the attached toilet cubicle. Quickly, before the guards could intervene, she swallowed a handful of hidden pills.

Shivering, heaving, covered with cold sweat and bleeding from the mouth, Maria began to convulse. Now swarmed by guards and the other women, she was forced to vomit up the poison.

Huddled on the floor in a fetal position, kicked by the guards in their anger, the world went black as Maria muttered, "God protect me."

Part One

CHAPTER 1

Hometown

THE WOMAN WHO ATTEMPTED SUICIDE on an extradition train in 1946 was guilty of many things: mass murder, atrocity, torture, and pitilessness in the face of suffering. She was also a lover of music, children, and family, and founded an orchestra in the unlikeliest of places—the death camp known as Auschwitz-Birkenau.

In her youth Maria Mandl was often described as a nice girl from a good family. Ultimately, like so many of her contemporaries, she was led astray by a thirst for power and visibility and took full advantage of the new opportunities which arose, even for a woman, in the Third Reich. Had Adolf Hitler never created the Nazi state, Maria surely would have lived out her life as a girl from a small town, unremarkable and unknown. Instead, she is now recognized as one of the worst perpetrators of the Holocaust.

Maria's story began modestly, when she was born in January 1912 in the beautiful Austrian village of Münzkirchen. Then, she was simply a country girl from a good family and there were few portents that signified she would one day become the most infamous member of her community.

Today Münzkirchen is a bustling regional presence. Founded in the Middle Ages, the town has always been a prosperous place for small business. In many ways Münzkirchen appears now as it did in Maria's lifetime. The community is surrounded by verdant rolling hills interspersed with dense dark green pines which stab the landscape. Beautiful ivory-colored homes with red-and-brown tile roofs fill the city center, while the agricultural roots of the area are much in evidence: chickens pecking about, the smell of manure in the air, giant rabbits bounding the surrounding fields—seemingly begging to become the next course of Hasenpfeffer (rabbit stew). Golden fields of corn and wheat shimmer in the sun; local roads are gorged with farm machinery.

True to its Catholic heritage the community boasts two churches: St. Sebastian's, the small branch church located on the outskirts of town, and a midtown parish church. The cemetery adjacent to St. Sebastian's is in many ways the spiritual center of Münzkirchen. Beautiful, meticulously tended graves tell the story of the village. Near the markers of people who died of plague in the Middle Ages is a general monument to all who were lost in various armed conflicts. Separate stones with discreet iron crosses mark soldiers who fought and died in the Second World War. The names and dates of villagers who were Maria's classmates are easily found. Many of the girls are also named Maria, and prominent surnames, still important in the community, recur.

The view is panoramic, the air melodic with birdsong. Bees buzz gently, a soft breeze rustles the leaves in the trees, a scent of honeysuckle is in the air. It is quiet and peaceful. Maria's parents are buried here, as are her brother and his wife. Their grave marker feels warm to the touch, alive.

In later years Maria would describe her early childhood and adolescence in Münzkirchen as "the most beautiful [time] of my life." The treasured and often spoiled youngest child in a family of four siblings, Maria thrived in the insular community. Her father, Franz Mandl, was an important man, a master shoemaker.

Franz's passport application from the 1930s reveals a man of stern visage, gazing challengingly into the camera with a slightly furrowed brow and a lean body, tanned and fit from hard work. His hair is closely cropped, his mustache small and defined, his ears well shaped and close to his head. Franz's suit coat, vest, and shirt are obviously well worn, but meticulously buttoned, pressed, and coordinated. His dark eyes are penetrating. In other images Franz is often shown with a work apron tied around his waist, arms prominent with ropey muscles, and a pipe in his mouth. The Mandl family grew their own tobacco for that pipe, later described by a grandson as not great quality but with a "*gute Duft*," a nice scent. Franz played the zither for relaxation, usually at the end of the day. He was undoubtedly the strongest influence on Maria and would remain so until her death. Later, in prison, Maria worried most about what her actions and fate were doing to her father.

Maria's mother, Anna Streibl, was the daughter of a country blacksmith from the nearby hamlet of Freundorf. Two years older than her husband, Anna suffered from depression throughout her lifetime.

Anna's passport image looks ineffably sad. Her face is careworn, her eyes haunted, moist, and overwhelmed by circumstance. Anna's hair is carefully slicked back and the posture of her body is beaten down, resigned. Within the Mandl family, Anna occupied a muted place. Plagued by illness, she was unable to cope with the realities and responsibilities of her life.

Shortly after the onset of menopause Anna had a nervous breakdown. Her depression accelerated, and she became irritable, short-tempered, and excessively sensitive to stimuli. Diagnosed with *Vervensach* (nerve disease) and other issues, Anna's final decline lasted seven years. Sadly, at that time and place, there were few treatments for what was labeled "evolutional melancholia" and she suffered greatly.

Despite this, Anna was well loved by her children. Maria once stated that, "[Although] my good mother was rarely approachable for us children, the doctor could not do very much about it. It had to get right again by itself. After that my good mother was for us the best on earth."

Throughout her life Anna remained devoutly Catholic. In later years, after Maria had begun her camp service at Auschwitz and changed in personality, Anna walked daily to Mass—praying for her daughter's eternal soul. She died before the end of the war, in 1944.

Anna and Franz's first child was a son named Georg, born in 1905. Seven years older than Maria, he remained the only boy in the family. Georg grew up to be a blond, muscular, and severe man, somewhat shorter than his father. In February of 1908 a daughter Anna was born, followed in 1909 by another daughter, Aloisia, nicknamed Loisi. Then, in 1912, Maria followed. She was a beautiful child, blond and well proportioned, with stunning light-colored eyes, who had inherited the high cheekbones and facial structure of her father.

The Mandl home, a large and sturdy house on Stiegl Street, had an attached barn, surrounding fields, and a beautiful view of the community. Franz Mandl was considered a very good friend who never quarreled with his neighbors.

Inside the home were spacious rooms with low ceilings. Franz's workshop and shoe store were located in the front, facing the street. A small room off the hallway stored leather used for the shoes. Farmers would bring partially cured skins from animals who had died or been slaughtered, and there was always "a certain odor from the fresh and salted animal hides" in the house. Decades later, in Birkenau, the scent of flesh in varying stages of decay would bring this smell back to Maria.

Franz was a fine craftsman and astute businessman. Men were employed as apprentices, to help in the store and with shoe manufacture. Additionally, they did odd jobs around the homestead and lived and ate with the family. One of his employees, who worked in Münzkirchen during Maria's childhood, described Franz Mandl as "strict, open, and fair. A man who treated everybody equally and was receptive to new ideas. An honorable man."

The Mandl homestead was also a working farm. Most people in the community, including the Mandls, grew food crops that could be stored throughout the winter: potatoes, parsley, red beets, cabbage, and carrots. Damp, cold cellars were used to keep the crops fresh, and root vegetables were laid in wet sand to preserve them. The Mandls had a pear tree in the yard, used for cider. Maria's chores included milking cows, making butter, caring for the poultry, and fetching fresh water from the pump.

An image from 1933 illustrates the hard labor needed to grow and harvest these crops. In an open field in front of a tree line, there is a large wooden wagon filled with hay pulled by a white ox. Franz and Georg Mandl buttress the sides of the wagon, leaning on their pitchforks and wearing sweat-soaked cotton shirts with sleeves rolled up on what is obviously a hot day. Both men are tanned and fit, and Georg has one hand cocked at his waist, gazing directly at the photographer, his blond hair and muscular frame hinting at physical power. Two of Franz's apprentices stand in the middle, drafted to help, likewise equipped with pitchforks. Atop the large mound of harvested hay sits Anna Mandl, Maria's sister, stabilizing the load.

The lifestyle was healthy and active. Children skied around the hills of Münzkirchen in the winter, and in the evening you could hear the drums and instruments of the town band rehearsing. It was a wonderful place to grow up.

Maria, like everyone else, was aware of the economic depression affecting Austria and Germany, but it had very little effect on her life. The farm fed the family, her father's business clothed them, her sisters protected and loved her. They were a nice family and she was a nice girl. A nice girl from a good family.

CHAPTER 2

Childhood

COURTESY OF MEMBERS OF THE MANDL FAMILY

EVERY SMALL TOWN HAS ITS own distinct rhythms and customs. While speaking with many of the current residents of Münz-kirchen, faces light up with memories, old conversations are recalled, stories—which have been handed down through generations—are shared.

For adults who came of age during the turbulent years of the Anschluss and the Second World War, who were Maria's classmates and
friends, life was not easy. This period and its hardships shaped everything they became. Their actions, in turn, left a lasting impact on
the community.

Details enliven our conversations, often shared in kitchens, a local
Gasthof (inn), on terraces, and—once—shouted out a second-story
window to the sidewalk below. A working farmer shyly relays his memories, dirt ingrained on hands hardened by years of toil, straw on his
shirt and shoes. We are offered Johannes berry torte and toast, spar-
kling water, and pear cider. Memories from parents and grandparents
abound about daily life in the insular community. Münzkirchen families were raised with these stories and are justifiably proud. These
memories are a gift, providing valuable insights into Maria's early life.

Many older adults speak of the local primary school, which is remembered with both fondness and shudders of trepidation. A
photograph from 1917, shortly before Maria's matriculation, reveals
a severe classroom and serious, well-behaved students with firmly
crossed arms on utilitarian wooden benches, girls on one side, boys
on the other. The girls are in braids, dresses, and pinafores, and the
boys wear jackets and shorts or pants. The teacher, Adolf Ilg, stands
sternly in the back, arms folded behind his body. All look intently
at the photographer.

Ilg was one of the teachers in the school during Maria's childhood.
It was common knowledge that Ilg often seemed more interested in
the small business he ran from his home, a kind of country general
store, than in his teaching. He would instruct the students to notify
their parents when new goods came in and urge them to shop in his
business.

Discipline was described as "very, very harsh – they hit the pupils!" That discipline carried over to academic subjects. Irmgard
Hunt, who grew up in a small village similar to Münzkirchen, remembered that "the proudest achievement of the day would be a
word of praise for a row of perfect letters that held strictly to the
limits of the three lines defining their lower, middle, and upper

spaces. *Schönschrift* [penmanship, literally 'beautiful script'] was an exacting art requiring rigorous training." She later summarized that "after all, '*Ordnung muss sein!* ['There must be order!')" Years later, when Maria was asked to write a pretrial deposition, that rigorous training in penmanship was still evident.

One of Maria's classmates, an older woman named Cäcilia, smiled while relating that if "the dumb boys" didn't know the answers, the teacher would take them by the back of the neck and force them to stand with their face to the blackboard in front of the class. She also feared Adolf Ilg as a strict taskmaster and remembers his detention of naughty students after school. That also meant those students got punished twice, first by Ilg and then at home by their parents. Students did not expect to play after school—they had to go home and do chores. If they were late, the whole rhythm of a household could be disrupted.

Cäcilia notes there was not a lot of contact between the children who lived in town and students who lived farther out. Her home was in a very rural area while Maria's was in the center of Münzkirchen and her family important in the community. Despite that, Cäcilia remembers that "Maria had a very nice face with red cheeks, [she was] a red-faced blond."

Most of the children would get one pair of shoes and wear them until their feet got too big and they would be handed down to other siblings. Franz Mandl made the shoes for Cäcilia's family after her father brought him the cured skin when an extra heavy pig was slaughtered.

Students attended school for just a half day, studying a variety of subjects. Boys got to participate in sports while girls mostly studied handcrafts: knitting, sewing, crocheting. Grade reports were sent home in a *Schulnachtrichtenbuch*, a small book with shiny green paper cover. Cäcilia still shows hers off proudly, revealing a string of *Sehr Gut* (Very Good) grades in all her subjects.

Most of the local children helped with farm work, and the more rural the family the greater their responsibility. Cäcilia cried when her parents held her out of school to help on the farm. One year alone she had sixty-six absences! A popular chore was for a child to lead the ox through the field as it was plowed. There were no real ball games, mostly they worked and had chores. Some children had a few marbles to play with.

As in many rural communities, the Catholic church and its services and celebrations dominated social and spiritual life. From an early age Münzkirchen children were taught basic Catholic fundamentals. Sunday Mass was an important part of the week—"you never missed church!" Many people in the community welcomed Sunday mornings; they didn't have to work, they could see others, there was a definite social component.

In 1919, when she was seven years old, Maria and her classmates received First Communion. Cäcilia smiled with pride when noting that the town band accompanied the ceremony, playing as they walked up the aisle. Then, when they reached fourth grade, they had confirmation. This was an even bigger thrill because most children were given a celebratory trip to a nearby town, Schärding. Cäcilia remembers this as a "very BIG deal," since these excursions were often the very first opportunity these children had to travel outside of the community in which they grew up. Usually a child's godparents would take them on this trip, or someone close to the family with a little extra money, and most traveled in a horse and carriage that was shared communally. When the children were twelve, they started attending Midnight Mass at Christmas.

Teenagers of the community got together in small groups, singing and talking. The young people sat on wall benches in a large room so everyone could fit, and there was cider to drink and a big loaf of bread. Refreshment was a slice of dry bread to eat. Someone usually had a guitar or a zither, the boys arm wrestled to impress the girls, and everyone played games. One popular entertainment was the "spanking game," where someone bent over someone else's lap so they couldn't see behind, then someone else sneaked up and spanked them and they had to guess who the spanker was. It is wonderful in 2005 to see ninety-three-year-old Cäcilia bend over and reenact this spanking game, erupting in giggles at the memory.

Like many of the local children and inspired by their father who was a member, Maria and her sister Loisi joined the local sports club, the *Turnverein*. Activities were organized, like gym classes, and leaders were usually affiliated with political parties. First, a man would demonstrate the exercise and then all the girls would mimic it. The students ran, jumped, did obstacle courses, hung on ropes, stood on their heads, and moved their bodies in special ways. "It was all about developing your muscles—no games—just exercises."

The women were permitted to wear pants for practices, a policy which proved controversial when men were forbidden to visit because of the "immodest clothing." For their rare public performances, the girls wore skirts. In an early photograph of the *Turnverein* Maria is standing proudly in the front row, wearing the public uniform with a sailor collar.

Most of the local children stopped their education after the age of fourteen since they had to help in the family homes and farms. Maria was no exception, and despite her obvious intelligence and promise, she left school after eight years on July 20, 1924, without an exit certificate.

Unexpectedly, Maria was given a rare opportunity in 1927 when Franz Mandl extended himself financially to send her to a Catholic boarding school in the German community of Neuhaus am Inn. Although Maria's sister Anna was also very intelligent, only Maria got this opportunity. It seems unlikely the Mandl family could have afforded to send them both.

The imposing edifice at Neuhaus, located across from the Austrian community of Schärding, was originally erected as a bastion defense to oversee the Inn River crossing in the Middle Ages. In the eighteenth century the structure was expanded into a magnificent rococo moated castle. In 1859 a convent acquired the castle and founded a school for girls.

The castle's wooded grounds are beautiful, while the Inn River has its own character; swift, fast-moving, deadly. The river's constant motion mirrored Maria's restless nature. As all the young women did, she often walked along the river's banks, gazing at the gray-green water and feeling both its strength and its inherent threat. Many people had drowned in the Inn, yet for those who managed to harness its power, there was respect.

In 2005 the convent is still run by the sisters of the Kloster der-Maria-Ward, who provide a warm welcome and show us around the beautiful grounds. The sister in charge has a lovely face which shines with a profound faith. She shares photograph albums from the period, and we marvel at nuns in severe habits teaching classes of girls in dark uniforms, sitting on hard wooden benches at the communal tables that served as desks.

The typical curriculum included sewing, secretarial skills, gym, theater, and music. Students attended daily Mass in the mornings, had evening prayers, and went to confession with a priest once a week. The nuns were very, very strict and were known to slap the students on the top of their hands with rulers when they misbehaved. Despite that, for these young women it was a privileged existence.

Skills Maria acquired at Neuhaus were evident throughout her life. She almost certainly learned to play the piano there and continued to nurture her love of music. The sewing skills she developed were often in evidence later in life. After the war, while in prison, Maria once constructed an entire women's suit for a friend, perfectly fitted, with only a needle and some unraveled thread.

Maria graduated from the program after completing three years of study. It remains unclear if she ever thanked Franz and Anna or appreciated the obvious sacrifices they had made which enabled her to attend this school.

CHAPTER 3

Coming of Age

MARIA'S SCHOOLMATE FROM THE MÜNZKIRCHEN grade school, Cäcilia, sits musing over her life in a chilly room on a long bench. On this day in 2005 she notes that in one week she will be ninety-three years old—exactly the same age Maria would be if she were still alive. Cäcilia's hair is short and gray, her eyes a little glassy. She wheezes when she talks but is very verbal and very much in her right mind. Seventy years later, she and other elderly women in the community vividly remember the difficult times in Austria as they came to adulthood.

"The 1930s were very, very bad. There was no work around. There was no money, it was always a struggle." At the age of eighteen Cäcilia owned only two "cheap" dresses, one for church and one for everything else. Her family lived on a diet of cabbage and potatoes, and eating meat was a major and rare event. "We liked that, it gave us strength to work."

Maria's family had more resources. In a photo taken shortly after she returned from Neuhaus Maria stands in a yard, casually holding a book under her arm in a relaxed but professional pose. She looks strong and well fed, carefully put together, gazing directly and almost sternly at the camera with a hint of smile on her face. Maria's outfit is stylish and appears store-bought. She wears light-colored opaque stockings and has stylish shoes with a strap across the top of each foot, which seem barely encased by the leather. Her hands are broad and strong. The shoes are decidedly not work shoes, nor is the dress.

Like the other women and despite her advantages and convent education, Maria also struggled to find work. Although she was decidedly better off than a girl from a rural family, employment was simply not available. In lieu of other opportunities, Cäcilia remembers that the young women of the community were always looking to marry for money. Women weren't allowed to say very much; if something bothered them they were supposed to keep it inside. The mother's job was to cook, clean, wash, and take care of the small animals and children.

One of Maria's best friends later remarked that if you were still unmarried at the "old age" of twenty-six you were considered a "leftover," an *übrig-geblieben*. It was a disgrace. "There was an old Bavarian saying, 'If your horse dies, that's a tragedy. If your wife dies, it doesn't matter.'"

Alison Owings, author of *Frauen: German Women Recall the Third Reich*, notes that economic hardships after the First World War meant a lessening of even marginal educational or professional possibilities for German (or Austrian) girls. Many villages had illiterate women, while others trained for jobs as clerks or saleswomen. There was a decided feeling that "any job was preferable to none."

In 1929, when Maria was seventeen, she applied for a passport. "I went to Switzerland where I was employed for 13 months as a house worker and a cook at Dr. Clausen's in Brig." Like Maria, her sister Loisi left home around this time because she too could not find work in Münzkirchen. Loisi would remain in Switzerland for the rest of her life. Maria's brother Georg had brought home a new wife, and the Mandl household was becoming crowded. Maria's sister Anna also married around this time and moved to her own home, although she stayed in the area. Throughout her life Maria remained very close to her sisters, and Loisi's presence in Switzerland helped Maria assimilate to her first professional position away from Münzkirchen.

Brig, Switzerland—Maria's destination—is a beautiful town located in the Swiss Alps. Today, the Brig tourist website boasts of the town's strategic location and the grand Italianate castle that dominates the otherwise simple town. Visitors and residents, then and now, can stroll into the triple-arcaded interior courtyard, which is especially beautiful when it catches the sun.

In an image from Brig, Maria is shown posing on a rocky outcrop overlooking the mountains. She seems happy and relaxed with a wide smile breaking across her face. Again, Maria's dress is stylish and well fitting and she wears fashionable and matching shoes.

Despite the steady employment and beautiful location Maria became very homesick. She later wrote that "after 13 months, because I missed home, I gave up this job and returned to my parents. I then worked in my parents' home until 1934."

During the months that Maria was living in Switzerland, her brother and oldest sister had started their own families. In 1932 Georg's daughter Franziska was born, and in 1933 a boy named Franz Josef was born to Anna. Maria was now an aunt and doted on these new arrivals. Always very taken with children, one of the great sorrows of Maria's life was her inability to have babies of her own.

Although happy to be home, Maria was still unable to find work. In 1934, after a brief respite, she "accepted a post as maid (*Zimmermädchen*) in a private villa in Innsbrück, Austria, where I worked until 1936." Then, with her mother's health worsening, Maria returned to Münzkirchen to help with the household and look after her father.

Nineteen thirty-six saw both great joy and great sorrow for the Mandl family. In September a second son was born to Maria's sister Anna. Sadly, it was also around this time that Anna's first son, Franz Josef, died at the age of three.

Franz Josef was a beautiful round-faced young cherub, who loved to dance excitedly around the farmyard with a flock of chickens. Although the family does not know exactly what caused the toddler's death, they think it may have been food poisoning. Franz Josef's body began to retain water and swell, to such an extent that his clothes had to be cut off with scissors. His throat was sore and filled with yellow pus. Child mortality was not uncommon in those days, and it is possible Franz Josef suffered an anaphylactic reaction to a food allergy. This would have explained his symptoms and death by cardiac arrest as his body filled with fluid.

Maria had always been particularly close to Anna, and the premature death of the beloved young boy was a tremendous blow to them both.

In 1937, when Maria was twenty-five years old, she had the good fortune to be hired by the Münzkirchen post office. Maria also embarked on her first serious romance, with a young man from the community. They soon became engaged, planning an optimistic future together.

A studio photograph of Maria taken around this time shows a beautiful young woman gazing directly at the camera, with carefully combed hair and light makeup. She is confident and has an assessing gaze.

In normal times Maria would probably have remained in Münzkirchen, living out her days in anonymity. History intervened, however, and Maria's life was overturned by the entrance of the German army into Austria and the Anschluss of 1938. Thus began for Maria, as she later described it, "a time of suffering. I could not find peace anywhere, I felt like a nutshell swimming on the waves of a big ocean."

CHAPTER 4

Anschluss

Anschluss: A joining. A connection. An annexation.

Ⅰ N MARCH OF 1938 AUSTRIA was officially annexed to Hitler's Third Reich. In the months preceding the Anschluss large rallies were held in several Austrian towns. All accoutrements of the Nazi regime were in evidence: swastika armbands, rallying songs, pedantic slogans. Hitler's photographs were a popular sale item, and in Graz, enthusiastic crowds marched through the streets with torches and flags.

Across the country as the Anschluss got underway, German troops were caught up in the population's paroxysms of joy that greatly exceeded Hitler's expectations. Bells sounded and manically exuberant masses in many towns greeted Hitler and his soldiers by yelling *"Ein Volk! Ein Reich! Ein Führer!"* ("One people! One empire! One leader!")

In Münzkirchen it had been common knowledge that German troops were gathered nearby, waiting to enter Austria. Then, on the morning of March 12, 1938, they began marching into upper Austria at Neuhaus, near where Maria had gone to school.

As in many small towns, Austrian troops were sent to Münzkirchen to keep law and order. The temporary commander in Schärding, Franz Jäger, kept a detailed account of the day's events. Jäger received a call from the division office and was told that if the German troops did enter his men were to offer no resistance but to retreat with all weapons and equipment in an easterly direction. From his account:

> Meanwhile one could already notice that large groups of people were underway on the street from St. Florian to Schärding, by foot, bicycle and car. One could also hear music and singing from the city plaza—already the Horst Wessel Song! [My] adjutant leaned cheerfully on the garden fence and sang along, which I had forbidden.

The soldiers later exited Münzkirchen and returned to Schärding, as entire convoys of German troops began moving in the street. A German flag was raised in front of the barracks as some officers were sworn in and raised their hand to the Führer, Adolf Hitler. Shortly thereafter Chancellor Schuschnigg's address came over the radio announcing the surrender of Austria.

Even before Hitler's ascent to power, the community of Münzkirchen had become increasingly politicized. Two major political parties dominated; the ÖVP (*Christliche Soziale Partei*) otherwise known as the "Blacks," and the Social Democrats, or "Browns," as well as other smaller parties, including the "Reds" and a few Communists.

As early as 1934 the *Turnverein* sports club had already divided into two: Nazi supporters and the others. The town band even divided into two groups—one for Hitler, one against. Community members later described this as "*Himmlische Musik und Hörliche Musik*" ("Music from Heaven and Music from Hell").

The Mandl family was Black, ÖVP. Seventy years later, neighbors and friends continue to state vehemently that "the Mandl family were NOT Nazis!" Franz even served in the District Council (*Gemeinderat*) of the ÖVP after the war. Because the Mandl family was well respected in the community, had a good business and were believed to be very honorable people, Franz Mandl's thoughts and beliefs held great weight with his friends and neighbors.

Before the Anschluss Maria's father had been outspoken and critical of the Nazis. "He was on a list of ten people who would be hanged if the Nazis came to power! He was against the Nazis coming into Austria!" This antipathy was undoubtedly grounded in issues Franz Mandl was having with a local official.

The mayor of Münzkirchen during the "*Nazi Zeit*" ("Nazi time"), 1939–1945, was a man named Anton Schiller. Schiller was a chimney sweep and member of the Nazi party. Franz Mandl, in the opposition party, was generally considered more rational and savvier than Schiller. Because of the respect he held in the community, Maria's father had the power to persuade other members of the ÖVP to vote against Schiller's platforms and ideas of how to run the town. Those things undoubtedly undermined Schiller.

When Maria Mandl later became an "important person" in the Nazi hierarchy, her hatred of Schiller was palpable. Returning from Auschwitz to visit Münzkirchen during the war, Maria presented a resplendent appearance with her black uniform, SS driver, and large black car. Her purpose was really to "rub their noses, and especially Schiller's nose," in her success.

After the war Schiller committed suicide, first killing his wife and then his dog. People in the community said he had a guilty conscience for actions he took during the war.

The Austrian Anschluss had enormous ramifications for Maria's life. She stated that "in 1937 I thought I was lucky, I was able to work at the post office and wanted to become Postmistress. The tragedy was that I was not considered politically spotless, i.e., I had no identity as a [National Socialist] so I was thrown out."

Many civil servants were fired after 1938, including the Münzkirchen postal employees, and it was common for local Nazis to snap up this sort of post. It is quite possible that Maria herself was apolitical at this time, simply echoing the beliefs of her father and family.

This is one of the great and ironic twists of Maria's life. Because she was not yet a member of the Nazi Party, she had lost her job and any chance for a normal future.

Or possibly, as many community members later conjectured, "she wasn't fired because she wasn't a Nazi, she was fired because her family were Blacks and belonged to the ÖVP."

For Maria, in addition to the emotional turmoil of losing her job and the tremendous upheavals of the period, she also lost her fiancé.

> My friend [fiancé] who wanted to have a career in the civil service after his military service, wrote to me after I described to him my misfortunes, and said that it would be impossible for him as a soldier in the Third Reich to sustain a connection with a girl who had to give up her position for... reasons. That would damage his future.

The identity of Maria's fiancé has been lost to history. Seven decades later rumors still fly about the insular community: Maria had a "*Verschmähter Liebe.*" She "loved someone who had left." "Her love was unrequited..." "Her fiancé was a policeman."

In recent years a credible witness emerged who claims that one of Maria's close friends identified Anton Schiller, the mayor during the Nazi time, as Maria's fiancé before the Anschluss. If true, this would explain the continued antipathy and the tensions between the Mandl family and Schiller.

Whatever his identity, the trauma to Maria's psyche was profound. Not only did she suffer the loss of someone she loved, Maria also lost the social standing and independence a marriage would have provided, not to mention the children she craved.

Understandably devastated and seeking a new direction for her now uncertain future, Maria made the decision to travel to Munich and look for work there. "When the German army entered Austria in 1938, I went in September to Munich, and the trouble continued."

Part Two

CHAPTER 5

Aufseherin

I was young. I was an opportunist. And once I joined, there was no way out.

—SS-Untersturmführer Hans Münch

I N September, devastated by her fiancé's rejection and the loss of her job, Maria traveled to Munich. The Mandl family had relatives in the city and Maria was hoping to find new employment. She later described this moment in her life:

> That same year [1938] I went to my uncle in Munich where he was a police chief constable and I asked him to find me a job in the German police. I wanted to get to the criminal police, I knew the works of this police department from my uncle's stories, I heard that criminal police officers made good money. There was no opening, therefore, at my uncle's advice, I accepted a job as *Aufseherin* [overseer] at the Lichtenburg KZ [*Konzentrationslager*— Concentration Camp]. I chose the job because I had heard that guards in the KZs made good money and I expected that I could earn more than as a nurse. Had I not gotten the job in the KZ, I would have studied to become a nurse.

Lichtenburg was a newly established concentration camp for female prisoners located in the small town of Prettin, southwest of Berlin. Housed in a deteriorating old castle with imposing stone walls and an angular and harsh courtyard, the new prison had a chronic shortage of guards. In lieu of qualified male candidates females were now being considered for these positions, and the Nazi hierarchy began to seek new ways to actively recruit and train overseers.

An ingenious press campaign was launched. Advertisements taken out in the newspapers stated that overseers were being sought for Lichtenburg, a camp for asocial and difficult women. The job was later advertised as light physical work with good pay, and interviewees were told they would only have to watch over prisoners. If an applicant asked about those prisoners, she was told they were women who had committed some violations against the racial community and now, to prevent further harm, had to be isolated. One job description simply read "female supervisory staff needed for a camp that will be newly erected for prostitutes."

A few of the newly hired guards were reluctant or taken aback when they realized that some of the women inmates had been arrested only because of their political leanings, not because of a history as a prostitute or "antisocial." A few pulled out at this revelation, but the majority, Mandl included, stayed. Most recruits had no other employment options, and eventually, the routine of the job and the pressure of the group dynamic made actions that had been previously unthinkable, normal.

Candidates were required to be in good health, have no criminal convictions, and be between twenty-one and forty-five years old. Mandl, twenty-six years old when she started her camp service, was typical—the average age for an overseer was twenty-five.

Most of the women who enlisted were not sophisticated or skilled. Many had a primary and secondary school education and several had worked as home help or in restaurants, but only a few had been employed by jails or social services.

One of the prisoners later commented that she was horrified to learn that "Hitler's creatures" were not born sadists or professional criminals, but rather from the middle class.

Heinrich Himmler eventually took the initiative of setting up a support group of women for the SS which came to be known as the SS *Helferinnen* (SS Auxiliaries). Himmler directed that women selected for this group were to meet the same racial criteria as the men and obtain their salary and full military uniforms from SS resources. They had the right to carry sidearms and be accompanied by SS dogs, but compared to SS men, the women's opportunities were circumscribed. The highest rank a woman could achieve in a concentration camp was *Oberaufseherin* (head guard), who would then supervise the lower-ranked female overseers.

Eventually candidates signed an occupational service contract after which the women were considered members of the SS staff, although not officially members of the SS. And despite the misogyny of the time, these women functioned as more than mere subordinates. Their responsibilities were extensive, and the new overseers had implicit authority over prisoners.

Maria later stated that "Before I started the job I was sworn to secrecy about whatever I would learn during my service in the camp. We were instructed that women prisoners were to be treated harshly but fairly [*streng aber gerecht*]."

Female guards who worked in the camps were attracted by the good salaries, the paid housing, the job security, and the chance to improve their lives and status. For an ambitious young woman like Maria, the rewards were great.

CHAPTER 6

KZ Lichtenburg

THE COMMUNITY OF PRETTIN FELT comfortable and familiar to Maria Mandl. Not too much larger than Münzkirchen, it boasted a congenial downtown area and many recreational and social opportunities. Brigitte Liebehenschel, whose father was stationed at Lichtenburg, remembered Prettin as a pretty town with a friendly tinker man who came around in a small rickety truck, trading old newspaper or tinfoil in exchange for small gift items.

Oskar Gröning, an SS officer who served in a small town similar to Prettin, enjoyed the primary form of off-duty entertainment, which was going to the cinema. "Because there was no television, the cinema was the only source of information by way of the culture films and, above all, the 'newsreels' that were shown before the main film. The films were either entertainment with revues, or trendy films."

The castle on the outskirts of Prettin—which had become KZ Lichtenburg—was a different world. Upon arrival, the newly hired female overseers discovered an aging but perfectly designed prison, an "ideal concentration camp." Hundreds of years old, the castle boasted towers, powerful walls, dungeons, and a large internal courtyard known as the *Appellplatz* (Roll Call Square). The castle was paved with large red ochre cobblestones which were uneven sizes, interspersed with walkways.

There was also a prison within the prison, the Bunker, which even on sunny days was dank and cold. High, vaulted ceilings over-

looked large gray slate floor tiles, slippery when wet; the air was described as rotting and fetid with decay and putrefaction.

By late 1938 Oswald Pohl, administrative head of the SS, had
recorded eight hundred inmates detained at Lichtenburg, including
political and social prisoners, Jehovah's Witnesses, and Jews.

Maria and the other new recruits were put through a training
program which was just now becoming standardized. Each took
courses in Nazi philosophy and proper attitudes toward the Reich,
followed by a twenty-question exam testing the applicant's knowledge of history and geography, dates important to the NSDAP, such
as Hitler's birthday, and her race and worldview. The new guard
then underwent an on-the-job performance evaluation. After all that
was successfully completed, a woman was deemed suitable to be an
overseer, an *Aufseherin*.

Once the Nazi oath was administered and the recruit officially
hired, she was issued an official gray uniform, a pair of long boots,
and various accessories, including gloves and field caps. During a
three-month trial period the new *Aufseherin* learned on the job by
total immersion into this new environment. New guards shadowed
more experienced staff members and adjusted quickly. This procedure normalized any disconcerting aspects of camp life, and most
women quickly lost any qualms they may have had.

Maria stated that "before I started service at the camp in Lichtenburg, I knew nothing about what the concentration camps were.
At first I worked there for a trial period of 3 months, and at that time
I had no independent function. I always accompanied one of my
friends/coworkers and became acquainted with the course of works
in the camp."

A prisoner who was there from the inception of the camp remembers Maria Mandl from her first days on the new job. She was
immediately struck by Mandl's beauty, and her youth. She spoke directly to Maria and told her to go home, that she was too pretty to
"play the supervisor here." Maria replied "No, I swore the oath to the
Führer, I'm staying."

CHAPTER 7

A Good, Orderly Life

Maria later described her initial impressions of Lichtenburg:

> (Prisoners were) Jewish women and professional criminals, mostly prostitutes. They had good accommodations, received the same food that we did, were able to shop in the canteen where there were handmade articles of all kinds: food, toiletries, patterns, and all possible things. Bean coffee and bakery items as much as they wanted. (At that time) there were only two working commandos: farming (only once in a while) and gardening. There were 12–20 prisoners (in those commandos). The others made things or sat around all day doing nothing. Newspapers and books could also be ordered and read. Life in Lichtenburg proceeded in an ordinary way. At that time beating of the prisoners was out of the question. In Lichtenburg prisoners were not beaten yet. Mortality was low, some would die but that was from natural causes, most frequently due to old age. The prisoners were treated strictly—but fairly. It was a good, orderly life.

Despite the rosy picture Maria painted, the reality of Lichtenburg was much harsher. Prisoners lived in large, inadequately heated, and drafty sleeping rooms with stacked beds they were not allowed to leave without permission. Daily roll calls occurred in morning and evening, and sanitary conditions were catastrophic, with two toilets in every hall for as many as 120 women. Some halls had only tubs for excrement.

Prisoners described considerable tensions due to their differing backgrounds. Food was inadequate and unappealing. Cabbage was the only vegetable or fruit, and once, after a fish meal, the prisoners had diarrhea and stomach pains for an extended period. Visitors were not permitted and mail from outside was censored. Medical treatment was minimal, from uncaring and insensitive doctors, who joined in the harassments and minimally and grudgingly treated wounds from beatings.

Most women worked inside the castle—kitchen, laundry, sewing, cleaning overseers' rooms, scrubbing toilets. Some of the hardest work was for the assigned coal-carriers, which was used for heating the large rooms. Other women worked in the gardens or outside in agriculture and in irrigation ditches.

In the beginning the punitive system in Lichtenburg comprised, among other things, food deprivation, dark confinement in a single cell, and time in the Bunker. After June of 1938, on Himmler's order, whipping on the flogging rack was added as an additional and intensified punishment.

The *Kommandant* rationalized that it was impossible to maintain order in the camp if the defiance of these "hysterical broads" could not be broken through strict confinement, because no other "delicate punishment" was allowed to be used in women's camps. He was also frustrated that food deprivation alone had not achieved the desired result.

Historian Werner Dietrich summarizes that the ignorance and arrogance of the authorities, against the mental and physical terror of the prisoners, symbolized daily life in the camp.

CHAPTER 8

"Rein kommt Ihr alle, aber niemals wieder lebend raus!"

"Lots of you are coming in, but none of you will come out alive!"
—SS PERSONNEL, LICHTENBURG

FOR MOST OF MARIA'S TENURE at Lichtenburg her commanding officer was a man named Max Kögl. From the beginning Kögl was an intimidating presence. Wearing a brown SA uniform which strained over his potbelly, and often wielding a riding crop, Kögl was always accompanied by two female guards and their dogs.

Maria's immediate female supervisor was Head Overseer Johanna Langefeld. Colleagues in the lower ranks varied in quality. One, Emma Zimmer, was an alcoholic who was often censured for getting drunk on the job. Another woman named Gertrud Rabenstein became notorious for setting her dog loose on prisoners and "other terrible things."

When new prisoners were brought to Lichtenburg, the overseers immediately established their dominance. Rules and regulations of the camp were read, female overseers postured with trained dogs, the *Kommandant* was presented—for purposes of intimidation. A favorite admonition was "Lots of you are coming in, but none of you will come out alive!"

Lichtenburg was utilized to detain many Jehovah's Witnesses. Unlike other prisoners, these women were offered a chance for release if they agreed to sign a document renouncing their faith. Very few took advantage. Because of this, the "*Bibel Forschen*" were subjected to a more severe prison regimen, including torture and appalling interrogations. When Himmler visited the Lichtenburg camp in 1937, he threatened the Jehovah's Witnesses that they would be oppressed and humiliated until they gave in and surrendered.

After the war, when Mandl was in prison, she told a friend, "You know, it was hard [in Lichtenburg]. There were nice people there, the Bible researchers [Jehovah's Witnesses]. They were so good and they wanted nothing more, and nothing evil, and nothing said. The ones from Hamburg that came from the Reeperbahn, they were simply terrible. Under them, we did nothing but dole out punishment."

All life at Lichtenburg was aimed at demeaning and depersonalizing the prisoners. Work details were made gratuitously onerous while various infringements of camp rules could cause incarceration in the Bunker. Many prisoners were subjected to "sport," or rather, punitive exercises, while Sunday beatings and whippings were now held regularly. Day-to-day psychological torture created great stress, and there was constant fear of harassment, denouncement, punishments, Gestapo interrogations, and death. Blood-smeared corpses became a regular site in the morning after the Bunker had reaped its nightly harvest.

When prominent Nazis visited Lichtenburg, inmates were forbidden to reveal any sign of mistreatment. The Bunker did not appear on the itinerary. Days before these tours commenced the prisoners were forced to scrub the barracks, and punishments were doled out for even the smallest offense. The guests would visit the barracks, where women were presented as healthy and happy in desirable living quarters. Everyone knew that to tell the truth would result in a beating or worse. Former prisoner Lina Haag remembered that "we stood there listening vacantly or with a smile; no one stepped forward to say: 'No this is not true,' the truth is that at the slightest words from an informer we are whipped; for the whipping we are strapped naked to a wooden post and Wardress Mandl beats us with the dog-whip until she can go on no longer."

Haag later summarized that "you can never forget you are nothing more than a handful of dust…"

CHAPTER 9

The Transformation

What does it take to kill another person? Or, to put it another way, what is it that prevents us from killing?
— KARL OVE KNAUSGAARD, "THE
INEXPLICABLE: INSIDE THE MIND
OF A MASS KILLER"

IT WAS IN LICHTENBURG WHERE Maria's patterns of behavior first veered toward depravity. By all accounts her family life before this period was warm and loving, with no background of physical violence. Maria, like most of the other young women hired for guard positions, had no formal training in police or prison work. In Lichtenburg, as in other camps, the young female recruits were gradually trained and indoctrinated into what came to be known as a culture of cruelty, where harshness and lack of compassion were rewarded. New overseers were instructed in *Lagerordnung*—the rules and regulations that ensured "camp order." A strict and abusive physical discipline became part of that training.

In some significant ways Maria's entry into camp life was atypical. Unlike the many women who only gradually assimilated cruel behaviors, Mandl descended rapidly into a full-blown state of brutality. Some severe and inexplicable transition in Maria's personality had taken place between the breakup with her fiancé and the beginning of her job at Lichtenburg. An abrupt moral breakdown was evident, a disintegration of ethical behavior.

One former prisoner, Emilie Neu, entered Lichtenburg shortly before Maria. Accustomed to working hard, Neu did what was requested and tried to make the best of her situation. Despite that, the vulgarity of the female overseers scared her. Then, one day, Mandl came and Neu was immediately quite taken with her. "She was so young and so blond and such a nice girl." Neu was horrified to witness the transformation of Mandl's personality and found herself speechless with horror. "At the beginning, she had been very sweet and I couldn't grasp that she had gone so far later on and done such horrible things. At Lichtenburg she began to beat people."

Shortly thereafter, Maria became known as one of the most aggressive and feared guards, fully brutal and fully remorseless. Her brutality, in turn, caught the attention of her superiors and allowed Maria to rise rapidly through the ranks to a position of authority.

One inmate commented that Maria immediately behaved in a mean and brutal way against the prisoners. She tells of an early incident in which Mandl hit a prisoner with a key until the woman collapsed into unconsciousness. "Then she grabbed both of the woman's knees and dragged her over the whole courtyard to the place the cells were."

Undoubtedly, Maria enjoyed her new sense of power and respect. Whenever an overseer entered a room, all of the prisoners had to jump up and stay standing until permission was given to sit. For Maria, accustomed to treatment as a subordinate female in a small village dominated by men, this was heady stuff indeed.

As she settled into her responsibilities at Lichtenburg, Maria's power grew. When *Kommandant* Kögl instituted public beatings on Sundays in front of all the women, Mandl often wielded the stick. When Maria was placed in charge, she ordered the victims be stripped naked and strapped to a wooden block, after which she would whip them thoroughly. Mandl also stipulated to other guards that the prisoners were always to be "whipped through." (*durchgepeitscht*).

Maria was finding herself well suited to this new life she had chosen. More intelligent than many of her colleagues, she spit back the rhetoric with ease, and with a body hardened by the *Turnverein*, the physical demands were easy. Unlike other recruits, Maria does not seem to have been bothered by feelings of compassion for the prisoners—any human warmth she may once have felt had been snubbed out by her fiancé's betrayal. Maria became hard, and tough, and fully committed to proving herself in this new environment. After all the traumas before and during the Anschluss, National Socialism was turning out to be a boon, providing her with a new path for her life and what she perceived as a bright future.

Perhaps more transformative for Maria's personality was the moment she first killed, when she took a human life. Man is a creature of habit and such things—even killing—can become a daily routine. But that *first* time... What makes someone cross the line and strike that first blow, or pull that trigger?

When asked if he had witnessed first kill moments among his SS colleagues at Auschwitz, Oskar Gröning stated that "the inhibitions to prevent something like that disappear in the moment they are allowed to go unpunished. The danger is that a person will succumb to this desire, and it becomes larger if he gains power and his need for recognition separates him out from the mass of the others."

Gröning, like all other SS men, was taught that killing was just part of a fight for the existence of the German people. The Jews (and other undesirables) were presented as the enemy who, like those on the fighting front, had to be destroyed in order to achieve ultimate victory. "That was the justification for the Holocaust. That is how it was presented to us."

James Waller, in his landmark study *Becoming Evil*, notes that an individual in such a situation is enormously influenced by the nature of the collective—personal identity is subordinated to the group, which radically affects individual behaviors. Functioning as part of a group can spread out blame and culpability and amplify the best and worst tendencies of a person.

In the creation of a "culture of cruelty," Waller describes extreme desensitization, which often leads to a perpetrator's perverse enjoyment and sadistic pleasure in his or her activities. These activities become an addiction and contribute to a larger social milieu wherein evil is encouraged and rewarded.

Killing is made easier as the distance—physical, moral, psychological—between perpetrators and victims increases. Victims are blamed, scapegoated, and dehumanized. In Nazi Germany this process started as soon as Hitler came to power, and continued to escalate, culminating in the Holocaust. Every person had to make a moral choice, to resist or to embrace these policies.

Where, when, and how, did Maria first kill? Was it a logical outgrowth or consequence of a beating she administered? Was it during a duty assignment in the Bunker? Was it a shot from a gun? Was it an accident? There is no way of knowing.

Killers interviewed after the genocide in Rwanda remembered "the first time": "Basically, that first time, I was quite surprised by the speed of death, and also by the softness of the blow, if I may say so." "I put the two children side by side twenty meters away, I stood still, I shot twice at their backs." "For me, it was strange to see the children drop without a sound. It was almost pleasantly easy." "We no longer saw a human being when we turned up a Tutsi in the swamps." "The hunt was savage, the hunters were savage, the prey was savage—savagery took over the mind."

Or was it, for Maria, perhaps more frighteningly, not profound at all? A U.S. veteran from the Iraq War remarked that "the truth is, it wasn't all I thought it was cracked up to be. I mean, I thought killing somebody would be this life-changing experience. And then I did it, and I was like, 'all right, whatever.'" He later equated killing people to squashing an ant.

Either way, Maria had become a killer and the path was set for the rest of her life. From this point onward, there would be no turning back.

And now Lichtenburg was buzzing with anticipation about a new concentration camp for women being built north of Berlin. The female overseers were to be transferred soon. When asked what the new camp was called, they were told *Ravensbrück* (Raven's Bridge).

Like a bird of prey seizing an opportunity, Maria was ready.

Part Three

CHAPTER 10

Ravensbrück

Deep into that darkness, peering, long I stood there, wondering, fearing…

—Edgar Allan Poe, "The Raven"

BEAUTIFUL SCENERY SPED BY AS the overseers from Lichtenburg made their way to the new camp of Ravensbrück. May flowers bloomed in profusion, contrasting with the darker greens of the Mecklenburg Forest. The warmer weather was welcome after a long winter in the dank and drafty castle, and the women sat, nervous and excited. Maria was twenty-seven years old, newly confident in her abilities and eager to prove herself in this new environment.

Curious to see this freshly built camp designed especially for women, the overseers craned their necks in anticipation. Built outside the small town of Fürstenberg, Ravensbrück was chosen for its proximity to a good highway and a railroad junction. It was also close to Oranienburg, a major headquarters for the SS.

Originally a spa destination, the centerpiece of the area was a beautiful inland lake, the Schwedtsee, which glimmered peacefully in the sun. Because it was part of a system of lakes linked by canals, barges were able to transport heavy goods, such as coal, to and from the camp. The smell of sawdust was still pungent in the air, and both trucks and feet got mired in the soggy sand by the lakebed. Old boathouses, from a happier time, were scattered around the shore.

Exiting at the train station, the women entered the village of Fürstenberg, which was picturesque and abloom with flowers. Continuing along a road that curved around the lake, the overseers encountered some of the local residents. Healthy children with pink cheeks gazed at the new arrivals curiously, while adults looked and then quickly glanced away, going about their business. After a mile or so the camp came into view. Now in the distance, the red tile rooftops and church spire of Fürstenberg gleamed on the sunny day. SS engineers and architects had been busy. The new camp already had an electrified fence, ugly low gray barracks for prisoners, and a high concrete wall, which contrasted with the physical beauty of the location.

True to its name, the first living creatures the women encountered were large black ravens, which swooped down with a shrill cackling. Their chatter mingled with the distant barking of guard dogs, already installed in their kennels.

As the overseers began to explore their new workplace, they discovered another large *Appellplatz*, which enabled the entire prison population to gather in the same place. The camp was laid out in a grid on either side of a *Lagerstrasse* (camp street). This design ingeniously allowed guards a constant sight line to the women they were guarding. An SS canteen stood to the left of the front gate, and there was a laundry, a clothing warehouse, a bathhouse, a hospital (known as the *Revier*), and an aviary to raise poultry and rabbits. Plots in front of some barracks were planted with red salvia flowers, and linden tree saplings had been placed at uniform spacings throughout the camp.

The women settled in, and by the time the first three months had passed, the flowers were well established and sand-covered paths near the front gate had been raked by prisoners into complicated designs, like a distorted and ghoulish Zen garden. Exotic birds had been added to the aviary, including peacocks and a squawking parrot.

The constant sound of the Schwedtsee splashing against the shore-line added a further touch of surrealism.

In her later deposition Maria mentions the beauty of Ravens-brück in those early days. Seeking to mitigate the subsequent horrors of the camp, Maria noted that prisoners "only worked weekdays, Sunday was free, they could linger in nature all day. The camp was very beautifully situated with grasslands, flowers, and bushes around every block and poplars on the main camp street on the left and right. There was even a zoo which had apes, ducks and various birds."

The new camp's location also provided ample building space for a large SS housing development. "There were 12 barracks for living, one was the kitchen with a good bath for the prisoners. We employ-ees lived initially in the first barrack [shack] where the police station was also located. Later on our room was moved next to the prisoner's bath until our living quarters were ready to be moved into."

By late 1940, those quarters were completed and ready for occu-pancy. Purposefully located a distance from the male housing, they could accommodate 112 overseers. Five women were assigned per floor, and each had a sleeping and living area, with a wardrobe and a sink, and access to a communal bathroom and tea kitchen. The de-sirable upper levels overlooked the lake, while the basement had a laundry room. Most evenings after work were spent in common rooms located in each apartment building. Each house also had a sewing room where the women could knit or crochet in their spare time. Head overseers lived alone or with a child.

Many of the women, who came from humble backgrounds, found this better than what they had at home; comfortable, independent, modern, and—for some—luxurious. They reveled in the fact that prisoners did all their laundry, ironing, and mending. For most, who had to do all those things regularly for their families, Ravensbrück was proving a very fine job indeed! Few other young women seeking employment in the difficult economic climate of the time could boast a private room, regular leisure time, and an attractive salary.

Although it is difficult to imagine that working as a guard in a concentration camp could ever be viewed as "normal" employment, it is obvious many of the women did. Ravensbrück and the surrounding area ultimately became what Jeannette Toussaint describes as a completely normal place to live and work.

CHAPTER 11

Daily Life

Of course, I was occasionally struck by doubt and I was unsettled, but the camaraderie and the togetherness in the community always swept away these doubts like a haze that disappears in the sun.

—SS-Unterscharführer Oskar Gröning,
after his first concentration camp posting

Daily life quickly fell into a rhythm of work and routine. The female overseers in Ravensbrück were issued practical and durable uniforms, as well as canes, pistols, and whips. Because the camp grounds were covered in hard dirt, puddles, mud, and various sharp objects, each was given a pair of high leather boots. This made it possible for the overseers to stride purposefully and confidently through camp. A side "benefit" was that they could also be used as a weapon, to kick.

Most of the initial camp personnel had simply transferred from Lichtenburg. Max Kögl continued in his role as *Kommandant* and Johanna Langefeld in her role as female *Oberaufseherin*. Maria was one of thirty female guards and twelve SS men in the initial work assignment. Kögl continued to bolster his reputation as a brutal sadist and rekindled his hatred towards the Jehovah's Witness prisoners. They were "especially tortured."

Kögl's strong personality and personal brutality had been a major influence on Maria during her days of indoctrination at Lichtenburg. Now considered one of the more seasoned guards, Maria became increasingly important to the running of the new camp.

Rumors flew about Ravensbrück that Mandl was having an affair with Kögl, but it is more likely she was having a liaison with another officer, Edmund Bräuning. Aleksandra Steuer remembers that it was common knowledge that Bräuning was the lover of Mandl, who accompanied him always and everywhere and never let him be one-on-one with any prisoner. At first, Bräuning was always submissive to Mandl, but by the end of her stay in Ravensbrück their roles had reversed. Steuer concludes, "Bräuning found himself another lover. This change had great ramifications on the prisoners upon whom Mandl unloaded her fury. During that time, both shootings and penalties increased."

Although the head female SS supervisor, Johanna Langefeld, had responsibility for the practical day-to-day running of the camp, she was not permitted to give orders to the SS men. This often created resentments and conflicts.

Langefeld was a paradox. Survivors described her as "not 100% SS" and more than any of the other high-ranking female guards, Langefeld seemed conflicted about the ethical consequences of what they were doing. Margarete Buber-Neumann, who worked closely with Langefeld, remembers that "she came to the camp every morning, praying and begging God for strength to stop evil from happening. What a disastrous confusion."

Despite these inner (and outer) reservations, Langefeld happily accepted the perks of her position. She enjoyed a private apartment with a wonderful view of the Schwedtsee and made a home there for her fourteen-year-old son, who attended a local school.

Langefeld's strengths, and weaknesses, would prove seminal to the career of Maria Mandl. In the end, when Langefeld's ability to enforce the brutality and structure required in the Nazi camp system proved inadequate, Maria stepped into the breach.

Maria's other colleagues at Ravensbrück ranged from young and inexperienced girls to hardened veterans. Overseers included Margot Drechsel (also known as Drexler), who "got along well with Mandl" and was notorious for boxing women in the ears, and Emma Zimmer, also from Lichtenburg, who became famous for striking prisoners with her leather briefcase.

Another overseer, Dorothea Binz, was known in SS quarters for doting on a little dog she loved and caressed. Former prisoner Zofia Ciszek wryly noted that "Binz loved that dog but liked to beat people; a dog was a dog—she loved the dogs! But a prisoner? No such love."

As in Lichtenburg, newly hired female overseers gradually seasoned into their jobs during a three-month trial period. Eventually, Ravensbrück became the designated place for a young woman to receive *Aufseherin* training. By the end of the war almost four thousand women had been trained or worked at Ravensbrück, and Maria Mandl assumed much of the instruction of new recruits in the first years of the camp.

Hermine Braunsteiner, later known as the "Mare of Majdanek," was one of those trainees in summer of 1939. Mandl was in charge of showing Braunsteiner how to make sure the prisoners completed their work duties and, in general, how to function as an overseer. "Maria Mandl was very strict," she said. "My training with her wasn't very good, and what I saw was also unfavorable. What I mean by that is she often hit the prisoners."

By September 1, 1939, when the Third Reich invaded Poland and the Second World War began, the work routines and procedures at Ravensbrück were well established.

CHAPTER 12

The Visit

Januar 4, 1940 was a landmark day for the female overseers at Ravensbrück. SS-*Reichsführer* Heinrich Himmler was coming to inspect the new camp. It was a bitterly cold winter's morning, with heavy snowfalls the night before and temperatures falling to twenty below zero centigrade.

Prisoners were already hard at work, clearing snow from the path or chopping ice from the frozen lake for the storerooms. It was not unusual for a woman to collapse from such efforts and freeze to death where she lay.

Himmler, oblivious to such sights, entered the camp, where Kögl stepped out to greet him. Followed by Johanna Langefeld, the men strode through the front gates to inspect a lineup of excited female guards.

In existing photographs from this visit the overseers are lined up in rows by one of the larger buildings in the camp, arms at sides, all wearing the standard camp uniform of culottes, jacket, cap, and boots. The day looks frigid—one of those dry January bitter colds where the snow is packed hard and the sky is gray. Many of the women glance shyly at the photographer and smile, obviously excited. Others crane their necks for the first sighting of Himmler. Some chat gently with their neighbors; all have an air of anticipation.

A few frames later, in a much higher-resolution photograph, Himmler has appeared and is beginning his inspection of "the troops," walking with gloves in hand, in his SS trench coat. The women's demeanor has now changed. All stand at attention. Most look forward although some eyes stray toward Himmler. Johanna Langefeld follows the small group of men, obviously subservient. The surrounding camp buildings are clearly delineated, and a guard is visible on top of an adjoining rooftop.

After inspection of the female overseers, Kögl and Himmler met in the main office to discuss various challenges facing the camp, including the ongoing resistance of the Jehovah's Witnesses. Kögl wanted permission from Himmler to institute the "*Prügelstrafe*," a process which strapped a prisoner down over a wooden horse and gave her twenty-five lashes on the buttocks with an oxhide whip. Although Johanna Langefeld had long voiced opposition to this idea, her concerns were dismissed, and Himmler made the decision to implement Kögl's discipline plan for all prisoners, not just Jehovah's Witnesses. Another topic of concern was the shortage of qualified female overseers and the difficulties of attracting new women for these jobs.

For much of the visit Langefeld was humiliatingly relegated to the sidelines while Himmler (a former chicken farmer) and Oswald Pohl, another high-ranking SS officer, engaged in a lengthy and impassioned discussion about the management of poultry stock at Pohl's nearby estate.

In her postwar deposition, Maria claims that she personally approached Himmler during this visit and interceded on behalf of a political prisoner. "A political woman who was supposed to have taken part in a demolition of a bridge during the invasion by the Germans was with us. During a visit by Reichsführer Himmler she was released within five days, at my request to him." Maria says that the prisoner later wrote her a letter of support and thanks which was confiscated by the police from her sister's house after the war.

This may have just been a smoke screen on the part of Mandl, who at the time was seeking positive testimonies that would bolster her defense.

There is documentation that Himmler did submit a release form for a political prisoner on this visit. However, in order to have the pardon appear on Hitler's birthday, as was customary, the announcement was postdated by four months. Whether or not this was done at the instigation of Maria Mandl may be impossible to confirm.

CHAPTER 13

"To work!"

*The head SS supervisor, Rabenstein, at outdoor work, set a dog
on a prisoner who had eaten a carrot. A mother of four children.
The prisoner died.*

—ERIKA BUCHMANN, FORMER INMATE, RAVENSBRÜCK

MARIA HAD A VARIETY OF jobs after arriving at Ravensbrück. She,
along with all the overseers, had to administer the roll calls
every morning and evening. Following roll call, the head overseer
assigned the women to different work commandos, which changed
daily, and was responsible for the "trouble free organization of
camp business."

In early summer of 1939 approximately one thousand women prisoners were detained in Ravensbrück. Since construction of the camp
was still incomplete, most were stationed to work at building sites.
One prisoner, transferred from Lichtenburg, remarked that in the
beginning "the camp was not even completely ready. It was just barracks in a sand desert."

Labor detachments at Ravensbrück typically had one armed
guard, although larger details would sometimes be assigned an
extra overseer. Prisoners seldom knew the proper names of the
guards since they were required to address all overseers as "*Frau
Aufseherin.*" Nicknames became common, usually inspired by the

guard's actions or appearance, such as "the snake," "the red-head," or "the mare."

Women in work details were intimidated and controlled by shows of violence. Overseers were instructed to keep a distance of six paces from prisoners but to always keep them in their sight. During any attempt at flight, the use of a dog or a pistol was allowed. Dogs were also used in the external detachments to prevent escape, a policy Heinrich Himmler promoted. He believed canines were particularly useful in intimidating female prisoners and helped reduce the number of necessary human guards. As a result, most of the female overseers at Ravensbrück worked with a dog, picking the animals up at the entrance to the camp on the way to outdoor work details and returning them to kennels near the camp boundary at night.

The dogs were always leashed and trained to run after an escaping prisoner on command, pin them down, tear their clothes. Typically, a dog was trained to bite three times: the first time on the foot, the second on the shoulder, and the third on the throat. Katharina Zeh, who was a political prisoner in Ravensbrück, stated emphatically that "Mandl ALWAYS had a dog with her!" and that many prisoners returned to the camp at night with dog bites.

Maria later denied that the dogs were used for punitive purposes. "In my time female supervisors at Ravensbrück were handlers of dogs and with pistols, but only for outside commandoes, so that the prisoners were not in danger. In case someone was escaping, dogs were used to find her. In the case of the pistols, three shots were to be fired, but not in the direction of the prisoner, but into the air to announce that something had happened."

Mandl supervised many outdoor work details. Although some of the overseers accepted and tolerated the outdoor service, others, like Hildegard Lächert, found the long hours on duty tedious and boring. "We had to stand there on duty, whether it was raining, snowing, cold, or hot. Just imagine, standing there like a mule, 12 hours at a time. At that point you don't care about anything, anymore."

Certain assignments became notorious for their difficult working conditions, especially the sand pit (*Sandgrube*). This was often one of Mandl's duties. "At the beginning in Ravensbrück I supervised the sand digging." This dreaded assignment had an ironic connotation, since many of the prisoners previously associated sand with the beach, summers, and fun. Prisoner Wanda Półtawska described the *Sandgrube* as pure torture, where hundreds of women were forced to shift sand from one pile to another for the entire day. Overseers with dogs constantly shouted "Faster! Faster!" as the women struggled to keep up. "The spades blistered the palms of our hands, and the sand, heavy and damp in the morning would, as the day wore on, be whipped by the fierce Mecklenburg winds into fine, shifting grains which choked our eyes, ears and mouths, and penetrated through our clothing. We returned home smothered in sand. We felt as though it were burying us alive."

Other inmates, harnessed to huge rollers in teams of twelve to twenty-four, built roads inside the camp from stones dragged up from the lakeside. Prisoners also unloaded ships full of coke, standing in the marshland along the shore, carrying rocks for days on end. These details were forced to work in the open during all seasons, including the "terrible winter" of 1939–40, in temperatures of thirty degrees Fahrenheit, wearing only a summer dress and a jacket. Hanna Burdówna remembered that "the tempo of the work was horrible. We always stood in water, then steam, heat, and then outside again. We were always getting colds and often feverish as well."

Another prisoner, Luise Mauer, relayed vivid memories of outdoor work details under Mandl. She had been assigned to unload the coal ships, a brutal and exhausting job. One day, after several hours of shoveling coal, Luise begged for a break. "*Aufseherin* Mandl gave me a reply: 'You may have additional shovels but no time for dallying. I have watched you the entire time and I have something that will help you. A kick in the ass often works wonders!'" She continued to work until Mandl, annoyed by the look on the prisoner's face, lunged toward Luise, roaring and bellowing and kicking her with the tread on her boots. Blood flowed from Luise's face and forehead and Mandl continued to strike her in a paroxysm of rage.

Zofia Ciszek, a young woman from Poland, remembered her Ravensbrück work details with anguish. "There were always guards with whips and dogs screaming 'Faster! Faster!' The labor was REALLY hard and I was never strong. I have always been a physically weak woman and I was totally out of strength—and she [Mandl] REALLY beat me then!"

A prisoner named Minnie Artner worked in an outdoor punishment detail for eight months supervised by Maria Mandl, who, one time, actually *improved* their conditions. The women were given the task of unloading bricks from cargo ships channeled from the Spree River. Artner unloaded 120,000 bricks herself. Since the prisoners had no protection, their hands were soon covered with blood. When the women requested bandages or hand protection, they were told, "There are no bandages for beasts." "It was only at the intervention of supervisor Mandl, who declared that the ship had to be unloaded and undoubtedly had a quota to fill, that bandages were given to those who had serious wounds. After two days, old mitts were given out for this work."

By 1940 various indoor industries had also been formed, including the SS-owned "Society for Textile and Leather Utilization." Special barracks were designated as cutting places, tailor shops, a furrier, a repair place, a weaving mill for manufacturing—among other things—Persian rugs for the SS, and a straw shoe factory. The tailor shops were particularly brutal. Prisoners were worked to the point of exhaustion and beyond, many pushing their heads against the machines until blood ran out of their noses.

Like all the overseers, Mandl also supervised these inside details.

CHAPTER 14

Leisure Time

FOR MARIA AND HER COLLEAGUES, life in Ravensbrück was satisfying. Despite the proximity of the camp, the carefully calculated design meant that the overseers could completely separate the two parts of their lives. After leaving work for the day, they returned to a cozy and inviting home. The women were proud of their new jobs, their uniforms, their living quarters, and of the newly acquired respect those things gave them in the community and in their hometowns.

The Nazi hierarchy had a vested interest in keeping the female workforce happy, and development of social infrastructure in and around the camp further contributed to their satisfaction. Women could have a supportive and domestic social life, they could keep their children with them—all contributed to a general air of warmth and family. The brutality of the camp could and did fade into the distance.

The geographical location of the camp also contributed to its allure. The glittering Schwedtsee provided endless hours of entertainment and beauty. When it was warm they could swim or boat on it, and when it was colder they could ice skate. The women went on strolls in the beauty of the surrounding woods; they could go to local fairs.

Fürstenberg, an easy walk from the camp, provided restaurants, coffee houses, and movie theaters. When the female guards walked along the streets of the town in their new uniforms, they received admiring glances from the local population.

The overseers availed themselves of the hair salon in Fürstenberg, and later a salon was set up in the camp itself. Former prisoner and hairdresser Edith Sparmann remembered that most guards had an appointment every two weeks. A popular and trendy style was something called an "Olympia Roll." "It was a single roll swept back from the crown." Maria Mandl and Dorothea Binz were often seen there, as well as wives of the male SS officers. It was one of the only places where the overseers acted human.

The women could also visit a cafeteria with a casino, a tailor, and a library. When an overseer had a weekend off, she could take a side trip to Berlin for a taste of city life.

There was ample time for outside interests, and Maria was able to engage in her love of music. Although the Ravensbrück camp did not have an orchestra, recorded music was frequently broadcast over the loudspeakers to the entire camp, and musical selections were usually chosen by Mandl. Survivor Wanda Półtawska remembers a recording of Robert Schumann's *Reverie*, one of Maria's favorites. The piece was once played immediately after an execution, and Półtawska felt strongly the contrast between the beauty of the music and the ugliness of the moment.

Mandl often found in music an emotional support which allowed her to distance herself from her increasingly savage actions. Prisoner Maria Bielicka related a story she heard about Maria's love for music. A friend of hers had the job of cleaning the overseers' living quarters, where a senior guard had a piano. "One day my friend went in and heard the most beautiful music. The woman who was playing was lost in a world of her own—in ecstasy. It was the same guard [Mandl] who had murdered the Jewish women a few days earlier."

In a few years Maria's love for music would result in the creation of the first and only women's orchestra in the whole concentration camp system.

In the meantime, for Maria and her colleagues, Ravensbrück had become both home and community.

CHAPTER 15

Christmas in Ravensbrück

*The holidays were very cruel. Everyone was thinking about
her own home. But we did sing Christmas carols.*

—Zofia Ciszek

ALTHOUGH ANY HOLIDAY IN A concentration camp was hard, Christmas was particularly difficult for prisoners. The guards, by contrast, attended festive parties which were arranged for all SS personnel, who were allowed to decorate their own apartments. In theory, the Nazi regime promoted the celebration of a more generic Yule or winter solstice holiday. In practice, prisoners were often charged with putting up Christmas trees and decorations for the SS and their families.

Wanda Półtawska remembers that cruelly and "perhaps to taunt us, the Germans had put up a tree in the camp street; a tree with fairy lights, which we walked past each day, weary with our duties."

December of 1941, Maria's third Christmas in Ravensbrück, is especially vivid in the memories of survivors. It was a bitterly cold month with howling winds that cut cruelly through the camp. On Christmas Eve one of the guards in a textile shed took pity on the prisoners and allowed each national group to sing a Christmas carol. Półtawska describes the moment: "The Germans sang first, though *Silent Night* sounded strangely ill-suited to those noisy surroundings."

The Poles chose a carol of their own, "But when we came to the words, 'Take my hand, O Christ Child,' we choked on our tears and could not continue."

Likewise, many prisoners were filled with a sense of loneliness and despair when "Silent Night"—probably chosen by Maria—was broadcast over the camp. As one survivor stated, "The loudspeakers played carols, the guards yelled at us," and people were beaten and killed.

In the days leading up to the holiday a Roma girl escaped. Although she was caught fairly quickly, the camp still had to do roll calls for three days in the bitter cold. On Christmas Day, in front of all the women, they killed the teenager by beating her in front of the Christmas tree.

CHAPTER 16

The Prisoners

RAVENSBRÜCK MADE AN INTENSE AND terrifying impression on prisoners entering for the first time. Trains would arrive at the Fürstenburg train station, usually early in the morning. Women guards screaming "*Raus! Raus!*" ("Out! Out!") flooded the platform, each with a barking dog and a whip. Prisoners were marched around the lake to the camp, greeted by the omnipresent cawing ravens, and herded through the gate, after which they were forcibly stripped, shaved, and showered. In the midst of this terror prisoners couldn't help noticing that the camp itself was orderly, and that flowers incongruously had been planted in front of the barracks. As one prisoner later stated, "Red salvia in bloom, and ever since then I just can't stand that particular flower! And the flower has no guilt!" By 1940, it was not uncommon for an arriving prisoner to see a charred body hanging on the electric fence, left there to act as a deterrent.

The new prisoner was often assigned to a barracks with little or no regard to her background, ethnicity, or profession. A sheltered young woman from a middle- or upper-class family could suddenly be living in close proximity with a prostitute, a career criminal, or simply with women who did not speak her language.

Certain barracks or blocks became notorious, such as the notoriously filthy Block Two, populated by prisoners labeled "asocials." One young woman remarked that entering this barrack was like "stepping naked into a cage of wild animals." Another was horrified that many women shit or pissed into their food bowls or in the bunks, and was taken aback by the aggressive lesbianism.

The new prisoners were forced to acclimate quickly to the camp. Any order given by an overseer or a block elder had to be promptly followed. All prisoners had to get up immediately at the sound of the wake-up siren at 4:00 A.M. and stay in bed after curfew. Prisoners were often disciplined for small or perceived infractions of the rules.

Mandl, in her later deposition, rather blithely and inaccurately boasts about the prisoners' living conditions. She describes adequate clothing, weekly baths and laundry, access to equipped kitchens, and claims that, to a large degree, the asocials (criminals) were the only women used for heavy labor. Mandl also calls attention to the "two free hours at mid-day when they could walk around the camp road and listen to the radio," and notes that twice a month they could receive mail, purchase things in the canteen to eat or drink, and that prisoners who did not have money could receive funds from a "welfare lady." She notes proudly that "everybody had Sunday totally off—they could spend the entire day in the open air."

A few early prisoners concurred with aspects of this assessment of the camp. Women lived for the weekends, when, after working a half-day Saturday, they were largely left alone until Monday morning. Prisoners could stroll on the camp streets, talk, and exchange gossip.

Most prisoners, including Wanda Półtawska, remembered their Sundays rather differently, when a radio loudspeaker was put up on the camp's main street. She noted that in a show camp like Ravensbrück, care was taken to provide "cultural entertainment" for the prisoners. "What a joke! The loudspeaker blared forth, blasting out our ear-drums and dragging us out of sleep. The nauseating tones of *Träumerei* jangled our nerves."

In the early months of the camp things ran relatively smoothly. Over the next two years, however, as additional and unending prisoner transports arrived, challenges arose. *Aufseherin* Jane Bernigau described the stresses this put on the overseers. She noted that, at first, the living environment was quite good and even the prisoners said positive things. However, when war broke out, conditions in the

camp became more serious. The situation worsened when Ravensbrück began to receive an overwhelming number of new prisoners.
This, in turn, created dissatisfaction among the overseers—who now
had a much greater workload. The greater demands and responsibilities caused some of the overseers to request transfers. "These were
always refused with the remark that we had to do our service where
we were placed."

Like all the overseers, Maria struggled with the overcrowding of
the camp. She later testified that on her arrival in May of 1939, eight
hundred prisoners were detained in the camp. By the time she left
in October of 1942, there were eight thousand.

CHAPTER 17

The Bunker

I also flogged the sentenced prisoners on several occasions, they were the asocial ones placed in the Bunker who were penalized because they were playing rotten tricks. Only sometimes it happened that I hit a prisoner in the face when she was behaving insolently.

—MARIA MANDL

IN EARLY 1940 MANDL WAS assigned as supervisor, along with Dorothea Binz, to the recently completed camp jail known as "the Bunker." She later described it as a building for punishment where "such elements were placed who did not want to follow the orders of the camp." Maria now had tremendous power and her own small kingdom to oversee. As such, she became more feared than even the higher-ranked Johanna Langefeld.

The Bunker, essentially a mini cell block, was equipped with all the accoutrements necessary for enforcing discipline in the camp. It was a sturdy rectangular building with individual cells on either side of a centralized two-story walkway and corridor. The lower level was purposely built to be largely underground. Small cell doors on both levels opened to the hallways, and lights in the ceiling were round balls on metal stems which cast circular shadows on ceiling. There were paned windows at both ends of the building.

The SS described the area immediately outside the Bunker as "The Garden." Flowers were planted in front, separated from the camp by an interior wall, and in a narrow corridor between the building and the main wall covered in barbed wire. These small green areas in the gray atmosphere of the camp provided space for the overseers to take a quick coffee break from their duties inside.

Mandl later described the Bunker in positive terms. "It contained cells, plank beds which could be lifted up during the day, a table, a stool, running water with a wash basin, WC. The floors were painted with varnish. They were clean and airy cells."

Of course, the actual conditions were decidedly worse, and the Bunker soon became one of the most feared destinations in the camp. A woman could be sent there for almost any reason: not responding quickly enough to an order, making excessive noise in the barracks, taking part in "lesbian swinishness" or not reporting lesbian activity in others, planning an escape, or even for "bad bed-making."

Upon entry the prisoner had her clothes and shoes taken away and she was confined in a dark, dank, and cold cell without adequate food or blankets. Prisoners were sometimes doused with high-pressure hoses, turning them black and blue.

In winter, frostbite was common, and it became a regular occurrence for guards to find bodies frozen to the floors of the cells or mummified from starvation. There was also a designated "ice room." The prisoner, for some minor offense, had to stand for hours barefoot on the ice. For more severe punishment women were stripped naked. If a prisoner lost consciousness after a beating, she was laid on the floor of the cell and a water tap was turned on. If she froze, so be it. Many of the Jehovah's Witnesses died in this way.

Prisoners later described other forms of abuse, including standing punishment with food deprivation, detention in the dark, or the cruelest of all, twenty-five blows with the rod. Soon, beatings became routine.

Before her trial in 1947, and seeking to lessen the impact of witness accounts, Maria downplayed punishments in the Bunker with descriptions the survivors found laughable.

> Prisoners were punished for 3–28 days. They received
> coffee and bread twice a day for 3 days and on the 4th
> day full board. They received blankets for sleeping.
> There were others who had to be kept in single cells (by
> order of the Kommandant, doctor, or other). They re-
> ceived the same food and were treated the same as in the
> camp.

Of all atrocities carried out in the Bunker, the continued beatings
left the greatest impression on survivors. Maria later stated that "In
1940–1941, I do not remember exactly, beating with a cane was introduced for women and for repeat offenders. This punishment was
carried out by a superior as determined by the head supervisor and
the camp commander; after the superiors refused, then it was done
by the prisoners. This was only done after Reichsführer Himmler
approved it."

In 1942 Himmler did initiate a policy stating that implementation
of the "intensified corporal punishment" should be done on the
naked backside.

The usual penalty was twenty-five strikes with a rod, during
which the prisoner had to count along. For many, already weak, sick,
or elderly, this became a death sentence.

Monday was "hit day" for penalties in the Bunker. At first, Mandl
and Kögl were present and did all the beatings; later they were aided
by Dorothea Binz. By the end of 1940 thrashings were so frequent
that Kögl arranged for women from the criminal or punishment
block to "help." They were given extra food for this duty, causing
many women to volunteer. One prisoner noted that "if they hit hard
enough they got extra food, if they didn't hit hard enough they
would be killed."

Today, a whipping table—designed for that purpose—is on display in the Ravensbrück museum. The wood is seasoned, worn
smooth from use. It is sturdy, constructed from wooden slats, with
leather straps designed to hold the person down. Two small holes
for the feet, like old-fashioned New England stocks, are in the

lower part of the stand. These were often clamped painfully around the woman's ankles.

A prisoner sentenced to a beating from the general camp population had to remove her underwear before leaving the barracks. After entering the whipping room, she was forced to lie face down, her skirts lifted, and she was flogged on her uncovered flesh. The victims almost always got hit in the area of the kidneys. Huge wounds and death often followed.

The flogging bench was placed in the middle of the room, and on the right wall hung a bullwhip with a strap the beater could wrap around her hand in order to strike with greater force. A pail on the other side was used to pour water on the prisoner if she lost consciousness. Another bench was layered with several blankets to muffle screams. The beatings were often administered in complete darkness.

All of the overseers, Mandl included, were continually indoctrinated with the necessity for this kind of violence. Overseers also received inspirational edicts, urging them to fulfill Nazi ideals and "beat down the enemy objectively and without exception."

It was primarily through her activities in the Bunker that Mandl gained infamy as a cruel sadist. Many women noted that after Maria personally executed the punishment by flogging, she would leave the Bunker looking radiant and happy.

At her war crimes trial, there were many testimonies about Mandl's time in the Bunker.

Survivors Aleksandra Steuer and Klara Schnippering testified that, when they were in the Bunker, horrible screams were heard from prisoners abused by Mandl. Steuer noted that Mandl had a special technique for beating where she would take one glove off. She also delighted in tormenting and mocking women confined to punishment cells, often withholding food until the prisoner starved to death. When prisoners complained about the lack of food, Mandl said that under her command a person "would swell with hunger!"

Nelia Epker, a Dutch prisoner, remembered that "supervisor Mandl beat me on July 21, 1942, terribly with a piece of wood, and that due to her [I was sent] for 6 weeks in the Bunker, which was the same as a death warrant, because at that time the bunker was so terrible that nobody up to then had lived there very long. For weeks I stayed there in icy cold temperatures in the basement and had only once in four days a little to eat. Only through a miracle did I survive."

Both Mandl and Binz had reached an emotional nadir, where the power and act of beating another woman gave them great satisfaction—physical, mental, and sexual.

In April of 1942 Mandl signed the Bunker administrative report for the last time. Her activities had brought Maria positive recognition and she had been awarded a promotion. Maria now became the head overseer, *Oberaufseherin*, of the Ravensbrück concentration camp for women.

CHAPTER 18

In Charge

Frau Langefeld's place was taken by a fury named Mandl.
You're never so badly off in a concentration camp that it can't
get worse, and this Mandl was a sadistic beast.
—MARGARETE BUBER-NEUMANN

MARIA MANDL'S TRAJECTORY THROUGH THE ranks of female over-seers had been swift and assured. When Johanna Langefeld was transferred in April of 1942, Maria was the logical choice to suc-ceed her as head overseer.

Earlier that year Himmler had come to Ravensbrück to recruit guards for the chaotic and unorganized women's camp in Auschwitz. Because Langefeld was the most experienced and highest-ranking female, Himmler arranged to transfer her to Poland, along with many of the seasoned guards.

Maria, recently returned from vacation, was promoted to *Oberauf-seherin.* Although she later stated that "I was not very happy about this and would have preferred to be sent to an office having nothing to do with the prisoners," the promotion undoubtedly provided her with great professional satisfaction. She had risen as high as it was possible to go at the camp.

Daniel Patrick Brown observes that "the senior overseer was roughly equivalent to a male officer (although she could never order a male to do anything). In addition, the Oberaufseherin was a member of the command staff of the camp. Her powers over all the women guards beneath her were close to absolute, and subordinate female guards had to ensure that they did not do anything that would anger her."

Both Mandl and Langefeld before her struggled with the challenges of overseeing and administering the often immature and contentious women recruited to be guards. Mandl later said that although the difficulties of hiring and maintaining good female supervisors and guards were worse in Auschwitz, they were already a problem in Ravensbrück.

Additionally, as the camp system expanded, many of the experienced guards were recruited or taken away to staff positions in other camps. This caused great resentment. Mandl complained that "as the female supervisors were engaged, they selected the best for themselves and sent the rest to Auschwitz, Lublin, or some of the other camps. There was a lot of trouble about it."

Some female guards were disciplined or released due to "moral turpitude" or various infractions of the rules. Maria expressed frustration about her inability to get even *more* women fired from their positions, when the male high command essentially dismissed her concerns about the women and simply transferred them to other camps.

> We had released female supervisors in Oranienberg after 5–6 days, often asked for their dismissal, since they were impossible [to use] for this purpose for moral reasons. It was not approved and they were transferred to another camp. It often drove me to despair, and in the summer of '41 I went to Oranienburg for this reason with Kommandant Kramer. We described to Glücks the impossible conditions. Nothing was done about it because the men had no trouble with it and their nerves did not suffer because of it.

Despite these challenges, Maria rose to the responsibilities of her new position with enthusiasm and diligence. She was now in charge, and she was ready.

CHAPTER 19

"The Mistress of Life and Death"

Ich habe Blut geleckt (I have licked blood—and found it good)
—Swabian folk saying

Maria strode onto the Appellplatz early one morning, well rested and ready to begin the day. Her golden hair, gleaming and freshly set, had been enhanced by the camp beauty shop. She was wearing a beautifully tailored uniform that showed off her figure, so tight you could see the muscles rippling underneath like well-coordinated snakes. Her light eyes glowed with self-importance, her cheeks were rosy and flushed with power.

As was her custom, Maria wore spotless white gloves and carried her favorite leather bullwhip. In earlier days Maria had often worked with a dog, but lately, as her status and rank had increased in the camp, she preferred using a bicycle. Her athletic body enabled her to jump on and off with great agility and to quickly cover large areas of the camp.

At first glance the camp street appeared deserted, a fact Maria relished. She had noticed that her unexpected appearance often caused women to scurry quickly into the closest available barrack. It appealed to Maria's sense of importance, that her presence alone could cause such terror. She perused the now wide and empty camp street with satisfaction. Time to get to work and ferret out some of these "*Sau-Hunden*" ("Pig-Dogs").

It was in Ravensbrück that Maria reached the apogee of her brutality. Skills developed in the Bunker equipped her well for the extreme cruelty that now became her trademark. Any trace of softness had long since fled her face and her character. Savagery was the order of the day, and Maria rose to the challenge and the expectation.

As the new *Oberaufseherin*, Maria administered the twice daily roll calls which counted and accounted for the number of prisoners. Final totals were presented to Mandl by the lower-ranked overseers, who then had to make sure the numbers tallied.

The prisoner's day began at 4:00 A.M. with the first siren. This kicked off a frenzy of activity in which prisoners were expected to use the bathroom, make their beds, and send someone to the kitchen for rations—all within the space of an hour. A second siren sounded at 5:00 A.M. that was the signal for everybody to gather in the roll call square to be counted. The leaders of each barracks formed the women in their group to line up in rows of ten to make sure everybody was accounted for. Crows and ravens would often fly around the prisoners in great numbers and caw unpleasantly.

After another hour, sometimes more, the overseers came on the scene and walked down and between the rows of the prisoners. Each overseer would receive a count from the block leader and would often cuff or punish one of the prisoners just for fun.

One witness, later interviewed in Dachau, remembered the young and beautiful Mandl riding a bicycle in front of nine thousand women. All knew that such a ride always abounded with disasters, and the Polish women muttered prayers under their breath as she went by. If Mandl saw the moving lips, she would hit the women on their faces while still on the bike. Eventually, after all the numbers tallied, the siren would sound again, dismissing the women to their daily work assignments.

After Maria's promotion, roll calls took on added terror and rigor. Once or twice a week, if it was raining or very hot, Maria would leave an entire block or the entire *Appellplatz* standing for hours. She would then agree to receive reports at the head table, saying sarcastically, if conditions were especially bad, "Nice weather isn't it? It's really good if you stand in open air." Every roll call would end with the beating of multiple prisoners, and one woman was horrified to observe that "beating us in anger gave her pleasure. After each execution she became more pretty." Maria had truly become, as the camp population described her, "the Mistress of Life and Death."

Prisoners endured as they were able. Many stared at the sky and took comfort in what were often magnificent sunrises and sunsets, filled with a radiant kaleidoscope of colors. The occasional late-night roll calls, for women assigned to night shifts in the textile workrooms, had their own kind of macabre fascination. Wanda Półtawska remembered a night when her work detail was standing under a dark blue sky full of stars, surrounded by the light of two lanterns and their own shadows. Someone "suggested that our row of worn-out skeletons would fit well into a horror movie."

Nicknamed "The Tigress" for her habit of stalking prisoners and sneaking around behind columns of women, Maria, daughter of a shoemaker, seemed to take great delight in creating agonies for the women's feet.

She often ordered roll calls be conducted without shoes or socks in the coldest days of winter, causing tremendous suffering, and initiated a policy in June of 1942 that banned all wooden shoes for prisoners. Regardless of her job, a prisoner now had to be barefoot. As a result, there were massive foot injuries and an ongoing lack of proper treatment. If a prisoner dared to line her feet on the bottom with a scrap of paper or cardboard as meager protection against the cold, Mandl would beat her savagely for her effrontery. Maria would even lie on the ground and peek to see if a paper was underneath anyone's feet.

Prisoner Urszula Wińska learned that Mandl had ordered the side streets of the camp, which they took to get to the workshops every day, be covered with cinders. Urszula described going through this torture four times a day and noted that when the women had smoothed the sharp edges of the cinder with their feet, a new layer was laid. One day a prisoner went to the side of the road to walk where there was less cinder. Unexpectedly from a side street, Mandl appeared on a bicycle, in white gloves and a uniform, and hit the prisoner on her cheek with a swift movement. "The poor woman fell face down in the cinders and Mandl rode away with triumph on her face." Urszula concludes, "She was intoxicated by her power!"

Survivors vividly remembered this torture and its horrific physical cost. "Bare feet on rough gravel of camp streets. If someone had paper or bandage on their feet Mandl and Ehrich would kick and beat and all blows were directed to the 'pussed areas.' Dust from the street accumulated in the wounds, flies laid eggs there, the wounds stank more and more and the poor victims couldn't walk."

Appalled by the terrible injuries sustained by these practices, the chief camp doctor twice intervened, begging permission for prisoners to wear clogs. He was turned down on both occasions.

All prisoners suffered the agonies of Mandl's shoe policies and terrible roll call conditions. Zofia Ciszek remembers those roll calls with horror. "In the fall and winter they were VERY early because it was still dark, and endless because the numbers never matched. And it was so COLD. Excruciatingly cold—especially in the morning, even in summer." Ciszek also shuddered when remembering that from the early spring to late fall, the prisoners were barefoot. She concluded, "The morning roll calls were the toughest ones."

CHAPTER 20

The Hunt of the Curly-Heads

We were told every day that we were nothing but numbers, that we had to forget we were human beings, that we had nobody to think of us, that we would never return to our country, that we were slaves, and that we had only to work. We were not allowed to smile, to cry, or to pray. We were not allowed to defend ourselves when we were beaten.

—JADWIGA DZIDO

JADWIGA DZIDO, A PRISONER, REMEMBERED that in 1942 great hunger and terror reigned in the camp. "The Germans were at the zenith of their power. You could see the haughtiness and pride on the face of every SS woman." As Maria settled into her position as *Oberaufseherin* she fed voraciously upon this terror of the prisoners and her ability to determine life or death. One woman remembered that Mandl liked it when they passed her with fear. She carried her head high with pride and looked down on the prisoners with contempt. "She reveled in her power. She was always in full regalia, including the gloves. Tormenting and abusing prisoners reassured her of her own importance."

Mandl's torture often contained a sexual element. "One time she undressed a prisoner during the strongest cold on the camp street in front of the entire roll call, which was more than 10,000 women, until she was naked and then beat her."

Other prisoners remember that under Maria's rule "women were ordered to 'perform' [have sex] for German soldiers! Anyone who refused was sent to the Bunker while those who agreed were promised release after three months. If a woman returned from the brothel with a venereal disease, she was killed with a shot of poison."

Almost any infraction, perceived or real, could result in punishment and usually did. Prisoners remember that it was impossible to tell what was forbidden and what wasn't, and as a result, they were constantly punished.

Maria Liwo remembered that one of Mandl's first orders after becoming *Oberaufseherin* was "that all bras and clogs be taken away. She also took away sheets and mattresses so the prisoners had to sleep on hard wood and often gave punishment of '50 whips.' The most common sentence was 25 whips, 4 weeks in the Bunker, and 3 months of Strafblock." Another prisoner remarked that Mandl's period as *Oberaufseherin* was "the time of the biggest hunger." "We were served over boiled and rotten potatoes. Every Sunday she ordered fasting/starvation."

Minnie Artner describes Mandl's tenure as a regimen of horror. The head overseer would appear unexpectedly in the barracks, examine the cupboards, confiscate any small treasures the women had organized, and issue reprimands. "At the counting roll call there was no column the way she wished it [up to her standard]. At the outdoor labor, she appeared and screamed with the supervisors, with the prisoners and distributed her very well-known slaps on the face."

Mandl seemed especially hostile toward the Polish women, often hurling insults like "*Sau-Hunde*," ("Sow-Dogs"), "Polish Gang," and "Polish Pigs," and giving them extra beatings. One survivor remembered that when Mandl encountered a mentally unstable Polish prisoner, "she killed the woman in front of my eyes. She had utmost hatred towards Polish women, beat us, persecute us."

According to camp regulations, inmates had to tie their hair up into a bun. Offended for some reason by curly hair, Maria would single out for punishment any unfortunate woman who dared allow even a small curl to escape from underneath her kerchief.

Mandl often embarked on this special sport—the hunt of the curly-heads. "Once Mandl identified an offender she would pull her out of line, rip off her kerchief, box her around the ears and head, and kick and bludgeon her with her boots. The inmate's prison number would then be recorded and she would be taken away and shaved. Afterwards the unfortunate prisoner would be forced to wear a placard around her neck stating that she had offended the camp order and grown her locks of hair.

It was also during Mandl's tenure as *Oberaufseherin*, in spring of 1942, that executions of prisoners by shooting started. Executions took place on Tuesday and Friday of every week.

"They did it in a wicked way, for example the names were brought of the people who were to be executed the following day. And they always did it so the sound of guns was heard during evening roll call." Executions took place on Death Row, behind the camp wall, where the victims faced a firing squad.

Wanda Urbanska, who worked in the camp office, was given the responsibility of locating the files of condemned prisoners and carrying them and the prisoners' names on a sheet of paper to Kögl for final approval and then to Mandl. Urbanska confirmed that Mandl would then escort those women to the Bunker, where they sat until evening roll call.

When the other prisoners were gathered, the convicted women were led behind the gate. "Then, after a dozen minutes or so, one could hear a volley of shots. I stress that on several occasions women prisoners were [personally] escorted by Mandl. The names of the executed prisoners were then crossed off the list."

Mandl seemed to delight in these executions. One prisoner remembers that before the victims were led to execution, Mandl would beat and kick them without a reason. "I stress that she did this often, however she would hit 'professionally,' that is, into the painful places/parts of the body. She would beat until loss of consciousness—the victims had battered, bleeding and bruised faces."

Wanda Półtwaksa remembered the executions vividly. How she and her friends did not weep when the lists of people to be killed the next day were delivered to their barracks. How they did not weep at roll call when the rifle shots rang out. "How terrible is the silence of a crowd of women!" She later summarized that "words may be eloquent, but how much more so is silence, especially the silence of many thousands of people." The carefully calculated cruelty of these murders, and the manner in which they were executed, remained seared in the memories of all the survivors.

CHAPTER 21

The Biggest Cruelty

She was a tall, strong person and was able to strike down the emaciated prisoners with one punch.

—MARIE WIEDMAIER

Beating with a hand on the face was not, in my opinion, such a big offense.

—MARIA MANDL

THE ABUSES CONTINUED, ONE AFTER another, in a seemingly relentless stream. Maria was caught up in a vortex of power, fueled by paroxysms of rage and the heady perks of her position. She continued beating dozens of prisoners daily, often in the face.

"I remember in 1941 Mandl beat one woman prisoner to the point she died in the camp hospital a few days later. She held her by the hair with her left hand and hit her with a fist in the face, which dissolved in blood, and when the woman fell, kept kicking her in the stomach a dozen or so times."

Maria was known for her omnipresent whip, often bolstered by a rubber club or plank of wood. Most prisoners avoided Mandl if they could, as she was apt to suddenly begin beating and kicking women with little or no provocation. The unpredictability of her attacks inspired terror, some of the women even fearing to breathe during roll call lest she sneak up soundlessly behind them. "Suddenly, like a hawk she would strike—beating, kicking, pulling out hair, before the person could figure out what had happened." Her physical presence magnified the horror. "White eyes gleamed like phosphorus at night. White teeth clenched, her voice would raise with the passion of a high falsetto."

Wanda Półtawska remembered that Maria "would stand straddled in her top boots and roar at us... She used to beat the prisoners with her horsewhip upon their heads and everywhere but she never beat me. In general, she rather wreaked her rage upon old women and we were young."

Indeed, a woman's older age seemed to be a catalyst for Maria's brutality. Perhaps this was a conscious or unconscious expression of resentment toward her own mother, who was still struggling with depression and illness back home in Münzkirchen.

Urszula Wińska was friends with Nelia Epker, who shared an incident about an older woman in the camp, greatly respected by the other prisoners. One day on the main camp street, Epker saw Mandl beating her. She ran up to Mandl and said "Why are you beating this old woman? She could be your mother!" Mandl raised her hand intending to hit Epker. Instead, Epker grabbed her by the hand and said, "I am a lady and you have no right to hit me!"

In retaliation, Mandl sent Epker to the Bunker for three months with almost no food and very harsh conditions. Every day Mandl rushed in and stopped by the cell and hit her in the face, saying "You are a lady and I can beat you!"

Occasionally Maria seemed to register a reality check. Hanna Sturm, a longtime prisoner who had known Mandl since Lichtenburg, described a winter roll call that went on for twelve hours in the snow and rain. It was very cold and many had already succumbed, bodies littering the *Appellplatz*. Maria was there, dressed warmly in a leather coat, beating according to her whim. Sturm decided ("what the hell") to take the risk of approaching as Mandl stood there smirking. "Frau Ober Mandl, you are Austrian." Mandl: "Shut up!" Sturm: "Please, let us leave the lines. Look how many dead bodies are lying there already. Your mother could be among them!" Mandl gave Sturm a kick and went into the office. Five minutes later the siren sounded and the prisoners were released back into the barracks. Sturm concluded, "Somehow one had to touch her insides as if they knew her."

Mandl seemed to bear a special grudge against the Jehovah's Witnesses, a legacy from her time in Lichtenburg. "Prisoners who wore crosses drove her crazy (total insanity). They made crosses from buttons, toothbrushes, etc. She treated this as sabotage and severely punished them." One survivor remembers Maria ripping a cross from her neck so viciously that she erupted in blood, further enraging "the Ober," who kicked her to the ground, causing lasting kidney damage.

After the war, prisoners described Mandl as "the biggest cruelty." Later, when Maria was on trial for her life, she stated that "as long as the prisoners were decent I was never malicious or nasty."

> I was nice to them and was always happy to help them. I have sometimes given a slap on the face when things were out of hand and were vicious. [But] I have never [seriously] hurt any woman, since I would have been held responsible for it. I would never have attacked a decent person or done any harm to them.
>
> According to camp regulations, which I was familiar with, we were forbidden to beat the prisoners, but I understood it in such a way that they were not supposed to be beaten with special tools, like a cane or a club. Therefore, beating with a hand on the face was not, in my opinion, such a big offense.

CHAPTER 22

Lab Rabbits

It was worse than the smell of rotting corpses. Our own legs.

—Zofia Kawińska, former Lab Rabbit

THE YEAR 1942 BROUGHT MANY new developments to Maria's life. After a major expansion of Ravensbrück, twelve new barracks were built, and a punishment and death camp, Ueckermark, opened on the camp's periphery. Maria's brother Georg went to war.

It was at this time that Maria took a necessary step to assure her future in the Nazi hierarchy. "In 1941 I joined a party organization the Deutsche Frauenschaft and in the summer of 1942 joined the NSDAP. At this time the SS men in the camp sent out a questionnaire stressing that all guards had to belong to the party."

It was only now, five years after the Anschluss and Maria's termination from the Münzkirchen post office for not being a member of the National Socialist Party—and the loss of her fiancé for the same reason—that Maria became an official Nazi.

Other developments in the war also impacted Maria's life. In May of 1942 SS-*Obergruppenführer* Reinhard Heydrich was assassinated by members of a Czech resistance group. In retaliation, Hitler ordered the complete destruction of a Czech village called Lidice. The men of Lidice were killed outright in a mass execution. A significant number of women and children from the Lidice area were brought to Ravensbrück, immediately becoming a severely persecuted minority, blamed for Heydrich's death and subjected to horrifyingly brutal treatment.

Although Heydrich survived his initial injuries, he died a few days after the attack from infection and sepsis. The Nazi doctors who treated Heydrich were criticized for not saving his life. One of them, Karl Gebhardt, was ordered by Himmler to carry out experiments at Ravensbrück utilizing some new sulfa (sulfanilamide) drugs. The intent was to create and then treat injuries which mimicked the catastrophic wounds suffered by men in battle, and also the wounds suffered by Heydrich. Thus began the so-called Lab Rabbit program, which ran from July of 1942 to September of 1943.

Women selected for these experiments were taken largely from recent transports of young and healthy political prisoners out of Lublin, Poland. Each had wounds deliberately inflicted on her legs or other extremities which were then infected with bacteria such as streptococcus, gas gangrene, and tetanus. Many were given authentic gunshot wounds. Blood vessels were tied off at both ends of the wound to cut off circulation and mimic a battle injury.

In addition to bacteria, foreign objects, such as ground glass or wood shavings, were forced into the wounds, which were then treated by sulfa and other drugs to study the results. Women were also subjected to unbelievably painful regeneration experiments in which bone, muscle, and nerves were removed from extremities, creating permanent disability.

Postwar photographs of these wounds prompt visceral incredulity and dismay, the observer's thoughts darting about like mice in a trap, the mind refusing to accept what the eyes are seeing. Young, healthy legs cleaved by enormous wounds, separated fascia, the mutilation pronounced and impossible to conceal. Of the many horrifying images to come out of the Holocaust, these are some of the worst.

The program began in July, when seventy-five of the Lublin women were summoned to the *Appellplatz* and subsequently subjected to leg exams and verification of their papers. Shortly thereafter, the women were divided into smaller groups and the first operations took place.

Wanda Półtawska, one of the Lab Rabbits, describes that round of operations and the girls lying there in pain, crying, moaning, screaming, and cursing. "Only our group, the first of the 'guinea pigs,' were fortunate enough to have a night-sister on duty. Our successors were simply locked in for the night, completely unattended."

A second set of operations was initiated to "learn more about regeneration." Muscles were severed and bones were broken, sometimes with hammers and resulting in permanent disability. Others were taken elsewhere for experimental surgeries involving amputations and bone transplants. It was hoped they could be used for "spare parts" for wounded German soldiers. These unfortunate women were classified as "mentally ill" and all were killed by injection.

Later, Maria Mandl stated that she had no knowledge of the experimental surgeries. "At the end of my stay in Ravensbrück there was some talk of experimental procedures taking place, but what they were I do not know, because these matters were handled directly by the doctors with the commandants. Even I, a senior supervisor, had no insight."

However, survivor testimonies during the Krakow and Nuremberg trials revealed that Mandl personally chose at least eighty prisoners for the medical experiments performed in Ravensbrück.

One survivor, Vladislava Karolewska, testified in Nuremberg that she remembered distinctly the first selection outside the camp office, at which Kögl, Mandl, and Dr. Fritz Fischer [the Ravensbrück staff physician] were present. Then thirty-seven years old, Vladislava was operated on six different times and subjected to sulfanilamide, bone, muscle, and nerve experiments. On the 25th of July, all the women from the Lublin transports were again summoned by Mandl, who told them they were not allowed to work outside of the camp. The next day they were summoned again.

Other testimonies concur that Mandl was intrinsically and proactively involved with the selection process. Two of the camp's inmate doctors verified that Mandl personally chose the women for these operations. "Mandl and Langefeld posted the list of names from the office. They knew about the experiments."

At Maria's trial Dr. Zofia Maczka stated firmly that "all preparations to conduct experiments were done under Mandl's rule and were started then. She oversaw moving transports from which women were selected for experimentation and was also surely aware of the enormous suffering these operations caused. The women were totally incapacitated, some in casts, pus flowing, some couldn't walk."

Zofia Kawińska was a Lab Rabbit. In the summer of 1942 she was a teenager, newly arrived from Lublin and still adjusting to camp life. Sixty years later she is a tiny woman with alert brown eyes, frail but not fragile, with an enormous strength of character that carries through into her body. Articulate and succinct in her answers, Zofia has short, dark gray hair, parted on the side. Her companion, a slate-blue canary with feather bangs, is very lively and contributes to the conversation.

For our interview she has provided us with a beautiful selection of cold meats, breads, and a homemade cheesecake. The smell of salami wafts around the room in a pleasant way, contrasting hugely with her descriptions of the extreme hunger in the camp. Even now, safe in her home decades later, she shudders at what was done to her and her friends. "They cut our legs, put dirt of different kinds in them, including iron scraps and so on, and then sewed them up and put on a cast. It was a HORRIBLE experience, the pain is... There are no words to describe the pain." Zofia remembers being half-conscious, locked up for the night, and calling for someone to help. She remembers her friends crying and falling from the beds, and still no one came.

Zofia survived Ravensbrück, graduated from dental school after the war, and started working in a clinic near Lublin. As with many of the surviving Lab Rabbits, the surgeries to which she was subjected altered the course of her life and her future. Zofia described postwar conditions in Poland as very primitive, where even the best dental clinics did not have proper equipment. She struggled to stand on her feet six hours a day. At first her office had an electric dental drilling machine, but this broke quickly and Zofia had to propel it by foot with a kind of a conveyer belt (shudder from the interpreter, who had been subjected to just such a dental drill). "Until this day I have problems with my right leg and hip [from the Ravensbrück surgeries]. So I didn't work long, maybe ten years—I quit because I just couldn't continue."

Zofia is representative of all the Lab Rabbits; horribly mutilated young women, whose lives were irrevocably changed due to policies administered by Maria Mandl and initiated by an uncaring ruler and regime. As fellow Lab Rabbit Wacława Gnatowska stated many years later, "That period has left an irreversible trace on my body and soul."

CHAPTER 23

The Transfer

Here Supervisor Mandl was selected for the extermination camp Auschwitz because she was the best representative for the gas ovens; corrupt, brutal, like an animal.

—Maria Wiedmaier

A FTER ONLY FOUR MONTHS AS *Oberaufseherin*, Maria's time at Ravensbrück came to an end. In Auschwitz Johanna Langefeld was struggling and fell into disagreement with the *Kommandant*, Rudolf Höss. As a result, she was transferred back to Ravensbrück, and Mandl was ordered to take her place in Auschwitz. Mandl was disgruntled. "I was upset because the supervisors Glücks and Pohl had ushered me into disaster and there was no chance to get out of it quickly."

The prisoner grapevine back at Ravensbrück buzzed with the news: Mandl was leaving from the camp and Langefeld was coming back! This created "heated excitement and joy in the entire camp" because Langefeld was widely recognized for her more humane treatment of prisoners.

Johanna Langefeld had been decidedly ineffectual in her duties at Auschwitz, and Höss often stated his disdain and lack of respect for the women under his command. "Spoiled," as Höss said, by the better conditions at Ravensbrück, the female overseers transferred to Auschwitz rebelled against the primitive conditions and did not fulfill their duties. Langefeld's tenure in the camp had done nothing to change his opinion.

Höss criticized Langefeld's ability to control her guards, saying they ran "hither and thither in all this confusion, like a lot of flustered hens." Langefeld did not disagree with this assessment and had to acknowledge, when many of the young women began sexual affairs with SS men, that morals had disintegrated alarmingly. The Auschwitz staff canteen became known for "drunken debauchery," and one female guard even began an affair with a male prisoner. As conditions deteriorated, the depravity of the female guards saw an exponential increase.

Langefeld also struggled with a crisis of conscience once she became aware of the systematic extermination in the gas chambers at Auschwitz. Later, she asserted that prior to this appointment she had not known "the reason for these camps." In Auschwitz, for the first time, she realized what was really happening. "The total impression," she stated, "made me so depressed that I couldn't close my eyes at night and I often hardly dared to breathe."

Three and a half months later, Langefeld finally got her desired transfer back to Ravensbrück after bungled management of the subsidiary labor camp of Budy and a subsequent riot and prisoner massacre caused a scandal in the SS hierarchy.

Originally, Ravensbrück *Kommandant* Max Kögl had planned to transfer Maria Mandl to Majdanek, where the women's camp lacked leadership. "Kögl requested that I be sent to Lublin but I refused to go to the East." Then, when Langefeld proved inadequate for the challenges at Auschwitz, Maria was told she would be sent there instead.

> My transfer to Auschwitz took place as a result of Langefeld's dismissal whose superiors considered her unfit for the position. I also heard there was an investigation going on against Langefeld for "organizing" Jewish property. The investigation was also going on when she was trans-

ferred from Auschwitz to Ravensbrück, where she was eventually arrested as a result of the investigation.

My transfer to Auschwitz was decided by [SS-*Gruppen-führer*] Glücks, who called me to his office in Oranienburg and informed me that, according to an order of Pohl, I had to go to Auschwitz. I replied that I didn't want to go to Auschwitz and that I requested a discharge. I returned to Ravensbrück where, some time later, Suhren informed me that my transfer to Auschwitz was a fait accompli. I went to Glücks again. He told me that Pohl had decided I had to be transferred to Auschwitz and that I could face worse consequences if I failed to follow this order. Once again I rejected it and returned to Ravensbrück. Finally, after continued persuasion from Suhren—who told me that Pohl was unpredictable and that he might lock me up in a KZ if I refused, I decided to go to Auschwitz.

I fought against this transfer because Auschwitz at that time had the reputation of being famed for being a nest, a hatchery of typhus and lice, and that the hygienic and sanitary conditions were awful.

Despite her protests Maria was ordered to proceed immediately to Auschwitz and soon was en route to Poland.

Part Four

CHAPTER 24

Anteroom to Hell

FLAT. GREEN. THE SCENERY PASSING outside of Maria's window had a depressing monotony to it. Dense woods, ground covered with ferns.

On the train to a new destination yet again, she fumed internally at this latest transfer. Accompanied by Emma Zimmer and dozens of hand-selected prisoners from Ravensbrück, Mandl arrived in Poland with the charge to "create order in the camp." But what an impossible charge, she must have thought, and how exactly was she to do that in the chaos that awaited?

By the time of Maria's arrival the Auschwitz complex had grown to comprise three main camps: Auschwitz I, constructed in 1940; Auschwitz II Birkenau, which became the main center for slave labor and extermination; and Auschwitz III, Monowitz Buna, a subsidiary factory complex of the I. G. Farben company.

The train station lay on the edge of the city of Oświęcim, renamed Auschwitz by the Germans. A river, the Sola, ran past the town, and an old stone bridge led into the closed downtown of the city. Ongoing construction projects lined the outskirts and, along with the houses, had been almost completely taken over for use by camp personnel. Maria heard through the grapevine that the current living quarters for female overseers were rudimentary, far from the *gemütlich* accommodations at Ravensbrück. A building called the *Stabsgebäude* was converted for that purpose.

Auschwitz II, called Birkenau, was located west of the main camp in a grove of birch trees on the former site of Brzezinka, a village. In 1942 the only connection between it and the town was one meandering fortified road which led over the frequently traveled railway line. "This path led from the main camp through various streets of houses to the utilities and past a few industrial plants."

Today, when visiting the camp site and on the surface, Birkenau can appear a peaceful, even bucolic setting. Upon Maria's arrival, however, the camp that awaited was the antithesis.

CHAPTER 25

Hell

…a catastrophic lack of water
—MARIA MANDL, UPON ARRIVAL IN BIRKENAU

THE SMELL. IT WAS THE smell that hit Maria first, reminiscent of overripe hides in her father's cure room or the outhouse on a hot summer's day, with an unsettling smoky and meaty undercurrent. The stench was a living presence, impossible to escape, impossible to ignore.

The women's camp had no water, no sewage disposal. Garbage and human waste lay everywhere, rotting where it had fallen. There was an absence of birds in the sky, as if other living creatures had rejected this fallow place as any kind of home. Underneath hummed a disconcerting and unceasing hubbub, like a bad case of tinnitus, manic and unrelenting. The ground was a bog of mud covered by a miasma of filth, upon which it was impossible to walk normally.

When the wind changed direction, a thick and oily fog made it difficult to breathe. Eyes began to burn, a smoky taste entered one's mouth.

Former prisoner Margot Větrovcóvà remembered that on the day of her arrival "all this seemed to me as a crazy mixture of devastated countryside and cold hell, mixed with an unprecedented circus." The female prisoners were wandering about wearing rags in unfathomable combinations, and only sporadically did she see women in the regular striped uniforms which looked "nearly genteel" next to the rags. "Sporadically a beautiful woman appeared, in silken tights, lady's shoes with heels, in a pink dress with frills and with nice curls and clean. She was a camp officer."

Antonina Kozubek was transferred to Auschwitz in the same group as Mandl. She and the others saw bodies left after the Budy massacre thrown out on the ramp as a "discarded black mess," and were dismayed by the conditions. "The barracks we were placed in were murky as there were no lights there. In Ravensbrück it was very clean so we could not get used to the filth and fleas in the barrack." Maria echoed her shock.

> The conditions were unbearable and I had to shake my head that this was possible, especially since I was used to having a clean camp in Ravensbrück. I did not believe my eyes—terrible conditions! About 7,000 women were cooped up in it, in such a state of exhaustion and apathy that they didn't care about life and showed it, as a result the entire camp was one huge manure pit.
>
> The terrain didn't have sewage and one was walking in boggy ground up to the knees—the soil was clay and one sank into the ground and could barely free oneself, there were no floors in the blocks, so they were wet and muddy and one could sense a catastrophic lack of water. All along the blocks and outside, corpses were lying around.

A German doctor incarcerated in the camp, Ella Lingens-Reiner, described ditches by the camp street, full of dirt, bowls, and food remains, used as a toilet. "The women often had to lick their food out of bowls like dogs. The only source of water was directly adjacent to the latrines and also had the function of causing one to have to use a finger-thick stream of water to flush away the excrement. The women stood there and drank and tried to take the water with them in some kind of container while their partners in suffering relieved themselves right next to them."

On her preliminary tour of the camp Maria was approached by some German women.

> They were placed in a wooden barracks without windows. At the entrance were two young girls who were sick. Their feet were frozen, the legs black up to the ankles. I was upset and wanted to have them brought to the hospital [*Revier*]. They refused to go there and wanted to die where they were. [They said] it would have been worse there. In the section were very sick people, poor desperate souls who asked me on their knees not to leave them alone and help them instead.

Entering another of the primitive barracks, Maria noticed that the structure had been erected in a haphazard fashion. There was no foundation to speak of, almost no floorboards, no water pipes. It was dark and musty, and smelled of unwashed bodies and urine. She could hear constant coughs and moans from all sides. The primitive shelves for sleeping looked like cages for cows or pigs. Women had hung their wet clothing on beams to dry, creating a macabre tableau.

Maria recoiled in disgust when she realized that the barracks and their occupants were infested with lice, bodies and bedding teeming with the ravenous creatures. Her guide explained that due to the lack of water in Birkenau camp, there were always a lot of lice. For that reason, all prisoners had been given an order to stay at least three meters away from any SS man or woman.

Kamp Kommandant Höss confirmed Maria's initial impressions that conditions in the women's camp were atrocious, far worse than in the men's camp, largely due to the extreme overcrowding. Höss described stacks of women reaching to the tops of the barracks and the lack of even the most primitive kind of sanitation. Urine and feces lay underfoot, while everything was black with lice. Typhus was rampant, as was suicide.

Höss blamed the terrible conditions on the prisoners themselves. "When the women had reached a point of no return, they let themselves go completely. They stumbled through the area like ghosts, completely without will, and had to be literally pushed everywhere by others until one day they just quietly died." Mandl, also, blamed the prisoners. "People looked bad, dirty clothes, lice and fleas. No washing facilities but the prisoners actually had no desire to wash themselves and were sliding further and further downhill."

Maria later said that "The first impression in Birkenau made me consider whether or not to go to Berlin to see Glücks to tell him that working there appeared to me to be impossible."

CHAPTER 26

Order and Discipline

*It is absolutely clear to me that in such a large camp there has
to be order and discipline.*

—MARIA MANDL

MARIA WAS OVERWHELMED BY THE chaos of Birkenau camp.
From a logistical standpoint, the challenges facing her were
monumental. Considering Mandl's response through the prism of
an administrative nightmare, removing the human—or humane—
quotient, many of her decisions appear to make sense.

Prisoner Antonina Kozubek confirmed that some of Maria's first
actions were to connect the electricity in the barracks so there would
be light, place stoves in the barracks for heat, and have a toilet area
made from wooden boards installed in the Latrine Block.

Mandl later stated that "I tried to get clean clothes and underwear for the women, but the camp laundry could not supply
anything so I organized an unused barrack for a laundry facility
with basins and soap." Male prisoners from Birkenau were assigned to aid in construction, and she arranged to have internal
walls torn down but "was caught by the building manager, so I received a report which went to Pohl. I received a letter from Pohl
asking why I had acted on my own initiative. I described to him
the terrible situation in the camp and received a severe reprimand.

[But] afterwards I received undergarments, dresses. Soap, combs and I relaxed slightly."

Sick prisoners in the camp were "selected by an SS doctor and prisoner Weiss and sent to Block 25, a walled quarantine barrack, to avoid transmitting diseases."

Mandl describes other early steps she took in the administration of the camp.

> I had the walls inside and outside washed and on the out-
> side I had them painted with…For inside I ordered
> chalk/whitewash. Beds were cleaned and 600 straw mat-
> tresses in awful condition were burnt. I organized spades
> from the construction site for cleaning of the camp, for
> which Tauber [SS-Obersturmbannführer Anton Tauber]
> was helpful.

Mandl received permission to let women in the offices wear their hair long and asked Höss and Dr. Eduard Wirths, chief SS doctor at Auschwitz, for improvements and a nurse for the *Revier*. They suggested she write a letter describing the conditions to Dr. Lolling in Oranienburg and request help. She did this and he turned the request down twice, citing lack of available nursing personnel and ordering her to staff the job from the camp population.

Maria was often frustrated in her other efforts to improve conditions in the women's camp. In her pretrial deposition she stated that

> in Auschwitz the male prisoners were better in every-
> thing as far as provisions were concerned. They had
> enough opportunities to get everything, since they were
> actively working in every department. That the male pris-
> oners were not at all concerned with the well-being of
> the women can be seen by the following: When the men
> had to leave the camp to make room for the women,
> every request for help working in our camp was refused.
> They tore out all electrical wires, switches, bulb holders

and bulbs. I had to turn to the management to repair everything.

We supervisors were faced with these terrible conditions in which to do our work. I had only been in Auschwitz barely four weeks and already seven supervisors were in the hospital with typhus. I had hardly anyone to deploy since some remained in the hospital for one year. We were not allowed to go into the rooms with our dresses and underwear since they were full of fleas and lice from the camp. It was awful.

Gradually conditions improved somewhat. Mandl continued to request cement floors from Höss, who ordered her to "approach chief building manager Bischoff directly 'because as a woman I had a better chance to get results.'" Bischoff refused. Eventually Maria received permission from Oswald Pohl to install stamped clay floors for the barracks, and she noted that "with them it was impossible to keep everything clean and free of lice. Doctors changed a lot. Mengele came and did a lot. Dr. Wirths helped with warm water so typhus and epidemics were reduced."

CHAPTER 27

Appell Was Torture

To save one another's life we dragged the sick, the dying along with us and held them up through those endless hours of numb, bestial suffering.

—GISELLA PERL, INMATE DOCTOR,

AUSCHWITZ-BIRKENAU

T HERE ARE FEW ACCOUNTS OF life in Birkenau that do not make reference to the daily roll calls. Prisoner Aleksandr Kinsky later observed that when Mandl entered the camp the commotion of the roll calls would start and she was always present at roll calls. The Nazi mania for record-keeping made this a high priority, and Maria knew that one of her major tasks as *Oberaufseherin* would be their administration. For the overseers, and especially for the prisoners, this was an onerous and difficult task. Roll calls could last several hours, often in terrible weather. The prisoners, in inadequate clothing and without adequate nutrition, endured as they were able. Later, these roll calls evolved into selections of who would live and who would die, separating sick and healthy prisoners. The extreme suffering during roll calls was a theme which would recur often during Maria's war crimes trial.

Maria stated that "When I took over the camp I could not even determine the exact number of prisoners. To ensure order, I had to catalog the prisoners. For this purpose and with the agreement of the political department, two Sunday roll calls were organized. With the disorder I found, and the lack of any organization, those roll calls were long, they dragged on all day. I state firmly that during these Sunday roll calls none of the prisoners died. It only happened that some of the prisoners fell down due to exhaustion."

Survivors remember the mayhem of those early roll calls. Helen Tichauer, a prisoner who was in the women's camp almost from its inception, remembered a chaotic administrative process in which the female guards floundered. Prisoners would hide, run from one group to another, and the numbers wouldn't match, so the entire process would have to be started over. Maria later stated that "it was terrible with the counting roll call."

On Saturday, February 6, 1943, Maria initiated and supervised a marathon roll call in the Birkenau women's camp which lasted from 3:00 A.M. to 5:00 P.M. in the bitter cold. Over two thousand prisoners died as a result.

Accounts of this terrible *Appell* (roll call) remained vivid in survivors' memories. Gerda Schneider remembers that when the day came all prisoners were ordered to go outside to "the meadows." Delousing was "on the program," and the women stood there all day, scantily clad. "Finally in the afternoon the march back into the camp was called and many women were so stiff and frozen they could not move. These people were pulled aside and gassed. This was the most horrible Appell anyone could remember."

Conditions continued to deteriorate in the camp over the next several months until finally, in September of 1943, Maria appealed to Höss. "I told him about the terrible conditions and he went with me to the camp. I believed he had never seen such conditions and he promised to help. On special order the healthy and sick prisoners were separated." From this point on selection roll calls also increased in frequency, duration, and intensity.

New components were added to make the process more onerous. It was not uncommon for Mandl to give an order for the prisoners to lift their arms above their heads for the duration. It was also regular practice for new prisoners in quarantine to be subjected to all-day roll calls in the " *Wiese* " ("Meadow"), a sarcastically nicknamed barren and icy field which lay near the end of Block 15. There, prisoners picked lice off one another, some fainted, some were beaten.

Helena Niwińska remembered that "during the counting no prisoner dared even flinch because every infringement of the despicable camp discipline could end in tragedy. We were completely terrorized." Anita Lasker-Wallfisch noted that, because the prisoners almost without exception suffered from dysentery, "in plain language, many of us just stood there with shit running down our legs, in complete agony ... It is impossible to convey how extreme our misery was."

Later in 1943, after a general roll call in which four thousand women were selected for the gas, Mandl ordered the kitchen to prepare four thousand dinners less for the following day. These roll calls, for her, had become routine.

CHAPTER 28

A Normal Life

*So that was the camp Auschwitz, in which one could feel quite
good, if one looks away from the other things.*
—Oskar Gröning

SS-Unterscharführer Oskar Gröning, stationed at Auschwitz
the same time as Maria Mandl, remembers that life at camp was
quite a "normal life," which he equated to a small, good, middle-
class German town. "There was one side of life in Auschwitz and
there was another (in the Lager [camp]) and the two were, more or
less, separate."

Living quarters and administrative offices for the SS were segre-
gated and carefully monitored. Solid brick barracks were
surrounded by blooming flowers and carefully tended lawns.

In the *Stabsgebäude*, where the *Aufseherinnen* were housed, female
prisoners were assigned to take care of the staff. The lower floors
were occupied by the supervisors, including at first Maria Mandl.
Later, at Maria's trial, one of the survivors commented that "in Breze-
zinka I knew Mandl because I often worked in the Stabsgebäude
where SS women had hairdressers, had servants, and were [treated
like] princesses."

Food was brought in from outside of Auschwitz, with an additional alcohol ration. A typical SS dinner was thick tomato soup,

half a fried chicken, and a scoop of vanilla ice cream. The SS personnel slept in comfortable beds covered with soft, checkered quilts. The "Auschwitz SS town" had a hairdresser and a special barracks where off-duty personnel could get together and socialize, containing a canteen, theater, and movie area.

Maria described the camp room as partly occupied with male and female supervisors, many of whom were ethnic Germans she did not know. Gröning described people playing card and dice games in the evening ("Scat" was a favorite) and various sports groups for male personnel. There was even a store in the inner area of the watch zone, *Tag*.

He noted that the canteen had small items like shaving soap, paintbrushes, drinking cups, and small snacks, but that personnel also frequented a vegetable shop where they could buy soup bones. Both Gröning and Mandl enjoyed communal dances and concerts in the main camp, which featured "a very good prisoner band [that] played marches, operetta music, and other pieces of music from 11:00 to 12:30 in front of the Kommandant's office. The concerts were comparable to a good concert in a spa city."

Artur Liebehenschel, who served as *Kommandant* of Auschwitz from December 1943 to May 1944, arranged other special entertainments for camp personnel, including performances of operas in Katowice, regional state theater performances, children's matinees for SS families, and a Katowice Symphony performance. He noted that "the Commander's Office of the Concentration Camp Auschwitz will be available to take orders for Christmas trees until 14:00 hrs. on Dec. 12, 1943; for the various companies, their departments and sections." Liebehenschel also remarked that he often went to dinner at Hotel zur Post, "a small quaint old restaurant in town."

Helga Schneider remembers her mother, a female overseer in Birkenau, boasting about their good conditions while many others in Europe were suffering from the most terrible hunger. "We had everything, the comrades made sure we wanted for nothing: real coffee, salami, butter, Polish vodka, cigarettes, scented soap. We had silk stockings and real champagne, although only at Christmas." She continued, "I was an absolute bookworm, for example, and the comrades when they came back from Berlin, always brought me something interesting to read."

After Maria had been in Auschwitz for several months, she procured a private villa in the region. Thereafter she left the *Stabsgebäude* and lived a distance from the other SS.

Many of the SS officers and female overseers received visits from family and friends. Irene, Josef Mengele's wife, visited her husband and described "happy days" in which they swam and picked blackberries to make jam.

Maria later wrote that she had visits from a cousin. Townspeople in Münzkirchen concurred, stating that "Maria Gruber was a cousin whom Maria took to Auschwitz where she was working. She couldn't take it and left." Helen Tichauer also remembers that Maria had people who visited "from time to time."

For visits by friends and family, Oskar Gröning and many others used a hotel across from the train station that bore the name "House of the Weaponry—SS," where visitors from the Reich could check in normally and stay overnight. Many of his comrades did so. He found the statements of the acquaintances of Maria Mandl about her guests "absolutely believable."

SS personnel and auxiliaries could also take vacations (Gröning was sent to a ski lodge for a few weeks to recover from a sickness) and many regularly visited Solahutte, a nearby resort where they could hunt, hike, sunbathe, and enjoy lakes and parks. In one photograph, female overseers in a large group are enjoying their time away from work, socializing with jovial male SS officers, one of whom is playing an accordion. Gröning later said that "the special situation at Auschwitz led to friendships which I think back on with joy."

CHAPTER 29

Oberaufseherin

As she had in Ravensbrück, Maria rose to the challenge of being *Oberaufseherin* of Birkenau. Despite the difficulties, Mandl was proud of her professional success and elevated status. She was now, arguably, the most important woman in Himmler's camps.

Prisoners took note of Maria's physical bearing. Survivor Stanisława Rzepka-Palka recalls that "from the first she was VERY, very straight and self-assured! She would always be MARCHING, it was not just a leisurely walk; VERY self-assured, VERY proud! She looked always very groomed and she ALWAYS carried a small whip." Zofia Cykowiak says, "She wore a skirt, a very elegant uniform, I remember it clearly, the others had crumpled uniforms and were run-down. She was a stickler for cleanliness, her uniform well-tailored, the jackboots shining in contrast to the others, as mud was up to the knees there." She always had to be addressed as *Oberaufseherin* Mandl.

Maria kept a handsome horse to ride for recreation and often cantered between the barracks, usually at conspicuous times. "She could ride perfectly." Maria also "excellently drove a car, and a motorcycle" and, as in Ravensbrück, utilized bicycles.

In a photograph taken during a dedication ceremony for a new SS hospital in 1944, two high-ranking SS officers, *Kommandant* Richard Baer and architect Karl Bischoff, are shaking hands in front of a large gathering of SS men, all in uniform, all looking rather smug and self-satisfied. To the left of the gathering, in between two larger men, stands Maria Mandl, hands clasped, uniform impeccable. In this setting her smaller physical stature contrasts strongly with the men in jackboots surrounding her. As the only woman in the gathering, her status as head female overseer is obvious. Mandl has a small smile on her face and a slightly obsequious air as she peers around the taller men in front of her. This was heady stuff indeed.

Interestingly, in other views of the scene, Maria has been totally eclipsed by the officers in front of her. No man moves to accommodate her sight line, and in some photographs, all you can see are her feet.

Like Langefeld before her, Maria struggled with the ongoing power struggles between male and female officers and the confidence of the Nazi male in his own superiority. Conflicts came from the top down. Höss continued to disparage the women under his command, and because he doubted their organizational abilities, he introduced parallel posts of camp director, report officer, and director of employment—all held by men—into the women's camp.

The post of camp director was held first by SS-*Oberstürmfuhrer* Paul Müller and after by SS-*Hauptstürmfuhrer* Franz Hössler. A memo from the *Kommandantur* notes Hössler's assignment, that Maria Mandl is the top supervisor, and—rather optimistically—that "she and Hössler work together in agreement with one another."

Hössler was a slightly built man with a high nasal voice and a weak chin. Mandl did not submit easily to his authority, and their continued jockeying for power was evident to the prisoners. "They hated each other! Because there was competition." Understandably, Mandl's relationship with Franz Hössler was fraught and would remain a source of ire and frustration for her entire time in Birkenau.

Other male colleagues with whom Maria worked closely were the suave, sophisticated doctor, Josef Mengele, and the more brutish Josef Kramer.

As Maria's power and sense of self-importance grew, she began to refuse to be dominated by Hössler, or indeed, almost any masculine figure. This was, perhaps, a result of the long simmering resentment coming out at last against her wayward fiancé.

Stanisława Rzepka-Palka remembers an occasion when Maria beat a male prisoner. Periodically, prisoners from the men's camp would visit to work on specialized infrastructure, like electricity. One day there was a tall, handsome man from Lodz who caught Mandl's attention.

"She had a whim. She started beating him, which was ridiculous and looked so funny because she was a short person in comparison to him and had to jump up to reach him, to hit him in the face. We thought—if he would just swing at her—she wouldn't have stood a chance!"

It is significant, as noted by Aleksander Lasik in his landmark study of Auschwitz, that "only Maria Mandel [*sic*] managed to establish a position of sufficient independence that she could enforce her own policies towards both the prisoners and the SS men in the women's camp."

CHAPTER 30

The Lover

He did anything to impress her. She did anything to impress him.

—HELEN TICHAUER

IT WAS IN BIRKENAU THAT Maria began the next serious personal relationship in her life. SS-*Obersturmführer* Josef Janisch was a tall and striking dark-haired officer from Salzburg, Austria. Janisch was employed in the Architectural Division (*Bauleitung*) of the Auschwitz complex, where he worked under the command of *Sturmbahnführer* Karl Bischoff—a fat boor and wife beater.

Janisch was three years older than Maria and had aided in the construction of the Birkenau crematoria and ovens. Coming from Salzburg, Janisch had a cultured background, and Maria's interest in music helped engage his interest in her.

Helen Tichauer, who worked in the camp office, later noted that Mandl "had a lot of natural ability and understanding for music, the Arts, to be partner of an architect [Janisch] ... She had to communicate, somehow, with him. She had understanding for law and order." As fellow Austrians, they had additional common ground.

The relationship between Maria and Josef was a boon to Tichauer, as Janisch had access to materials she needed in her office work. Mandl asked Tichauer what she needed, and the next day, to her amazement, Helen had been supplied with the best possible architectural equipment procured by Janisch.

Other prisoners described Janisch as very handsome and not particularly cruel. Rather, "he was just building things" and spent most of his time in the *Bauleitung.*

As news of their liaison spread throughout the women's camp, prisoners delighted in the gossip that Mandl had gone to the SS medical office to be treated for pain during sexual intercourse.

A few survivors believe that Janisch was a moderating force on Mandl. Ella Lingens-Reiner noted that during the period of Maria and Josef's relationship, "some of the prisoners who had known her in Ravensbrück Camp found it difficult to recognize her in Auschwitz. It was generally assumed that her fiancé had forbidden her to

Oberstürmführer Josef Janisch, a fellow Austrian, was Mandl's love interest at Auschwitz. BUNDESARCHIV BERLIN* NSDAP-ZENTRALKARTEI/BARCH R 9361-VIII KARTEI/13590141.

take an active part in beatings. Unfortunately, he was transferred later on, as a punishment, because he had 'organized' something, and she resumed her practice."

Prisoners often saw Maria and Josef riding together on Sundays, with Maria wearing a white blouse and a real red rose. At other times, Maria and Josef rode early in the morning before *Appell.* Tichauer elaborated, "Felt like in Hollywood. Beautiful people. Beautiful horses."

They were also seen riding in the evenings and at sunset, behind the active crematoria belching their smoke, where the camp hierarchy had ordered the digging of huge pits for the burning of human bodies. The crematoria capacity had not been sufficient for some time, and many earlier corpses were buried in mass graves. Oskar Gröning remembers that "for some reason, an order came that the mass graves should be opened again and the dead ones burned. Probably a fear of contagion played a role in the order."

Gröning has graphic memories of those nights, when the pyres were in full blaze, crackling, smoky, and tended by the Sonderkommando, who seemed dazed by their work. The air was hot, humid, black, as if a scene from Dante's *Inferno* were being enacted. Many corpses looked like they were trying to sit up in the heat, as though still alive. Gröning vividly describes a moment when "suddenly, a man's member unfolded into a life of its own, catching my eye. Things were so backed up that the supervisors had ordered overflow from the transports be thrown alive into the blazing pits. The burning unfortunates were screaming like lunatics, the people waiting their turn wailing and pleading." These scenes were undoubtedly observed multiple times by Maria and Josef on their evening rides through the back of the camp.

Maria had long since ceased to question the morality of the camps. It was now routine, the prisoners no longer human at all, just problems to be managed. If in the end they had to die, so be it. If it was her hand or actions that helped them along, so be that. She was secure in her actions, secure in the righteousness and necessity of what she was doing. At that point, seemingly, she had no regrets. Maria could not see what she had become reflected by the victim's eyes in the light of the fires.

CHAPTER 31

The "Ladies"

You know, it's like this. If a girl is a street-walker, she's sent to the camp as a prisoner. If she only did her stuff in a bar, she gets sent to camp as a wardress.

—ELLA LINGENS-REINER

MARIA'S ATTENTION TO ORDER AND discipline carried over to her interactions with the other female overseers. One survivor noted that "she...was also a terror of the Aufseherinnen. Seeing her, they all became very diligent to get into her favors, to be promoted. She was an omnipotent mistress in the camp."

The women under Mandl's charge ranged from nineteen to forty-two years old, with an average age of twenty-eight. As in Ravensbrück, most were unmarried, uneducated, and came from working- or middle-class backgrounds. The majority were German or Austrian.

In Rudolf Höss's postwar testimony he noted that the women who came to Auschwitz were supposed to adjust to the difficult conditions, but from the time they arrived most wanted to just run away, back to the "quiet, comfortable, and easygoing" life they'd had at Ravensbrück. However, "the senior camp guards were head and shoulders above those who came after them."

Ella Lingens-Reiner remarked in 1948 that the intellectual level of the *Aufseherinnen* was remarkably low and that she had seldom seen such a number of genuinely stupid women in one place. She also noted that many were sexually free and sought trinkets from murdered women to enrich their own coffers. "They lived their inane little life, were greedy for anything which could be 'organized,' knew no limit in taking bribes; and nearly all of them hoped to accumulate a tidy little sum which would help them towards acquiring a household of their own."

Maria listed her minions in a pretrial deposition: "Subordinate guards to me were Margot Drexler [Drechsel], Brunner, Stange, Brandl, Ruppert, Kick, Hasse, Franz, Volkenrath, Weniger. The strictest one was Drexler, whom I often scolded for that."

Although both Hasse and Drechsel were known for their cruelty, it was Drechsel who became most notorious. Five years younger than Maria, Drechsel was a bucktoothed, unattractive, vulgar woman, notorious for her brutal beatings and selection of women and children for the gas chambers. She also went out of her way to torment the musicians in the women's orchestra, whom she resented.

Survivor Klara Pfortsch noted firmly that "the female supervisor Drexler was in one word, a bitch. She beat people terribly. I myself was beaten by her and in such a way that my left eardrum was destroyed." She noted that she, Drechsel, and Mandl were all around the same age, and that the two overseers "got along with each other." Antonina Piatkowska also believed that "Mandl was close friends with Drexler."

Gerda Schneider remembers a more contentious and competitive relationship between the two. "The fact that Mandl had been given the instruction 'to get order into the camp' became known all over the camp because Rapport leader Margot Drexler could not hide her disappointment since she had definitely counted on getting the advancement to senior supervisor herself. From now on the situation in the women's camp got much worse. Beats, kicks, disrobing at entrance, confiscating any small possessions a prisoner tried to accumulate."

Other women under Mandl's command included Alice Orlowski, a heavy and plodding woman somewhat older than the rest. Orlowski quickly acquired the nickname "*Krowa, Die Kuh*" ("The Cow"), and would later be tried in the same war crimes trial as Maria.

Perhaps the most notorious *Aufseherin* was another subordinate of Mandl's, Irma Grese, one of the youngest and most beautiful of the female guards. Grese had also been stationed at Ravensbrück and was in her early twenties during her camp service. Blond-haired and blue-eyed, she delighted in the power she wielded over the inmates in her charge.

Prisoners remember the scent of her perfume and hair spray, both of which she applied liberally. She also had her SS uniforms tailored and molded to her figure, an extensive wardrobe, and the exploitive use of an inmate dressmaker from Vienna.

Mandl tried with varying degrees of success to rein in Grese and moderate her various requests for "perks." One commodity Grese monopolized was French turpentine, which the overseers used to clean their boots and uniforms. Eventually, after complaints, Mandl intervened and evaluated each request personally, thereby limiting Grese's access to the hoarded substance.

Another colleague, Therese Brandl, paralleled Maria's course through the camps. Brandl was a slight, mousy woman who spoke in an irritating high-pitched voice. Although she "morally and physically abused women by insulting their dignity, by beating and kicking, and by refusing to ration them necessary underwear and clothing," her less forceful personality remanded her to the background. At the end of Mandl's life, Brandl took on added importance when she shared a prison cell with Maria. Condemned in the same trial, they were executed on the same day.

Maria was responsible for all of these women and for their behavior. Their excesses, often sexual, fell under her purview. The promiscuity that had been common in Ravensbrück continued in Auschwitz. Many of the female overseers had one or more SS lovers.

During Auschwitz testimony at Maria's trial one woman noted that the overseers "often came home late at night, drunk, after different parties. They would throw empty soda bottles all over the place. The SS had bottled soda water delivered by train cars and always had a dozen or so cases stacked up in the apartment or the hallways." After each party, the prisoners had to carry out baskets of broken glass.

Seweryna Szmaglewska also described the *Stabsgebäude*, where nightly orgies, gluttony, ribald sexual games, and free-flowing alcohol all contributed to a dissolute atmosphere. This loose sexual climate did not enhance any small amount of respect the male officers may have had for the female overseers. The SS men often referred to the female overseers as "*Hurren* (whores)."

During her trial, testimony emerged about activities at Maria's private residence. "But the next witness told about orgies at Mandel's [*sic*] richly furnished villa near Auschwitz—orgies becoming especially wild after 'good' executions, when Mandel would beat up and whip the women before sending them to their deaths."

There had been various ineffectual attempts by the Auschwitz command to curb the promiscuity. Artur Liebehenschel wrote a memo reinforcing that the living quarters of the SS women "are off limits to male personnel. Visiting hours remains until 22:00 hrs. in the recreation room." This edict was largely ignored.

One survivor concluded that "Maria Mandl was charming and accommodating to the SS people who were her superiors, as far as they had any influence. She had a need to call us prostitutes and whores when she herself could be found nearly every night in bed with a different Sturmbannführer."

CHAPTER 32

"Mandelka"

> *The more we saw people die, the less we thought about their lives, the less we talked about their deaths. And the more we got used to enjoying it. And the more we told ourselves, deep inside, that since we knew how to do it, we really should do it down to the very last one.*
>
> —JEAN HATZFELD, MACHETE SEASON: THE KILLERS IN RWANDA SPEAK

HER OWN OFFICE. PRISONERS REMEMBER Maria viewing the space with pleasure, puffing herself with pride. Located in a free-standing wooden building called the *Blockführerstube* [the Block Leader's Office], the office adjoined a room where prisoners' files were kept. Mandl's office contained ample space for conducting interrogations and punishments, as well as for administering the camp. In Birkenau slang Mandl's office was "*on Vorne*" ("in the front"). Due to its location, everybody who entered or exited the camp had to pass by.

The *Blockführerstube* was located across from the infamous Block 25, also known as "the Death Block," an area isolated from the rest of the barracks by a tall stone wall. Block 25 was used as a holding pen for the gas chambers. Before doctors did selections for Block 25, they reported first to Maria in the Blockführerstube for her approval.

A malevolent spirit emanated from this block as well as a terrible odor, since the women confined to the courtyard during the day were forced to use an open latrine pit next to the wall. The barrack contained only brick-and-wooden plank beds and prisoners were kept there naked.

Survivor Szmaglewska remembered seeing processions of Jewish women carrying their dying companions to Block 25. "They carry the fading human remnants in blood encrusted blankets. Sometimes they must stop, rest their load in the mud for a while. The blood and excrement on the blankets mix with the mud."

More than any other place in what remains of Birkenau today, Block 25 has a palpable presence. If there are such things as uneasy spirits, they reside here. Even on warm days, the temperature drops by several degrees upon entrance.

In 1943 Maria could not have avoided hearing, seeing, and smelling the reality of Block 25. The unfortunate women trapped inside were fully aware of their fate and tortured by thirst. "They sobbed for water, begged for water. Dozens of hands reached out through the barred windows." Cries for help and female voices calling out "Murderers, murderers, you must die in your own blood!" were common. When the block had enough for a "full load," trucks arrived in the night to take the women to the gas chamber.

A woman who worked in the office adjoining Mandl's remembered the horrors of Block 25. Every night, always at 8:30, a truck would arrive with an SS guard. "Shortly after I would hear the cries of the victims who, beaten with guns and truncheons, were pulled by their hair and limbs and flung onto the truck. I would also hear the callous laughter of the SS who were usually given a supplementary ration of brandy to carry out the job... Truck after truck would leave with its cargo until Block 25 was empty."

CHAPTER 33

The Embodiment of Satan

The most frightening and worst nightmares from the entire camp staff came from Mandl. She had a strange sadism with the prisoners and beating and was always looking at us with hate-filled eyes. Always looking for an opportunity to "unleash" her anger.

—MARIA GAKIEWICZ, FORMER PRISONER
AUSCHWITZ-BIRKENAU

MARIA'S YEARS IN THE TURNVEREIN and her subsequent work as an *Aufseherin* had created a woman of great physical strength and power. A hard and muscular body and an increasingly corrupted spirit resulted in a woman who was feared throughout the camp. "She was generally considered the embodiment of Satan."

Maria always carried a short leather whip in her boot and used it frequently. She had the quick reflexes of a prey animal and would strike when least expected. Once, when leaving a performance of the orchestra, she suddenly drew a whip out of her boot and hit some of the prisoners "just for fun." Another woman remembered seeing Mandl stop her car before a working prisoner just to beat her. "And then she would get back in her car and drive away."

Although the SS personnel were encouraged to use whips, sticks, or truncheons rather than hitting the prisoners directly with their hands, Maria often used her strong fists to inflict harm and seemed to enjoy hitting prisoners in the face. The victims would often dissolve in a pool of blood, falling to the ground, where Maria continued kicking them.

Prisoner Genowefa Ulan remembered being beaten by Mandl and Drechsel during an inspection. "They were punching my face alternately, like a boxer, with their fists. I started losing consciousness, blacking out, but I didn't fall. Then one of them poured the boiling soup on the floor and both kicking me, made me lose my balance and sit in the boiling liquid." The heat shocked Ulan, and when she tried to get up Mandl and Drechsel held her by the shoulders in the scalding liquid. After tiring of this activity, they went away.

Anna Szyller described the atmosphere of fear Mandl created in the camp. When she hit "then she was breaking jaws." Another prisoner, Wanda Marossanyi, remembered Mandl's secretary, Karolina Wilinska, observing Maria beating German women prisoners so badly that streams of blood had to be washed off. Szyller once heard another overseer asking Mandl for advice on how to keep roll calls organized. "Mandl said that this is what the stick is for—that each block supervisor has; 'One has to beat, to break the sticks, or to kill to death.' 'Kill to death' was her favorite phrase that she would repeat and realize. With her there was no rite of mercy or pardon."

Mandl and her subordinates took pleasure in subjecting the prisoners to searches which lasted several hours. Most had tried and managed to organize a small collection of items called their "treasure," things that helped them to survive and often meant the difference between life and death. Seweryna Szmaglewska remembered that the overseers were not interested in the treasure, per se, rather they wanted to see if the prisoner begged for mercy or trembled with fear. If she did that, they burst into loud laughter, wrote down her tattooed number, and went away. If she remained proud, "they beat, torture, lash with their whips until the blood runs."

Once, in the summer of 1943, a group of five hundred female prisoners was returning to camp in the evening when Mandl ordered an inspection at the main gate for contraband. Nothing was found on any of the prisoners. Enraged, Maria ordered the arbitrary whipping

of every tenth prisoner. "Accordingly, Tauber chose every tenth one
and on a stool next to Block 25, whipped them. Mandl stood next to
the Blockführerstube and watched."

On April 4, 1943, in Block 20, Section A there were fifteen hundred prisoners. A panic broke out because a fire extinguisher had
blown up. Prisoners thought that a fire had started and ran from the
barracks, breaking the windowpanes. The SS gave the alarm and the
staff arrived, including Mandl, who wanted to punish the women for
the uproar. She, Drechsel, and Tauber stood at the entrance to the
barrack and beat every returning prisoner. "Beat them with sticks.
When Mandl got tired, they stopped letting in prisoners. She rested,
then continued her activity."

CHAPTER 34

"We ALLOW
you to work for us!"

It was a world of polar opposites and extremes of great clarity,
with no room for reflection of any kind. Hardened by the war,
molded by the harsh discipline the Khmer Rouge imposed, and
pumped by a righteous rhetoric underscored by fear, the young
guards were unstoppable.
— NIC DUNLOP, THE LOST EXECUTIONER:
A JOURNEY TO THE HEART OF THE KILLING FIELDS

MARIA HAD NOW ENTERED A psychological state where brutality
was the norm and excess encouraged. Prisoner Władysława
Janik observed that the abuse of prisoners brought her visible pleasure. Aberrant behaviors carried over from Ravensbrück, such as her
antipathy toward and punishment of anyone with curly hair.

Maria's abuse of the prisoners took many other forms. Mandl ordered the cleaning women to take refuse out of the ditch with their
bare hands. "This was particularly cruel, because in the ditch there
was infectious human excrement from people ill with typhus and diarrhea and other diseases. Water and soap were very difficult to
come by so prisoners could not clean their hands properly. Many
got ill afterwards and died."

A highly educated chemist was caught writing an imaginary account of Paris being liberated by the Allies. Mandl was furious and

summoned the prisoner to her office. He remembered that she asked him with great anger, "How dare you write such a thing? I understand that you dream about your homeland [but] that for the past 2 years, ever since you've been in this camp, you haven't understood that not one prisoner will leave this place! We ALLOW you to work for us!" Mandl was further infuriated when the chemist stated that he thought his actions were understandable in the circumstances and that had he been in her shoes, he would have forgiven. This provoked Mandl to respond that "we Germans are too human towards you! You would hang us. But we give you a chance!" She then escorted him out with the words "I hope you will be hanged."

Small infringements of the rules could lead to serious consequences. Improperly buttoned clothing could bring on a savage beating. The prisoners who worked in the laundry room were often abused. "Once she beat a prisoner for the improper ironing of a handkerchief. She beat until unconscious and threw the prisoner against the wall for the wrong ironing. She did this in front of us all."

Mandl's depravity grew. One survivor described a bath in the Sauna (the Delousing Block) where Mandl ordered SS men to brand women with a hot iron, noting that a female physician died from such a burning.

Once, a penalty was ordered for all kitchen workers. "From 12 noon until 6:30 pm we had to carry and run with large rocks, then crawl in the mud and jump like frogs with hand up in which we were holding the rocks. Mandl assisted during the penalty and beat mercilessly the prisoners who were losing strength. Only 1/10 of all these prisoners managed to hang on until the end."

Mandl often ordered prisoners to kneel with bare knees on gravel, with hands above their heads holding bricks. One woman had to kneel with hands up in a place visible to the SS from ten in the morning to four in the afternoon. When she angered Mandl by succumbing to hysterical laughter, Maria ordered additional stones for the prisoner's hands and then beat her around the elbows.

Routine events like delousing caused great misery. "I remember when I saw a few thousand naked women standing in front of the

Sauna where they were shaved and covered with some disinfectant:
so-called de-lousing... It was very cold—lots of mud, rain. And
when the women were shaking from the cold the Kapos were beating them with sticks." The female overseers would show off with
greater beatings if there was a handsome SS man present but "if a
'Clumsy One' was leading the Kommando they were calmer and did
not show off."

CHAPTER 35

Humiliated,
Appalled, Helpless

*I complained on several occasions that Hössler and Moll used
coarse language towards the prisoners, it was not right to do it.*
—Maria Mandl

CONVENT-EDUCATED MARIA WAS FAMOUS FOR her profanity and de-
rived enormous pleasure from her ability to insult the prisoners.
A common epithet was "*Du kleine Mistbiene!*" ("you little shit bee!"),
usually yelled at a prisoner who could not control her bowels after an
attack of diarrhea. Mandl peppered her speech with other favorites
including "*Die Luder*" ("hussy," "minx," "poor stupid creature")," "*Hurweiber*" ("whore-bitch"), and "*Dreckige Saujudinnen!*" ("loathesome pig
Jews!"). Maria would erupt when the labor columns returned and she
found an illegal carrot or beet. "Then, that's when she would curse."

Daily roll calls offered many opportunities. "During the roll call
Mandl verbally abused us, calling us damned Polish pigs and other
vulgar names, emphasizing that this kind of disorder could only exist
in Poland, but now that we are on 'German soil' we have to follow
the German system."

There continued to be a sexual component or undercurrent to
Maria's punishments. She seemed to take delight in having women
disrobe. Individual punishments often involved placing the woman
in a naked or vulnerable position. Stripping off in front of the SS was

a standard part of the camp intake procedure, as was the accompanying rude and vulgar commentary and insults. In subsequent and regular delousings, Mandl reveled in placing the prisoners on public view and in telling the men where to cut or shave the women's body hair. Many women remember their feelings of shame and mortification. Many women used three simple words to describe the process: humiliated, appalled, helpless.

Even Mandl occasionally reached saturation point. Margot Větrovcóvà remembers that her first encounter with Mandl was while she was marching naked after showering. Mandl remarked, "I cannot see naked women ANY more!"

Ella Lingens-Reiner noted that Maria's sexual jealousy of young girls was conspicuous. "She never tired of inventing new and unbecoming ways of tying the head scarves, she decreed nun-like hair styles, she hated every woman prisoner who was relatively well-dressed, and in particular she hated our very attractive Jewish chief doctor."

Bordellos had been erected in Auschwitz I and Auschwitz III (Monowitz-Buna), and Mandl was charged with staffing these facilities with prostitutes. Some prisoners, like Hermann Langbein, believe that Mandl paid strict attention to ensure that those who reported to the bordellos did so voluntarily.

Helen Tichauer remembers Maria lecturing women, experienced prostitutes from Germany, who were volunteering for these positions. Mandl stated that they should be ashamed of themselves—that she would NEVER recommend this. That they now had a chance to become *good* German women. "She [Mandl] was very moral—she was trying to be a good woman. A decent woman. To persuade other women to turn away from prostitution."

CHAPTER 36

A Pause, to Acknowledge Courage

How ironic, that something that happened to me when I was 17 years old has come to define my life.

—ZOFIA CYKOWIAK

No one who was ever in the camps has ever entirely left them. No Auschwitz survivor has ever been healed once and for all of the effects of evil.

—HELGA SCHNEIDER, DAUGHTER OF FORMER *Aufseherin*

IT IS POSSIBLE, WHEN READING multiple testimonies of atrocity and suffering, to become numb, inured somehow to the real physical and emotional cost Maria's actions had on these women. That distancing or numbness dissipates quickly when speaking directly with survivors of her cruelty.

Several women who made it through Auschwitz agreed to share memories of Mandl. Their reactions and backgrounds are as different as the stories they describe; their courage and willingness to relive these experiences humbling, and profound. These interviews revived nightmares and kindled visceral feelings of loss, still fresh after six decades. The women vary in appearance, but all have tattooed numbers on their arms.

One stunning woman makes an *entrance* after an announcement
by her husband, beauty still intact at eighty-nine, the pearl buttons
on her shirt works of art, her tattooed number small and propor-
tional. This survivor worked as a secretary in a camp office and
acknowledges she would not have survived had it not been for her
beauty. Her fondest memory of the camp is of clandestinely spitting
into the food of a Nazi overseer in the office.

Another survivor is small, alert, spry, cautious. Her eyes are alive
with curiosity and warning, her arm tattoo large and sloppily done.
"We were one of the first transports to arrive and the ladies did not
have experience." She is able to speak with us only briefly before
memories overwhelm and overtake her. In her we see most clearly
the great toll reliving these memories takes, and the extraordinary
courage of these survivors. When she curls up like a wounded animal, we leave quickly, not wanting to contribute further to her hurt
and despair.

Some survivors welcome the chance to share their memories,
and one, a rangy thin woman with reddish-brown hair and keen
brown eyes, welcomes us warmly. This woman is brilliant and well
read and used to work as a librarian. She lives in a large apartment
building where we hear a violin practicing in the distance. At first
she laughs a lot and quickly begins to speak in depth, all she can remember about Mandl; thirty minutes nonstop, almost stream of
consciousness.

Then, suddenly, she switches off. The mood in the room changes,
darkens, and she becomes glum and monosyllabic. She abruptly asks
to end the interview, needs to "take her medication." Our meeting
ends on a low note; she wants us out of her apartment, away, fast!

One survivor, who in coming years would become a dear friend
and fierce advocate of memory, is just the opposite at her first interview. She is retiring, shy, not eager to volunteer information. This
woman has a beautiful face: high cheekbones, relatively unlined skin,
pure white hair, and a gentle smile that tears at our hearts.

After stopping the interview several times, she retires to the
kitchen to gather herself. Then we calm her down, talk of more

pleasant things. She is like an injured bird in hand; vulnerable, damaged, fragile, and yet in every way a survivor. She has not made peace with her Auschwitz experience, nor will she ever. Instead she uses it as a catalyst for education and remembrance, stopping only when she dies at the age of 103 in 2018.

Another survivor, who lives in a resort town in the Czech Republic, is in her midnineties and very, very frail. Still, she summons the strength for an interview and arranges a beautiful spread of sandwiches. After thirty minutes she asks for a break, to somehow gather the strength to continue.

One woman shares her memories on the anniversary of her arrest. "It is a very special day for me, but I am not saying that to make you feel guilty or stir up some emotions in you or apologize. It's just that today, after all these years, I look at things differently. I am grateful for every day that I have been alive for such a long time."

Zofia Cykowiak, nicknamed "the philosopher" by her friends in Birkenau, was beaten several times for staring a Nazi official in the eye. Her presence is luminous, her spirit as strong as her body is weak. Zofia surrounds her bed with chairs at night, makeshift protection against the nightmares which often drive her suddenly out of sleep and out of bed. She tells us about a recent hospital stay, "where they had no chairs and I jumped out of bed from a bad dream and broke my nose."

Zofia who is more concerned at the end of our interview with who the author *is*, not what she has done or any credentials, but simply asking insistently, "Yes, but what *kind* of person are you?" When the author answers, after some thought, that "I would like to think I am the kind of person who would have hidden Jews during the war." Zofia gazes at her assessingly, all the sorrow in the world contained in her eyes. Both doubtful, and hopeful.

Zofia, unknowingly, has echoed the thoughts of James Waller, in his seminal work *Becoming Evil.* Waller examines these essential questions about fundamental human nature, about who we are and of what we are capable. Rather than judging others he rightly asks us to look at ourselves and ask,

Could I? Could you? These are the ultimate questions that—as we seek to answer them—make it impossible for us to ever think the same again about societies, other human beings, and ourselves.

CHAPTER 37

The Whip

- *She always carried a small whip!*
- *I was beaten by Mandl with a whip on many occasions.*
- *Mandl came, leading a dog herself. Dogs jumped on prisoners and bit off pieces of their bodies.*
- *She was siccing dogs, she would beat with leather and with sticks.*
- *She always, constantly, walked with a whip in her hand, with which she beat prisoners left and right for no apparent reason.*
    —FORMER PRISONERS, AUSCHWITZ, ABOUT MANDL

I never had a whip or a dog in the camps.
    —MARIA MANDL

ONE OVERCAST DAY IN POLAND, sixty-five years after the end of the war and after reading numerous testimonies of abuse, the author and her translator directly confront the harsh and visceral reality of what it really means to beat a fellow human being. Many survivors remember Maria's whip, especially notable for its tensile strength and power.

After a drive through a gentle rain we arrive in late afternoon at a local leather goods store, located in a small town about thirty kilometers outside of Krakow. A wiry, muscled, smallish man greets us and explains that this is a family business which has been in operation for several generations. Given its proximity to Oświęcim, it was often patronized by Nazi soldiers for any leather goods they might need, including saddles, materials for boots, and whips.

The proprietor notes that they rarely work with the special leather utilized for Maria's kind of whip because it has a "nasty consistency" and is slimy and smelly when uncured. There is a cured strip of this material in the corner of the shop, two to three feet long. It has a yellowish color, a stringy texture, and is as hard as a pliable ruler. Its tensile nature makes it the ideal material for a whip. Not only is it exceptionally durable, its ability to be wielded with great speed makes it especially deadly when used on human flesh.

Our new acquaintance demonstrates, swinging this piece of raw material through the air and slapping it onto the floor. When wielded with appropriate velocity, it whistles, or rather "it sings." He makes it look easy, but when we try, neither of us can garnish the necessary speed and force. More than anything, this illustrates how very strong Maria must have been.

A similar whip survives today in the Auschwitz-Birkenau State Museum. Photographs reveal a carefully crafted implement, with a braided knob on the handle and a "stinger" of loose leather strips at the end. The whip in the photographs is cracked and battered from extreme use, yet still serviceable. The physical reality of this whip, and the graphic nature of the man's demonstration, drive home the harsh purposes to which it was put.

Later that evening, after leaving the leather shop, we interview a survivor who describes a whipping she once received. It is a memory no less vivid for its being sixty years in the past. She notes, almost in passing, that during the incident her back was broken. Physically she is shrunken; elderly, hunched over, still suffering the pain and aftereffects of that beating in a most concrete way. She is, in fact, a living link to the atrocity of the whip and to the person who wielded it.

CHAPTER 38

Selections

Help me, because these stinking Jewish women don't want to go by themselves!

—MARIA MANDL

DURING MARIA MANDL'S WAR CRIMES trial considerable attention was paid to her active participation in the selection process. In camp jargon, "selection" meant selected for death. In Maria's case this took many forms, including selecting weaker women for the gas chambers from general roll calls and targeting sick women in the hospital block. Maria also took part in the general selections from incoming transports on the main rail spur in the camp.

Prisoners later testified that "Mandl was present at almost all of the selections from the camp to the gas chamber. She ACTIVELY participated! Such selections took place at least twice a month, usually with Mengele, Tauber and Drexler."

Maria denied culpability in the selection roll calls. "As the Oberaufseherin and Lagerführerin, I had nothing to do with this mass extermination of the transport Jews, I didn't even have access to the terrain where the extermination equipment was located. I only saw the crematoria when it was being built." Mandl later claimed that prisoners selected for death were sick, or were marked "SB" (special handling) and that this status was determined by the doctors, and not her.

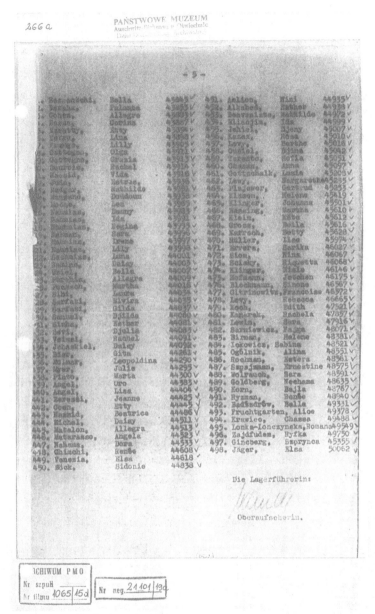

The death list, signed by Mandl in 1943 consigning 498 Greek women to the gas chamber, became a major piece of evidence at her trial. COURTESY OF THE ARCHIVAL COLLECTION OF THE STATE MUSEUM AUSCHWITZ-BIRKENAU IN OŚWIĘCIM. NR 1065/15D, NEG 21101/19A.

One of the most damning pieces of evidence against Mandl was a document from August 21, 1943, on which Maria signed a death list selecting 498 Jewish women from Greece for the gas chamber with the annotation "G.U."—"*gesonderte Unterbringung*" or "*gesondert Unter-gebracht*"("special placement"), meaning a sentence of death. The Polish underground in the camp found out about this list and arranged to have it stolen from the camp office and smuggled outside to their contacts.

The selection from the Greek transport was precipitated by two SS guards who caught typhus in an epidemic that had engulfed the Birkenau women's camp. Mengele—seeking a vacant barrack—ordered Maria to send the current occupants, the Greek women, to the gas chambers. The plan was to then disinfect that barrack, transfer the next barrack in, and in that way to work through the camp.

An observer later noted that when Maria signed sheets of death lists for gas chamber, it looked like the converse of Schindler's List. "You did not want to be on THIS list!"

Later, Maria consciously sought ways to cover up her incriminating behavior during selections. Maria Zumanska, who worked in the camp office, in the Records Division, remembers that on September 11, 1943, she was called to Mandl's office, where she was given a list of about a thousand women prisoners and ordered to find them in the files which they had marked "SB." ("Special Handling," or death by gas). "I was ordered to remove those letters without a trace, scrape them off with a razor blade—and replace them with 'verstorben' (dead)."

CHAPTER 39

All Begging
Was in Vain

Here pity only lives when it is dead.
—Virgil, as quoted by Dante Alighieri

Perhaps someday we'll meet, then I will suck the blood from your veins, and I will open the door of revenge. Only I don't know what to get even for first, the fact you were a beast. Or because I gave that beast my weakness and cowardice.
—Fradel Kiwetz, former prisoner,
Auschwitz-Birkenau

M ARIA, NOW SEASONED INTO HER position as chief overseer, had totally suppressed any small crumb of compassion or empathy she might have once felt. If a woman selected for Block 25 was unable to walk, Mandl ordered the working prisoners to lash her hands and drag her along the ground. She also delighted in overseeing or participating in the process of removing the women from Block 25 and loading them onto the trucks that would take them to the gas chambers.

I remember seeing Mandl standing with her leg resting on the stairs which the women prisoners were climbing

to get onto the trucks, with a cigarette in her mouth, in-
differently watching the "loading" of the truck.

Once during such a scene, Mandl turned to the SS man standing
next to her and with a mocking look on her face said, "That prisoner
stinks!" After another large selection when many women from Block
25 were gassed, a prisoner in a work detail observed that "when I entered the gate I met Mandl and Hössler who were leaving with
content faces. Mandl was saying to Hössler, 'They deserved it.'"

With any kind of selection Mandl was immune to outcries from
the prisoners. Wanda Marossanyi categorized her response as "implacable. She ignored begging or pleading."

She would choose prisoners for death on the flimsiest pretense,
a scratched heel or a frozen finger. Anyone who was elderly or
weak did not stand a chance. One woman who worked in the Sauna
remembers an incident in December of 1943. "I was witness to selections in which Mandl participated. Mandl was then in gloves
with a stick in her hand, with which she was pushing it into the
stinking pus-filled abscesses/wounds of the prisoners while Mengele made the final decision. At that time they selected 3,000
women."

Barbara Iboja Pozimska later submitted testimony for Mandl's
trial about a particularly terrible day on which many healthy and
young prisoners were chosen for death. It was a Sunday in the fall
of 1942, and Mandl came with a dog and ordered all the prisoners to
gather in the yard for a roll call.

Barbara sensed that something bad was about to happen and hid
in a lower bunk with a friend. From there they began to hear screams,
dogs barking, and an angry Mandl taunting the prisoners. "She
started squirting (with a hose), washing and throwing the weak and
those who were not able to stand on their own strength so could not
move by themselves, so they were thrown into nearby cars and the
prisoners were shouting and trying not to enter the cars and then
both Maria Mandl and SS men, the latter with guns, would beat the
prisoners by force and push them into cars and sicced the dogs on

the prisoners. I could see when the dogs attacked the prisoners. And biting off pieces of flesh in that block."

Barbara remembered that there were about eight hundred prisoners, almost all young women, aged sixteen to twenty-five, among them many healthy, strong, and young girls, still able to work. Mandl loaded all of those girls onto the cars and transported them to the gas chambers. Only Barbara and her friend survived.

Sometimes Maria's brutality even caused chagrin among the male SS. Maria Stromberger, a witness at the trial of Rudolf Höss, related a story told by an SS man named Riegenhagen, who had been assigned head of disinfection and delousing.

In the winter of 1943 800 Aryan women came into Birkenau on a transport from Paris. Under Mandl's supervision they were placed in a "cold, iced-over" barrack where they remained for several weeks. Eventually they were ordered to undergo a selection, to see who might be capable of work. The women had to stand with their backs towards Mandl, who proceeded to kick them with her foot in the small of their backs. If the starved, weakened women were able to withstand the kick and did not fall over, they were declared able to work. Those who fell down, were taken to the gas chamber.

Riegenhagen and a colleague challenged Maria about her treatment of the prisoners. Afterward, she complained to Höss, who then summoned Riegenhagen and said that "Frau Mandl had such a good reputation in Berlin and did such good work here, the two should go to her immediately and apologize." Soon after that, Riegenhagen was transferred.

CHAPTER 40

"I often cried"

*I often cried because of the women supervisors... Sometimes
I lost all courage and wished to stop working because, what
was a matter of course in Ravensbrück, had to be gotten by
force in Auschwitz... Auschwitz was for me the most difficult
time of my life.*

—Maria Mandl

MARIA'S CHALLENGES AS HEAD OVERSEER no doubt contributed
to her more abhorrent behaviors. Difficulties controlling the
female overseers under her command, the treacherous hygienic conditions of the women's camp, and the mental effort necessary to
exert control over higher-ranking prisoners and *Kapos*, all lent to her
general stress level. In addition, the ongoing adversarial relationships
with the misogynic Hössler and other male officers were a constant
aggravation.

By far, Maria's greatest frustrations came from the female overseers under her command.

> Among the female supervisors were very decent ones but
> the others were mostly impossible in their behavior. It
> became worst in 1943–44 when they could not be distin-
> guished from asocial elements. In Auschwitz it became

especially bad. There was great danger they would get into some disaster through dealings with prisoners. Several ended up in court and were severely punished. Many were sent to another camp because of suspicion, to avoid temptation. [There was a lot of] bad behavior, professional and privately.

We got supervisors who were always drunk, I do not know where they got all the liquor—officially it was impossible. One supervisor in Auschwitz—in 1944—disappeared for 4 weeks, during which time she was hanging out with men, was caught near the camp and brought into the hospital. She had venereal disease. I was ashamed facing the prisoners because they knew all about it. I often cried because of the women supervisors.

Theft and corruption had become commonplace among the overseers. In postwar testimony former *Aufseherin* Elfride Kock described how she and seven other female supervisors were arrested for stealing prisoner's belongings. These were not isolated incidents, and although Himmler warned that "those who fall short will die without mercy," it remained a huge issue. Maria ordering the SS women to stop siphoning turpentine from prison sources was just one example.

Eventually things deteriorated so much that SS-*Gruppenführer* Richard Glücks sent a letter to all *Kommandants* stating that "in recent times there has been a worrying increase in the incidence of criminal cases against female SS supervisors in the concentration camps." He stressed that these employees be reminded of their obligations and especially to respect the property of others.

As titular head of the female overseers, Mandl came under great pressure to control this behavior. Nonetheless, Oskar Gröning points out that "the acquisition of things, food and alcoholic beverages, were illegal [but] up to a certain point it was accepted by the SS personnel–they tolerated it—looked the other way."

When the stealing got too egregious, Höss would order searches of the SS barracks for contraband. "One day—during the end of

October 1943—the SS-quarters in the Auschwitz camp were searched in a lightning operation by people of the SD Security Service and Gestapo. Lockers were opened (in the presence of their owners) and they were searched for 'residue' from the Canada-stock. During this operation, a whole lot of SS-members fell and were arrested."

Although Maria was not swept up in this particular action, she also was subject to the temptation of easy goods. Prisoner Gerda Schneider heard talk of two instances: a package was placed in her car by the messenger Liane Pollak, which contained two duvets. "She drove home with this package without saying anything." Other supervisors remarked that Mandl had appeared on a reunion evening in an evening dress and silver fox fur and that "these items had definitely not been purchases out of her salary."

Previously, before leaving Ravensbrück for Auschwitz, Maria was rumored to have sent some "spoils of war" back to Münzkirchen. Inmates remember that she took some valuables that belonged to prisoners. "However, she didn't keep [personal things but did keep] a bar of gold which was found on her. The news came from prisoners employed in the place where prisoners' belongings were deposited and those prisoners had to give them to Mandl at her command."

Several townspeople in Münzkirchen remembered that during the Nazi times, many packages from Maria were delivered. One neighbor remembered that "I picked them up and delivered them... Around 1944... I don't know what was in them, but each was around 8–10 kg and were sent through the train station in Schärding."

Despite her high position, Maria was also vulnerable to censure from the upper echelons of command. Often, she would commandeer an SS car to drive around the camp. An edict from Camp *Kommandant* Höss dated July 28, 1943, mentions a statute concerning the withdrawal of motor vehicles: "According to an order of the Wirtschaft, driving without a license is forbidden. The following SS members are not in possession of a proper license:... [on the list] Maria Mandl... The vehicles in their possession are to be confiscated immediately and deposited at the service station."

Mandl continued to struggle with the horrific hygienic conditions. Survivors remember that in March of 1943 things were
particularly grim in the camp, even for Birkenau. Rats, lice, fleas, and
other vermin thrived in the unsanitary environment. Oskar Gröning
stated that as the weather warmed into summer it became especially
bad. "The fleas were on the sand streets and would hop in the sand
on the sand streets—and onto us."

In her trial testimony Mandl notes several occasions when she
lobbied Höss, Glücks, and Pohl with Dr. Wirth about her ongoing
concerns with the conditions in the women's camp: "The health of
the prisoners deteriorated." She calls attention to the bad conditions
in the *Revier* and how, in part, the "women in the camp had to be
forced to wash and take baths."

> I was often quite desperate, because I and the other super-
> visors suffered mentally and physically in this environment.
> I often wondered whether the people realized [I] wanted
> to help them.

Maria's colleague Margot Drechsel contracted typhus from the
conditions in the camp. Maria herself suffered from various medical
problems as recorded in her SS medical records. Along with treatment for "pain during intercourse" during her affair with Josef
Janisch, Maria was seen at different times for hygiene-related problems, including dysentery (May '43), a large nose boil ("*Nasenfurunkel,*"
September '44), and—most annoyingly—several treatments and
tests for intestinal ascaris worms and worm eggs in July through October 1944. Ascaris worms are long, thin, and pale, with tripart mouths.
They look disconcertingly similar to mobile white string beans and
cause intense itching and other discomfort. Maria must have recoiled
with disgust during every trip to the bathroom.

Eventually, Maria's efforts in combating all of these problems
were recognized by her superiors. Beginning in April of 1943 she
began receiving overtime and a raise of 100 RM to her current salary.
Like others, she had received the regular overtime pay of RM 35,

which was not reflective of her weekly working time of at least sixty-eight hours. The health dangers of working in close proximity to possibly infectious prisoners was also noted "as payment for considerable additional work and the danger of infection connected with this activity."

Maria's supervisor asked that this higher pay rate be continued throughout 1944.

> Fräulein Mandl is subject in her occupation as head supervisor to a greater danger of epidemic, especially as the sanitary and hygienic conditions in the women's camp are still inadequate. The extended amount of work also requires daily a number of overtime, which is further required since she has the added responsibility of supervision of the female managers in the office building after the end of the working day. The otherwise usual monthly amount of RM35 is in lieu of her services, entirely inadequate. Signed by the SS Obersturmbannführer.

CHAPTER 41

The Orchestra

There are many publications which claim, not without a certain emphasis, that music kept up the spirits of the emaciated prisoners and gave them strength to survive. Others assert that music had a directly opposite effect, that it demoralized the poor wretches and contributed instead to their earlier demise. I personally share the latter opinion.

—SZYMON LAKS, CONDUCTOR OF THE
AUSCHWITZ-BIRKENAU MEN'S ORCHESTRA

I remember the camp orchestra, which was hope.

—JANINA LENC, FORMER PRISONER,
AUSCHWITZ-BIRKENAU

HOW TO COMPETE WITH THE smug overbearing SS men? Even holding the coveted rank of head overseer, Maria still had to answer to a lesser man like Franz Hössler. One of her strategies came with the idea of forming a women's orchestra.

Upon her arrival in the Auschwitz complex, Maria had been surprised to learn that the men's camps in both Auschwitz I and Auschwitz II (Birkenau) had orchestras and music ensembles. These orchestras had various responsibilities in the camp. They entertained the SS in regular Sunday concerts and special functions and helped increase the efficiency of forced labor by playing music while labor details marched to work. Some groups were used to lull incoming transports into a sense of normalcy. They also—however inadvertently—allowed prisoner musicians a chance to survive and provided distraction to the inmate population during concerts.

Maria proposed the idea of a women's orchestra to Franz Hössler, who immediately recognized the potential benefits and prestige. Hössler then took the initiative of organizing the necessary paperwork and helped Maria make her case to the higher administration. Camp *Kommandant* Höss approved the request, and by the end of April 1943, he gave Mandl and Hössler permission to move ahead.

Recruitment of female musicians from the camp population began. Instruments and music were obtained from the men's camp and from incoming transports, while female prisoners were allowed to consult with the male musicians for advice.

A prisoner named Zofia Czajkowska was the first conductor, chosen, according to rumor, because of the resemblance of her name to the famous composer Tchaikovsky rather than for any pronounced musical talent.

Czajkowska was an anomaly in Birkenau, an "old number," someone who had survived from the inception of the women's camp. What Czajkowska lacked in musical talent, she made up for in authority and organization. Helena Niwińska remembers that Czajkowska would shout at and insult the women only when the female overseers were present—thereby deflecting further abuse on their part. Niwińska stressed that Czajkowska did not steal from the women; instead she helped several to survive by turning a blind eye to extra activities or covering up sickness. "As a Block elder, Zofia Czajkowska remained a human being with a capital H."

At first, concerts presented by the orchestra sounded less than professional and the musicians struggled to present a polished product. The new players were almost all young and inexperienced. Although they were very grateful for this new assignment, which got them away from other work details, few had significant or even any professional experience.

Helen Tichauer later noted that "we could not be proud of our playing under Czajkowska. It was Katzenmusik. We were playing and we tried hard, but we were like monkeys to an organ grinder." Margot Větrovcóvà concurred, hearing the orchestra in concert shortly after its inception: "I heard the group under Czajakowska, the quality was terrible."

Since women assigned to the orchestra had no other duties (a cushy job in a place like Auschwitz), Mandl knew they would need to excel and prove their worth. If unable to do so, the orchestra would not survive.

CHAPTER 42

Hope

HOPE CAME IN THE FORM of an accomplished violinist and conductor named Alma Rosé, deported to Auschwitz in July of 1943. Rosé was the daughter of well-known violin soloist Arnold Rosé and the niece of famed composer Gustav Mahler.

Upon arrival, Alma was assigned to Block 10 in the main camp, Auschwitz I. Block 10 was an imposing two-story brick building which housed 395 Jewish women utilized in medical experiments. One side of the building faced the courtyard of "the death barrack," Block 11, and the execution yard and black wall where hundreds of prisoners were shot to death. Block 10 and its activities were administered through the Birkenau office and reported administratively to Maria Mandl.

Alma learned the truth of what was going on in Block 10 and, believing she would soon be dead, asked an overseer if a violin could be brought in so she could play "one last time." The overseer, Magda, sent a message to the main office in Birkenau stating that Alma Rosé was now in Auschwitz and had requested a violin.

This was exciting news to women in the office and to members of the orchestra. Struggling to survive and desperate for substantive musical direction, an experienced talent like Alma Rosé could mean the difference between life and death.

Alma was given a violin and began playing in Block 10 that very evening. The women were enraptured, transported emotionally to a different and better world through her music. The informal concerts continued, expanding to include other performers and dancers, and soon the SS took notice. Maria, notified of Alma's presence, attended a concert and arranged to have her transferred to Birkenau.

Aware of the potential pitfalls of assigning a Jewish musician to such a prominent position, Mandl arranged for Alma's classification to be changed from Dutch Jew to *Mischlinge* (part Jew) and insisted on the use of her maiden name, Rosé. Alma now became conductor of the orchestra.

CHAPTER 43

Alma

No conductor has ever faced a more formidable task.
—HELEN TICHAUER

WITHOUT DOUBT ALMA ROSÉ PROVIDED the leadership that made the women's orchestra a viable unit. The task was Sisyphean—to create and maintain an artistic ensemble in a group where most of the musicians had little formal training and an average age of nineteen. Alma herself was only thirty-six years old when she arrived in Auschwitz. Gradually, by sheer will and steady discipline, she was able to mold the players into an orchestra.

After her arrival the group expanded to include forty-five to fifty players. Instrumentation was an eclectic combination of violins, cello, bass, guitar, mandolin, flute, accordion, drum, cymbals, two pianists, and six singers.

The orchestra had now been assigned a permanent barrack; walls were planks painted gray, electric lights hung on exposed wires, and a big rehearsal space was arranged in the front, while beds were placed in the back. The block had a wooden floor in the rehearsal room—a rarity. Hygienic conditions were superior to the rest of the camp. The women were allowed to go daily to the washrooms and could keep clean.

Maria Mandl ordered that women in the orchestra be (by camp standards) relatively well fed and excused from the brutal outdoor roll calls. Maria also facilitated the construction of an interior heating stove which kept the instruments at a stable temperature, bedding for the musicians, and a table where they could eat. As one young woman later exclaimed, "That was a luxury!"

Margot Větrovcóvà remembers that the period after Alma joined the orchestra was wonderful. "She was a great musician and a great artist. All this music was in her head. She was able to choose programs well suited to what her audience wanted and what the group was capable of doing."

To everyone's shock, the Nazi officials began addressing the new conductor as "Frau Alma," which was a complete sensation. After Alma's arrival, Mandl visited the Music Block and "came to ask how recruitment for the orchestra was going. She spoke in a calm voice (for her), with a gentle smile."

Within weeks improvement in the orchestra was discernible. Mandl was delighted, and relieved. Alma took several controversial steps, including replacing many of the Czajkowska era musicians with better qualified Jewish musicians. However, cognizant of the fact that the orchestra was a safe haven for those women, she had them reassigned to clerical or copyist duties.

Rosé also expanded the repertoire of the orchestra. She continued to include traditional German favorites and marches, but now began to venture into more sophisticated repertoire from operas and symphonic works. Since Alma was a virtuoso violinist, she included several pieces for solo violin and orchestra.

The German officers would often come to the music block during rehearsals to listen to Alma play. "With satisfaction, they would bring their guests and clearly 'boasted' about having a women's orchestra, especially a violinist of such class." Zofia Cykowiak notes that "after very good concerts in the German's opinion, we would get an extra spoonful of marmalade or liver sausage."

Alma remained very conscious of the fact that these extra privileges came at a great price. Having always been a dedicated and

hardworking musician, she became even more so at Auschwitz. Demanding long hours and absolute dedication from the young
musicians under her baton, she "did not tolerate the smallest care-
lessness. During the day Alma would conduct rehearsals with the
orchestra, in the evenings she practiced her own solo pieces, and at
night she worked on music for the whole orchestra."

The women's orchestra began presenting regular Sunday afternoon concerts in front of the Delousing Block, or Sauna, which was
located between the men's and women's camps. When the weather
was particularly bad, the concerts took place inside the building. On
Sundays most of the SS men were off-duty and most of the women
prisoners did not have to do forced labor.

Performances lasted two to three hours, with chairs and stands
being brought by the musicians from their block. Mandl arranged
for the girls to wear special concert clothes, including dark blue
skirts, white blouses, black stockings, gray-and-blue striped jackets
from the prison material, and heather-colored kerchiefs. Because
Mandl wanted them to "look pretty," the women were permitted to
grow their hair.

The SS men sat in the front rows, and sometimes SS functionaries from other parts of the camp were invited. Musicians
distributed programs which they had made themselves. Behind the
SS the "privileged" prisoners sat on benches, and behind them "the
gray mass," women prisoners, stood.

Audiences at these concerts varied in behavior. Sometimes the
SS listened with glowing faces. Sometimes disturbances took place—
SS women talking, laughing, walking around, or prisoners humming
along. Alma would occasionally ask the audience to be quiet and respect the efforts of the musicians. There was no applause at the end
of performances since the SS had forbidden this.

Mandl usually listened intently to the concerts. However, Maria
and the other SS also felt free to criticize performances. Katarina
Grunsteinova remembers a "very pretty young French Jewess" who
played the violin. "At the end she sang '*J'attendrai*' which was a great
success. However, Mandl did not agree and said—which I re-

member exactly—"*Dir Hüre flieht aus, von Kommando!*" ("The whores fly off on command!").

The Birkenau Sunday concerts had become a "social event." In a daily atmosphere of terror, the presentation of concerts lent a veneer of respectability. By attending concerts, the perpetrators bolstered the image that they were both normal and civilized.

For female prisoners in the camp these concerts were a balm to the spirit. Listening to the music, they could escape the harsh realities of the camp and of their daily life. "One can say these were something unusual in our camp life as it was difficult not to be deeply moved or to forget this experience. It was like a piece of freedom. To return to the sad reality was bitter."

CHAPTER 44

At the Gate

She liked listening to music. She must have especially liked it when the orchestra played to the commandos returning from work, which were dragging behind them women who were killed or who died of exhaustion in the fields, and she was standing in front of the Blockführerstube counting whether the number was right.

—WALENTYNA NIKODEM, FORMER PRISONER, AUSCHWITZ-BIRKENAU

ONE OF THE MOST TAXING duties of the orchestra was to play at the entrance gate of the women's camp as the prisoner's work details marched out for the forced labor of the day, and back again at night. Every prisoner remembered the unceasing chant of *"Links-zwei-drei-vier"* ("Left-two-three-four") required of work details entering or exiting the camp gate. The orchestra played a dozen marches repeatedly and prisoners were required to march in step as they were counted by the official in charge. "The most important thing was to cross the threshold of the camp with the left leg... During such times Mandl was often laughing."

Since much of the camp population had been assigned to outdoor work details, every person had to endure the gauntlet of the gate. "The marching rhythm set by the orchestra sped up the ranks of the prisoners and got them in step, making it easier for the SS women to count and supervise them." Since there were approximately ten thousand women in the daily work details, this was no small contribution.

Margot Větrovcóvà remembers these duties well. "Early in the morning, in winter it was still dark, we were carrying the instruments and music stands to the gate and we played. The SS men did not mind that when playing the stringed instruments in winter our fingers froze to the strings. After coming back we played in the block, [and then] in the evening again at the gate—ten hours a day."

These shifts at the gate were often the scenes of cruelty and depravity on the part of the SS guards. Sylvia Wagenberg remembered many horrible incidents, especially one day when, as the orchestra was playing a quick march, a prisoner could not keep up. "The overseer gave her dog the order to attack the poor girl. The demonic dog mauled her to pieces. For my whole life, I have not been able to forget this horrible sight."

Seweryna Szmaglewska described early frost-covered mornings in which her work details passed through the gate to the beat of the orchestra. "They march rigidly, mechanically, past the formidable blond Head Supervisor Mandel [*sic*], who condemns to death without moving an eyelash." The women looked straight ahead, fearful of catching an overseer's eye, and jockeyed for position in the center of the columns, where it was easier to dodge the blows. "At both sides of the gate, as if at the portals of the mythical Hades, great dogs of various breeds howl, bark, foam with rage and strain at their leashes. These dogs are trained to attack people when released ... It is daybreak, but the sun is not yet visible, only pink streaks of dawn."

Mandl served many shifts at the gate, and violinist Zofia Cykowiak remembers a time when they were playing a jazzy piece and the women prisoners simply couldn't catch the beat to keep in step. Tauber jumped into the formation with his whip, along with other supervisors, who also had whips. "Then I saw her [Mandl], the same person I had seen in our little room, also among the rows of prisoners ferociously hitting them. Then I was terrified." Cykowiak continues, "When Mandl would jump into the formation and began beating you can't say that she was screaming. That was a...I can't find a word that was more than a scream. It was more like a bellow, like animal behavior—out of control, totally out of control."

Other responsibilities of the orchestra included playing concerts in the hospital building, or *Revier*. Most of the women were too sick to hear the music, others did not want to hear it. Quite often, music in the Hospital Block coincided with selections for the gas. The music distracted, speeded up, and diverted the camp officials from what they were really doing. The orchestra also played occasionally at the arrival of transports.

For the young musicians, and for their conductor, making music at a place like Auschwitz would prove to be a moral crucible, and for some a crucifixion. Helena Niwińska remembers tremendous moral suffering. "Playing music in a place like this...Marks of profound depression were evident in Alma Rosé and many others."

Alma, like all the musicians, struggled. Manca Svalbova likened Rosé to a bird that cannot get used to being confined in a cage and repeatedly bloodies its wings. Alma channeled her anguish, and her fear, into her work and the intensity of rehearsals and expectations. For many of the young woman under her supervision, unaccustomed to the harsh discipline music requires, "the physical and mental effort involved in daily rehearsals and performances was enormous." Niwińska notes that fainting was a frequent occurrence, and many passed out from sheer exhaustion and the physical and nervous strain of all-day rehearsals.

The general camp population also showed tremendous resentment toward the orchestra women, who had better conditions. It was the basis for the musicians' daily conundrum: Should they protect their lives and play, or refuse to play and doom themselves to a harder life or death? Helena Niwińska, a close friend of Zofia Cykowiak, said that Zofia was tormented until the end of her life by these issues.

Zofia, only eighteen in the camp, truly loved Alma, a huge figure in her life. Fifty plus years later there is still a lot of unresolved emotion there: guilt, sadness, anger. Zofia remembered that one night, when they were under *Lagersperre*—a ban on leaving the barracks, she and Alma slipped out of the block and stood in its shade to watch a transport of Jewish women being selected from the camp for the gas chamber—fully aware of their fate. "They were being transported in open trucks, naked. They were screaming. She told me then that she did not want to die in such an inhuman way."

CHAPTER 45

"She Would Look Beautiful"

When Mandl listened to music her face would change, angel-like.
—JANINA LENC

*After their hard actions in the crematorium, it was then they
came to us.*
—ZOFIA CYKOWIAK

MARIA SEEMED TO DRAW STRENGTH from the orchestra for her
other duties. She would enter the music block, sometimes
after a difficult selection or action, and request music to calm her
nerves. Several prisoners noticed the change in her face when Maria
listened, concentrating with great intensity and contentment upon
the music.

When Maria neared the orchestra barrack, she was preceded by
a messenger crying "Mandl's coming!" or "The *Ober's* coming!"
"When she walked in a sense of danger would emanate. When she
left, Maria seemed more relaxed, content. Somehow the music
reached her—it was a peculiar form of therapy."

Sometimes Mandl would request a specific piece from Alma for
the orchestra to play. Other times she would simply ask, "What's
new? What new can the orchestra play?" Helena Niwińska remarked
that all the musicians knew if they didn't play well they risked

Maria's wrath. "Once, Mandl threw a baton at a Greek girl who couldn't master a piece. She was very upset at the girl's ineptitude."

Maria's taste in music ran the gamut from traditional repertoire like Mozart and Bach, to more sentimental and popular songs. Zofia Cykowiak remembers that two pieces, in particular, made her expression change very much: "*Mein Peterle*" and the popular dance-hall "*Jalousie Tango*," which featured a virtuosic solo for the violin. During these pieces Mandl would fall into a reverie and her face would soften and become distant. "As for the remaining pieces, Mandl put a good face on it [laughter]. Then her face was more serious, focused/pensive. She wanted to show what a connoisseur she was!"

Mandl rarely sat down for a performance, rather she would stand and listen—sometimes not even remaining for the entire piece. She preferred to come alone, rather than with Hössler, and often visited early afternoon or when she was getting off a shift. "She usually came before noon. Since she worked practically all the time, she would stop by on her way to some place else." When Mandl was leaving, they had to stand up.

On one occasion the orchestra prepared a modest theatrical performance. The musicians made small paper hats and wore them, waving small flags around and performing a farewell song. Maria got very upset. Violinist Zofia Cykowiak stated "She did NOT like it! She got spots [hives]. She thought we were waving to her and wanted her to go away."

The musicians of the orchestra discussed Mandl's reasons for supporting the orchestra. They agreed that at least, in part, she used it for prestige purposes. Seeing the lack of respect with which Mandl's subordinates were treated, they observed Maria seeking ways to avoid this. She always presented herself in a specific way and looked "absolutely intelligent." "Mandl tried to make the impression of being important, dignified, inaccessible. She would flaunt with a severe expression on her face, implacable lips, a cold look on her face. She wore a skirt, a very elegant uniform—she was always elegant."

Cykowiak surmises that sponsoring the orchestra added to her feelings of cultural self-worth and that Mandl wanted to project the image that "well, [if] she is knowledgeable about music, then the woman is up to scratch."

When Mandl brought representatives or high-ranking officials from Berlin to hear the orchestra, she would stand very proudly, accepting all credit for the musicians' performance. The members of the orchestra would whisper among themselves that "now Mandl is puffing herself with pride."

> I saw her cheerful, not to say joyous, when she would bring her guests to us. And she would act as if she was [totally responsible], she would "puff up." To show off, that she had SUCH an orchestra! And SUCH a conductor! And then I saw her smiling, FULL, because normally they were half smiles. She was very proud, despite the fact that she would stand on the side, not speak to the musicians or interact. Her expression was "I achieved that."

CHAPTER 46

The Men

*When she came to our barracks with Hössler, she didn't act like
his subordinate, rather as an equal. Over time this orchestra became the apple of the camp authorities' eye, and they showed
it off during visits by various higher-ranking SS officials.*

—HELENA NIWIŃSKA

MARIA'S SPONSORSHIP OF THE ORCHESTRA raised her standing in
the eyes of her superiors in Birkenau—including Josef Kramer
and Josef Mengele. Mengele's love of music was well known and he
attended several concerts of the camp's orchestras. Maria's relationship with Hössler continued to be both competitive and contentious.
Little love was lost between the two, and they existed in an uneasy if
symbiotic relationship where matters of the orchestra were concerned.
Although Hössler outranked Maria, and by virtue of his gender would
always be considered superior, Maria refused to act as his subordinate.

Survivor Anna Palarczyk believes that Mandl and Hössler hated
each other because they were always in competition. Maria's refusal
to be dominated by Hössler during her time at Auschwitz reveals
how her own sense of self-importance had grown exponentially during her time in camp service.

The highest-ranking Nazi official to hear the orchestra was Adolf
Eichmann, who toured Birkenau at the end of February 1944. Mandl

arranged to have Eichmann visit the Music Block, perhaps the culmination of her pride in what she had achieved. Alma prepared the
orchestra with great intensity, everyone aware of how important it
was that they make a good showing.

Although Eichmann only stayed at the Music Block a few minutes, he received a positive impression of the orchestra. As a reward
the women were granted an extra ration of camp coffee and—more
importantly—the opportunity to take a walk in the country under
light guard away from the perpetual grayness of the camp into the
burgeoning spring outside. The musicians believe that this taste of
freedom was the result of Alma stressing the suffering of the young
performers in talks with Mandl.

Ultimately the orchestra women were given two walks in the
country, one in early spring, one a little later. Today, these memories
are cherished by the survivors. "It was warm, there were many ponds
in the area and the girls were permitted to swim and just generally
relax, talk to one another, sit down and rest. It was something fantastic. Fantastic…"

On the second walk the prisoners were accompanied only by two
female overseers, one of whom was Irma Grese with a dog. Zofia Cykowiak remembers that while some girls swam, she didn't, she sat by
a tree. When it was time to go, Zofia lagged behind, then slipped.
The dog lunged for her (as it was trained to do), but the rope was
around Grese's wrist and it pulled her down after Zofia and the dog.
Everyone went flying, flattened out by the pond! "A moment of
shared sense of humor in the midst of the madness. A comedy of er-
rors! All were lying flat!" Everyone, *including Grese*, laughed, struck
at that moment by the absurdity of the whole situation. There were
no repercussions.

CHAPTER 47

"The Orchestra Means Life!"

If we don't play well, we'll go to the gas.

—ALMA ROSÉ

MANDL WAS DELIGHTED WITH ALMA's leadership of the orchestra. She developed a genuine respect for Rosé, despite the fact Alma was both a prisoner and Jewish. The women were close in age (in 1943 Maria was thirty-one, Alma thirty-seven years old), and both were Austrian and native speakers of German. Alma, a good-looking woman with longer dark hair beginning to show signs of gray, and Maria, the very stereotype of the blond-haired blue-eyed Aryan, forged an unlikely relationship. Niwińska recalled that "Alma had a very strong personality. She was also pretty but in a different way and taller than Mandl. With her posture full of dignity, she demanded respect."

The entire camp buzzed with gossip when Alma was seen in Maria's office, sitting in a chair, simply enjoying a normal discussion. This created a sensation. Mandl addressed Alma as "Frau Alma," and Alma would tell stories of her performing career, the stages and courts of the world where she had performed. The women were *incredulous* that Alma was seated! "There was also no such example in the history of the camp. THIS IS INCREDIBLE! UNBELIEVE-ABLE!" Maria had a kind of reverence for Alma, telling her repeatedly that she would be the very last person ever to enter a gas chamber.

Alma's music and her performances, especially, affected Maria deeply. "When I observed her during a successful concert, especially with a new performance by Alma, then her face would radiate, literally radiate. She would take on an expression of deep soulfulness. When Alma performed her solo, there was surprise (astonishment) in Mandl's eyes—that the product was so good."

Hélène Scheps remembers that "Mandl greatly admired our director Alma Rose. This is without doubt the reason that she 'favored' the members of the orchestra. She would often offer little parcels that were probably from deceased people!" Alma, in return, put a lot of effort into making interesting programs for the Sunday concerts. Some of the musicians rebelled at the inclusion of lighter fare, given the backdrop of the death camp. But Alma always reinforced that "The Orchestra Means Life!"

Alma occasionally used her influence with Maria to request extra food for the musicians but seems to have been careful not to overuse this privilege. Mandl had already allowed significant privileges for the orchestra women, including the nature walk after Eichmann's visit. Therefore, she was reluctant to ask the SS for too many favors.

Violinist Violette Jacquet remembered Mandl once saying to Alma, "If you need bread, ask me. I will have it distributed." A few days later the girls reminded Alma of this offer and she refused, saying that they hadn't played well in the last concert. This caused some resentment. In the judgment of those closest to Alma, she declined SS favors in an effort to keep her dignity and focus and to inspire the same decorum among the orchestra women. Alma believed that such a rigid discipline was necessary to protect all of their lives. She also had a finely honed sense of just how far she could push in her interactions with Mandl.

Alma was also courageous in her dealings with Nazis other than Mandl. During one Sunday concert some SS women in the audience began laughing and swearing. Alma stopped the music, took a deep breath, and said, "Like that, I cannot play." The interruptions stopped, the orchestra continued.

The camp inmates were always surprised when Alma stood up to the SS. Anita Lasker-Wallfisch stresses that "she commanded an absolute and total respect from us, and by all appearances from the SS as well. I am sure I am right when I say she occupied a unique position." On her part, Mandl dealt with the other overseers and SS, particularly Margot Drechsel and Anton Tauber, who were openly opposed to the orchestra and considered its members lazy. Tauber pushed to have the musicians assigned to normal work details.

Believing she had to build the quality of the performers to maintain the performance level of the orchestra, Alma created some conflict when she started adding more Jewish members. This became an inflammatory issue when Mandl noticed there were new players in the orchestra who had Semitic features. Whenever Maria became upset, agitated, or moved by something, large red spots or hives would appear on her face. At this moment the spots appeared, and in a raised and angry voice she accosted Alma and told her that she didn't wish to have a "Jewish orchestra." Surviving musicians remember the blood draining from Alma's face at that moment.

In a further conversation between the two in the camp office, Mandl again "yelled at Alma for scheming against Polish women and taking on a new preponderance of Jewish musicians" and accused her of releasing Aryan prisoners and putting Jews in their place. Maria declared that Alma was forbidden to reassign any Aryans without her permission. Eventually the two women came to an uneasy truce; Alma would be allowed to accept Jewish musicians but was ordered to keep a better balance of Jewish and non-Jewish performers.

It was an impossible tightrope for Alma to walk, daily balancing the needs of her girls in the orchestra with constant pressures by Mandl and the other SS. She always knew that the relationship she had developed with Mandl was only as strong as the next performance. "Alma mentioned several times that the orchestra must work well, because as long as it works we are needed. If the orchestra does not work, we will all be gassed, go to the crematorium."

As for Maria, Alma's talent made the orchestra something of which she was proud. Proud of the respect it gave her. Proud that the high-ranking male officers in the camp now made an effort to come to concerts. Proud that, because of Alma, the final product was so good.

In music Maria also found escape, even solace. The music made it possible to leave the camp, the filth, the procession of death, and to dream of a different life, where her responsibilities did not come at what she perceived as such a great cost.

CHAPTER 48

Christmas in Auschwitz

Outside the flames burned one-meter high, young people [burn-
ing] in the crematorium, its presence in this dark night stood
out terribly, and whose bad smell wafted across the entire camp.
Not even on such a day did they stop.
These were, at that time, my Christmas candles.

—ERMINIE SCHULUNG, FORMER PRISONER,
AUSCHWITZ-BIRKENAU

CHRISTMAS OF 1943 FELL IN the middle of a very cold winter. On
Christmas Eve Maria, the female German overseers, and the
Volksdeutsche (the most deserving non-Germans) were invited to the
Delousing Block for a party. Onion soup was on the agenda, and an
address by *Lagerführer* Hössler. Seweryna Szmaglewska remembers
that Hössler made trite assurances and promises of rewards for good
behavior, while frequently repeating "*Wir Deutsche! Wir Deutsche! Wir
Deutsche!*" ("We are Germans! We are Germans! We are Germans!")

Musicians were drafted for entertainment. One young musician
in the orchestra had vivid memories of this, her first Christmas in
the camp. "I was only little and very young, my head shaved. The
SS organized a party...they asked me to play a Christmas carol on
the flute. They put a pink dress on me, and a pink ribbon—with a
ribbon tied all around my face, like a dentist." The young woman

played the carol and watched as, that same night, the Berlin Theatre Troupe was sent to the gas.

Christmas was the only day in the camp that did not start and end with a roll call, and Szmaglewska later described a special concert presented by the women's orchestra that all the women, except for those in solitary confinement, were permitted to attend. The crowd of women was excited by the absence of the SS men and listened attentively.

Alma began conducting a sad and melancholy tune which featured Puffmutti Musskeller, notorious prisoner and *Kapo* from both Ravensbrück and Auschwitz. Musskeller, an accomplished yodeler, had been petitioning Alma to join the orchestra for months with no success. This performance was a concession on Alma's part.

Seweryna Szmaglewska vividly described how Musskeller, with bloodshot eyes and spread arms, swayed and panted and threw her head back to sing. The song was the "essence of yearning": "*Wien, Wien, nur du allein*" ("Vienna, city of my dreams"). Musskeller's writhing, and passionate animal shouting rather than singing, gave "a touch of despair to the song." The orchestra followed Alma's lead and played with passion, echoing the mood of the song and their own despair. The inside of the bathhouse became stuffy as snow continued to fall outside.

Eventually, Musskeller's singing got out of control and hysterical, and she began substituting vulgar words for some of the lyrics. Alma burst into tears and stopped the music. After the performance Alma nearly collapsed, saying in despair, "We are going home." Orchestra member Rachela Olewski remembered that "I looked at the face of Alma Rosé. She was so miserable, she cried afterwards. 'What did she [Musskeller] do? She ruined the orchestra!'" Now, after being summarily silenced, Musskeller became a fierce enemy of Alma.

Later, one prisoner remembered that on Christmas everybody was hoping for an extra potato. "But it was already dark and there was no meal. It seemed that these hours were twice as long." Finally, dinner came, but it consisted only of a small ladle with turnips and water.

"In the meantime, it had become completely dark and someone began with a Christmas song. These voices I will never forget. While in all different languages, one still heard the same sound with children's voices, 'Silent Night, Holy Night,' whose end disintegrated into heartrending sobbing."

CHAPTER 49

The Paradox

Everyone who was there did something good at some time, and that was the worst thing. If the SS men in Auschwitz had always committed only evil deeds, I would have told myself that they were pathological sadists and could not act differently. However, these people were able to distinguish between good and evil.
—ELLA LINGENS-REINER

Thus they would seem brutal monsters to one prisoner, fairly decent persons to another, and both things would be true of them.
—ELLA LINGENS-REINER

You only have the power of life and death if you SAVE a life occasionally! The power is the thing. The "joy" is in the choice.
—JOHN GROTGEN AND FAYE ALTMAN, PSYCHOLOGISTS

I have, especially in Auschwitz, tried to help people...I have helped many prisoners, as much as I was able, in every way.
—MARIA MANDL

DESPITE THE MANY ACCOUNTS OF Mandl's brutality in the camps, and the deaths for which she was responsible, Maria also had a kind side. Emerging rarely but definitely in evidence, prisoners who experienced it never forgot it. Survivor Helen Tichauer had only positive things to say about Mandl. "I never experienced any cruelty or anything which really made me hate her. She NEVER engaged in brutality in Birkenau! She was top management—very ladylike"

Tichauer, who worked in both the camp office and played in the orchestra, remembers a day when she illegally remained in her barrack due to severe menstrual cramps. Mandl caught her there, a huge infringement of camp rules. However, to Tichauer's surprise, instead of any kind of punishment Mandl simply touched her gently on the forehead in a motherly way and allowed her to stay in bed.

Another time Tichauer was summoned to Mandl's office. She went nervously, and Mandl was holding a book in her hand called *The River Pirates*. Helen was asked to decorate it and insert an embellished dedication to Josef Kramer, because it was his birthday on November 10. Tichauer dared to say that it was her birthday too. Surprisingly, Maria told Helen to go choose a "birthday present" for herself from the array of packages sent to prisoners and stored in Block 5.

Tichauer also benefited from the walk in the country given to the orchestra women. "We went swimming. It's unbelievable what she did for our well-being!"

Tichauer stressed that "I never witnessed any beatings. She was [simply] too high up [the ladder] in Auschwitz" and that she never used profanity in her presence. "No! Just the opposite! I heard much of her in the office. [She talked often] to German women, on their discharge from the service—she gave advice."

When asked in 2003 about an earlier interview done in Feldafing shortly after the war, in which Tichauer stated that Mandl took part in several selections of incoming transports for the gas chambers, Tichauer revised her comment: "She never took part in a selection!"

Anita Lasker-Wallfisch described one face-to-face encounter with Mandl. Anita discovered that her sister, Renate, had arrived in the camp. Seeking a way to help, Anita made the brave decision to approach Mandl directly and ask if Renata could become a *Läuferin*—a messenger, a desirable position in Auschwitz, with better conditions.

Anita was a native German speaker, which undoubtedly helped her case, as did the fact she was the only cellist. "Improbable though it may seem, she [Mandl] was quite polite, and she said she would see what she could do." Shortly after this exchange Renate did, indeed, become a *Läuferin.* "Naturally I was worried that Mandl would change her mind the moment she clapped eyes on Renate. However, she didn't and that was the difference between life and death."

Aleksander Kinsky, aide to a *Blockführer,* remembers that "once I had to appear before Maria Mandl about a penal report filed about me, as a result of an accusation from Kramer who alleged I was drunk. I denied the accusation, saying that if it had been true Kramer would undoubtedly have punished me. Mandl lectured me that I was too lenient towards the women prisoners and that I should conduct myself professionally and not engage in any conversation with the prisoners." Afterward Mandl ordered Kinsky to get some sleep and didn't give him any punishment.

Hilde Simche, a percussionist in the orchestra, later stated that she didn't see Mandl's brutality. "I was not afraid of her. When she came to the orchestra, she behaved OK." Hilde also remembered that Mandl sometimes allowed special parcels from Canada to be directed to the orchestra as a favor.

Hermine Markovits, very young when she was sent to Birkenau, remembers pulling a muscle in her leg and being selected for the gas chambers. She was taken to the quarantine block to await her fate. Markovits was sitting in a corner, surrounded by a crowd of around two hundred prisoners, when Mandl came in. Spying her, Mandl asked, "What is the green vegetable [*das Grüne Gemüse*] doing up there?" Markovits's youth stood out because she was the only young girl among so many older women. The Slovakian physician told Mandl that Markovits had only pulled a ligament and would recover quickly. Surprisingly, Mandl had Markovits separated and sent to the *Revier* (prison hospital). And just like that, her life was saved.

When she returned to her normal barrack Markovits was told that Mandl had been looking for her and that she was supposed to report to the gate as they were 'hiring' secretaries. Hermine stood in line together with the others and ten were selected. She was not one of them so began returning to her block when Mandl shouted, 'Hey, you with the stiff leg, come back!' Markovits concludes, "Thus I got an office job."

Anna Palarczyk, when interviewed in 2003, related what she described as a "very nice and beautiful story about Mandl." Palarczyk was working in a special barrack, Block 4, that had extraordinarily good conditions for Birkenau. The bunks had blankets, there were showers almost daily. One day Mandl came in with a twelve-year-old German girl. "She tells me that this girl will be in my block, and you have to take care of her and it's best if you do homework with her. [laughter] I couldn't understand this—here! Where we had the crematoria and they were murdering people."

When Palarczyk asked if the girl was German, Mandl responded that she came from the Siemens family, that her mother was a Siemens and her husband was a Jew. When the couple got divorced, the father was taken to Auschwitz together with his daughter. "I didn't know what to do with her! She was with me for maybe a week [always saying], 'Ich bin ein Deutscher Frau!' ['I am a German woman!'] And I wanted to laugh, and I was surprised that Mandl told me to teach her German while I could hardly SPEAK German!" Eventually Anna heard that the family had secured the girl's release.

Ella Lingens-Reiner had several encounters with Mandl. Ella was a prisoner with unusual status, being "the only non-Jewish, German doctor among the prisoners." She was surprised to learn of an incident in which Mandl protected and arranged an early release for a young Austrian girl who refused to make munitions. It became a bit of a scandal, which was later glossed over. Hössler, still in rivalry with Maria, wanted to report the incident to Berlin. However, at that time he was also in hot water over a timber theft and shortly thereafter was sent away for a time.

Lingens-Reiner clearly remembered that Mandl liked to give presents, especially of things which were not hers. "I sometimes forced myself, for the sake of my child, to ask permission to write my son special little letters illustrated with drawings. The Head

Wardress would not only give me permission every time, but she would show her sympathy by slipping something into my hand, such as dried fruit or a tin of sardines. I would take it with a shrug and go away." Mandl also gave Lingens-Reiner a voucher for the parcels depot and told her to go get "a nice parcel."

Stanisława Rachwałowa, a prisoner who had many negative interactions with Mandl, also acknowledged a moment of kindness on Maria's part.

"I remembered that in this woman human feelings existed as well. Once, when she was at the selection of Hungarian Jews on the ramp, she had mercy on a teenage girl who suddenly started to dance barefoot in front of her, among packages, people, chaos and screams of prisoners being separated, she danced some beautiful, fancy dance and in the end she bent down to the Oberaufseherin's feet with a silent appeal to let her enter the camp with her mother. One gesture from Mandl saved their lives and they walked in happy because [they were] together. She [Mandl] even remembered about them later and they were both barracks chiefs in the Krätzenblock."

In Auschwitz, a low prisoner number was a sign of having lived way beyond the normal life expectancy for an average inmate. Even from the staff, there was a certain grudging respect for those who had survived that long. After Maria had been in the camp four months, she gave an order to pass through selections any healthy woman who had a low four-digit number. This was a significant break for the three hundred or so young women left from the first official transport into the camp, and allowed many to survive.

Although orchestra violinist Zofia Cykowiak was very conscious of Mandl's brutality, she also thought very deeply about Mandl's motivations. Her belief was that there were two Mandls: a Ravensbrück Mandl (more brutal) and an Auschwitz Mandl, who was simply too high-ranking to engage in the same kind of brutality.

Zofia witnessed many of Mandl's beatings at the gate and later observed that "she would do it for show in front of her subordinates, to model how they were supposed to behave, rather than from innate sadism—we talked among ourselves. Tauber was a sadist for sure, and Drexler, her deputy. But I wouldn't say that Mandl had some sadistic inclination." Zofia acknowledged that when Mandl acted in such a moment it was horrifying. "But I couldn't say that she tormented with delight. Rather, that she cared about making an impression of a very important person towards her personnel."

CHAPTER 50

The Children

Green grass, green grass under my feet, I lost my lover, I will have to look for a lover or for my love. He is not here, he is not over there, among them all, there has to be someone out there for me.
    —SONG MARIA MANDL USED TO SING TO THE
    CHILDREN AT AUSCHWITZ

MARIA'S LIFE HAD ALWAYS BEEN marked by a yearning for children. Becoming a mother was her dearest wish, yet it was never something she achieved. Instead, Maria often substituted the children of family members as recipients of her affections. Extremely close to her sister Anna's three boys, she sent her beloved nephews a red truck and pair of skis procured in Poland. Those skis still survive today—dusty but serviceable.

In Birkenau she was often distracted from her professional duties by this continuing obsession with children. After her failed engagement in Münzkirchen, Maria spiraled into a series of affairs with high-ranking men in the various camps in which she served. With none of these men did she conceive, and her childless state, or what may even have been her inability to have children, precipitated numerous interactions with children who came through the inmate population.

Maria would carry cake and chocolate and often visited the children's barracks to hand out treats. Stanisława Rachwałowa reported that "I saw her several times in such a situation with smiling children on her knees, beautiful in her joy, because the children ran to her joyfully with their hands stretched out for the gifts, in cheerful commotion."

Maria could also be protective of the children in the camp. One day, the prisoner in charge of a quarantine barrack had taken the children outside to play. As they were hugging in a group, all lost their balance and everybody sprawled to the ground. Suddenly, what had been a gaggle of laughter and giggles turned to dead silence as the prisoner looked up and saw Maria, standing there screaming in anger. "You are a Polish mother! How could you be so careless? The kids could have been hurt!" The prisoner was sure she would be punished, but in the end, she was only reprimanded to "be more careful."

Another time Maria approached an "extremely pretty and flighty" pregnant German woman. Maria tried to explain the folly of making her life in the camp more difficult by having a fatherless child and then suddenly asked her to "give me the child. I'm so unhappy that I haven't got children—it would be like my own."

Maria would occasionally "adopt" a child who caught her eye, such as an engaging orphaned Roma boy who spoke fluent German. The boy was around five and became a pet of the SS, who gave him cuddles and rides on their horses and assigned a prisoner to care for him. In December of 1943 Zofia Ulewicz personally witnessed Mandl riding the Roma child on a sled, heavily bundled in blankets to keep him warm, and tied to secure his safety. "She would purposely tip the sled, pick him up and laugh loudly. The gypsy child enjoyed it and was laughing too. He was a nice kid, he was lucky, he could live." Then, the order came to liquidate the gypsy camp, and he was burned too.

Several survivors of the orchestra have vivid memories of Maria pulling a different small, fair boy from one of the transports. For seven days they were inseparable, going everywhere together while Maria dressed him in special clothes and showered him with warmth. On the eighth day, Mandl sent the child to the gas chambers.

Violinist Zofia Cykowiak remembered that it was already fall when she came with the boy, "a lovely child, very trusting towards her, very open." Maria requested that the orchestra play a short composition, and the child, under the influence of the music, started to dance. "To move as children do. And what's interesting—the child kept holding her hand. I remember it because after a while, I can't say how long it took, I saw her on the road at the rail side leading him to the crematorium and that paralyzed me. And I asked, 'How is it possible?'"

The village of Münzkirchen, Austria, as shown on a postcard, circa 1918.

The Mandl family home, as it looked in Maria's time. Franz Mandl's shop was located in the front of the house.

Maria's father, Franz Josef, was stern, compassionate, philanthropic – and always a central figure in her life.
Courtesy of members of the Mandl family.

The Mandl homestead w.
also a working far
In this harvest phot
Franz stands on the far le
brother Georg is on the far rig
and sister Anna is on to
stabilizing the load of ha
Courtesy of members of the Mandl fami

Maria's mother, Anna Mandl, struggled with depression and illness, yet was always a loving presence in her family.
Courtesy of members of the Mandl family.

Münzkirchen's schoolroom in 1917. Maria would matriculate there he next year.
Courtesy of Franz Ruhmanseder.

Münzkirchen's Communion Class, circa 1919.

Münzkirchen's Turnverein, or sports club. Maria, age 17, stands in the front row, fifth from the right. Her sister Aloisia is second from the left.

Neuhaus am Inn,
the Catholic boarding school
Maria attended.
Photo by Author.

After graduating from Neuhaus,
Maria appeared strong and confident.
Courtesy of Franz Ruhmanseder.

Maria's first job away from home
took her to the town of Brig
in the Swiss Alps.
Courtesy of members of the Mandl family.

Anton Schiller, the Mandl family's nemesis,
was mayor of Münzkirchen during the "Nazi Time."
Courtesy of Marktgemeinde Münzkirchen.

The death of Maria's beloved nephew, Franz Josef, at age three was a painful loss for her and her family.
Courtesy of members of the Mandl family.

A studio portrait of Maria, around the time of the German annexation of Austria in March 1938.
Courtesy of members of the Mandl family.

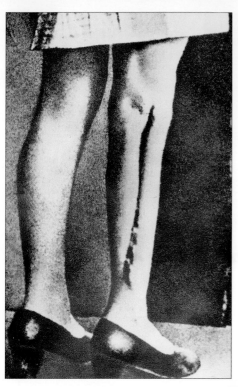

At the Ravensbruck camp, Maria Mandl oversaw a program of medical experiments in which horrific injuries were inflicted on the prisoners, supposedly for the sake of research.
The subjects were known as lab rabbits.
Yad Vashem Photo Archive, Jerusalem.

Alma Rosé, conductor of the Birkenau Women's Orchestra, was a virtuoso violinist.
Osterreichische Nationalbibliothek.

The only known photograph of Maria at Auschwitz shows her attending a dedication ceremony for a new SS hospital. Although to prisoners Mandl appeared larger than life, in this image she looks diminutive among the men. *United States Holocaust Memorial Museum.*

Maria, an accomplished equestrian, used her leather whip on prisoners. *The Archival Collection of the State Museum Auschwitz-Birkenau in Oswiecim.*

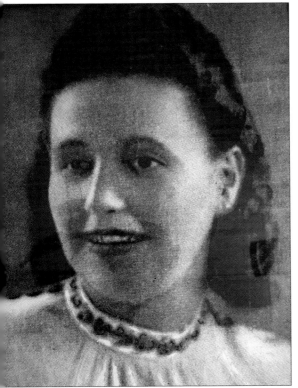

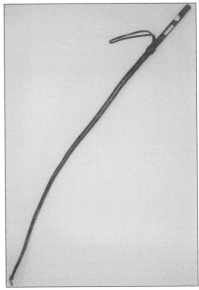

ala Zimetbaum.
d Vashem Photo Archive, Jerusalem.

The Mandl family shortly before mother Anna's death in 1944. By this time Maria had been a hardened killer for years. Yet still, she tenderly rests her hand on Anna's shoulder in a loving and protective gesture.
Courtesy of members of the Mandl family.

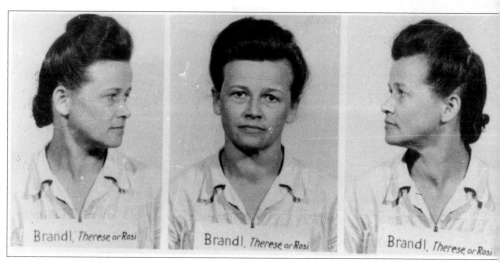

Brandl, *Therese or Rosi*

Brandl, *Therese or Rosi*

Brandl, *Therese or Rosi*

Therese Brandl was an overseer under Mandl's leadership at Auschwitz and later became her vexing cellmate in the Montelupich Prison. The two were executed on the same morning.
The Archival Collection of the State Museum Auschwitz-Birkenau in Oświęcim.

These haunting photos were taken at Mühldorf, Maria's final posting in the last months of the war.
Despite the exhaustion she expressed, she found the energy to pose in a party dress and to wade in a nearby pond.
The National Archives and Records Administration.

A still image taken from a video made at the POW enclosure located in the former concentration car of Dachau after Maria's arrest. Mandl is shown at left. At right is Elisabeth Ruppert, another overseer from Auschwitz. *United States Holocaust Memorial Museum, courtesy of National Archives and Records Administration.*

SS Obersturmbahnführer Otto Skorzeny, who slipped Maria some poison when they encountered each other at Dachau. *Archiva Państwowe, Narodowe Archivm Cyfrowe.*

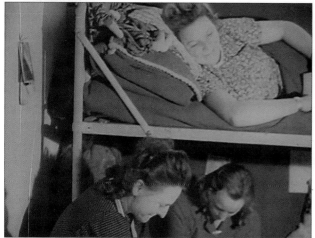

Maria's cellmates at Dachau. Her friend Margit, later acquitted, was also held in the cell. *United States Holocaust Memorial Museum, courtesy of the National Archives & Records Administration.*

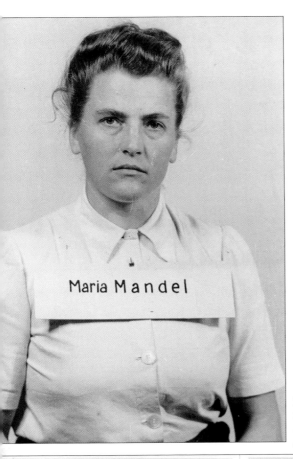

Mugshots taken upon Maria's arrival at
Montelupich Prison in Krakow, Poland.
*The Archival Collection of the State Museum
Auschwitz-Birkenau in Oświęcim.*

Maria exits the truck that transported prisoners to their trial each day. For security reasons, the defendants were brought in through a rear door. Still, they drew jeering crowds. "March of Time – outtakes – Krakow scenes; War Crimes Trial" "Butchers of Auschwitz." *United States Holocaust Memorial Museum, courtesy of the National Archives and Records Administration.*

The Second Auschwitz trial begins. Maria in the defendant's dock, with former camp Kommandant Arthur Liebehenschel to her right. *The Archival Collection of the State Museum Auschwitz-Birkenau in Oświęcim.*

Overflow crowds listened to the trial of the Auschwitz perpetrators, while seats inside the courtroom were packed to capacity with survivors, the international press, and the dock of forty defendants. "March of Time – outtakes – Krakow scenes; War Crimes Trial" "Butchers of Auschwitz." *The United States Holocaust Memorial Museum, courtesy of the National Archives & Records Administration.*

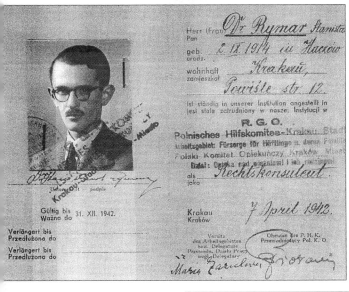

The ID card issued to Stanisław Rymar, Maria's court-appointed defense attorney. *Courtesy of Stanisław Rymar, Jr.*

Maria stood to hear the charges leveled against her during the proceedings. *The Archival Collection of the State Museum Auschwitz-Birkenau in Oswiecim.*

Stanisława Rachwałowa, a former prisoner at Auschwitz and later Montelupich, created controversy when she forgave Maria "in the name of all the prisoners," shortly before Mandl's execution. *The Archival Collection of the State Museum Auschwitz-Birkenau in Oświęcim.*

A page from the datebook of Father Marian Stark, the priest assigned to be Maria's counselor and reluctant attendee at her hanging. The entry for January 24, 1948, notes simply: "Execution, Auschwitz perpetrators, 5:45 – 10:00 am, seven Catholics." *Zgromadzenia Księży Misionarzy, Krakow, Poland.*

1948   Styczeń   31 dni

Niedziela 18 Katr. św. Piotra — 9.8 św. Laren (x. Mortinajti's) KRZESZOVICE. Dzieci złych rodziców będą cierpiały za ich złe czyny.

Poniedziałek 19 Ferdynanda

Wtorek 20 Fabiana i Sebast.

Sroda 21 Agnieszki

Czwartek 22 Wincentego

Piątek 23 Zaśl. N. M. P.

Sobota 24 Tymoteusza

4 Tydzie

CHAPTER 51

The Child
Was Eaten by Rats

*Which is why, believe me, I could not allow myself even the
slightest weakness over mothers and children. When I saw the
littlest ones going into the bunker, all I could think was: "There's
a few less Jewish brats; there are some kids who will never become repellent adult Jews."*

—HELGA SCHNEIDER, LET ME GO, QUOTING
A FORMER AUFSEHERIN

STANISŁAWA RACHWAŁOWA, WHO WAS TO feature prominently in
Maria's future, had always noted this dichotomy in Maria's personality. How she "adopted" a child one day, and then—on the
following day—"participated in selections on the rail ramp where
also there were children who, however, walked straight to their
death and she calmly watched it—that too was Mandl."

After the war there were many reports of incidents in which
Mandl was particularly cruel to pregnant mothers and newborn
babies. Although she denied this at her trial ("From the time of
delivery, mothers were placed in a hospital, where they had ensured medical care and child care") there was ample evidence to
the contrary.

Anna Palarczyk testified that she often saw newborn babies in
the camp placed in the ambulance as a kind of storage. "They were

laid there and they continued to lay there until they died. In 1942, when a woman came to the camp expecting a child, then neither she nor the child would remain alive."

Dr. Kosciuszka remembered newborn babies drowned and then burned in a stove and babies a few months old being taken away from their mothers and killed. Aleksandr Kinsky later testified that Mandl starved a child to death, and Antonina Piatkowska told of an incident in which Mandl ordered a newborn child thrown outside the barracks, where the child was eaten by rats.

Piatkowska also testified that "in 1942, on Mandl's order, pregnant women and babies were killed with phenol shots." Dr. Kosciuszka concurred, stating that Mandl sent pregnant women to the gas or had them killed with phenol injections and that the conditions in the women's camp caused nearly all children born there to die.

Several specific incidents were noted at Mandl's subsequent trial. These included Maria's brutal actions during the liquidation of the Czech family camp, and another time when a transport of Russian women arrived from Witebsk and she took children away from their mothers, throwing them "like stones" into the cars that were standing ready to transport them to the gas chambers.

Luba Reiss testified that in one selection Mandl noticed among the prisoners a young Greek girl, very pretty and healthy, in an advanced state of pregnancy. Mandl sent her to Block 25. "The woman explained that she was in her ninth month of pregnancy, and that after giving birth she could work. She pleaded for her life. Mandl kicked her in the stomach and put her in the group going to the gas."

How can one explain these paradoxical actions on Maria's part? Psychologist John Grotgen conjectures that Mandl couldn't let soft emotions affect her, things like a child's curly hair, and she tried hard *not* to feel compassion. Anything that triggered compassion was dangerous, personally and professionally. She had to fight against it. "The way Maria saw herself, was as someone who would not likely be a parent. One of the tragedies of Maria's life was the premature death of her sister's son, Franz Josef. These actions were a playing out of that loss—a way to escape from her reality."

Grotgen notes that they were also a way for Mandl to be even MORE powerful. To take a life, nurture it, and then kill it. To have the POWER to do that! "Regarding her interactions with children—doing that is like an emotional vacation. Hanging out with a child for example—fun stuff, a simple, happy world. Many guards had their 'guilty pleasures,' this was hers; that and a visceral need for power."

CHAPTER 52

An Untimely Death

She was the savior of the orchestra, she managed to save us—
but not, alas, herself.

—HELENA NIWIŃSKA

O N APRIL 5, 1944, THE women's orchestra suffered a huge blow
when Alma Rosé died.

Three days before, Alma had conducted a successful Sunday concert. She was proud of her musicians and that evening was asked to
attend a birthday celebration for Frau Schmidt, a *Kapo* in the Canada
compound. When she returned to the orchestra barrack Alma became terribly ill with a headache, nausea, dizziness, and seizures.
She was delirious, moving her hands in conducting motions. Mandl
was summoned and arrived with an SS doctor, who ordered Alma
be taken to the *Revier*. Maria was extremely upset and assigned Alma
a private room in the Hospital Block with an unheard of luxury—a
cot complete with bedding.

Over the next two days Alma's condition worsened. Dr. Mengele
came to consult, and Alma wavered between consciousness and unconsciousness. After various unsuccessful treatments, Alma died
shortly before dawn on April 5 at thrity-eight years of age, probably
of botulism.

Mandl returned to the Music Block and announced that orchestra members could go to the *Revier*, where Alma's body had been laid in state, on a white cloth—covered pedestal consisting of two stools. The orchestra women, many weeping openly, said goodbye and placed small bunches of wildflowers on Alma's body. Anita Lasker-Wallfisch later noted that "even the SS seemed upset."

Afterward, Maria distanced herself somewhat from the orchestra, while the musicians struggled to maintain a high artistic standard without Alma's presence and guidance. It became increasingly apparent that Alma had *been* the orchestra. Without her strong leadership, the group floundered.

CHAPTER 53

Mala

Mala Zimetbaum. YAD VASHEM PHOTO ARCHIVE, JERUSALEM. ARCHIVAL SIGNA-
TURE 2986/84, ITEM ID 4062116.

There were no executions in the camp. I knew only one, and it
was a former woman prisoner who escaped in the uniform of
a supervisor during the day from the camp and was picked up
some weeks later together with a male prisoner. She was kept
for some time in the Bunker at Auschwitz. Why she was con-
demned to die, I don't know. It was an order that anybody who
tried to escape was punished with death.

—MARIA MANDL

IN EARLY SUMMER OF 1944, prisoners in Auschwitz-Birkenau were riveted by the escape and capture of prisoners Mala Zimetbaum and Edek Galinski. The story of Mala and Edek is now recognized as one of the most profoundly moving examples of love and courage in the Holocaust.

Mala Zimetbaum was a young woman renowned for her linguistic abilities, sharp intelligence, and personal assurance. Mala's primary position was as *Läuferin*, a camp messenger. This was both a difficult and privileged job. The messenger had to stand near the front gate, in all weathers. As soon as an overseer like Mandl would bellow "*Läufer!*" the woman had to run up and do whatever was ordered. Mala's position and influence evolved to the point where she, unlike the general prison population, was allowed her to keep her hair long and to dress well. She was also respected by the other prisoners, who appreciated her efforts to help improve their conditions.

Mala quickly became Mandl's favorite messenger, and because Maria trusted her, she enjoyed a large degree of freedom in the camp.

Mala had fallen in love with Edek Galinski, a Polish political prisoner. After conceiving and implementing a carefully orchestrated plan, she escaped with Edek, both of them disguised in German uniforms. When the SS discovered what had happened, they were incredulous. Margot Drechsel even initiated a search, worrying that Mala had fallen somewhere and was sick. "They simply couldn't believe she had escaped!"

After an extraordinarily long roll call during which the camp buzzed with the news, the sirens wailed and everyone knew they had escaped.

Rumors spread that Mala and Edek had taken lists with them to tell the world about Auschwitz. Calls were quickly made by the SS to military outposts in the area, spreading news of the escape and ramping up the pursuit.

Mala and Edek succeeded in eluding their pursuers for two weeks; days of hope and elation for prisoners in the camp who identified emotionally with the escapees. The couple managed to reach the Slovakian border but then aroused the suspicion of the

border guards. Sadly, Mala and Edek were arrested and returned
to Auschwitz.

Edek was tortured and then hanged in Birkenau. Mala had her
hair cut off and was detained in a barrack. One prisoner later said
that "I took advantage of the opportunity to speak with her privately.
She only said: 'I'm doing well.'" She told everyone she met she
wouldn't allow herself to be hanged.

Because Maria Mandl had trusted the *Läuferin*, she viewed Mala's
escape as a personal betrayal. Holding a very public execution would
allow Maria to vent her anger and serve as a warning to others.

Mandl ordered the prisoners to assemble at a special roll call on
the camp street, some in a circle so everyone could see and hear well.
"It wasn't cold, there was no rain, the weather was good."

Mandl came, along with other officials followed by Mala, re-
strained and very pale. After everyone had assembled, an unearthly
quiet descended and Mandl read the sentence from a piece of paper
in her hand.

"This Mala, in whom we had such great confidence, escaped. An
order has come from Berlin that a Jewish woman who dares to escape from our camp must be hanged."

As the prisoners began speaking quietly among themselves, Mala
suddenly brandished a stolen razor blade and slashed her wrists. She
raised her hand to Maria, blood dripping, as the guards tried to wrest
the blade from her. Mala fought hard and screamed, "I know that I
will die but that is unimportant. You also will die, your hours are
numbered!"

Two men finally succeeded in handcuffing Mala and beat her viciously. Mandl's carefully planned spectacle was ruined, chaos
ensued, and she was livid with anger. Prisoners were ordered back
into their barracks as Mala was carried away in a wheelbarrow to
Block 4. "They wanted to stop the bleeding so that they could carry
out the sentence. So that she wouldn't die from her own hand." "She
wasn't a human anymore. She was a bloody lump, a mess."

Mandl followed, and through the door, which was ajar, witnesses
saw her beating and kicking Mala, screaming with hate at the bleed-

ing woman. "Get this swine into the chimney alive!" Mala was taken away on a carriage. No one is quite sure exactly where or how she died, but die she did that day.

During Maria's subsequent war crimes trial, she downplayed her role in the execution of Mala and Edek. "I learned in the political department that Mala had been sentenced to death in Berlin. Arbeitsdienstführer Reuters called and told me that Mala wanted to cut her wrists or veins. So I caused her immediately to be taken to the hospital for medical attention. Later, I had an order from the political office to transport her in order to do the execution at the crematorium."

In private Maria was enraged by Mala's defiance and by her actions. How, inexplicably, with blood streaming down her arms, Mala had remained alive. How the whole women's camp had stood in silence, frozen by the spectacle, seeing the *Oberaufseherin* humiliated in this way.

After the bungled execution Maria was spent, sweaty, covered with Mala's blood, heart still pounding with rage. Strangely impotent in the face of Mala's courage.

CHAPTER 54

Summer of '44/
Homecoming

She came back to Münzkirchen like an Empress, in a beautiful
uniform and beautiful long boots!

—MÜNZKIRCHEN CITIZENS

THE SUMMER OF 1944 WAS seminal for Maria Mandl. Large Hungarian transports had begun arriving and the entire camp of Auschwitz-Birkenau was mobilized for mass slaughter. The escape, capture, and botched execution of Mala Zimetbaum added to Maria's stress level.

Still reeling from the death of Alma Rosé, Maria struggled to support the floundering women's orchestra. The conductor appointed as Alma's successor could not maintain the quality and discipline of the ensemble. Sunday concerts were canceled, although the musicians continued to play marches for arriving and departing work details. Physically, Maria continued to be plagued by intestinal parasites.

Most jarring on a personal level was the death of her mother. Maria returned to Münzkirchen for the funeral, a visit which is still remembered today. Inflated with a sense of her own importance and aiming to impress the community, Maria came escorted by two male SS officers and clothed in full dress uniform.

Maria's feelings toward her mother had remained conflicted. Her love for Anna was tempered by the distance she felt as a child when her mother suffered episodes of depression and illness. As an adult Maria became protective of Anna and helped her father as much as possible.

Her family was bewildered by the path Maria's life had taken. "Maria's mother really had trouble with her nerves. And she really suffered by her daughter being a part of the Nazi Party." During the last two years of her life, after observing the changes in Maria's character, villagers remember that Anna walked daily to Mass to pray for her daughter's soul.

Maria had returned to Münzkirchen periodically during her time at Auschwitz, and these visits always made a great impression on the community. She went to great pains to present herself as an *important person* when entering her hometown. It was a great ego boost, to suddenly find herself both feared and admired. The townspeople and the mayor she hated had to stand there and (kind of) honor her. "That made her feel good."

Maria often came with an entourage in a commandeered SS automobile; "she always had decorated SS officers with her." Once a friend of hers, an SS officer (presumably Janisch) came with Maria. Franz Mandl said they couldn't stay at home, so they went and stayed with her sister for two days. Maria's father said, "You can come anytime but your friend can't."

For casual dress on her visits Maria often wore jodhpurs with boots and a "Teller-Mutze" hat. One young boy also vividly remembered seeing her in uniform. "She was VERY proud!" Another boy, whose father was a friend of Franz Mandl, remembers that "she wore a black uniform, not brown, and one of those taller plate-like hats."

"She was a very big and tall, a real GERMANIC woman! And nobody knew what she was up to, or what she did, or had any idea in what she was involved. NOBODY knew that!"

On earlier visits, when Maria traveled through the train station in Schärding, different people were paid to pick her up in a wagon and drive her home. One time, in 1943, a local man was engaged to do just that. His daughter remembered that her father had heard stories about what was happening in the East, and, curious, he asked Mandl a lot of questions. Maria became angered by his inquiries and threatened deportation if he did not stop. Subdued, the man was scared to death he would later be picked up and taken to a concentration camp.

A photograph exists from what was possibly Maria's final visit to Münzkirchen before her mother died. The nuclear family is gathered by the front door of the family home. Her father and mother are seated on wooden chairs and the children are gathered around, now adults. They have made an effort for this occasion and everybody is wearing good clothes; the men in ties and jackets, the women in dresses with embellished necklines.

Loisi stands on the right near her father, on a visit from Switzerland. She has a pleasant smile and her sweet personality is evident. Georg and Anna stand in the middle behind the parents, both with somber expressions. Georg looks confident, Anna a little beaten down. The mother has a small smile and carefully clasped hands in her lap. Franz Mandl has a pleasant yet stern look on his face.

Maria stands on the left, now a mature woman in her early thirties. She has filled out but looks strong rather than heavy and has an agreeable smile on her face as she gazes directly at the camera. Most tellingly, her left hand has reached out and rests gently on her mother's shoulder, in a tender moment of protection and love.

In 1944 Maria came to Münzkirchen for several visits, once for her mother's funeral, once in October, and again in December for Christmas. On her visits home Maria and her father often visited one of Franz's good friends, who lived nearby on his farm.

That farm is still a substantial holding, located on the outskirts of Münzkirchen, past fields where large rabbits run and cavort. It is a beautiful property with a large interior courtyard. Today it appears much as it did in 1944. The scene is peaceful, with an old farm dog lying sentinel.

The current owner is an energetic and articulate man in his late sixties. He has great personal charm and welcomes us warmly. Once, in 1943, as a teenaged boy, he drove Maria to the train station—one horse with a buggy. "It is a forty-five-minute trip to Schärding, about ten kilometers. She did not say one word!"

From 1944, when he was fifteen, he remembers very clearly the visits of Maria and her father to his home. Maria was wearing her black uniform. When the two fathers were chatting, the son recalls that Franz Mandl said that the war was going to be over very soon. The farmer's son notes that "if Franz had said that in public he would have been deported!"

On Maria's December visit home, one of her schoolmates, Paula Bauer, remembers an encounter between Maria and Anton Schiller. "After midnight Mass, Maria Mandl was meeting her ex-lover. They had an angry dispute with one another. She had become very distant and rigorous."

Community members also remarked on Schiller's restlessness as the war came to a close later that spring. "We saw him driving up and down. Schiller shot himself when he knew the Americans were coming." One person recalls that Maria "had threatened him several times with taking him to a concentration camp. And she swore to take revenge on him for dumping her. But it didn't come to that."

CHAPTER 55

The Living Hell

Arriving transport on the Birkenau ramp, 1944. YAD VASHEM PHOTO ARCHIVE, JE-
RUSALEM. ARCHIVAL SIGNATURE 4522, ALBUM FA 268/4, ITEM ID 33237.

*That was an action which made everyone involved feel eerie,
and made shivers run down their backs, because of the incon-
ceivable scope of the annihilation of masses of people.*

—OSKAR GRÖNING

I thought I was in the living hell.

—HELEN TICHAUER

L ATER THAT SUMMER, BACK IN Auschwitz, Mandl achieved a professional triumph of sorts when she received a high party
number and was awarded the Cross of Merit, 2nd Class, for her service in the war. The war merit cross was a variant of the Iron Cross,
which could be awarded to civilians as well as military personnel.
The merit medal, created by Adolf Hitler, was a routine kind of
award rather than a true distinction for superior services.

Mandl later noted in her deposition that "I received a Party
Number higher than 8,000,000 in the summer of 1944 and I also got
the Order of War Achievement, Class II. Apart from me; Drexler,
Kock and Franz received this and, I think, Brandl. I was handed the
cross by Kommandant Kramer." In her service evaluation the Nazi
authorities "assessed her work positively."

In addition to the large transports of Jews from Hungary arriving
daily for extermination, Birkenau was involved in several significant
actions during what would turn out to be the last year of the war.
The Czech family camp was liquidated on July 11, 1944, and the
Roma camp was liquidated on August 2, 1944.

All of the personnel at Auschwitz began to feel the pressure of
"processing" the huge influx of people. Oskar Gröning remembered
the strain, as did *Kommandant* Rudolf Höss, who noted in his journal
that in the summer of 1944, during the Hungary action, train delays
caused five trains to come within twenty-four hours instead of the
expected three. "On top of that, the five trains had more people in
them than ever." Höss summarized that "we executed about 400,000
Hungarian Jews alone at Auschwitz in summer of 1944."

Birkenau's primary function as the largest extermination facility
in the Third Reich was already a fact of daily life. Incoming transports of Jews were omnipresent and long lines of people walking to
the gas chambers a common sight. "The transports were announced
at the Kommandant's office by the railway management in Auschwitz and by the train personnel on the railway line and then driven
onto the sidetrack on the ramp. The wagons, up to a count of 40, in
which up to 80 Jews were pent-up, remained standing on the ramp
and the locomotive traveled back to the Auschwitz train station."

The SS and assigned camp prisoners then started the selection process. By now, the accompanying mayhem had become ordinary.

After long journeys without food or water, the doors to the trains were thrown open violently by SS officers carrying machine guns and screaming "*Raus! Raus!*" Dogs were barking, the sounds were deafening, orders came thick and fast, there was often smoke and the smell of burning flesh in the air.

Gröning remembers things getting much more hectic when the Hungarian Jews started arriving, and that often two transports stood on the ramps while another waited in the train station in Oświęcim. "During this period, even seasoned officers began to feel a twinge of conscience."

This methodical annihilation of the Jews left little time for reflection on the part of the SS, and Gröning remembers working to the point of exhaustion. He describes many days where the responsibilities detailed under a *Special Assignment Roste* assigned officers duty from six in the morning until six the next morning, a twenty-four-hour shift. "It is only too understandable that the quality of the supervision suffered enormously from this."

Whenever a transport came and the preceding one wasn't yet handled completely, the new arrivals had to wait. Gröning later remarked that everything was done in this situation to prevent the new arrivals from figuring out about the procedures.

Some of the musicians in the orchestra remember being used as a distraction to lull the incoming transports, while many survivors of those transports remember the sound of the orchestra juxtaposed against the backdrop of women and children screaming and crying, dogs barking, and Germans yelling orders.

On one occasion the orchestra "played all night during the selections of the Hungarian convoys. [We] saw all the convoys arriving. Played outside, our entire repertoire—everyone." Another purpose was to divert the SS, who also had to stay outside all night.

Because of the location of the orchestra barrack, across from the crematorium, the women were always aware of the massive slaughter going on outside their windows. When the Hungarian transports arrived, so many people were being burned that the crematoria could not keep up. The overflow of bodies were thrown into a nearby grave and burned there. One musician later remarked that the sight of, and the horrible smoke of, burning corpses haunted her whole life thereafter.

The orchestra practiced and played from morning to night during this period.

> These hours gave us a short relief from the horrible occur-rences that were being played out in our direct proximity. A member of the orchestra, she was called Ariala, was no longer in a condition wherein she could endure the cir-cumstances of Birkenau. She threw herself against the electric fence and died there.

Oskar Gröning concurs that the crematoria were not sufficient to process the task at hand so the "old technology" of open burning of corpses in pits and pyres was reinitiated. Helen Tichauer con-firms this and notes that, at night, the sky was red from the flames. "I was out in the late evenings while they were burning bodies, with those flames high in the sky. The red was all around you. I thought I was in the living hell."

During the transports of Hungarian Jews, prisoners saw Mandl "directly participating in selections on the ramp."

Maria dealt with the pressure in her own way. In her separate villa, staffed by female prisoners, parties took place after selections, and alcohol—taken from the incoming trains—was consumed. A German woman named Klimaszewska, who worked in the villa for about a month, remembers that Mandl kept a diary in which she took notes about the incoming transports, selections, and numbers of people sent to the gas.

CHAPTER 56

Dissolution

THE LAST SIX MONTHS OF Birkenau camp were a tumultuous—
and by Nazi standards—disorganized time. Increasingly, the
Auschwitz complex was coming under aerial reconnaissance by Allied forces. Oskar Gröning remembers that during the Hungarian
transports there were many flights by the Allied pilots who, by this
point in the war, "could fly unhindered without a German fighter
[plane] being seen, even attack planes."

Approximately three kilometers east of Auschwitz lay the large
Monowitz-Buna factory run by I. G. Farben. Bombing raids began
there, targeting this industrial part of the camp.

Gröning notes that "there were one or two attacks on the factory
and once even on the main camp Auschwitz I. The damages were
minimal, and no important installations were hit. Two blocks of
houses near the main camp were hit in which prisoners performed
some kind of work—so the Jews were caught in between two fires
of the war." Danuta Czech verifies that on August 20, 1944, I. G.
Farben was bombed for twenty-eight minutes by the Americans, late
on a Sunday afternoon with good weather conditions. Other bombing raids took place mid-September.

Gröning later remarked that although "a few bombs fell after or
during attacks on the Buna factory (5 klm away), no one took the
bombing danger seriously—we were too far spread out."

Maria, however, did take the bombing danger seriously. Anna Palarczyk relates a "funny story" about an air raid when the prisoners
were told to walk into the block. They were joyous that the RAF was
coming closer and that they would bomb the camp. "However, the
SS... [got very nervous during raids]. The girls in the main camp
saw Mandl crawl on all fours to the bunker!"

In August Maria asked for a transfer out of Auschwitz but was ordered to remain for a few more months. At the beginning of October
the prisoner work detail (*Sonderkommando*) responsible for working
in the death apparatus of Crematorium IV revolted and blew up the
installation. Brutal reprisals were taken and female members of the
resistance were arrested and killed for providing the explosives.

Sometime in October Maria again visited Münzkirchen. By this
point the pressures she faced were beginning to crack her tough veneer. One of Maria's nephews remembers that Mandl came in
uniform, in a jeep, accompanied by a man also wearing a uniform
and carrying a weapon, who waited outside while Maria visited with
her sister inside. She didn't stay too long, and Anna, Maria's sister,
cried when Maria left because she wanted her to stay and not go
back. Her nephew clearly remembers Maria saying, "*Ich kann nicht
mehr weg*" ("I can no longer go on").

After Maria returned to Birkenau, she initiated the final dissolu-
tion of the orchestra, which took place during one of Franz
Hössler's absences. Hössler, furious when he returned and discovered what had happened, frantically tried to reactivate the orchestra.
"It was a parody, a parody!" one survivor later exclaimed. "Here they
are burning documents, destroying traces, one could see panicky
preparations for the evacuation, and he is creating a new orchestra."
One musician, Wisia, said that Mandl had purposefully dissolved
the orchestra while Hössler was gone, to play a joke on him, and to
get even with him. "[We did think] that it was solely her decision
[to dissolve the orchestra] without communicating with Hössler."

Helena Niwińska remembers how it transpired. "At dinnertime
on October 31, 1944, a member of the SS garrison unexpectedly came
into the orchestra block and issued the command '*Kapelle antreten!*

('Band, fall in!'). We immediately went out in front of the block and had barely lined up there before we heard another portentous order: '*Jüdinnen austreten!*' ('Jewish women step forward!'). The Jewish women were then led to the main camp street and transferred to Bergen-Belsen. The Aryan women were transferred to a vacated men's barracks. And just like that, the orchestra ceased to exist."

As prisoners were sent back into Germany, the population of the camp began to decrease. Several of the most hated guards, including Irma Grese, were transferred to Bergen-Belsen. To a small degree, conditions for prisoners eased and the constant harassment lessened. One survivor called it an "idyllic period."

Helen Tichauer remarked in a 2003 interview that had Germany been winning the war, there were plans for a new women's camp which Mandl was to administer. "At the end of '44 Mandl was promoted to become leader of the future largest women's camp in the Reich; Kaufering. This was on the drawing board." Mandl had already selected a group of women from Birkenau that she would take with her, and Tichauer was one of them. "She respected me because I had my skills. [I had] won her over."

Germany was decidedly not winning the war at this point, however, so any plans for a new women's camp at Kaufering were scrapped. As Birkenau begins to ebb its way out of existence, accounts of Maria dwindle. Like many SS officers, she was keeping a lower profile and trying to figure out what came next, especially given the increasing yet rarely vocalized likelihood that Germany would lose the war.

One of the last accounts of Maria at Auschwitz comes from Ella Lingens-Reiner, late that fall. All German prisoners had been ordered to the camp gate, when Mandl appeared. After asking if everyone was present, Mandl "took a cardboard box and said 'Well, here is some chocolate for you, and if you behave, you'll get some again.' Each of us was given a small piece of chocolate taken from Swiss Red Cross parcels. First we were dumbfounded, then we had to suppress laughter."

The prisoners quickly recognized that Mandl, like many of the other supervisory personnel, was getting nervous. As Lingens-Reiner summarizes: "Now those gaolers were frightened and attempted to placate and suborn us in the twelfth hour—with a piece of chocolate! This was how those brains imagined the world."

Records show that Maria was largely off-duty for the month of November and then, on November 30, left Auschwitz for the last time to begin a new duty assignment in the German camp of Mühldorf.

Part Five

CHAPTER 57

Mühldorf

In August I asked Glücks for a transfer and came to Mühldorf.
Since there was already a manager of the camp as well as a fe-
male supervisor, and the commando consisted of only 200
women, I remained without work until the end of the war. I
wanted to go home but did not get permission. Here everything
was under duress. Everybody had to go where he was told to go.
This is what Himmler was saying. There was no consideration
shown for us at all, no matter if you were physically or emo-
tionally breaking down.

—Maria Mandl

The only joy I found was to see how our brave guards scattered
like rabbits when the air raid siren began to howl. By 1944, they
had been in, or seen their share of [enough] Allied air raids to
dazzle their superiority to shreds. I was amazed how thin was
the line that separated the super Aryan braves from the super
Aryan chickens.

—Bill Gluck, survivor, Mühldorf

N INETEEN FORTY-FOUR. As summer turned to fall and the war entered its final stages, members of the SS were systematically transferred back into Germany. On November 30, 1944, Maria left

Auschwitz for the camp at Mühldorf, where she remained for the duration of the war. Her presence there went almost unnoticed in the hectic closing days of the Third Reich.

Mandl was assigned to Mettenheim, a women's sub-camp of Dachau located near the town of Mühldorf and charged with the production of armament and bunker construction. Maria was titular *Oberaufseherin* in the last months of its existence.

By the end of the war over eight thousand primarily Jewish concentration camp prisoners had been transported to Mühldorf, among them eight hundred women. Although some worked in the cement brigades, the majority worked in the camp's own infrastructure, including the kitchen, laundry, tailor shop, and debris rooms. The death rate in the Mühldorf camps was very high, almost 50 percent of the prisoners sent there lost their lives.

Survivor Bill Gluck remembers that "it was a work camp. Our task was to build an underground aircraft maintenance bunker. The camp did not need gas chambers—people were dying quicker than flies."

On January 10, 1945, a month after her arrival in the camp, Maria observed her thirty-third birthday with little reason to celebrate. The approaching front loomed, causing deep depression among the overseers.

There are two photographs of Maria that exist from this period. Obviously taken during some downtime, by a friend or colleague, they reveal further insights into Maria's state of mind. Both pictures are staged in the wooded area surrounding the camp. In the first she is wearing a beautiful white dress with matching shoes, a watch, and a string of pearls. She is seated naturally on a picnic blanket and has a pensive look. She appears pretty, calm, even feminine—the furthest thing you could imagine from a woman known for her brutality.

There is a disconcerting innocence about the other photograph. Maria sits on the bank of a pond, wearing a casual dress, hiking up her skirt as she dips her bare feet into the water. She looks like a country girl, enjoying a simple pleasure, lost in a daydream.

Soon there was little time for such diversions as the Americans began bombing railways and all roads surrounding the camp.

Maria survived harrowing air raids in March and April and describes terror, depression, and insomnia. "In Mühldorf we had horrible bomb and flying airplane attacks, so that I could hardly sleep for days. The camp was located near the airport. We were cut off from the world and found ourselves in a trap."

On March 19 a wave of twenty-seven American planes began bombing the railway at 11:38 A.M. By 12:20 P.M. there had been eight bombing raids totaling 760 bombs. One hundred and thirty people were killed outright and over three thousand were wounded. Prisoners from the camp were brought in to help rebuild the rail line, joined by able-bodied citizens. A second wave of bombings began on April 20 and killed twenty of those prisoners. Mühldorf was largely destroyed by these bombings.

Conditions in the air raid shelters were terrifying. Attacks could last over two hours with people packed "like sardines in a can." The shelter itself had only one door, no windows, and very dim lighting. One survivor remembered that everybody looked angry and everyone had trouble breathing, with bombs falling the whole time. The "hellish noise of the iron door gives us a scare every time [when people run in], the bombs fall and fall. People come in continually, there is no room, it's so narrow. Some people get claustrophobia, some pray."

As for the SS, "When the all-clear sounded, they came out of their holes, dusted themselves off, raised their chins in the best Mussolini fashion, and continued parading up and down as if nothing happened."

Kate Bernath, a Hungarian prisoner, was transferred to Mühldorf in the beginning of April. She describes the prisoner population as "walking corpses," and remembers being taken to the town, where they were forced to clean up rubble of buildings that had been bombed. Bernath and her cousin survived several bombing raids. "But we didn't care about the bombs. We were happy that there were bombings... We wanted to see the Germans defeated."

Bill Gluck, like Kate Bernath, was part of a prisoner work detail assigned to clean up after the bombing raids. "Mühldorf junction must have been one of the most busy and important centers, judging by the urgency with which the Germans reacted to its demise—the place was completely devastated; railroad tracks were twisted and turned in every direction imaginable, including toward the sky, and trains were ripped to pieces, cars buried partially or completely in the ground, and contents strewn in all directions. What a marvelous sight it was!"

As the Allied forces advanced, the SS began to leave the camp, all dignity forgotten in the scurry to save their lives. With only minutes to spare, Maria fled.

Liberation by the American army of the various camps in the Mühldorf system took place between April 29 and May 2, 1945. Accounts by U.S. servicemen are vivid, describing charred remains of Jewish prisoners stretched out in misshapen forms, "some with their mouths open in agony, others shot and burned, still others burned so badly you could not recognize them at all."

Photos taken of the liberation of Mühldorf show a heavily wooded area with farmland in the background. Images of squat barracks and crematory ovens alternate with a whip woven of electrical wire used to beat prisoners and a body pulled from the Inn River, head cleaved open with an ax. Piles of corpses, male and female, are evident as well as bodies removed from mass graves in preparation for reburial.

For the moment, at least, Maria had escaped retribution for her crimes.

CHAPTER 58

Escape and Capture

Ten minutes before the Americans reached the camp I left and became the victim.

—MARIA MANDL

ARIA'S ESCAPE FROM MÜHLDORF AND her life in hiding commenced with the liberation of the camp. She was
accompanied by Walter Langleist, the *Kommandant*, and a former
prisoner named Mase, who had a privileged and protected status.
Many in the camp assumed that Mandl and Langleist had been
having an affair.

In her deposition Maria stated that the group tried to "cross
the... [river] together with several others from the camp with a boat,
[under] heavy bombardment from tanks." Mühldorf is located on
the left bank of the Inn River, and Maria wanted to go toward Schärding and then on to her home in Münzkirchen. The distance between
Mühldorf and Münzkirchen is about eighty kilometers (fifty miles),
in a straight line.

When Maria finally arrived, she stayed one night only. Neighbors
later conjectured that her father had denied sanctuary, stating, "You
must now stand up for what you have done." There is no way to confirm the exact details of any conversation, so these rumors were
almost certainly the result of local gossip rather than anchored in

fact. Franz, a man of high morals and profound love for his family, undoubtedly suffered agonies over his daughter's situation.

Maria then fled to her sister's farm in the tiny hamlet of Luck. It was the last time she would see her home.

She remained in hiding for the next three months. Her sister Anna and her husband were afraid when Maria showed up at their house because there were harsh penalties for harboring fugitives, including deportation. Nonetheless, Anna loved her sister, and the family made the difficult decision to help. Langleist and Mase had accompanied Maria to Luck, and all were wearing uniforms, which they promptly removed. The car was hidden in the back.

After the turbulence of the last few months Luck was an oasis. The community is located about 4.5 kilometers from Münzkirchen, along a scenic road of rolling hills alternating with dark, lush woods. Maria's sister's farm was situated in a corner of the settlement, with a self-contained courtyard.

In the spring, despite the privations of the war, there was a wonderful scent of flowers, manure, and fresh air. Anna's house was large, with low ceilings and corner tables, and a stunning view of the countryside from the back of the barn. The three escapees settled into the home, with Maria later claiming that "I registered under my own name." Langleist, described as "having a stern look about him, dark-rimmed glasses, and piercing eyes" interacted naturally with Maria's family.

At the same time, American servicemen in the area began establishing law and order, repairing roads and infrastructure, detaining thousands of German POWs, and setting up camps for displaced civilians. Many war criminals tried to blend in with these larger groups. Once captured, the SS men were detained and interrogated and former inmates were questioned, large numbers of whom were still living in displaced persons camps.

Why didn't Maria run? Perhaps a clue lies in the comment she made to her sister during their visit near the end of the war, "*Ich kann nicht mehr weg*" ("I can't go on"). She was tired, she was home, she was out of the camp environment. There was also a bit of hubris in her decision. During her time in the camps Maria felt herself so secure within the cocoon of the ideology of duty and country that she never thought of herself as particularly vulnerable.

For three months Maria did escape capture and retribution. In the end, however, she was arrested on August 10, 1945. Mase, the ex-prisoner, had reported their whereabouts to the Allies. Maria remained indignant over this betrayal for the rest of her life, especially over Mase's socialization with her family and how he had taken advantage of the safe haven of her sister's home.

> I was betrayed by a former prisoner, Mase, from the camp Mühldorf and then arrested. Mase was with me, as well as with an SS leader who was always in Mühldorf... He was sitting at the table with all the people from the house, was able to move around from morning to night, as and where he wanted. I would never have believed that a person who had never suffered any injustice and had all the advantages which were possible offered to him, who was drinking schnapps with Sturmband leader Langleist in his room, would then take revenge for the harm done to him by others.

Perhaps Mase was having second thoughts about hiding with two well-known Nazi officials, perhaps he was concerned about the fact that Maria had once found him inebriated after drinking with Langleist and the fraternization that implied. For whatever reason, Maria's haven was gone and she would spend the rest of her life in captivity.

CHAPTER 59

Dachau

*There's never a day that I don't think about Dachau in one
way or the other. [It's] one of those psychological things, I'm sure,
but you hear voices. And they leave the suffering, even though
it's cleaned up.*

——Lavan Robinson, U.S. serviceman stationed
at Dachau after the war

Soldiers of the American army now occupying southern Germany were issued a gray manual from the War Department with
lists of mandatory arrestees, persons from all echelons of the Nazi
Party to be detained for future trials. Many people suspected of war
crimes, including Maria Mandl, were taken to a new detention
center built on the site of the former concentration camp of Dachau.

The area surrounding Dachau and its closest city, Munich, had
been heavily bombed. Roads were clogged with debris, and initially,
the camp looked much as it had at liberation. Bodies had been removed, but the crematorium chimney was still standing, while the
ground underneath the execution wall was "stained rust red and the
smell of blood was still strong."

The War Crimes Enclosure constructed inside of Dachau had a
capacity of thirty thousand and served as a prison for Nazi personnel for the next three years. Within that enclosure were barbed wire

subdivisions with barracks separated into "cages" for women and men. Maria Mandl was placed in War Crimes Cage PWE-29 and assigned prison number #29-1277.

To engender a sense of guilt, POWs were immediately taken to see the Dachau crematorium and gas chamber, where the Allies had replaced bodies found at liberation with wax dummies. For someone like Maria, accustomed to the "excesses" of the Birkenau extermination machine, Dachau's more modest facility probably made little impression.

The barracks in which the detainees lived were clean and well built, had heat and electric light, basic furniture, gravel-covered walkways, and adequate sanitary facilities with running water and toilets with seats. The food was adequate if not tasty. One detainee later exclaimed, "It was really something you could stand!"

Prisoners were permitted to walk outside between the barracks for exercise, and by the end of 1945, restrictions instituted by Eisenhower were relaxed enough to allow some censored postal communication between them and their families. Maria later acknowledged that during the period of her incarceration with the Americans, she received three letters from her father and sister.

The Red Cross regularly sent officials to monitor conditions and ensure the prisoners were being treated humanely. "They were very, very regular, very faithful about that."

For Maria, this period was marked by illness, her body finally succumbing to the stresses of being on the run and in hiding. "For four days I was lying in bed unconscious with angina and nervous breakdown in the bunker at Dachau, without being treated properly by the prison doctor. He was furious, because I had counseled a fellow prisoner in my cell not to start a relationship with him."

Increasingly, the world press began to cover the Nazi prisoners in Dachau. Although not as notorious as other SS women, like Irma Grese and Ilse Koch, Mandl did attract some attention. The Polish journalist Melchior Wankowicz was granted a permit to visit Dachau and conduct interviews with the imprisoned Nazis. His secretary, Zofia, had been in Ravensbrück and insisted they interview "this monster in a skirt." Wankowicz forbid his secretary to taunt Mandl and then got sidetracked by the beauty of Maria's cellmate—Elisabeth Ruppert. In the end, he never wrote about Mandl.

Polish filmmaker Wanda Jakubowska spoke with several former SS men in the summer of 1945 about their motives and inner conflicts. She tried to carry out an interview with *Lagerführerin* Mandel [sic], but Maria refused to cooperate.

There is a film clip of Mandl and Ruppert in one of the detention cells, made during their time in Dachau. The doors to these cells are solid, with a variety of locks and a small open square filled with a metal grid. In the first frame a woman is seen smiling through this opening.

In a subsequent scene, the door has been opened and Mandl and Ruppert are sitting on one side in casual conversation. Maria, on the left, is talking and Elisabeth is smiling convivially. Both wear regular dresses and Elisabeth also wears an apron. Maria, resting her arm along a ledge, looks up at the camera, raises her eyebrows, and makes a gesture of dismissal. Then, as if to give the cameraman what he wants, she widens her eyes and glares demonically. Shortly before the video ends the façade comes off and the real Maria emerges, looking down, all artifice aside, visibly swallowing.

Another cellmate of Maria's, Margit Burda, remembers that "we had it very good. There were extra blankets. We had good food. Even the Americans didn't have it so good! We were four to a cell, with running water and a toilet. I got to know Maria there."

Margit

She was the Personification of Evil.
—Elsa Berkomiczowa, former inmate,
Auschwitz-Birkenau

She was my good and kind friend.
—Margit Burda

MARGIT BURDA WAS ONE OF many young women drafted by the German government to serve in an administrative capacity in occupied Poland. For most of the war she worked as a secretary for the police station in Krakow. Margit remembers that "I was 20 years old when I came to Krakow. We earned well and had a lovely apartment. I was in love and the years of my youth until 1945 were wonderful. As the war came to an end, the Russians came. And I came into imprisonment. Why I became a prisoner, I have no idea. I never did anything bad to anybody. The lovely time was over. My wonderful life had come to an end."

Transferred to the Allies, Margit was sent to Dachau, where she was detained in the same cell as Maria Mandl. Over the next two years Margit and Maria were together almost without pause, and a warm and supportive friendship grew between them. Sixty years later, through some serendipitous luck and diligent detective work,

Margit was found—alive and well at the age of eighty-six and willing to speak about her friendship with Maria.

Margit, born in 1920, was eight years younger than the friend she loved. She now lived by the Olympic stadium in Munich with her companion and "Love of My Life," Helmut. Like many young men coming of age in the 1940s, Helmut had been drafted into the Wehrmacht and sent to the Russian Front. He was apprehended and spent the next five years as a POW in Russia. Today he is solicitous of Margit, yet also willing to talk about this turbulent period in both their lives.

The couple greets us warmly in the foyer of their apartment building. Margit looks like an aging film star: curly auburn hair, *perfect* makeup, a pretty roundish face, and stunning eyes—gray with a yellow center. She serves coffee and a variety of cakes—berry torte, cheesecake, a croissant—confiding as an aside that she loves sweets. We immediately bond over the mood and the sugar. For the next four hours she warmly and without reservation shares her memories of Maria.

When we finally leave, Margit and Helmut walk us down to our car, where she waves and waves and *waves* as we drive away. Over the next nine years, until Margit's death in 2016, we forge a friendship of our own, nurtured by frequent visits and an extensive correspondence. It is a wonderful and direct link to Maria, and a rare opportunity to learn more about a different part of her character.

As a teenager Margit had been a musician, playing clarinet and piano in a female wind orchestra in Germany. In 1938 her group was asked to play the opening march for a speech and rally Hitler was giving in Dresden. The young musicians were asked to prepare "The Badenweiler March," and the event made a vivid impression on the fifteen-year-old Margit.

> We practiced half the night. I was already tired and half dozed off, scolded for the first time ever. The performance was very rousing. Hitler was so pleased and shook each of our hands. We were just happy we didn't have to play

anymore! The encounter with Hitler was not very exciting for me. I didn't have a good opinion of a lot of what
he did. Plus, Hitler's handshake was slack and he was wearing gloves.

Margit's background as a musician, and Maria's love of music,
formed the initial basis for their friendship.

Margit had no previous knowledge of Maria or the crimes of
which she was accused, so her impression of and affection for Maria
was gleaned solely from their interactions during incarceration. Now,
when thinking back, Margit remembers that Maria always made direct eye contact, walked with a resolute and self-aware gait, was
disciplined in her speech and physical motions, and didn't use her
hands to talk. She was a little taller than Margit herself. "Mostly she
missed her freedom and her relatives."

Eventually, after they got to know each other, the subject of the
camps came up. When Margit asked, "Was everything really that
bad?" Maria responded, "Yes it was, but I couldn't—as an individual
person—I couldn't do anything against it. Everything was an order
and if I didn't follow the orders, I would have been punished. I was
responsible for order and if [the prisoners] didn't do what I told
them to, I *had* to punish them."

Margit has many good memories of Maria and describes an immediate rapport. "She was quite honest—and she did everything for
me. Her personality [to me] was very good. She was really a dear person. It [seemed what came out later] really backwards... *Sie war 'ein
liebe Mensch.* [A very nice person.] Everything she did, she did 100%."

Margit remembers taking walks with Maria before they went to
the showers, during which they shared conversations about music.
"Maria was quite musical!" There was little chance for humor. "We
couldn't really have a real laugh there. From down in your heart you
couldn't laugh about anything."

"The conversation was always about her father. She also talked
about her siblings, but it was always more about how she had hurt
her father."

Later, after Margit was exonerated and released, she returned home to Germany and wrote a letter to Franz Mandl.

> I was with Maria for two years, we shared our greatest sorrow and only a little joy, and it is only in such conditions that one really gets to know another person. I must state that Maria was in EVERY way a good comrade. I maintain that everything that [was said about her] were lies and deceit.

CHAPTER 61

Treated with Respect

I could have gone into any fashion show in that suit—that's how lovely it was!

—MARGIT BURDA

DAY-TO-DAY LIFE CONTINUED, AND FOR the most part, the Nazi prisoners were treated with civility. A former serviceman stationed at Dachau remembers that "we respected them because they were soldiers too—and we were taught to respect every soldier. You don't demean them, you don't kick them like they did the Jews and all that. And I know they did that, but they were treated normally like I would have liked to have been treated." Margit concurs, stating that:

> The Amis [Americans] permitted us to read books and we had toilet paper. There was an old financier and he had a bunch of notepapers with him. We stuck notes in the back of those books.
>
> The Americans trusted us. They let us write the cell number down. In front. And then they would send the notes out and back again, acting as postmen between cells.
>
> Nearby was a great hall and almost every evening the Germans gave concerts. They sang and made music for

the Amis and we heard everything. In Dachau I lay up on
the top bunk where there were windows. We opened them
and heard the singing. *"Die kleine Stadt will schlafen gehen."*
("The little city goes to sleep.") I can still hear that...

Prisoners, including Margit and Maria, received many perks. "In
Dachau we got a lot of things. I got everything you need in the way
of undergarments from the Americans—underwear—such warm underwear and shirts and everything. And we also got blankets—the
green blankets."

Margit admired Maria for her skills as a talented seamstress.

> She was able to do a lot with her hands. She was very tal-
> ented. Although I was in good health I didn't really have
> any warm outer clothes to wear once the winter months
> began. Maria said, "you know what? I have a good, green
> blanket from the Amis and it is very thick and double ma-
> terial." The border of the blanket had a kind of woven
> pattern and the edges were very nice.

The two women took the end pieces apart and unraveled enough
thread for the project. Margit had hidden a small piece of a razor
blade and a sewing needle in the cuff of her pants. That gave them
everything they needed. Maria, somehow, died the material brown
so it "didn't look so American."

Working in their cell, with very little light, Maria made Margit
a suit. Never using any kind of tape measure to make measure-
ments, she was able to tailor the suit simply from her imagination
and her talent.

> I had to stand in front of the viewing hole in the door of
> the cell and Maria tailored first the pants and then a little
> jacket with the razor blade. I could have entered any fash-
> ion show in that suit—that's how lovely it was! Maria
> could simply do everything! It was perfect and it fit me so

well! Yes, it was very chic and so lovely. It was incredible
what she did with no light! I was very proud of it.

Margit wore the suit throughout her time in prison and for several
years in Germany after she returned home. "Then, when I earned
money, I could buy something to wear. Heavy hearted, I donated
my still wearable suit to a clothing collection."

Days in the cell passed by reading, talking with each other, and
covert activities like the sewing project. Evenings were harder. The
air carried a foul odor that was nicknamed the "Dachau Aroma,"
causing insomnia. When it rained, the smell became more pronounced and made the previous horrors of the camp more visceral.

By this time, the detainees were well aware of the prosecutorial
actions taking place across Germany against other Nazi detainees.
On November 20, 1945, the Nuremberg Trials began. These highest-
ranking Nazi officials had been the face of the regime. Now they
were answering, and paying, for their crimes.

Maria followed the proceedings in Nuremberg closely. A list of
her personal effects includes a tablet with notes written in shorthand
on the course of that trial, probably taken while listening to the radio
in Dachau. She learned of the death sentences for many of her former
colleagues, including Josef Kramer, Franz Hössler, and Irma Grese.

On June 26, 1946, Max Kögl, Maria's former *Kommandant* at Ravensbrück, hanged himself in his cell at Dachau. A few months later, in
late August, the women began to suspect they would be transferred.

This relocation was briefly delayed when Margit became unexpectedly ill. She and the other women in her cell, including Maria,
would regularly take midday walks on their way to the showers.

One of the girls really stole a lot, and as we were passing
the kitchen and the flower and vegetable beds, she stole
a cabbage and hid it in her pants. When we got back to
the cell she took the cabbage out of her pants!!
    Well, and, naturally, we had breakfast: Muesli with lots
of fruit in it and strong coffee and pastries, or whatever

else is sufficient for a breakfast. But we had nothing fresh, nothing green and we were excited about the salad, all five of us.

Shortly thereafter, when Margit was in the showers, one of the physicians was alerted that she had red spots all over the front of her body. She was taken to the infirmary, where scarlet fever was suspected, but ultimately it was determined that her sickness came from the illicit cabbage and was not contagious. Then, they discovered that Margit had appendicitis. The infirmary doctor learned that Margit and the others in her cell were on a list to be moved soon. He arranged an operation for Margit to have her appendix removed, and this—in turn—delayed the entire transport. "The whole transport waited on me. Everyone waited until I recovered."

Finally, on July 26, 1946, the women were transferred to the American Detention Center in Ludwigsburg. Margit remembers this as a time of lessening tensions. "In Ludwigsburg we laughed and messed around."

CHAPTER 62

Extradition

Only with great effort did I live through this transport from Germany to Poland.

—MARIA MANDL

IN JULY OF 1946 MARIA and Margit were sent to Ludwigsburg, where they were held for two months. On September 2 they were transferred to Regensburg, and then, on September 4, 1946, they were extradited along with seventy-seven men to Poland. "The transport went through Czechoslovakia, lasted a long time, and was dreadful."

On departure day guards discovered that five of the prisoners had escaped. U.S. Second Lieutenant Chester P. Bednarczyk, the American officer in command, reported that the escape took place at the Schwandorf railway station. "Investigation showed that the escape was made through an opening in the floor of the railway car through which the prisoners escaped. Further investigation was handed over to Polish authorities." The transport lost one more man to suicide.

By the time the prisoners were transferred to Polish authorities in Dziedzice on September 7, there were seventy-one people plus the dead body. Of those prisoners four were women: Maria, Margit, Erna Boden, and Johanna Langefeld.

The train journey itself was traumatic. Margit remembers that "the train was full of thousands of Berliners. All the compartments were full, and only four of us were women. We had armed Amis at our heads, machine guns and everything. We were in a normal train compartment in a normal passenger train. We had the whole compartment in the train! [Because] Maria was there, they had to leave the door open. When she went to the bathroom the door also had to stay open. They stood in back of her with machine guns. We never knew what would happen next. No one told us anything."

CHAPTER 63

Selbstmord

Nazi whores! Murderers! Kill them!
—Camp survivors screaming at the
transport of war criminals

A FTER THE WAR, AND ESPECIALLY after the very public trial of the
Nazi hierarchy in Nuremberg, camp survivors closely followed
coverage of other apprehended war criminals. News of the extradition of Maria's group to Poland, where they would stand trial for
their crimes, became well known in the zones of occupation.

The Polish press covered these transports extensively. One article,
filled with inaccurate information, is typical. "Maria Mandl, a young
woman of fascinating looks, was once a known sportswoman and famous pilot. Yet, to satisfy her sadistic inclinations, gave up the
Luftwaffe and sports at the beginning of the war and volunteered for
work in KZs..."

Sensationalized press coverage like this meant that the transport
was mobbed by crowds screaming for revenge at every stop. Margit
remembers this vividly.

> In *every* train station we went through there were people
> who had been in the concentration camps. They were yel-
> ling and screaming and Maria got scared. They said

"We're gonna jump in and grab you and tear you apart!"
And she was scared. It was stressful. Many of the former
prisoners were on crutches. The soldiers constantly
threatened that they were going to throw us to them!

Stanisław Kobiela rightly notes that "all the Nazis interned in the
German occupied zones feared return to the place of their crimes,
especially Poland. Some SS men preferred to commit suicide [*Selbts-
mord*] rather than find themselves in Polish hands."

When Maria was detained in Dachau, she had somehow made
contact with Otto Skorzeny, an Austrian SS officer. Skorzeny was an
imposing man, tall, with a dramatic fencing scar on his cheek. He
slipped Maria some pills and told her to "take these tablets, don't let
them kill you! Commit suicide!"

Frightened by the mobs at the train stations, and fearful of what
lay ahead in Poland, Maria made the decision to end her life.

Sixty years later, Margit describes what happened next. While
speaking she makes a sound like a train whistle coming into a station.

Maria took the pills because she really thought the former
prisoners were going to reach in and grab her and tear her
apart. Maria said "God protect me," and took the tablets.
[Her hand was to her mouth] and she came away with a
handful of blood. Once the pills were gone she said, "ah,
not so bad, not so bad." Then she couldn't stand upright
anymore.

I said "I'm coming!" And I took her halfway on my
shoulder and dragged her to the toilet where she threw up.
Everything broke out, everything came out again. I had
the feeling, I thought she was dying. She seemed fragile—
quite bad, quite bad. The faces outside the window [of the
train compartment] changed, and she couldn't stand or
walk anymore. Gradually the faces went away...And gradually, [she] got better...We were underway for 7 days.

CHAPTER 64

The Beater
Becomes the Beaten

O N AN EARLY KRAKOW MORNING in 2006, weak sunlight is filtering through the clouds on a humid, close day as the author and her translator follow another research lead. The traffic slows, and off to the left, in a park, an unkempt woman suddenly begins beating the dog at her side. The dog yelps, whimpers, and cowers as the blows shower down. The traffic begins moving again and soon we are a block away. We are shaken, horrified by the dog's pain, our inability to help, and the woman's callous disregard for its suffering.

Then the parallel of all we have been learning strikes us. Maria beat human innocents with equal disregard. They cried, they cowered, they were equally powerless to escape. We think about Zofia Cykowiak, the orchestra survivor, who described her great shame at having been beaten like an animal.

"And once I was mauled. Even today it's hard for me to say I was beaten, I say rather that I was mauled or petted." Zofia later confides that this "petting" by the Gestapo broke her back in five places. The shame remains fresh, sixty years later and for the rest of her life.

A few days after her suicide attempt Maria too experienced that moment. Some American soldiers entered the railroad car where the women were riding and asked who among them had been in Auschwitz. When Mandl was identified, they singled her out for special punishment. Maria described the incident:

The American officer entered a stop in Czechoslovakia together with a civilian woman and another man into the
compartment where we four women were sitting: Langefeld, Bode, Burda and I. He asked who among us had been
in Auschwitz. I said yes, [but] Langefeld and Bode said
Ravensbrück and denied being in Auschwitz. Then they
hit us, especially on the head, pulled our hair, until blood
came out of nose and mouth.

Maria later noted that as a result of the incident, she developed
problems with her vision and that "I was beaten so hard on my head
that my hearing is impaired." The injuries sustained in this beating
would bother Maria for the rest of her life. At long last and however
briefly, in a paradigm shift of karmic reprisal, the beater had become
the beaten.

Perhaps Maria thought back to the first woman she had beaten
with her hands at Lichtenburg. More likely, she was still filled with
the hubris that she was *nothing* like that woman and had done nothing to deserve treatment like this!

In her trial deposition Maria also refers, obliquely, to the effects
of her suicide attempt. "After the beating I got heavy head pain and
took 2 pills which…I had asked for in Regensburg. It did not help,
although it may have been 8–10 pieces. I could find some peace, tem-
porarily lost consciousness and was very sick." This may have been
her way of acknowledging the ingested pills she had been given by
Otto Skorzeny.

CHAPTER 65

Cieszyn

O NCE LIEUTENANT BEDNARCZYK TURNED THE prisoners over to Polish authorities, the train backtracked to the town of Cieszyn, which lay on the Czech/Polish border and where the prisoners were detained. After being held in quarantine for four weeks, they were put to work. Maria, still suffering the effects of her beating and suicide attempt, consulted the prison doctor.

> My eyesight is temporarily very bad, I already reported that to the doctor in Cieszyn, where a nervous condition was determined. I am suffering from this since the transport from Germany to Poland... [He] found a nervous condition which had to heal itself. My terrible headache got better gradually. In Czechoslovakia I could not walk by myself at first, since I could only see a little bit. I did get better in the meantime, but I believed [during] these difficult times it would not heal completely.

Records show that Maria was examined twice while she was in Cieszyn. The doctor's notes describe what he found. "Health Condition: Beaten by Czechs. Bruises on her nose, near her right ear, the left eye, and on the chin and neck, pains in the back and spits blood repeatedly. Sees worse in right eye." Despite these injuries he noted that she was fit for (further) transport.

Maria does little self-reflection during this period. Instead, she bemoans the lack of contact with her family and concerns about her father. "There are also worries about my father who is 64 and my family from whom I have had only 3 letters from my father and sister in August 1946 before traveling to Poland."

Margit remembers that "in Cieszyn, in the vicinity of Möhr-Ostrau, we were unloaded and put into jail. For four weeks it was terrible and then we were allowed to work. Maria worked in the laundry and I worked in the tailor's shop. I was again with Maria in a cell and we were happy when we could be together in the evenings."

After spending almost two and a half months in Cieszyn, the prisoners were transferred to Krakow. This journey, although shorter than the transport from Germany, was both cold and uncomfortable, and filled with apprehension.

Margit confirmed that "at the end of November we were transported again in an open truck and brought to a jail in Krakow. We were all very afraid but established later that it actually was not as bad as we had imagined. We couldn't say that things were going well for us, but we could stand it."

CHAPTER 66

Montelupich

*I have felt the same with my own imprisonment which has
lasted two years. I have now lived through everything the prisoners complained about during my years of service.*

— MARIA MANDL

AFTER ARRIVING IN KRAKOW, MARIA was held in Montelupich
Prison, where she would remain for the rest of her life. There
she awaited the trial that would determine her fate. SS *Untersturm-
führer* Hans Münch, imprisoned at Montelupich the same time as
Maria, remembered that the rough times at Auschwitz—"strange as
it may sound"—were easier to bear than the times immediately after
war's end. "When I finally ended up in a Polish prison, things got
really bad—to be confined in a very small space, in a narrow cell
with many Auschwitz guards and leaders," all of them loudly pro-
claiming and discussing their innocence. "We suffered some severe
emotional stresses."

As German prisoners, both Mandl and Münch received better
than average treatment, although both were also subject to various
indignities by fellow inmates who were survivors of Auschwitz and
the camps.

Montelupich, present day. The large prison dominates its neighborhood. Surrounding streets are very busy, congested. We are

admitted to the prison ahead of a long line of civilians waiting for visiting hours—our official visit request categorized as high security. Escorted to the director's office, we discover a tall, high-walled corner room, filmed for the movie *Schindler's List.* The guard confides that everyone finds the décor ugly but it must be retained "because it's famous."

The director is in his late forties, tall and good-looking. Keen brown eyes appraise us. He wears an open-necked shirt and talks with his hands; his manner is gracious, accommodating, charming, urbane.

We sit around a table, drinking tea. A PR man also sits in, offering information. He is younger, chatty, and very observant. We evidently make a good impression because all doors open for us. The translator urges the author to "drink in the experience." She does.

The director has a sense of humor. "I must call ahead to make sure they don't shoot me!" He, in contrast to everyone else we see, does not carry a gun. We are given a tour with few restrictions. We are allowed to take photos.

The corridors are long and dark, with black-and-maroon floor tiles dating from Maria's time. We pass through heavy security. The cell block has no interior windows; there are visible pipes on the top of the corridors, some thick, some thin, with intermittent dim lights and peeling paint near the ceiling.

The smell overwhelms, a combination of musty bodies, confined spaces, nervous perspiration, despair.

Our guide shows us a cell currently occupied by two men. It seems impossibly small—the same size as in Mandl's day. These prisoners are kept here twenty-three hours a day. The translator apologizes to them for our intrusion and the author is ashamed she has been oblivious to their discomfort—distracted by the drinking in of this experience.

There is a fairly large courtyard not currently used by prisoners, who are now consigned to a rooftop exercise area. Some executions were done in the courtyard in Mandl's time; others were done in an execution room no larger than a typical cell. Although we walk by those areas, we are not invited to enter.

Some things are the same now, some different. The fact remains that this building saw the last years and end of Maria Mandl's life.

CHAPTER 67

Arrival in Prison

U PON ARRIVAL IN MONTELUPICH the war criminals were finger-
printed and photographed in a series of formal mug shots.
These photographs were intended for use as identification, to be
shown to former prisoners during the gathering of evidence for the
preliminary hearings and subsequent trial.

A major aim was to help potential witnesses recognize the camp
staff as they looked *during* the war rather than from their current appearance, which was disheveled and in civilian clothing. Former SS
men were supposed to be photographed in uniform, but most of
those had been discarded or hidden. Finally, someone found an SS
man's cap, which many of the men wore, regardless of rank.

Each prisoner was photographed in three positions: full face forward, a profile with the head turned right, and a profile with the
head turned left. The photographs were then displayed in all the
larger communities in Poland.

Mandl's mug shot reveals a steely gaze, a strong-looking woman
who is beginning to wear around the edges. There are no visible
signs of the facial beating she received three months prior in Czechoslovakia, but there are bags under her eyes. Her hair is pulled back
and up in a traditional style. It is wavy with a fine texture, tendrils
escaping above her ears. Her jaw is set and she has beautifully
shaped lips and nose and a strong but not pronounced chin. The eyebrows are close to her eyes. Her name on the plaque is spelled

incorrectly (Mandel). She is wearing a white shirt, buttoned all the way up, tightly fitting. Her neck is strong. She looks not thick, but muscular. Maria is staring down the camera—in a direct gaze as if challenging the photographer.

In the profile shot her chin and brow are more pronounced. The cheekbone looks high, her nose has a slight bump near the top. Maria's eyebrows are thick, and at this angle, her earlobes look disproportionately large. The white blouse has large buttons spaced far apart, and short sleeves—about four inches above the elbow. It is somewhat wrinkled. She also wears a somber skirt with a square pattern on it. Her hair looks darker than in earlier photos; it has been a while since she could use peroxide.

Today the originals of these prison intake records are stored in the city archive of Krakow. Located behind a rusty fence in a small parking lot on a city street, the weather-beaten and stuffy building is filled with men of various ages. An older man in the reading room clings stubbornly to his papers, sharing bits of unsolicited advice and information. The archive itself is guarded by a Cerberus of an attendant, both loquacious and opinionated.

The original documents are crumbling and yellowed and feel slightly oily. The author gently places her hand over Maria's original fingerprints, still vivid all these years later. The translator observes of Maria's name, "That was not a happy signature!" The signature was done with a special kind of pen in which the ink comes out purple and doesn't wash out—rather like a thin laundry marker.

The intake document notes that Maria, aged 34, was 5 feet 4.5 inches tall, had dark blond hair, blue eyes, dark blond eyebrows, healthy teeth, and average features. She weighed 132 pounds, walked normally, and had normal speech. The thumbprint was of her right hand.

Flaking away around the edges, the old documents appear bent on self-destruction. It seems impossible they will survive another sixty years.

CHAPTER 68

Harsh, but Better

The crowding was indescribable. Everybody had a blanket; the nutrition was barely sufficient, but nobody starved.

—HANS MÜNCH

IN DECEMBER OF 2004 THE prison director at Montelupich oversaw a meeting of former political prisoners. Twenty-four men, mostly octogenarians, came to talk—often at the same time—and described in great detail conditions at Montelupich during the period of Maria's incarceration. Many noted that although prisoners found the conditions harsh, they were much better than in other Polish prisons of the period.

Everyone remembered that heating was minimal, with one brick stove for every two cells from a hearth in the hallway. The stoves were made of tin and "were scratched all over. Everyone who was imprisoned wrote something, with whatever they had to scratch or carve with." The winter of 1946–1947 was very severe, so the cells were cold too. With no glass in the windows the temperature was often the same inside as outside.

Breakfast typically consisted of black coffee with three hundred grams (ten ounces) of bread. At midday soup was served, variously consisting of "black UNRRA [mashed corn from transports of Rumanian corn rejects], pea soup. Rutabaga, cabbage, groats [barley or millet] in 2 colors: blue or green [from disinfectants], and at times, smelly cod." In the evening prisoners would get a portion of " *Wasser zupka*," water soup made of rutabaga.

One of the Polish political prisoners, Hanna Wysocka, remembered that "in 1947 this soup caused mass food poisoning among the prisoners and disappeared from the menus. Then, at the order of Dr. Dormicki, high quality sauerkraut and fresh carrots were served in great quantities. Unfortunately, these delicacies only lasted twelve or so days."

Zofia Moskała also remembered the decidedly terrible condition of the food the prisoners were given to eat: "The soup had worms, but we closed our eyes and drank it, we wanted to cry but we were hungry. The bread was small and black and sprinkled with oat bran—sometimes with tiny wood shavings—impossible to eat. We would pick it from each other's lips, it was horrible."

Former prisoners described the daily routine: 6:00 A.M.—reveille and collection of "cubes." (The inmates left their clothes outside cells, folded in cubes.) Breakfast. Between breakfast and lunch—do nothing. 1:00–2:00 P.M., lunch. Between lunch and dinner—do nothing. 4:00–5:00 P.M., dinner. 6:00 P.M.—roll call. After assembly, leave cubes outside cells.

Every day the guards checked the cells by hitting the bars with some object to hear the sounds. The director remarks they still do that today. The guards were not armed. German prisoners were allowed to receive packages and sleep on straw mattresses; Poles were not and slept on bare boards. There were no toilets in the cells, and prisoners were permitted to bathe only once a week.

Orders had been given that Nazi detainees receive better treatment. "All war criminals, when receiving food, should have an added portion of raw cabbage. Their walks in the fresh air should be lengthened in time and that [we must] make the utmost effort to make sure their looks and health are good for the trial." Jadzia, a former guard at the prison, stated that "we were not allowed to raise our hands on them in any way."

Margit notes that in the first weeks after arrival in Montelupich they were assigned five people to a cell and that the other three women with her and Maria were former overseers from Auschwitz. "I had the feeling," she says, "the [prison] was stretched to capacity."

CHAPTER 69

The Escape

MARIA'S PREDECESSOR IN BOTH RAVENSBRÜCK and Birkenau, Johanna Langefeld, had been extradited to Poland in the same transport. Margit remembers Langefeld: "She wore white stockings with high shoes. She was something else for the Nazis and for Germankind."

Upon arrival at Montelupich, both Langefeld and Mandl were assigned to outdoor work details in and around the prison. Christmas Eve, 1946, Johanna and Maria were given the task of cleaning the private apartment of the director. Margit remembers this vividly.

One day before the holy night of 1946 [Christmas Eve], Maria was allowed to work outside of the jail—in the private apartment of the director. Maria went together with Oberaufseherin Langefeld from Auschwitz to work. Both of them washed windows, it was already dark, and suddenly Langefeld ran away [escaped] and wasn't caught. She had unusual luck—was unusually lucky.

We couldn't find her! We had to look all over the train station [deserted because it was a day before Christmas Eve], and I froze. It was freezing. After this the Germans were not allowed to work and we had to sit the entire winter in our cells.

Langefeld ran through the cold and snowy streets of Krakow and found shelter at a cloister, which put her in touch with a Polish Catholic organization. She subsequently went into hiding, resurfacing in Germany in 1957 and dying in 1975 without further prosecution.

In addition to the furor caused by Langefeld's escape, some inmates were upset that Mandl had been assigned to a regular work detail. One of the former Auschwitz prisoners complained to the officials of the enormity of Maria's crimes. That, along with Langefeld's escape, condemned her to an extended period of cell isolation. On April 16, 1947, former Auschwitz Kommandant Rudolf Höss was hanged at Auschwitz, and at the end of April the interrogations of Maria began. She remained in solitary confinement.

Margit had been placed in an adjoining cell with some other women. "Every evening when the air was pure we spoke with each other through the stove opening. I felt sorry for Maria and always consoled her."

After several months of solitary confinement prison officials noticed that Mandl was struggling. The director of the jail, concerned because he was charged with keeping the Nazi prisoners in good shape until the trial, asked Maria which of her cellmates she would like to have join her in the cell. She chose Margit. Margit still remembers this with gladness and a touch of pride, "She asked for *me!*"

Having a companion helped Maria recover from her depression, and for Margit, who was delighted to be reunited with her friend, there were other benefits.

> I had come in with very bad acne from puberty. At 25 years old I had thought that the worst was over [but] nothing was over—quite the contrary. In the face it was not quite so bad, but my back and shoulders were still quite bad. I showed Maria and she was shocked at how bad it looked...I always needed [to get] a piece of silk linen from the laundry and everyday Maria rubbed my back with my urine and it got better. I was very grateful to her and I won't forget that. Even when we didn't have anything, Maria always knew how to help.

CHAPTER 70

Time Passed Slowly

EVENTUALLY BOTH MARIA AND MARGIT were relocated to a four-person cell where, due to the overcrowding in the prison, they had to sleep two to a bed. The bottom bunk was used by Margit and Erna Boden, and the top shared by Maria and Therese Brandl. Margit can "still see Maria sitting on that bed with her hair styled on her head." There was a crucifix in the cell, and "we had a tin window that was only open a crack at the top. But there was only the wall, and the tin was so lopsided that we could only see from that little bit [of light] whether it was day or night."

A neighboring prisoner remembers that the bunks were wooden, with many bedbugs living behind them—so many they fell from the ceiling. The women had long johns and tied the legs at the bottom, to keep the bedbugs from creeping up. "They would bring stinking rags [with disinfectants] to put in the corners. The smell gave us awful headaches, splitting heads. When the nice guard was on, we were allowed to bring knitting needles from the sewing room and pick the roaches from the gaps in the walls and floors and kill them one by one."

As for the food, Margit remembers the cabbage. "We only had cabbage soup. The whole time, only cabbage soup," and occasionally bread and black coffee. "On Christmas Eve, there was a spoonful of sauerkraut and half of a salted herring."

"In the beginning we were not allowed to keep any of our things in the cell and we wore clothes that we already had. Later when the trial was spoken of, we got new institutional clothing; a uniform skirt and jacket (green) and with it, a white blouse." Margit also remembers that although they had to "wear our underwear for weeks," they were permitted to wash every day. Margit had no shoes and had to wrap her feet in rags. "If you had them from home, you could wear them. If not, you were out of luck."

Toilets were rudimentary, essentially buckets kept in the cells. A few had lids but most did not, and Margit would steal old and torn shirts from the laundry room and use them to cover the bucket "so the smell wasn't quite as bad."

Zofia Moskała remembered that after a bath they had to use towels of very poor quality. "When you wiped yourself with it, you could wring it out and the water would flow. [Then] the guard would put some kind of powder in our hair."

As time went on, the cells and prisoners were shifted around, and some women, including Margit, although not yet Maria, got work assignments. Margit was placed in the prison laundry, where she was responsible for washing the clothes of the male guards. "We did not have fleas, but the guards who watched us did! When we did their laundry, the fleas were very large and floated on top of the water!"

When there was an execution, a car would arrive with a blue cross on it. "And the driver always stood on the step. Because they would take the corpses. A blue cross—I remember for sure." Another prisoner remembered that "during the walks, under the wall of a bakery, one could often see traces of blood. That's where the executions took place."

Time in prison passed slowly and was governed by the sounds of administration (meals, hitting of the bars, emptying of the toilet, the sounds of other women evacuating in the cell) and any noise that bled through the walls from outside the prison. One woman was woken up every morning by "a far-away squeaking sound of an electric car turning onto the turn of the last stop of *trojki* (three) at Kamienna Street."

Any incident that provided variety to the day was welcomed, dissected, and remembered. Danuta Wojnar-Górecka wrote about a sunny day in April when the sounds of birdsong and passing planes were in the air.

> For a few weeks somebody was training a dog right beneath the windows. "Crawl, crawl"—the same command was given time after time. The women felt sorry for the poor animal. Finally, one woman could not control herself and yelled out loud through the bars:
>
> "Crawl yourself, you idiot, and give the dog some peace!"
>
> Quite a laugh broke in all cells within her voice's reach, but the training went along. However, none of these incidents were so intriguing to prisoners as the presence of these Germans beneath their windows. Where were they from? What were they arrested for? For how long?

CHAPTER 71

Cellmates

CHALLENGING CONDITIONS IN ANY PRISON are exacerbated by one's cellmates and long hours spent in confinement. Even for the German prisoners with marginally better conditions, life was difficult. Danuta Wojnar-Górecka remembered that "there were no talks about loneliness at that time and the lack of space was causing other issues as well. One could not walk or exercise, and there was not a spot for a person to isolate just for a moment from the rest. And there was absolutely nothing to do. Studies and other "cultural exchanges" had ended, books and magazines were prohibited.

> On top of all this, the lack of information about the future fostered an atmosphere of uncertainty and was worsening at the same time already difficult existential conditions of four people on an area of barely six square meters [twenty square feet]. Constant presence of the same people during every hour of day and night was gradually becoming more and more difficult to handle. The best friends would begin playing on each other's nerves. To every complaint and grumble Kunda [one of the guards] would respond non-changeably in the same way: "Now, you will not forget you are in prison."

Many of Maria's former colleagues at Auschwitz had also ended up in Montelupich. One, Therese Brandl, was—to Maria's annoyance—constantly paired with her in Montelupich.

In her mug shot, Brandl is in an open and wrinkled light shirt, dark hair in the same style as Maria. She is a somewhat mousy woman, with small features set together closely in the middle of her face, a ski jump nose, and a timid mien. Therese does not look at the camera in a confrontational way, rather she looks sad and perplexed. There are wrinkles in her forehead.

Margit remembers quite definitely that Mandl and Brandl did NOT like each other! Brandl had always been noted for her shrill, high, and annoying voice, and Margit describes Brandl as "Strange. Quite strange. She was crazy!"

Margit describes one incident in their cell when Brandl "took her shoes off and prayed and worshipped them. They were high shoes with laces. She kind of got crazy and then they took her away from the communal cell (for a while). That was Brandl. She prayed to the shoes!"

For Maria, forced not only to live with Brandl in the cell but to sleep with her in a single bunk at night, these eccentricities were a huge annoyance.

CHAPTER 72

"*Pani* Jadzia"

*Whatever else they say Mandl did in Auschwitz she was a
classy woman! She liked me! She told me I deserved to wear a
uniform!*

—"Pani Jadzia," guard, Montelupich Prison 1947–48

H ANNA WYSOCKA, EIGHTY-SEVEN YEARS OLD in 2006, is a tiny,
wiry woman with a keen intellect and great mental strength.
She is *very* aware, extremely articulate, sharp as a tack. In 1939 when
Poland was invaded by Germany, Hanna had been a student at Jagiellonian University. During the Occupation she studied in the
underground cultural department, and in 1941 she joined the Home
Army as liaison officer of the military unit in Krakow. After 1945 she
transferred from her group to WiN, an underground Polish anti-
Communist organization which was persecuted by both the Soviets
and the Polish Communists. Hanna participated in an opposition
election campaign. For this she was arrested on December 15, 1946,
and sentenced to eight years in Montelupich. Upon her release and
in poor health, Hanna struggled to find employment, eventually
working in an industry for the disabled.

After embarking on what would become a series of interviews
with Hanna Wysocka, we are immediately captivated by her

strength, her kind nature, her self-effacing personality, and her vivid recall.

The courage she showed as a young woman is still evident. One day, while shopping in Krakow, Hannah encountered one of the former Montelupich guards, Jadzia. A voice accosted her saying loudly and stridently, "My lady is here!" Three times. Hanna and Jadzia spoke briefly on the street. Over the next few months Hanna would occasionally encounter Jadzia, and Jadzia would always greet Hannah the same way. "My lady!" Three times.

As we came to know her, Hanna agreed that if she saw Jadzia again, she would request an interview for us.

Hanna did not stop there. Despite a spell of harsh winter weather, she went to the neighborhood where she had seen "*Pani* Jadzia" and began walking from house to house, looking at all the mailboxes until she found the right one. Hanna, more than anyone, convinced Jadzia to speak.

This, in itself, was a miracle. In early 2005 a document called the Wildstein List had just been published on the internet. Wildstein, a reporter, had compiled a dossier listing the names of tens of thousands of secret police collaborators, workers, and agents of the former Stalinist and Communist era. Its publication created an unprecedented upheaval in Poland as people sought to clear or hide their names and background. Thousands of lawsuits were filed and the country was boiling with apprehension and distress. *Pani* Jadzia, who had been a worker in an institution of that oppressive system, must have been running scared herself.

The interview with the former guard was set up with great secrecy. She agreed to meet only if her identity could remain unknown and she could use the fictional name "*Pani* Jadzia" (Mrs. Jadzia). Hanna Wysocka graciously offered her apartment as a neutral meeting place.

From the first moment, the quiet dignity of *Pani* Wysocka contrasted with the coarse vulgarity of *Pani* Jadzia.

Jadzia was an odd woman, large-boned with dark features and a loud and nasal voice. She was very impressed with her own importance: "*I* have a crest! *I'm* from nobility!" Periodically, Jadzia would cackle for no obvious reason except perhaps nervousness. There was an impatient quality to her responses.

Hanna had arranged some delicate tea cookies on a serving tray, and Jadzia dumped multiple cookies onto her plate and slurped tea loudly throughout the interview. She tried to blackmail our translator almost immediately: "Get my daughter a job!" Had Rachwałowa (a fellow prisoner) been alive, "*she* would have found a job for my daughter for sure!"

When Hanna asked Jadzia about her children, she responded that she and her husband had not told them about their time at Montelupich. Jadzia did stress their children were "being brought up religiously."

Jadzia was twenty years old when she worked as a guard at Montelupich and had vivid memories of Maria Mandl. From the outset, Jadzia stated loudly and often, "Whatever else they say Mandl did in Auschwitz, she was a *classy* woman! She liked me. She told me I *deserved* to wear a uniform!"

Jadzia remembered Maria as "very, very handsome. VERY pretty! Very nice. Very kind. [She was] always smiling and kinds towards me. She was not depressed. Just normal. Smiling." Jadzia never heard Maria use any profanity and described her as "extra cultured!" "She was very quiet, sitting there like a church mouse. Not a dumb person. She was a CHIEF . . . She liked me SO much! I was always smiling at her and she at me."

Pani Jadzia's future husband, a high-ranking guard, would speak German with Mandl in her cell. Jadzia stressed that "we were not allowed to raise our hands on them in any way," although she did remember other political prisoners in Montelupich saying, "Let us in and we will kill the whore, the bitch!" Jadzia stressed that Maria was never attacked in prison—"we were too AFRAID to let anyone into her cell."

Jadzia claimed that, eventually, she lost her job because she was "too good" (too nice) to the prisoners.

With that statement, Jadzia made her exit. Left in her wake, we were preoccupied with thoughts of an earlier time and place where women like Jadzia held the power. It had taken great courage for Hanna to have this former jailer in her home, and her great sense of dignity remained intact. The translator, Lidia, hugged her gently and we left.

CHAPTER 73

Always Full of Ideas

Maria was always full of ideas and always found something for us to do or talk about, so that we would not end up walking in circles and going crazy.

—MARGIT BURDA

ALL OF THE PRISONERS AT Montelupich sought ways to make their incarceration tolerable. The authorities granted certain privileges to inmates, including a daily ten-minute walk in the courtyard, but it was never enough to offset the stress and boredom.

Maria, who after Langefeld's escape was not permitted to go on a work detail, chafed at the confinement and monotony of her days. Once, looking around the cell, she said to Margit, "You know what? We're going to make the cell clean now! I can't stand this, just standing and sitting!"

Margit later mused that "they were wooden floors and could be cleaned with spoons. So with our spoons we cleaned the floor. With water. It was 'blood white.' The floor was really white. And then that cell was shown to everybody because it was so clean! Everything at that time was said three times. So they said '*Sauber, sauber, sauber!*' ('Clean, clean, clean!')"

With Margit, Maria spoke about the things that gave her life meaning—including music. Maria often expressed a fondness for

Mozart, church music, folk music, and once, she mentioned the women's orchestra she'd founded in Birkenau.

They often "pretend cooked" in their cell; "Maria liked to cook!" Planning imaginary meals, Margit and Maria would always piece together a Sunday menu. "In our minds and in our fantasies. Then we ate our cabbage soup. Whenever we cooked together in spirit on Sundays, we were a family. There were differences between poor and rich, nevertheless, we cooked."

Margit remembers that Maria liked to "eat" Wiener schnitzel with potatoes and cucumber salad and that her favorite food was Kaiserschmarrn, a sweet dish of chopped pancakes. Sixty years later Kaiserschmarrn is ordered from a *Gasthof* in Austria. It comes sprinkled with powdered sugar and fruit preserves and is VERY rich, very fattening, and *very* good!

In 2005 we are privileged to leaf through the *Kochbuch für Anny Mandl* (*Cookbook for Anny Mandl*), handed down through several generations. It is easy to envision the Mandl family enjoying these foods, which use basic ingredients readily available from the farm or from what they could grow. One marvels at the ingenuity of cookery before the age of artificially created chemicals. For example, if a woman wanted to make a green icing glaze, she would simply color the sugar mixture with spinach juice. For red glaze she would use beets. The Mandl family Schnitzel recipe still sounds inviting, advising the cook to dredge thick pork cutlets in salt, egg, and breadcrumbs and bake until "beautifully yellow."

In addition to their imaginary meals, Maria also spoke to Margit of her desire to have children. Together, they often said wistfully that "if we were free now, we would probably have children and a husband and a job." Margit noted sadly that "in normal times she would have been a good wife and mother."

"Worst sound for us was the rustling of the keys when the overseers passed by the cells. When the cell was locked up for the night. That didn't mean anything good."

CHAPTER 74

Personal Encounters

We were so happy to have something to keep us busy and occupied!
—Margit Burda, letter to Franz Mandl, 1948

EVENTUALLY, AS THE MONTHS WORE on, the authorities relaxed and Maria was again given work assignments. She sewed for a while in the tailor shop and then rotated through various cleaning details. Although the work was dirty and menial, it provided a relief of sorts and helped pass the time.

Often as she was engaged in some task, Maria was accosted by other prisoners who had been in the camps. Hanna Wysocka remembers that former Auschwitz prisoner Stanisława Rachwałowa "was shouting, terribly shouting, when she encountered Mandl in the halls. She got it off her chest really well!"

Danuta Wojnar-Górecka, who shared a cell with Rachwałowa, remembers one incident in particular. Rachwałowa came into the cell and said she had seen Mandl cleaning the floor on the second level. "A pail of water in front of her, a wet rag in her hands, knee deep in dirty water. Such a beautiful picture and such a rapture for me! The chief of the women's camp in Auschwitz! I told her at least in no uncertain terms what I'd thought of her all along. 'Oh you SS whore! How nice it is to see you here on your knees, sopping up the dirt and filth from the floor. It's better than you deserve, you haughty Auschwitz Duchess!'"

A few days later Danuta was summoned for an "assignment." Kunda, the head guard, had chosen her because she spoke German. "Follow me then. I have an assignment for you. The German women need scissors to cut their nails. I'm not supposed to leave them alone with any dangerous objects. So you're to stay and watch them." Danuta remembers being terrified and that her very nature revolted against the idea of meeting these women. Kunda the guard chided her, laughing, "Don't be afraid you fool! They won't do you any harm. Aren't you at all curious to see these women? If you see anything suspicious just knock on the door."

Danuta, writing after the war about the encounter as an exercise in learning English, related what happened next. Four women were sitting in the cell, Mandl on a folded straw bag. Maria looked taut, toughened, still pretty, with blond and wavy hair. Brandl looked young and gentle, with big dark and doleful eyes, while Alice Orlowski had the "face of an evil troll."

Danuta introduced herself and stated that she had scissors for them. "Good morning. Our pleasure. It's so nice that you speak German." Mandl's voice was expressionless but polite. "Were you ... (she hesitated) a Reichsdeutsche or a Volksdeutsche?" Danuta responded, "Neither. I'm a political prisoner who happens to know German."

An awkward silence followed, broken finally by Danuta, who addressed Mandl to break the silence, "Where are you from?" "*Ich bin aus Wien*" [I am from Vienna] responded Mandl, disregarding Münzkirchen. Danuta was disappointed. This was not like her picture of Vienna—Strauss, waltzes, charm, elegance. Was Mandl really Austrian? How had she become involved in the SS? But she asked none of these questions. Instead she replied: "I too am from WiN!" (The anti-Communist organization, pronounced the same way as the German *Wien*.)

Mandl looked questioningly at her and then burst into a belly laugh, out loud, the other women laughing along.

Danuta could not resist telling Mandl, "You know, you're just as I pictured you." Maria responded, "You've heard and read a lot about me, I imagine."

An awkward conversation followed, set against the backdrop of clicking scissors. Orlowski disparaged the Jews, Mandl defended Brandl, who sat there meekly, and then criticized the meanness of the Americans during the extradition to Poland.

Mandl mentioned that she'd met a woman in Montelupich she knew in Auschwitz. Danuta asked "Rachwałowa?" "Yes, that's her name. Every time she passes our cell she looks through the peephole and says something offensive to me. Tell me, why is she so obnoxious?? Aren't we both in the same situation now??"

Danuta pushed her, "Have you ever tried to put yourself in her shoes?? She was in Auschwitz for four years!" "So what?" snarled Mandl. "We were all in Auschwitz! And we had to obey orders as well. I never did anything wrong!"

Danuta brought up Hans Münch, a doctor at Auschwitz, and cited his efforts to save prisoners and follow his conscience. She asked Maria if she knew him.

"Oh yes, I know him," interrupted Mandl. "Who doesn't?" Her face got tougher. "That traitor! He was always like that. You couldn't possibly respect someone like him? Disloyal, unfair, untrustworthy— could you?" Danuta closed the conversation, gathered the scissors, and stated before leaving, "We see the matter differently and [I] respect and admire the man. Throughout his service in Auschwitz he jeopardized his own life by choosing to remain human."

CHAPTER 75

The Dirties

She [Mandl] was always making a fuss, constantly had some claims or resentment.

—HANNA WYSOCKA

OTHER PRISONERS, INCLUDING HANNA WYSOCKA, remember that one of Maria's work assignments was to clean the cells of random inmates. For a period of time after Hanna had been moved to the third floor, Mandl and Brandl were brought weekly to clean her cell. Hanna noted that Mandl wore basic prison clothes, a skirt and a blouse, and when she was finished would say, "*Już?*," which means done, or finished.

Mandl was once summoned to clean Hanna's cell of "the Dirties"—vomit, after she got sick. At the time Wysocka was sharing a cell with an elderly Polish lady who got a package containing a typical Polish sausage called metka, a kind of raw meat, slightly smoked. When Mandl came again, *Pani* Wysocka thanked her for cleaning the cell—gave her that sausage.

"Mandl left with the sausage and then came back, FURIOUS! If not for the guards she would have unleashed on me, because in that sausage there were worms!" Hanna later said "that only shows how little was necessary for her to unleash on people. She thought it was a trick, a revenge that I was playing on her."

Despite the fact that Mandl got preferential treatment as a German war criminal and, in theory, was permitted outside reading materials, a prison inventory of her possessions from May of 1947 lists only four letters to Mandl from her family; a notebook of twenty-two pages, handwritten in chemical pencil in German; several pieces of paper covered with shorthand and script; a calendar from 1944 with notes in shorthand on individual pages; and a certificate related to work.

Although after Maria's death a clerk recorded a copy of Goethe's *Faust* in her possessions, Margit is adamant they had no other reading material in their cell.

One of the few sanctioned "outside" activities in Montelupich were visits to and from the prison doctor Eryk Dormicki, Catholic and politically smart, a man who "played the game." Hans Münch rather admiringly described Dormicki: "That pseudo physician who had been in the camp for years and years was a real slick customer; he knew all the tricks, and even I could learn a few from him."

Hanna Wysocka remembers Dormicki as very kind and respectful, "but when they were sending the medications, somehow the medications would disappear. He would walk in, he would check on us, he would leave."

Maria consulted Dr. Dormicki several times during her stay at Montelupich. Shortly after her admission she visited the doctor with a complaint of rheumatism. In May and June of 1947 she visited the doctor with complaints related to her eyesight; "Can't see, can't read, from the time of her visits with the prosecutor," and "until now could sew perfectly." She was given aspirin for headaches. In May of 1947 she was also given a typhoid inoculation.

CHAPTER 76

"Virgin mother of my God, let me be fully your own"

I dragged on my ruined life in darkness and grief, wrathful in my heart.

—VIRGIL, THE AENEID

As THE WAR CRIMES TRIAL of Mandl and her colleagues approached, interest from the press increased. Various journalists were permitted access to Montelupich. Their coverage was sensationalistic and often smug, and reveled in the fact that Maria's beauty had diminished. "Now when I stand in front of her in the door of a prison cell in Monte, it seems to me that this robust female figure is wreathed in this smoke that chokes with odor of burnt bones. 'Mandelka' is gray."

Zofia Moskała, the prisoner across the hall, also noticed that Maria often seemed depressed. Elfriede Koch, her cellmate, remarked about how much both Mandl and Brandl changed during their time in prison.

Margit remembers that as the trial drew ever closer, although they did talk, "mostly Maria prayed. She prayed a lot." She did not pray on her knees, she prayed in bed. "I can still remember one prayer quite well. We always prayed it together, 'Virgin mother of my God, let me be fully your own.'"

Maria talked about her family to Margit, especially her father, and said "she was so sorry; that he was so good and she wished she would have acted differently somehow. It was more about how much she had hurt her father. She was so sorry her father was suffering. We did not speak about her mother, Maria stated only, 'Oh my mother has been dead for a long time.'"

Maria did not speak about her fiancé. Margit believes that she had already tuned out her private life. "She knew that she would not get out of this place alive." Maria avoided talking with Margit about how she got into the camp system.

> She couldn't talk about it at all. First because it was em-
> barrassing, and second because it ruined her—really her
> whole life. She told me very little. It was my impression
> that she was occupying herself with her past.
>
> She cried a lot. Not really in the open, but still...Maria
> (seemed a little surprised?) that she had achieved such a
> high position.
>
> Well, I really can't imagine what they accused her
> of—what (they say) she had done. Maybe it was the im-
> prisonment or, I don't know what, but she couldn't have
> been—she wasn't a bad person—not at all.
>
> She was not a bad person.

Part Six

CHAPTER 77

The Tribunal

Gradually the interrogations began and Maria had to go to the Tribunal often. She was, however, in no way sad about that. The opposite. She wanted to know, finally, what she was dealing with.
—MARGIT BURDA

ON JANUARY 22, 1946, THE *Najwyzszy Tribunal Narodowy* (Supreme National Court) was created to administer trials of special significance in Poland, including the prosecution of Nazi crimes committed on Polish soil.

The first prominent Nazi to be tried under this court was Rudolf Höss, *Kommandant* of Auschwitz, who was hanged for his crimes on April 16, 1947. Most observers expected a new trial of other Auschwitz perpetrators to follow shortly thereafter. However, it quickly became apparent that a rapid second trial would not be possible.

There were practical reasons for this, remarked former prosecutor Jan Brandys. "It took a while to gather all the materials for the staff trial. They also wanted to make Höss the show trial, describe the scope of his crimes and quickly punish him." Stanisław Kobiela, who interviewed Brandys, remembers that the lawyer privately resented Höss's quick execution, believing he would have been a good witness for the second trial.

The extradition of war criminals was also problematic. Along with communication difficulties between the new Communist

regime and countries governing the western zones of occupation, defendants were scattered across Poland and throughout Europe. One
defendant, Maximilian Grabner, was even extradited to Yugoslavia
by mistake. Of the 320 persons cited in the case, which included
Maria Mandl, only 120 were actually *in* Krakow. The prosecutor requested that all of these prisoners be immediately transferred to
Montelupich, but of course, this took time.

The Polish government was very aware of the high-profile nature
of this particular trial and the attention it would engender from the
world press. It was critical the defendants appear to be treated fairly
and humanely. In reality, many of the prisoners were in poor physical and mental condition. Because of this, the chief prosecutor
instituted regulations improving their condition, including increased calories, new clothing, exercise periods, and better medical
care. Maria Mandl benefited from this directly, as it precipitated her
move from solitary confinement after her initial incarceration and
the escape of Johanna Langefeld.

A man named Jan Sehn, instrumental in initiating and documenting the atrocities at Auschwitz, was nominated chief investigative
judge for "cases of exceptional significance," including the upcoming
high-profile trial of the Auschwitz defendants.

Sehn's other responsibilities included pursuing and extraditing
persons accused and suspected of these crimes. Fluent in German
and described as a stern taskmaster and stickler for details, Sehn was
"also quick to help any staffer in need." Sehn's linguistic fluency was
a huge advantage, because he had the ability to process large
numbers of German documents and also to communicate directly
with the defendants.

A photograph from 1946 reveals a lanky man with dark hair and
thick eyebrows. Sehn was a chain-smoker, soft-spoken and mild-man-
nered, who pursued his task with great resolve and brilliant
competence.

Ryszard Kotarba, Sehn's biographer, notes that "the personality
and the competence of Jan Sehn was a key issue here. At the time of
the proceedings [he was] the main person collecting and leading the

preliminary work. So he was the one who collected those volumes of materials." Sehn's knowledge, and competence, affected every facet of the trial. He oversaw all proceedings as they unfolded, and witnessed the final verdicts and sentences. In the end, Sehn—as Andrew Nagorski notes in his book *The Nazi Hunters*—meticulously laid the groundwork for victories in the courtroom.

On Sehn's directive, officials began fanning out across Poland to gather witnesses and solicit survivor testimonies. Mug shots of the Nazi prisoners were enlarged, mounted on posters, and then displayed in the town squares of larger cities. Many survivors came forward, recognizing Mandl and others from these photographs.

Witnesses were interviewed in regional courts. Each person gave a deposition (*Protokol*), which included a date, the name of the court, the witness's personal information, the name of the prosecutor, and the recording clerk.

Damning testimonies about Maria's actions began to flow into Krakow in an unstoppable torrent. Survivors (and at least one *Aufseherin*) described the atrocities that would feature prominently in the upcoming trial. Beatings, brandings, selections, the agony of the roll calls and Maria's lack of mercy and compassion—all were detailed in great depth.

By the time the trial began, Maria's dossier of depositions was more than twice as large as that of any other defendant.

CHAPTER 78

The Lawyers

We viewed this generation with a lot of respect. [They became]
some of the most famous political defense attorneys and helped
a lot of people by their wits and wisdom.

—Władysław Bartoscewski, former minister
of foreign affairs, Poland

Jacek Kanski, a stocky man with short white hair and the demeanor of a gruff bear, was a young law student at the time of the
trial. In later years he became vice dean of the Regional Bar Associ-
ation in Krakow and one of the senior statesmen in the city.
Interviewed in 2004, Jacek remembers many of the lawyers who
were tapped to serve as defense counsel for the Auschwitz staff.

It was a difficult appointment. Although the right to defense
was accepted, even for heinous criminals, most defense lawyers
struggled to function within the volatile climate of public opinion
after the war, the attention of the world press, and from being given
the task of "defending" people whose acts could be considered in-
defensible.

Kanski remembers that "a number of Krakow attorneys took part
in the trial as defense lawyers because it was their DUTY. It was a
show trial. The court would order a particular attorney to take a case
(and he had to take it)." And despite any qualms the appointed law-

yers may have had, Prosecutor Jan Brandys stated that "I have to admit, with all respect, that the defense was on a high standard."

Jolanta Ostrowska-Jazwiecka is the daughter of one of those lawyers, Dr. Kazimierz Ostrowski, who was forty years old in 1947. Like her father, she is now a lawyer. And like Kanski, Jolanta was a young student at the time of the trial. Nonetheless she states firmly that "I do remember my father's dilemma—he was not a defense attorney by his will/choice but was appointed by the court. Anyway, at home there were huge discussions before my father decided to defend in the trial. There was a possibility to file a petition to be released from this duty."

For most attorneys, recusal was not a real option and there was little freedom to refuse this appointment. "One lawyer, Dr. Henryk Wallisch, submitted a letter asking for recusal because his brother had been brutally murdered by SS troops and therefore he could not be objective. He was granted a release but this was not common." Another was a defense attorney named Rappaport, who was elderly and very well known in Krakow. Rappaport "requested the court to be exempted from service because he was Jewish and it would be very difficult for him to be impartial, and to defend people who had persecuted the Jews. His petition was not even considered!"

Ostrawska remembers the atmosphere in her home as tense and filled with tremendous uncertainty. "And when the trial had started, I do remember the talks my father had with my mother, about not knowing quite what to do. On one hand, having this full aversion to those people [the Nazi prisoners] but on the other hand, deciding that everyone had a right to defense." One of Jolanta's friends taunted her, asking "How can your father defend those people?"

"I think the majority of the appointed defense attorneys had a similar dilemma."

CHAPTER 79

Rymar

As a criminal defense attorney he worked in difficult times, so understanding the historical context is crucial for understanding him.

—Stanisław Rymar, Jr., son of Mandl's
defense attorney

THE MAN APPOINTED AS MARIA Mandl's defense attorney was named Stanisław Rymar. Rymar's identity card photograph from 1943 reveals a man with a direct yet cautious gaze, dark hair carefully combed to the side, a meticulously manicured and closely trimmed mustache, a wedge-shaped face with delicate features and prominent forehead, and black-framed glasses. Born in 1914, Rymar was two years younger than Maria and thirty-three years old at the time of the trial. He was known for his fierce intellect and integrity.

When reading Rymar's opening statement from the trial, it soon becomes apparent that defending these prisoners was a political minefield for the lawyers. Hoping to understand the man and the impossible pressures he faced, in 2004 we seek out Rymar's son, who is now an assured lawyer in Warsaw. Stanisław Rymar, Jr., is a fit man, with salt-and-pepper hair, a vibrant personality, and discreet glasses. He is one of the most important lawyers in Poland, having served for several years as president of the Supreme Bar Council and now as judge of the Constitutional Tribunal. The law was definitely the family business, and Rymar mentions that his grandfather, father, and uncle were all lawyers, and now he and his eldest daughter are lawyers as well.

Stanisław speaks of his father as a man with a mission in life who was dedicated to his clients, spending long hours with them when preparing a line of defense. Rymar Jr. suspects that his father, who had a superb command of German and got his doctorate in Germany before the war, would have spoken to Mandl many times. "He always talked a lot with his clients, in depth. He liked to understand a case the best he could. And he could only do it by entering a close relationship with a client."

Rymar Jr. was born in 1941 and, like Jolanta Ostrawska and Jacek Kanski, was a young student at the time of the trial. He remembers that "these were very difficult times, Stalin times. So my parents, for my and the family's safety, didn't talk to anyone about those issues."

We discuss Rymar Sr.'s opening statement from the trial and its literary references. Rymar states proudly that his father was a superb speaker who liked to quote and attended a classics high school where all students had to have a very good command of not only Latin but also Greek.

"Yes, he had an oratory talent, he was a pedigree defense attorney. Very emotional—he did it with conviction. One could learn from him how to be engaged in conducting a case, but he burned himself out easily, and in those days it was not easy to be a defense lawyer."

Despite that, and the tremendous and very public challenges this trial presented, Rymar Jr concludes, "Yes, he was young at the time, but such was his character. His character was already shaped then; he was tough, noncompromising, with a deep unshaken belief in what he was doing. For me, my father was always an example of character, courage and uncompromising character, intelligence, and knowledge."

Dr. Wojciech Dudek worked as a lawyer in Krakow during the postwar period. In 2004 he is a slight man with receding white hair and filmy gray eyes. He knew Stanisław Rymar well, met him often for coffee, and was impressed by his courage. Dudek remembers Rymar as very dignified and tall; a man who carried himself straight, who always wore a fresh shirt and a bow tie and maintained direct eye contact. "In court Rymar acted in a brave manner which brought troubles upon him (disciplinary actions). He never surrendered or yielded to anyone."

Because it was the Communist period in Poland, Dudek de scribes certain limitations on the ways an attorney could speak in court, e*specially* when it involved a military court or cases where the suspects were detained on political grounds. That was the reason for Rymar's disciplinary problems. "Because his appearances were very, very courageous and not 'politically correct.'"

The dangerous legal climate forced every lawyer to parse his language, with the care of a person creeping through a minefield. "It was very easy to use the wrong words—all the time you had to stress the goodness of Socialism. So political correctness was the thing and he could not adjust to it. He defended his clients just as if he would do it today—as if he could do it any way he wanted."

Despite that, Dudek does not believe that Rymar's appointment for the Oświęcim criminals was punitive. He remembers that these defense attorneys were chosen randomly from a list, so it was just coincidence that Rymar was assigned to the trial. Rymar Jr. is not sure if the appointment was punitive or not.

> I don't know. My father was always a man of reaction. At that time our family was on a list of intelligentsia, prepared by the Russian communists, of people who were to be thrown out of Krakow. My grandfather and father were on the list as political activists from before the war. My father had always been considered a political enemy in those days, and he always was there where he thought it was necessary for him to be, where people needed help. My father had a non-mercantile attitude towards people, so first it was to help people then the fees, he somehow didn't pay too much attention to it. And I was brought up

in such atmosphere. We could barely make ends meet. During my studies I worked as an extra at the Słowacki Theater. So first of all it was service to other people, and that's how I was brought up too.

Maria Mandl and Stanisław Rymar soon began their meetings in preparation for the trial.

Deposition

As we got closer to the date of the trial Maria changed. She got
quieter and more contemplative. I would gladly have consoled
Maria. But how?

—MARGIT BURDA

MARIA MANDL'S INITIAL QUESTIONING TOOK place on May 19 and 20, 1947, in Montelupich. The deposition was attended by Mandl, Jan Sehn, prosecutor Helena Torowicz, and recording clerk Krystyna Szymanska. These interrogations took place on the first floor in two rooms—one separated by a grill, located next to the administrative offices.

Szymanska remembers that "the questionings at Montelupich went very smoothly [calmly] No guards were even necessary. They were sitting in one room, we were questioning in another." At this stage of the investigation Mandl was still showing arrogance and cynicism.

Over the next two days Maria was shown different documents that implicated her in various crimes, for example her signature on penal reports and selection lists. She either denied complicity outright or stated that she was only following orders and enforcing decisions that had been made elsewhere. Maria downplayed her use of force and made several complaints about Höss's strictness.

She was most appalled by the testimony of former prisoner Stanisława Rachwałowa. When Maria learned that Rachwałowa had accused her of doing selections for the gas chambers, she started crying, which was noted in the report.

At Sehn's instigation, Maria was urged to write an account of her activities in the KZ system. This document was completed before the trial but after her conversations began with Sehn, between June 13 and July 19, 1947.

Mandl's remarks clearly reveal a desire to manipulate and obfuscate perceptions of her actions, as well as her underlying fear about what may lie ahead.

> I thought and think today that there is justice. I have, especially in Auschwitz, tried to help people. There were not all [good people] and there were many among them who did the opposite of what the orders were. They never thought about the cost that they first did harm to themselves and also to their fellow prisoners.
>
> It is absolutely clear that in such a large camp there had to be order and discipline. I have helped many prisoners, as much as I was able, in every way. I also hope that there are among the many people still some good ones who did know me at some time. I myself could not give orders. I was in all matters dependent on the Kommandant. I also could not know always what was going on in the camp, it was too big for that. I did not kill anybody, and always made an effort to make life easier for the prisoners.
>
> I joined the SS only for the chance to make money, I was never active politically.
>
> I am now in my eighth position, I had to try out everything, take part in the worse times; prison, penitentiary, bunker, camp. Now I have the worst before me, and that is my future fate.

As the trial approached, the prosecution gave the defense attorneys an indictment and list of witnesses for each defendant. When asked why there were so few testimonies *for* the defense, attorney Jacek Kanski replied that "probably the accused didn't request any witnesses—or knew of anyone who would testify for them. If they had had witnesses, they would have been required to file a regular report or *Protokol.*" In the end, Maria had few defenders Rymar could call upon to explain or defend her actions.

In November of 1947 the last indictments were handed down. Proceedings were scheduled to begin on November 24, 1947, and officials stated that henceforth this would be known as the Second Auschwitz Trial.

CHAPTER 81

The Trial

I am standing in my life for the first time and probably the last time before a Polish court. Whatever the decision is, I do not know. I only believe in justice.

—MARIA MANDL

Maria did not appear to be afraid during the trial—she didn't really show it. But I knew her very well, so I tried to help. She tried not to show that she was scared.

—MARGIT BURDA

IN THE TWENTY-FIRST CENTURY THE building where the trial of the Auschwitz staff took place is a well-tended national museum. Located across from the library of famed Jagiellonian University, and utilized for varying functions including high school dances, the pigeon spikes on the roof take one's mind to a darker place and time.

In the 1940s the building was one of the most imposing on the block. In preparation for the trial, the interior of the building was reconstructed as a courtroom. A specially elevated platform was built with sides for the defense and the prosecution. In front of the defendants' benches a long board provided a place to take notes, rest books, and hold pads and pencils. Uniformed guards were stationed at the corners and behind the defendants. The attorneys' tables were located in front on a lower level, below the defendants and judges, and a long rectangular table was placed for the press along one side. Wooden slat chairs for spectators were arranged in rows below.

An imposing docket was built for the judges. Two large circular stem lights on either side illuminated the proceedings. Above the judge's table, placed up high, on a dark panel surrounded by light walls, was a prominent Polish eagle. Large windows extended from floor to ceiling behind the defendants, the glass easily allowing street sounds to be heard. One spectator noted that, although it was quite overcast, it was often difficult to see the defendants because they sat right in front of the windows and were against the light.

Jan Brandys remembered that the large number of perpetrators being tried at one time precipitated a huge amount of interest. The trial was open to the public, and every day a finite number of entry permits were issued, not at all sufficient to meet the demand. As a result, the entire building was wired for radio, and loudspeakers were placed outside to broadcast the proceedings to people gathered

Maria and other accused war criminals in the defendant's dock. COURTESY OF THE ARCHIVAL COLLECTION OF THE STATE MUSEUM AUSCHWITZ-BIRKENAU IN OŚWĘCIM; 21 258/70.

on the steps. Every word was translated into four languages—Russian, French, German, and English—and the trial was observed by many international delegations and correspondents.

The proceedings were scheduled to run until December 20, 1947. Every day the trial sessions were divided in half, beginning at 9:00 A.M. There was a two-hour break at midday, followed by a second session lasting until 7:00 or 8:00 P.M.

Along with Maria, there were forty defendants including Artur Liebehenschel (the second camp commander), Maximilian Grabner (head of the camp's *Gestapo*), Dr. Johann Kremer (the camp's physician), Hans Aumeier, Karl Möckl, Erich Muhsfeldt (head of the crematorium), and female overseers Therese Brandl, Luise Danz, and Alice Orlowski.

Thirty minutes before the beginning of each session the defendants were transported from Montelupich in regular canvas-covered army trucks, lined with hard wooden benches. These were unloaded in the rear of the building.

Jerzy Ludwikowski, then a student, stood in a crowd at the back and watched prisoners exit the trucks. On both sides of the walkway barriers of barbed wire had been constructed, and the accused walked through this tunnel separating them from the public, "who certainly would have torn them to pieces as the mood of the citizens was very hostile." The men wore green Wehrmacht uniforms without rank insignia. The women wore civilian clothes. Some carried papers or notebooks in their hands.

Margit remembered that the female defendants were issued new clothes for the trial, a light gray suit and white blouse. "I remember Maria when she got them. They were cute, they were proud of them at first. They weren't jail clothes."

Newsreel footage was taken of the prisoners unloading. The November weather is messy; slush and snow cover the stairs and walkways and it looks cold and slippery. Guards hustle the prisoners quickly into the building. They are guarded but not handcuffed. Some women are wearing a scarf, some have fur-lined collars. There is a huge step down from the truck that transported them. Alice

Orlowski, whose weight and age prevents her from exiting gracefully, scoots inelegantly on her behind and jumps to the pavement.

Maria Mandl can also be seen exiting the transport truck. She is flanked by armed guards, wears what looks like a wool trench coat, and is holding a thick sheaf of papers under her right arm. Mandl's posture is erect, her hair carefully styled, her expression grim but determined, mouth closed. Her stride is purposeful. The session will begin soon.

CHAPTER 82

In Session

Defendants' faces were blank, all the time. Like they were wait-
ing for a bus.
—BEN FERENCZ, PROSECUTOR, NUREMBERG TRIALS

THE SECOND AUSCHWITZ TRIAL IS heavily documented in film
and still photography. In one picture Jan Sehn, hands clasped
in front of his body and wearing a dark suit, is listening keenly, his
strong, oval face, with heavy brows and chiseled features, intent on
the proceedings.

The docket of accused war criminals sits in three rows of
benches. White plates with carved names of the accused indicate
their required seats. The first row consists of the highest-ranked senior staff, and the back rows contain lower-ranked staff and support
personnel. The first defendant on the end is former camp commandant Artur Liebehenschel. Maria Mandl was next, followed by
Aumeier, Moeckel, and Grabner.

Jan Brandys later remarked that the dock in Krakow consisted of
people from all walks of life and society: professor, waitress, clerk,
tradesmen, etc. The defendants, except for the leaders, were "petty,
primitive and vulgar."

All the defendants wear large black headphones for translation.
One image has Liebehenschel and Mandl looking downward with

great focus. Mandl has what looks like a heavy wool pea jacket on over a blouse. Her hairstyle remains the same.

A different view shows that the prisoners have large sheaves of papers in front of them. Lead wires for the headphones extend across the desk board from their ears and plug into circular outlets on the shelf.

In front of the docket are cameramen and press, some using movie cameras, which are pointed toward the defendants. The policemen on guard are wearing brimmed hats with prominent black patent leather chin straps. Their uniforms look vaguely sinister.

Onlookers lucky enough to get a day pass are packed onto benches with no separation between people. They sit arm to arm. The benches for both onlookers and defendants look uncomfortable, with straight backs and wooden slats.

The panel of judges is formidable. The men wear heavy liturgical-style robes with velvet hats and a fancy sort of tied scarf around their necks. There is a huge medallion in front of the main judge.

Impressions from the newsreel footage are even more vivid. At first the accused are mostly calm, vacantly looking ahead. Maria is the exception, occasionally talking animatedly to her neighbors Liebehenschel or Aumeier. Liebehenschel, the *Kommandant*, remains quiet and balanced, behaving with decorum.

On the other hand, Max Grabner made a very negative impression. Jan Brandys exclaimed years later "He was *a coward!* He tried at all costs to defend himself from the testimonies. He behaved dishonorably!"

Here is Mandl again, blinking, but not often. Her breathing is visible. She swallows. A dimple comes out below her lower left lip as she does so. Her face is fuller than expected. Her hands are resting in front of her on the wooden platform, not clenched or flat, fingers curved slightly under.

Her breathing gets faster, she breaths from the throat up. Occasionally, she holds her breath. Her eyes narrow slightly. Almost a wince, not quite. Visible breaths, almost a flinch. Fast breaths.

She has gold-colored eyelashes, a face devoid of makeup.

CHAPTER 83

Opening

*One by one the accused stood up and with a quiet "jawohl" ver-
ified their personal data and pleas. In general, all pleaded not
guilty. Most denied certain facts or accepted the facts but took
refuge in an "I was only following orders" defense.*
-SŁOWO POWSZECHNE, NOVEMBER 26, 1947

D URING INITIAL SPEECHES OF THE prosecution, observers noted
that the accused sat motionless, most faces showing no expression. When the court left for a break, the defendants took off their
headphones and continued their indifference. Maria Mandl did
seem aware of her situation but stared stubbornly at the window as
camera flashes went off in the courtroom. Employees of the Polish
film industry set up spotlights, and next to them American film-
makers working on a documentary started filming the trial.

Indictments read against the defendants were comprehensive,
and damning. Various offenses were detailed including conspiracy
to wage aggressive war and participating in criminal organizations
such as the NSDAP, which had as a purpose organizing and committing crimes against peace, war crimes, and crimes against humanity.

Additionally cited were the exploitation of prisoners by creating
camp conditions that caused illness and death; specific torments
and systematic starvation; slave labor abuses; medical experiments

causing great disability, illness, or death; the ridicule, shame, and moral tormenting of inmates; and a detailing of the various ways prisoners were killed, including, shooting, torture, hanging, and the gas chambers.

The list of charges against Mandl was particularly damning:

> Ravensbrück, guard then senior guard
> Senior guard at Auschwitz then head of women's camp
> Taking part in mass and individual murders
> Selecting prisoners for the gas chambers and medical experiments
> Causing prisoners to die from hunger and exhaustion, or by beating them
> Abuse of prisoner's personal dignity by calling them names, depriving of food or clothes, and sentencing to inhuman punishments

In the opening statement against Maria, attention was drawn to the death list of Greek women she signed in 1943. "Due to a lack of inadequate documentary evidence, it is impossible to establish the number of victims in whose killing the accused participated. However, taking into consideration that the accused had been developing her activities in the concentration camps for several years, and that on just that one list there were almost 500 names, and that tens of thousands of women lost their lives, it can be concluded by this way of reasoning that the accused is co-responsible for the death of thousands of people."

On December 3, 1947, after two weeks of proceedings, prominent Polish lawyer Tadeusz Cyprian received a confidential report regarding the course of the trial. He was informed that the first stage of the trial had proceeded with no unpleasant incidents on the part of the defendants because they were frightened and shied away from the accusations that were piled upon them.

Cyprian, a well-respected and influential personality, resented the press, who he felt were twisting testimonies and formulating their own conclusions. He wryly noted that "the American press left Poland even before the announcement of the sentences, with full recognition for the Polish way of conducting the trial and ... for the quality of Polish vodka."

Cyprian summarized that the trial was very difficult because it was taking place in the circles of former prisoners and survivors. Therefore, it was inevitable that dissatisfaction stirred among those omitted. He noted that "if the defendants found themselves in a crowd, they would be torn to pieces."

During the trial many witnesses underwent what was termed a psychosis of collective experiences and identified with what they saw and heard. Excited by the courtroom atmosphere, by the sight of the accused, and by the necessity of appearing in public, they sometime gave facts about things that had taken place or hadn't taken place or had taken place at a different time/place. The defendants' lawyers began trying to discredit the witnesses through these inconsistencies.

In Cyprian's opinion the accused could be divided into two groups. The first were those who had a chance to be sentenced only to prison—they were more composed. The others, in light of the graphic witness testimonies, became more and more aware that they would probably face death. Thus, as the proceedings continued, their anxiety level increased.

He remembers that Maria Mandl, from the first day of the trial, was restless, moved around in the dock, nervously turned over her notes, covered her nervousness with haughty faces when photographed, or ironic smiles that irritated the audience.

CHAPTER 84

The Case Against Mandl

The accused are sick people for whom there were no basic ele-
ments of moral conduct.
  —STANISŁAW RYMAR, MANDL'S DEFENSE ATTORNEY

A S IS OFTEN THE CASE in war crimes trials, female perpetrators received extra notice and sensational coverage. People across the
world had heard of Buchenwald's notorious Ilse Koch and her pen-
chant for making lampshades from prisoner's skin. Irma Grese, the
beautiful young blond guard, was especially notorious and had already been tried and hanged at Belsen. Mandl and her female
codefendants were not as widely known but generated substantial
coverage in Krakow.

One of the prosecuting attorneys in Mandl's trial began his statement by remarking that "we are used to viewing women as more
subtle creatures, sensitive to human pain and suffering. In pain,
women give life to new human beings. [A woman] is hardly ever a
Master of Death or Suffering." He then stressed that these SS
women had made the conscious choice to be executioners and to
take an active part in beating, killing, and abusing human dignity.

After conjecturing on possible reasons for this depravity, the attorney stated simply that "I can only say that in the soul of these
women we cannot find any human feelings. The instance in which

one of the witnesses described that another woman was crawling at Mandl's feet, begging for her to spare her life and Mandl wouldn't listen, is for me, the most drastic example revealing that in these women there were no human feelings."

He went on to summarize the many charges against Mandl and concluded by stating that "as far as Mandl is concerned, she is especially 'privileged' in this trial. She has two volumes of files, half of which is testimonies of witnesses who can be counted in the rest of the line."

After the break on December 12, Stanislaw Rymar presented the opening defense statement in the case against Maria Mandl. He spent several minutes describing the difficulties he and the other attorneys were facing, and his realization that "the defense attorney in this Auschwitz trial must [go against his own feelings and instincts] but also against those of the entire Polish people. If not for the power and ability to forgive, this most beautiful manifestation of our faith, I do not know if I would have had the courage to proceed."

From the beginning Rymar stressed that, in order to understand the defendants, including Mandl, one had to study their actions in the context of the Nazi system and ideology. He rightly noted that from the very beginning of humanity there have been cruelties and atrocities.

Rymar, drawing from his background in classics, now expounded on historical examples. He quoted Caligula, who often said "*Oderint dum metuant*" ("Let them hate me, only let them be afraid of me").

Later noting that the defendants were members of the SS, the Auschwitz staff, and the Nazi Party, he summarized, "The accused are sick people for whom there were no basic elements of moral conduct."

The lawyer bolstered his argument by calling attention to the fact that in this trial, prosecutors had put forward the concept that belonging to the Auschwitz staff was in itself a crime equal to belonging to the SS or the Nazi Party. Rymar then discussed his doubts about the validity of prosecuting Nazi war criminals based on current Polish laws, rather than the laws they adhered to as

members of the German country/people/government. Rymar concluded by saying:

> I am supposed to defend the accused who—let's be open
> about it—are facing the rope. So I shall try to fulfill my
> duty as their defense attorney completely because we are
> talking about human life.

Once Rymar had wrapped up his opening statement, the case
against Maria began in earnest, with a parade of witnesses presented
by the prosecution.

CHAPTER 85

The Evidence

Whenever I asked Maria about her actions in Auschwitz she always said "I made a mistake. I got an order from above. It was very hard to keep so many good and evil people in check."
—MARGIT BURDA

BY THE BEGINNING OF THE trial, many survivors had emerged to go on record and testify publicly about Maria's actions in the camps. The eleventh day of the trial was particularly brutal to Mandl's defense.

One witness was a woman named Janina Frankiewicz, thirty-four, almost exactly Maria's age. Janina had been a prisoner at Auschwitz for a long period, beginning in October of 1942, and first encountered Mandl while in the Hospital Block suffering from typhus. Janina remembered Maria selecting prisoners to receive lethal injections. "This happened very often." After she recovered, Janina saw Mandl frequently in the camp and testified to many specific examples of cruelty, including an incident in which Mandl and Brandl were in Block 9 selecting "Muslims" [prisoners who had given up and were nearing death] for the gas. She saw one of these women kneeling in front of Mandl and begging her to either leave her mother in the block with her or send her to the gas too. In response, Mandl beat and kicked her.

Janina described Block 25 and a few other specific beatings that
Mandl did, including twenty-five to fifty strokes, after which most
of the victims were never seen again (died).

> In April of '44 Mandl came again to the hospital and
> chose sick prisoners to go to the gas, this time about 800
> people. Mandl, Tauber and Drexler [Drechsel] were
> doing it, and directed the trucks to the crematorium.
> They caught and beat and shot a woman who was trying
> to hide behind bricks on the road.

Janina talked about incoming transports on the ramp where selections were done by Mandl, Tauber, and Brandl. She described the
story of Mala/Edek, then afterward when Mala was taken to Block
4. "Through that door, which was a little ajar, I saw Mandl together
with Ritas beating and kicking this Jewish woman who cut her wrists."

One of the lead attorneys asked Janina how she knew that the selected prisoners were being sent to the gas. Janina responded that
they were taken to Block 25, which she stressed was a holding area
for people who were to be gassed, and that it was emptied regularly.
She reinforced that "prisoners were kept there naked. They were
walking around naked. From there they were taken on trucks [to the
gas chambers]." She described how the trucks came back and forth
and emptied the block.

Janina testified that after the large general roll call and selection in January of 1943 Mandl came to the kitchen and said that
they were not supposed to cook so many dinners because there
would now be fewer people. Brandys questioned her further, clar-
ifying the numbers: 4,000 women had been selected and Mandl
ordered the kitchen to prepare 4,000 fewer dinners? "Yes, 4,000
dinners less and coffee."

Perhaps the most damning accusations against Mandl were charges
that she took part in the selection of prisoners for the gas chambers,
both from Block 25 and on the main ramp from incoming transports.

Rymar, in an attempt to soften and refute this testimony, questioned Frankiewicz intensely. He asked that she provide details about her descriptions of Mandl at selections and if she had seen these actions personally. Frankiewicz responded that she *had* seen them, and that this was in 1944, when Mandl was participating in selections from the Hungarian transports.

> RYMAR: But, were *you* there?
> WITNESS: I saw it from the Sauna where I was working and the Sauna was directly on the other side of the ramp. As far as the Hungarian transports were concerned, the entire [staff were there]—all of them and among them Mandl, whom I would recognize even in the dark.

After Janina was finished, the chairman asked if any of the defendants would like to make a statement in relation to the testimony.

Maria spoke up, denying the accusations. She denied kicking prisoners and ordering guards to commit brutalities. She denied doing selections during general roll call and stated that the whipping punishments did not come from her but from higher-ups in administration, that the doctors were there, did the exams, and ordered the punishments.

> Never did I do selections in the hospital with a doctor nor was I present during such selections. Never was I present when a doctor gave prisoners shots.

Mandl described the Mala/Edek episode in general terms and said that after Mala cut her wrists, "I caused her to be immediately taken to the hospital with an order to provide her with medical attention. Later I had an order from the political office to transport her to the crematorium." She noted that Mala's death sentence had come from Berlin.

Maria refuted testimony that the witness could have seen what was going on in Block 25, due to the wall and internal courtyard, and denied doing any selections from the Hungarian transports.

After Mandl's rebuttal the chairman asked Frankiewicz, "Does the witness sustain her testimony?"

Janina said simply, and defiantly, "Yes!"

The chairman excused the witness.

Witnesses and testimonies against Maria continued in an unstoppable torrent. Felicja Pleszowska described Mandl rushing into her block and demanding valuables, screaming, "Money, foreign currency, jewelry—return it and whoever doesn't will be shot!" She described Mandl kicking and abusing the bodies of sick and dying prisoners in front of the blocks. "Everything was done with her knowledge and her order."

Antonina Piatkowska described a bath in the Sauna where Mandl ordered SS men to brand women with a hot iron, and that a female doctor died from such a burning.

Seweryna Szmaglewska, who later wrote a book called *Smoke Over Birkenau* and who was one of the few Poles to testify in the Nuremberg Trials, spoke in a high but well-modulated voice. A finely boned woman with delicate features and light hair, Szmaglewska presented thoughtful answers, enunciated carefully, and sat with straight posture, hands clasped in her lap. Szmaglewska had been in Auschwitz since fall of 1942 and worked in a variety of jobs and noted that the camp staff had a "very detailed system for annihilation." She described Mandl often escorting people to the crematoria and remarked that, from 1942 on, there was an increase in epidemics (typhus, malaria) because the German SS themselves were spreading the epidemics. "It was also a way in which the SS could control the prison population [because so many died]."

For example, at "the crazy searches at the gate, which Mandl exercised with pleasure, taking away any 'treasures' the prisoner had managed to accumulate, bowls, etc. were thrown into a ditch, and some were thrown into the latrines—into excrement, then the newly arriving transports would be given these bowls, the bowls were not rinsed first with water which was very sparse in the camp, so the bowls would be used again to distribute the food. Not disinfected, like the clothes were not disinfected. So the dysentery, etc. would continue to spread."

Szmaglewska remembered Mandl doing selections "between those who were to go to immediate death in crematorium, and those who would go into the camp and have a slim hope to stay alive."

Janina Unkiewicz from Lublin described "Mandelka," as the "Terror of the Camp." Unkiewicz described the agonizingly long roll calls, the freezing weather, and Mandl selecting women from this for death.

Rozalia Huber described the "frog game" as ordered by Mandl. "[You] jump like a frog with heavy stones in each hand, jumping for 3 hours. If you could not do it or continue, [you were] beaten with a whip."

Krystyna Zywulska described Mandl as "very diligent" in her beating, "Mandl would stand at the camp gate when labor details returned, and it was critical they enter on left foot, at such times Mandl was often laughing, and then she would beat or kill the women who were out of step."

Mandl was accused of falsifying records to cover up guilt, and Maria Zumanska testified to being ordered to alter the "Special Handling" cause of death on a list of one thousand women prisoners.

Wanda Marossanyi described the beatings and selections and noted that Maria ignored begging. She mentioned Mandl's secretary, Karolina Wilinska, who had witnessed Mandl beating German women prisoners so badly that streams of blood had to be washed off.

Janina Kosciuszkowa, Jozefina Wegierska, and Anna Szyller all described beatings, kickings, and selections. Janina noted that the "military rigor" was so strict that Mandl beat and broke jaws every time. Anna heard her order that beatings should either break the sticks or result in death: "Kill to death." Mandl was "ruthless. No pleading by prisoners who were kissing her shoes helped."

Wegierska described Mandl holding a prisoner with one hand and beating with the other. She "beat in the face until it was covered

with blood, when the woman prisoner fell to the ground she kept
kicking her in the stomach."

Many women cited the horrific conditions in the women's camps
of both Ravensbrück and Birkenau, the lack of sanitation, and the inadequate food. Hunger, and the lack of edible food, is an ongoing
thread in the prisoner testimonies. The condition of starved prisoners liberated after the war was undeniable proof that few people
were able to sustain a healthy body on the meager rations provided.

In response Maria stated that "I would like again to stress that
never had I let any prisoners to die of hunger in Ravensbrück."
Laughably, in her pretrial deposition Maria had even claimed that
"the prisoners in the women's camp could eat as much as they wanted.
Every prisoner who wanted to eat more, could come to me. I tasted
the food every day myself and approved it or complained if it hadn't
been cooked to perfection."

At night, back in Montelupich, Margit remembers Maria speaking to her about the witnesses who had been called to testify against
her. Maria mentioned that none of the "nice people [Jehovah's Wit-
nesses]" from her time in Lichtenburg and Ravensbrück were called.
"But from the others… They hauled us into the pan proper."

CHAPTER 86

Defense

My job was awfully hard...
—MARIA MANDL, ON THE TWENTIETH DAY OF
THE TRIAL

OVER THE NEXT SEVERAL DAYS of the trial Rymar and Mandl
sought to rebut or minimize the horrific testimony from the
parade of witnesses.

Mandl stated that she was not directly responsible in Ravensbrück
or Auschwitz for prisoners' deaths, did not take part in selections for
the gas chambers or in other executions or selections for medical experiments. Maria emphasized that she was only present at selections
a few times and then by order of the commandant or doctors.

Maria discussed her signatures on the "Special Handling" lists
and said it was just a "formality," that the doctor was the person who
selected the names for the lists. One of the prosecution attorneys
wryly responded, "As a result of those 'formalities,' the chimneys of
the crematorium were smoking day and night."

Mandl also challenged specific testimonies. In one, a woman
named Liberak had testified she had seen Maria kill a prisoner in Ravensbrück. Maria responded, "Had I done this I would have been
immediately arrested and received a severe penalty." Maria also
denied knowledge of the medical experiments on Polish women at

MISTRESS OF LIFE AND DEATH

Ravensbrück, denied doing selections in that camp or ordering penalties for the prisoners, and concluded "I was only responsible as chief guard over other guards."

Consistently, Mandl rebutted testimonies about the large roll call selections and often threw the blame to the doctors, to *Obersturmführer* Hössler, "who was removed from the women's camp for the reason of his cruelty which can also be confirmed by the Defendant Liebehenschel," or to *Kommandant* Höss. "The harshest punishments took place under Höss."

She stated that "the doctor sent some to the hospital and some for SB [Special Handling]. [When I first got to the camp] the first selection was conducted by Kommandant Höss. I was only the chief guard of the camp and I told Höss that I would take no responsibility regarding the selected prisoners. To this Höss replied to me that I can never sentence a prisoner to death and that I should leave that up to his exclusive power."

> Especially, in particular I would like to say that my service in Oświęcim was made very difficult by the extreme severity of Kommandant Höss. In my entire activities I was dependent upon Kommandant Höss and I could not give any punishments.

Mandl and Brandl discussed the trial proceedings between sessions, burying their animosities in a feeble effort to protect each other. Brandl requested to make a statement, expressing that "I would like to say that I have never been an associate [coworker] of Maria Mandl and I never received any orders from Mandl." Earlier, Mandl had testified that "as far as the accusation of Brandl—that she took part in selections—I must say that I have never seen her in those selections, during them, and that I had never heard about it. It's quite possible that the matter pertains to a different person, Drexler, or some other guard."

On the fourteenth day of the trial Rymar called several witnesses to bolster arguments against some of the testimonies. He was trying

to make a case that during selections Mandl's function was only clerical, a formality, and that she was never a person who would have a
decisive voice. Also, as pertained to the evidence relating to the abuse
of prisoners, it didn't "reflect reality because defendant Mandl never
had a dog in the camp, never walked with a key, a whip, or a revolver."
That statement prompted a scathing response by Szmaglewska. "To
say that 'Mandl didn't carry a gun,' or do other atrocities, is a naïve
assumption. We prisoners know that all of these defendants are responsible for an immense amount of deaths in Auschwitz."

The portrayal of herself that Maria presented in her pretrial affidavit was the image she continued to project in the trial. She blamed
the prisoners for their own misfortunes, stressed that anyone who
followed the rules was safe from punishment, and continued to den-
igrate the women as "asocials and criminals." Maria declared herself
innocent of the charges of brutality and deflected all acceptance of
responsibility away from herself.

Eventually, as chief prosecutor Lord Hartley Shawcross, had concluded in the Nuremberg trials, "there comes a point where a man
must refuse to answer to his leader if he is also to answer to his conscience." Maria had yet to reach this point. Near the beginning of the
proceedings when Prosecutor Gacki asked Maria directly, "In general,
does the accused feel guilty or not?" She simply responded, "No."

Krystyna Szymanska, the recording secretary, remembers that
in Mandl's preliminary deposition "Judge Sehn asked her because
in response to one comment she said she didn't want this (or hadn't
wanted to do these things) but she was ordered to, she had to. So
then Judge Sehn asked her, 'Well then, couldn't you give up this job?'
And she covered her eyes with her hand, thought for a moment, and
replied, 'I could give it up if I had a baby.' Sehn: 'Then why didn't
you do it?' And Mandl lowered her eyes and in a quiet voice she said
'I was trying but nothing would come of it.'"

CHAPTER 87

The Game Is Lost
(Final Innings)

D URING THE COURSE OF THE trial Maria projected an air of distance. Survivors who attended the proceedings observed that she sat with a stiff posture and often seemed deep in thought. When asked to testify, she held herself very erect, any nervousness manifested only by the red spots, or hives, that appeared on her face and neck. Occasionally she would answer with arrogance, impudence, and self-assurance, but as she held herself straight the telltale spots would reappear, giving away her inner turmoil.

Some defendants delivered passionate speeches, Liebehenschel was concentrated and serious; the other female overseers appeared mostly scared. Several witnesses remarked on Grabner's cowardice. Stanisław Kobiela notes that up to a certain point in the testimonies the defendants didn't attack each other, but put the blame on already dead Höss, Hössler, Kramer, and Drechsel. The first to break solidarity was Grabner, who, in his testimonies, clearly indicated that Aumeier and Mandl had participated in the selections. When the defendants were once again led out of the courtroom at the conclusion of a session, "Aumeier gave Grabner, who was walking ahead of him, a kick as a sign of his contempt."

It appears that Mandl first became aware that she had probably lost the battle for life the moment she was shown the list of 498 women prisoners selected for the gas chambers with her signature. Afterwards she appeared more nervous and kept her head down.

From prison medical records, we can see that on December 12 Maria complained about headaches and on December 8 and 14 Dr. Dormicki wrote on her chart a Latin abbreviation, "palp. Chr.," for palpitations or cardiac arrythmia brought on by stress. Press accounts of Mandl's demeanor near the end of the trial and before the sentencing note strong blushes, nervous facial tics, fast and broken breathing.

CHAPTER 88

The Press

One can go mad, really. What does he want?
—Survivor and trial attendee

Press coverage of the Second Auschwitz Trial was extensive. In addition to news sources in Poland, there was intense interest from the international press and audience. The added allure of female defendants was significant since, as Daniel Patrick Brown observes, very few female guards were brought to trial compared to SS men and it was much easier for female guards to simply walk away after the war.

The press seemed especially fascinated by Mandl and the juxtaposition of beauty and brutality. At first many articles contained false information, such as Maria being identified as a famous pilot and aviator for the Third Reich, an Olympic-caliber athlete, or a professional boxer.

Mandl, with her Aryan beauty, blond hair, blue eyes, and trim figure was sensationalized as "a beast in a gorgeous woman's body." One journalist even joked that "one could fall in love with her." Much of the press adopted the camp's derisive nickname, "Mandelka."

As the trial proceeded, coverage got more negative. Mandl was described as stout, with the face of an aging prostitute, and neither beautiful nor shapely, "a typical waitress from a second rate *Bierstube.*" One article was titled simply "Monsters in Human Bodies."

Many reporters commented on Mandl's demeanor during the proceedings. Her occasional nervous laughter was described as "carefree," and "cheerful." Several noted that Maria was exceptionally active in the dock, taking notes and laughing to her companions during recesses.

Dramatic moments from the trial made for dramatic press coverage. The periodical *Słowo Powszechne* described witnesses walking slowly in front of the accused and pointing their fingers in identification and accusation. "The courtroom was in deep silence, and the faces of the accused were frozen in terror."

Mandl was confronted directly during several testimonies. The more graphic the description of atrocity, the more extensive the coverage. During the testimony of a witness named Marchwicka, who described Mandl taking a newborn baby, dipping its head in a bucket of water, and throwing it outside alive to be bitten to death by rats, the spectators stirred with horror. When the judge asked if Marchwicka recognized the accused, she responded, "Supreme National Tribunal, I recognize the accused Maria Mandl! The accused Maria Mandl is a demon in a human body! When she ruled the camp we thought it was the end of the world for us!"

The press was also captivated by prurient details about the moral lifestyle of the female defendants; the more salacious the better. "They

One of the many press caricatures of Mandl at her trial. ECHO KRAKOWA, Z 3 GRUDNIA 1947. COURTESY OF POLSKA PRESS, FROM THE COLLECTION OF STANISŁAW KOBIELA.

talk of drunken orgies and moral morass that ruled at Mandl's . . . But her insolence doesn't leave her. She shrugs and yawns each time she hears her name mentioned by the witnesses."

Paraphrased descriptions of specific testimonies were also published. After being challenged by one of the prosecutors who asked if Mandl still maintained she did not beat women prisoners, Mandl said that "I admit that once in a while I slapped one of them across the face." When the prosecutor responded that "I heard that jaws broke as a result of this slapping," Maria responded, "I don't recall this. I beat when the women prisoners stole from one another." Prosecutor: "Did you have the right to beat them?" Maria Mandl (after a long pause, in a firm and upset voice): "No."

As the intensity of the testimonies increased and the severity and breadth of the charges, especially regarding the selections, became apparent, several reporters noticed a change in Maria's demeanor. She began to show her emotional distress, no longer appeared arrogant, and no longer smiled or chatted during recesses. When she asserted her innocence, her voice was shaking.

When Rymar consulted with Maria between testimonies, she interrupted him violently. "Yes, I beat because the women were insolent. I was signing the lists of those destined for death and lists for the doctor's medical experiments, but it was only pure formality."

After the witness testimonies concluded, Mandl asked to address the court. She stood and adjusted her hair, then worked her way through to the microphone. "When asked by the prosecutor whether she pleads guilty she responds that she is completely innocent. After her response, the courtroom is filled with loud laughter."

Once again, Mandl's signing of the death list for the Greek women drew notice. Several papers observed that Maria "became deadly pale" and in a shaking voice admitted she had signed the list.

One newspaper article, titled "From Our Perspective," reveals most keenly the emotional and psychological effect this trial had on survivors. Most could never have imagined that one day they would be sitting in a courtroom where their oppressors from Auschwitz were being tried. In many cases, these defendants had murdered members of the survivor's family and his or her friends or tortured the survivor personally. Even with the safety of the court guards, and the prisoners in a reinforced dock, the survivors experienced feelings of "uncanny terror."

Several bystanders observed that it was difficult for the witnesses, who had lived through this horror, to speak objectively and not become too excited or emotional. Most tried to suppress their nerves and speak calmly. Few looked at the defendant's bench.

A witness described a mother who lost her mind after her child was killed, after which a lawyer probed further, asking the witness to explain *why* the mother went mad. At this point the witness looked perplexed and asked him to clarify the question and stated again that the mother "went mad because they killed her child, is that clear?"

Although the lawyer thanked her for her testimony, it was obvious he did not accept the explanation. "One of the former prisoners leans over to another; 'One can go mad, really. What does he want?'"

CHAPTER 89

Challenge of the Orchestra Women

As THE TRIAL DREW TO a close, Maria's body showed signs of the stress she tried to mask in public. Plagued by recurrent headaches, she also complained of eye problems ("can't see") to the prison doctor. Occasionally Maria still delivered testimony holding herself straight and answering with arrogance, impudence, and self-assurance. Increasingly, however, when she was excited, upset, or moved, the telltale large red spots appeared on her skin, giving away her inner turmoil.

One former prisoner who had close contact with Mandl in the camp noted that "during the trial she made an impression of being alienated. She was very nervous as seen by the spots in her neck. They gave her away. She tried to put on a brave face with her posture, sometimes you could see her re-straightening herself. She maintained control over her statements, she was very terse, she said, 'I was an officer, it was my duty.'"

Maria often chose to remain in the dock during breaks rather than relocate to a holding room as the other defendants did. It was during one of these breaks that Maria, once again, came face-to-face with some women from her orchestra.

Three former musicians attended the trial and, at one point, attempted to speak with Mandl. The women wanted recognition from Maria; recognition of their place in the orchestra, recognition of their humanity, and recognition of the role they had once played in her life and she in theirs.

Wisia, a violinist, lost family during the war in addition to her own persecution and "couldn't handle or cope with her hatred towards them." Fifty-seven years later Zofia Cykowiak, Wisia's close friend, related the scene vividly.

> During a recess the prisoners were walked out some-where next door, and Mandl stayed in the dock. Wisia pushed in some, in a kind of trance, and spoke to her loudly because I was trying to hold her back/stop her. She managed to reach the entry for the press. Someone heard what she was saying, or heard me trying to stop her, got interested, and let us into where the press was sitting.
>
> They arranged something with a guard so that we were allowed to get closer [about six feet from Mandl], and Wisia said to me, "Ask her! Ask her!" I said, "What am I supposed to ask her about?" Wisia: "Whether she recognizes us." I thought I could ask that. So in German, I spoke quietly. I asked again. She did not react. Wisia: "Ask her again!!" So I did. Then Wisia noticed that I spoke to Mandl using the word "*Frau.*" Wisia spoke to me in a raised voice, "What are saying to her??! Talk to her as she named us!" I couldn't, I didn't know such a German word [a profane expression that Mandl used in the camps to refer to the women]. I said, "Wisiu, calm down!"
>
> I saw what was about to happen and didn't want a hys-terical scene, there had already been a hysterical scene when one of the women prisoners started yelling and the judge warned us that he would remove us all from the courtroom. So I repeated the question. One of the journal-ists repeated the question and Mandl turned towards us and looked.
>
> And she didn't turn her head away from us anymore, she just looked-stared. We knew she recognized us from the spots, which appeared on her neck, which were very characteristic for her. I noticed because in our room in the

camp, such spots would also occur, I noticed them too. So, the spots. Yes, she recognizes us, recognizes… She didn't utter a word. So Wisia kept struggling with me, "Tell her!" So I say, "We were in the orchestra! You visited us very often." Silence.

But all the time she didn't turn her head away; she kept looking at us, but she wouldn't say a word. Wisia had already lost control of herself, she started pulling at me. I saw what was about to happen and asked the men there for help, and we led Wisia out.

That was my last encounter with Mandl.

These brave women challenged Mandl, forced her to acknowledge them and to look directly into their faces and see their humanity. Perhaps this was the moment Maria really began to reflect on her choices. For if these women were indeed human, so too were all the other prisoners she had beaten, or tortured, or killed. And if that was the case, she did deserve to pay with her life.

CHAPTER 90

Closing Arguments

*Can't we just, for one moment, forget all the hatred and dislike
and rise above her crimes? Can't we understand that this country
girl, a shoemaker's daughter who for a long time was a servant
and a maid, who got a post through her uncle, went through the
Hitler schooling, moving through the camps in an accelerated
way because war broke out—[can't we understand] that she was
a slave of the system, a psychopath, a very sick person?*

—STANISŁAW RYMAR

O N THE NINETEENTH DAY OF the trial Stanislaw Rymar took the
floor to present his final arguments in defense of Maria Mandl.
Rymar began by reinforcing that he had been appointed by the tribunal to be Maria's defense counsel and that "before I spoke with
Mandl the first time, I wanted to make sure that I knew what she had
done and against what I had to defend her."

Rymar correctly categorized the accusations of Mandl's participation in the selections as the most damning charge against her. He
stressed that—as Mandl had stated—the doctors were clearly in
charge, but reassured the court that nonetheless, "Mandl *will* [an-
swer for her crimes]."

As her defense attorney Rymar acknowledged that he had to
"tackle the problem of Mandl's participation in the selections as this

will decide her ultimate fate." He also discussed the sheer volume of testimonies against Mandl (two volumes) and the fact that very few of the witnesses described in identical or substantial ways her participation in the selections.

He acknowledged that Mandl did work at the gate and abuse some women, but asserted that she did not have the power to make the decision about who was to go, and in what numbers, to the gas chamber.

Rymar postulated that although Maria did participate, "all the others did too. They were poisoned by the same kind of German psyche. It influenced them to act in this way." He pointed to a testimony where Mandl told the prisoner to submit to Germany and its ideals. "Isn't this a true confession of Mandl herself? This true Austrian woman Mandl? For her, all she was doing was surrendering to the system, [actions that were] normal and necessary."

Rymar ruefully noted the lack of testimonies in support of Maria Mandl, wishing he had had "a trifling detail—some unnoticed rays I could have clung to as her defense counsel." He reflected on the interactions that Mandl had with children in the camp and concluded from that behavior that she still had a "spark of femininity" and was still a human being.

> Can't we [remember] that Mandl was fired from her job at the post office for NOT being a member of the Nazi party? Wasn't it only the system and she a tiny wheel? The instinct [for self-preservation] of life is so big, that one can't demand these small people risk their life to oppose orders.

Having expressed those final thoughts, Mandl's defense rested.

CHAPTER 91

Guilty

I N THE END, THE COURT chose not to accept Rymar's arguments for the defense. The evidence against Maria was simply overwhelming in its breadth and depth. It goes on for pages, fully documented by witnesses, inescapable.

In a final synopsis before the penalty phase of the trial, the court concluded that Maria Mandl was guilty of the following charges:

> In nearly all the selections at Ravensbrück or Auschwitz Mandl took an active part and was by no means limited to passive assistance. The accused, equally with the doctors, selected prisoners for death. She assisted at hurrying or pushing victims to cars to transport them to the gas chambers, was also on the ramp for the Hungarian gassings and the liquidation of the Terezin family camp. She also took children from mothers, beat them and threw them like stones on cars. On her own initiative she sent pregnant women to the gas chambers or to receive injections of phenol.
>
> Testimonies from witnesses prove incontrovertibly that Mandl personally chose and assigned more than 80 prisoners for the limb regeneration medical experiments at Ravensbrück, the Polish women from Lublin, 5 died from them and 6 were shot afterwards.

The Supreme National Tribunal also determines that Mandl was responsible for many deaths in Brzezinka [Birkenau]. Large numbers of deaths in big roll calls, and specific instances of deaths such as mother and child.

She also caused other deaths in Ravensbrück and Auschwitz by the conditions at the roll calls, freezing, whipping, no shoes, etc. Long roll calls and delousings in harsh conditions and depriving of clothes and blankets resulting in deaths.

The following are also cited:

> Special cases of babies burned, inhumane tortures
> Willfully misusing her power to the prisoners, disadvantaging them through severe camp regulations
> Mandl was a terror to all prisoners because she kicked and tortured them relentlessly
> [Instituting] other major torments (kneeling on sharp rocks, etc.)
> Beating with cane or whip, transferring to penal brigade
> Sending women to the brothel
> Made rules more harsh and severe and beat prisoners herself, especially to face and jaw
> Shoe/feet abuses in Ravensbrück and the gypsy and insane women deaths

In light of such charges, it is difficult to imagine that Maria could have had any doubt about her ultimate sentence.

CHAPTER 92

Sentence

Not Revenge, but Justice
—Echo Krakowa

O N THE DAY THE SENTENCES were announced, December 22, 1947, Maria Mandl wore a patterned scarf, tied low on her neck, knotted once, and tucked into the top of her jacket.

Sentences against all forty prisoners were announced, and a Polish newspaper, *Wolni Ludzie*, published a large two-page article with caricatures of the defendants. It captured the mood and reality of the courtroom on that day.

Outside of the trial venue, crowds gathered from early in the morning to await the court sentences. At 9:40 the proceedings began as members of the Supreme National Tribunal took their places. The courtroom was profoundly silent and the defendants appeared anxious, darting nervous looks in the direction of the judges. The room was packed.

On the dot of 9:50 A.M. the head judge began reading the sentences, which were loudly and clearly broadcast to the crowds outside. "The Supreme National Tribunal, under Article 6 … finds the accused guilty."

In the end, twenty-three persons were proven guilty of participating in mass murder and received the death sentence, including

Liebehenschel, Aumeier, Grabner, Moeckel, Brandl, and Maria Mandl. Of the other female defendants, Luise Danz was sentenced to life in prison and Alice Orlowski and Hildegard Lächert each received fifteen years. The camp doctor, Hans Münch, was the only person acquitted.

In an article published on Christmas Eve 1947 the local newspaper, *Echo Krakowa*, described the moments when the sentences were read. The faces of most of the accused were frozen and pale; Liebehenschel was motionless.

> Maria Mandl behaves differently. She does her best to be
> in control of herself but her efforts are futile. The woman
> who with a single gesture would sentence women pris-
> oners to death now cannot control the accelerated breath,
> unnatural blush and a nervous twitch of her whole face.

Jerzy Ludwikowski was present for the sentencing, which was crowded with so many people that most had to stand as the room became stuffy with heat and tension. "Some of the accused couldn't breathe, they breathed nervously, they had unbuttoned the collars of the uniforms and Mandl had, if I remember well, an unbuttoned coat and a burning face. I think one of the accused, after the sentences had been read, yelled 'Heil Hitler!'"

Zofia Cykowiak, former member of Maria's orchestra, was also there. In 2004, fifty-seven years later, the moment is vivid in her memory. It is late at night, her small apartment lit only by a dim electric light. Outside the open windows, in the darkness, a cat (or possibly a child?) howls.

> Mandl was standing VERY straight and THIS time she
> didn't just have spots, she was all purple!

Maria Mandl had been sentenced to hang.

Part Seven

CHAPTER 93

The Waiting

It is a terrible thing to see a man condemned to death, even when you are certain he has been responsible for the death of millions.

—ANN AND JOHN TUSA, IN TIM TOWNSEND,
Mission at Nuremberg

Now I have the worst before me and that is my future fate.
—MARIA MANDL

DESPITE ITS SEEMING INEVITABILITY, THE shock of receiving a death sentence must have been overwhelming for Maria.

Hanna Wysocka, the Polish political prisoner held at Montelupich, also received a sentence of death at a previous trial. For Hanna, it was the worst moment of her life. In her anguish she unexpectedly began to sing a song as the judge yelled for her to be quiet. "'It was merry at my funeral, the birds were singing trill, trill,' and I wanted to laugh—all from stress. The judge shouted, 'Has the prisoner understood?' And I said with calmness, 'Un-der-stood,' and in my head went the song again, 'It was merry at my funeral'; very difficult, very, very difficult."

Maria Mandl and Therese Brandl were now moved to a "Death Cell" on the third floor of the prison. It was a single room, small, with only a very narrow bunkbed, a sink, a toilet bucket, and a chair. There was a two-foot passage between the bed and the wall. "That's all." Another prisoner who later occupied the same space remembers that "it was signed Brandl and Mandl, their dates of birth, on the boards of those bunks. They had carved their names."

As word of the death sentences spread rapidly through Montelupich, the condemned persons began to be subjected to abuses by other prisoners. Several remember that a soldier came and said that if any of them wanted to take retribution "now was the time, because in Oświęcim the German women had been terrible sadists."

One woman, Helena Jędrzejowska, declared that her husband and son had been shot by the Nazis and she wanted to take action "for my son, for my husband." The guards let her into Mandl and Brandl's cell and she hit them and pulled their hair. Afterward, Jędrzejowska returned to her cell and said, "I have taken revenge, so much they have had enough."

In the week after the trial, Maria and the other condemned prisoners wrote and filed pleas for clemency to Polish President Bierut. Stanisław Rymar submitted Maria's. "Fulfilling the convict's request as their ex officio defense attorney, I request Most Distinguished Mr. President to exercise the right for pardon in relation to the abovementioned convicts."

Maria's letter is written by hand, in chemical pencil like her other testimonies. The penmanship is very polished—she obviously took a great deal of care to make it as neat as possible. In her letter Mandl asks for a reprieve, cites that she had to earn her own living, and explains that after the Anschluss she lost her job in the post office for not belonging to the Nazi Party. She notes that her uncle then helped her to find a new job at Lichtenburg. "In 1942 all KZs were taken over by the SS and at that time by my own agreement, I was made a part of the SS—but only as a civilian employee."

Maria stated that others had more responsibility and that she only followed the orders they gave. Listing some of the abuses of which she was convicted, Maria pleaded that "I can only think that it must have been a different person, since none of the accusations had to do with me." She further referenced letters written in her defense which were submitted to the court. Finally, she asked for mercy for the sake of her elderly father. "I refer to my old father, who relies on himself. Therefore I should like to ask Mr. President to have mercy."

At no point did Maria express regret, apologize, or accept responsibility for her actions.

Then, filled with anxiety and hope, she awaited a response.

CHAPTER 94

Christmas Eve 1947

It's snowing and the sun is going down on this last pre-Christ-mas Sunday. What morale is in the hearts of man, the worries as we now bear them with no idea how to devote oneself to the magic of Christmas?

—KOMMANDANT ARTUR LIEBEHENSCHEL, LETTER, DECEMBER 21, 1947, POST-VERDICT

CHRISTMAS EVE, 1947, ONLY ONE day after many of the Auschwitz defendants were sentenced to death. Danuta Wojnar-Górecka remembered that night vividly. The cell block was quiet, with no one shouting or slamming doors as usual. The inmates were alone. In Danuta's cell the women became pensive.

It was 4:00 and, although the darkness of the night was slowly advancing on them, the light had not yet been turned on. The twilight of Christmas eve brought mem-ories of the past, recollection of events and people with whom they used to share the joys of holiday. Happy child-hood, promising years at school, the years of war...

Suddenly a distant, beautiful sound disrupted the thoughtful silence in the cell. It was a choir of a few male voices at first, but getting stronger and stronger every second. Did someone bring a group of carol-singers to the prison walls to cheer up the inmates on Christmas eve? Suddenly, the light went on in the cell and guard Kunda appeared at the door. "Listen, the Germans are singing their carols. Isn't it nice? I will leave all the doors open so everybody can listen."

A choir of robust male voices descending from the second floor cells seemed to engulf the prison. "Stille Nacht. Heilige Nacht." There was something touching in the sweet melody of this carol indeed, in the situation as well. 23 of these 40 singing men had been sentenced to death just a few days before.

CHAPTER 95

Zaba

My parents' set phrase for what had happened to them was a
blow dealt by fate, a fate beyond the reach of personal influence...
Everything was dreadful for the very reason that you had been
a victim yourself, the victim of a collective and unavoidable
fate... And you felt that fate had treated you unfairly."
— Uwe Timm, In My Brother's Shadow:
A Life and Death in the SS

LATER THAT SAME CHRISTMAS EVE, Mandl and Brandl were struggling emotionally. It was the custom in Montelupich to place a
political prisoner into the cell of persons condemned to death. This
prisoner was supposed to prevent any suicide attempts before execution. Kunda, the guard, came to Danuta Wojnar-Górecka's cell and
demanded she serve in this function. "You are to take all your things
right now and leave here to live with the two German women who
have been sentenced to death. They can't be left alone. Come
quickly." Danuta contemplated the idea with horror, and after some
discussion with her cellmates, a woman named Maria Żabianka, nicknamed "Zaba," volunteered to go instead.

The guard agreed, stating that the only criteria was fluency in
German. Zaba was a psychiatrist and accepted the assignment
calmly, stating that it would be a unique professional experience. "As

a psychiatrist I am eager to meet them. It is not a sacrifice on my part. I'm really looking forward to seeing these two women."

Maria Żabianka was a kind woman with a brilliant intellect. Described as "not compromising, with sympathy for people, but also sympathy for the SS," Zaba had a rangy build, dark hair cut short and parted on the side, and round dark-framed glasses. Like many of the political prisoners at Montelupich, Zaba had been arrested for activities with the WiN organization.

Both Hanna Wysocka and Danuta Wojnar-Górecka remember Zaba's vivid accounts of what transpired during the time she spent with the condemned women. Hanna later remarked that "when they were in the death cell, she calmed them down, and even cleaned for them."

Zaba had several discussions with Mandl and Brandl about their actions and what had happened in their lives. Both stated that, in war, every form of extermination is justified.

Mandl, in particular, could not understand why she was being punished. Mandl told Zaba that the political prisoners were in the same situation she was, that she had been in a service, she didn't regret it, that's how it was supposed to be. She thought the Russians would be nicer to her than the Americans, because "with the Americans she would get the death sentence for sure." So she expressed a good opinion about Stalin to Zaba, because she thought it would predispose the secret police political system to be more lenient.

During her visit Zaba found the women to be perfectly sane, even as they continued to deny being guilty of any crime. She found Mandl so fanatical that she soon gave up all efforts to explain the prisoner's feelings about Auschwitz. Zaba later told Danuta that "they prayed a lot and didn't believe their sentences would be carried out. Mandl even studied Polish."

CHAPTER 96

Father Stark

Undoubtedly, the job was difficult and undoubtedly Father Marian was sent there as a person competent to perform the job. In such matters a priest counts more on God than himself.
—FATHER WŁADYSŁAW PIOTROWSKI

ALL OF THE CONDEMNED PRISONERS were now given the opportunity to visit with a clergyman. As a former Catholic, Maria was assigned Father Marian Stark. A photograph of Father Stark from this period reveals a man with an intent and compassionate gaze framed by wire-framed glasses, wearing the dark suit and round white clerical collar of the time. Stark's hair is thinning on top, his chin has a pronounced cleft, he looks aware and intelligent.

Although Marian Stark died in 1984, he is still remembered fondly by one of his students, Father Władysław Piotrowski. Piotrowski describes Stark as very energetic with lovely manners. He was "a man of big kindness towards people, very outgoing. As a professor he was extremely well educated, his area of expertise was moral theology and he often dealt with the moral aspects of being a priest."

In 1947–48 Marian Stark was a professor, not a parish priest. "He was probably selected for Montelupich because of his background. It was a special case."

When asked how he thinks Father Stark might have counseled Maria, Piotrowski responded that "he reminded Maria of great God's mercy and helped her correctly judge the scale of her crimes in order to prepare her for the sacrament of reconciliation. I think that in every human being, in every man, there remains some little spark of goodness, and therefore we are not allowed to judge or condemn anyone. This is a matter for God himself."

Catholic deacon Luis Baerga also conjectured about how Father Stark may have counseled Maria. "He probably started by asking her questions about her childhood, upbringing and the degree of Catholic training she may or may not have received. How strong her faith was initially, how strong it was now. He would then try to find out if and why she had a loss of faith."

Indeed, Maria had always offered conflicting statements about her faith. In the beginning of her pretrial deposition she states that "from my birth until this day I am a believer in God." However, shortly thereafter Maria also states that "my past life led me on such a path of trial and tribulation and misfortune that I lost all faith in the Almighty God." Later still she says that "under the influence and as a result of all my experiences in the KZ at Auschwitz, and finally, due to the death of my fiancé and my mother, I doubted in the existence of God and in 1945 officially stepped out of the Catholic church. I did it during my stay in Mühldorf. [Although] I continued to believe in God, I divested myself of the faith in Mary, the immaculate conception, and the like."

Baerga believes that Father Stark had a monumental task convincing Maria of the enormity of her crimes. If Father Stark succeeded in having Maria acknowledge her crimes as sins, he may have gained a toehold in having her admit culpability. He could then begin the task of trying to bring her soul to repentance.

Baerga summarizes that Catholics believe God is all loving and all merciful, therefore willing to forgive sin, no matter how great or how heinous, provided the sinner has truly repented. "The Catholic church considers sins of Mandl's magnitude forgivable if her contrition is true."

Father Gerecke, a priest assigned to many of the condemned Nazi officers at Nuremberg, believed that God alone should judge, so the question of guilt was not in his domain. He prayed to avoid all pride and any prejudice against those beings in his care. Gerecke was described as approaching his tasks in a "spirit of humility, a battle for the souls of men standing beneath the shadow of the gallows." It seems likely Father Stark did the same.

CHAPTER 97

Final Goodbye

Our parting was very bad, very sad.
— MARGIT BURDA

MARIA'S FRIEND MARGIT, WHO HAD been with her since Dachau, was exonerated, released from prison, and scheduled to leave on the same train as the acquitted prisoner Dr. Münch. She later noted with great regret that "I couldn't say goodbye properly. It's always difficult when one person can leave and one can't. And I was completely alone when I had to go. I had my trunk and the truck came quickly and I was gone."

January 10 was Maria's thirty-sixth birthday. On January 13, 1948, the Supreme National Tribunal was notified that the president had not exercised his right to pardon twenty-one of the convicts, including Mandl.

It is not known when Maria and the others found out their pardons had been denied. On January 17 the newspaper *Trybuna Robotnicza* published an article titled "23 Criminals from the Auschwitz Camp Staff Will Be Hanged." So at least by that date word was out about the denial of the pardons and presumably the accused had been notified as well.

The time and date of the executions was set for January 24, 1948, at 7:00 A.M. From this point forward lights were left on at all times in the death cells.

CHAPTER 98

Rachwałowa and the Shower Room

It has become virtually an article of faith, at least among a great many Jews, that no Nazi war criminal should ever be for-given, no matter what the individual went on to do. And this point is finessed by the commonplace observation that only those who have been wronged can forgive those who committed the wrong in question. In the harrowing words of Jankélévitch: for-giveness died in the death camps.

—Laurence Thomas, "Forgiving the Unforgivable?," in Moral Philosophy and the Holocaust

From the beginning of her time at Montelupich, Maria's life intersected with that of a woman named Stanisława Rach-wałowa. Rachwałowa was a former inmate of Auschwitz-Birkenau now held on political charges. She was a striking woman, possessed of great strength of character and personal courage. Rachwałowa's daughter, Anna, described her mother as "very optimistic—always smiling. Very tough."

Anna, now living in the country with two formidable guard dogs and a tick-laden cat who weaves in and out as we speak, remembers a story from her childhood that sheds great light on Rachwałowa's personality. During the Occupation, her mother gave Anna their very last money to buy milk. When she was walking to the store, however, she saw a very skinny little cat. "I gave the owner the money and took the cat and came back home." As her mother opened the door, Anna said, "Mommy…," and she looked at me, and she asked, 'So now you have a cat?' And we laughed."

Rachwałowa had the misfortune to be detained in several different prisons and camps. Prison photos taken in 1951 show a strong face, heavy features, a long head, a beautiful profile, dark shoulder-length hair in a flip with a headband, and circles under her eyes. Her 1942 intake photo from Auschwitz shows hair that has been cropped unevenly to a length of about an inch, striped prisoner garb, and in one shot, a direct and defiant gaze into the camera lens, much as Maria Mandl had in her subsequent Montelupich photo.

Although originally from Lwow, Stanisława had married a Polish army officer named Zygmunt Rachwał and moved to Krakow. Two daughters were born from this marriage. After war broke out, Zygmunt was deported to Siberia, where he died of tuberculosis. Stanisława became active in the city underground movement, acting as a courier using a variety of aliases. She was arrested twice, first in 1941, after which she served a short sentence in Montelupich, and then again in October of 1942, when she was sent to Auschwitz-Birkenau.

When Rachwałowa arrived in 1942, the conditions were extremely harsh. She survived the difficult quarantine period in an overcrowded barracks infested with vermin, no climate control or heating, and brutal morning roll calls. Due to the terrible conditions, sleep was not possible, so prisoners spent entire nights sitting awake. After the quarantine ended, Rachwałowa was assigned to various grueling outdoor work details. Ultimately, due to her strong personality and fluency in French and German, Stanisława rose to a high position overseeing the influx and registration of new prisoners into the camp.

Danuta Mosiewicz-Mikusowa remembers Rachwałowa's kindness when she entered the camp. "Rachwalowa told me that the worst time when you arrive at Auschwitz is the first seven weeks because this is

the quarantine period and that's when you stay in the 'Lice Barracks.'"
After questioning her, Rachwałowa made an inscription that Danuta
had an excellent command of languages and told her, "Hang on for
the first seven weeks—and then we will try to place you somewhere."

Danuta noted that when the Jewish women came in, Rachwałowa
wouldn't register them. "She was exceptionally brave. If they didn't
LOOK Jewish, she would not register them as Jewish women, she
would register them as non-Jewish. Rachwałowa was EXCEPTION-
ALLY brave!" Stanisława also started networking with the camp
underground movement.

She served as a kind of surrogate mother for the younger women
and elevated their spirits by telling fabulous stories which allowed
them to escape the daily realities of their lives. Privately, she
mourned the separation from her daughters who were barely surviving outside of the camp. Due to her connections Rachwałowa was
able to send and receive letters from her daughters, several of which
exist today. Anna remembers that although some were censored,
they did indeed get through. "I don't know how she did it, but when
the camp was emptied she carried our letters out with her. The
letters said 'I am healthy, I am managing, I love you very much…'"

Rachwałowa was evacuated from Birkenau in January of 1945, to
Ravensbrück, then to another camp, and finally liberated in May.

She returned to Krakow and continued her underground activities with different anti-Communist organizations. Rachwałowa now
adopted the alias of "Zygmunt," a nod to her dead husband. Her aim
was to collect information about army, political, other intelligence,
also personal data about members of the Party and functionaries of
the Secret Police. A hand-drawn document from that period shows
Rachwałowa as the undeniable leader and center of a large spider-
web of underground contacts.

Stanisława was arrested again in October of 1946, incarcerated in
Montelupich, tried in court proceedings twice, and sentenced to
death in December of 1947. After several months, her sentence was
commuted to life in prison.

Rachwałowa states in her written memoirs that it was the dream of every prisoner in the camp to one day see his or her persecutors in jail and degraded. Later, her dream was fulfilled in a totally unexpected way when she encountered her former supervisor at Birkenau, Maria Mandl, in just such a position—on her hands and knees washing the floors of the prison.

Rachwałowa struggled with feelings of vengeance and with her memories of Mandl's brutality in the camps. Maria recognized Stanisława immediately and seemed to shrink from her gaze. Stanisława admitted that

> I had ceased to be a prisoner who had to observe prison regulations, I was a prisoner of the Oświęcim-Brzezinka concentration camp, and the women in front of me were the SS-women, our oppressors, murderers. The damn had broken and my words set off like an avalanche; evil, brutal, cruel, boorish, the ones we were treated with in the camp on any occasion.

Rachwałowa was occasionally taken to join the German women during exercise periods and noted that Maria would go for walks separately, away from them. "She walked quickly, her hands behind her back, her head down low, her eyebrows knitted. She had become ugly since Oświęcim. Only her hair was still golden, eyes big and blue, though in her look there was no former Mandl; there was some sadness and always an expression of surprise which would appear when she looked at me."

When Rachwałowa received her death sentence and was moved to a higher floor, she "awaited in solitude mercy or death." Mandl and Therese Brandl were placed next door. For Rachwałowa, neighboring by Mandl and Brandl was difficult because she "felt their restlessness behind the wall. I could count on pardon, they probably not. Now there was only a common fate, common waiting." Rachwałowa also believed that her presence next door added to Maria's contemplation of her actions and her fate. She heard Maria pacing, back and forth, back and forth, all day long.

One afternoon Rachwałowa was taken to a bath in the prison showers along with Mandl and Brandl. They walked before her and stood in the showers at the opposite end of the room. The guard turned on the water and, called by someone, left for a few minutes. Rachwałowa describes what happened next:

> Warm water was flowing from the shower giving me a nice relaxing sensation, but at the same time I could sense that a feeling of restlessness and fear was taking me over. I didn't take my eyes off the German women through the pouring water and steam. The situation was amazing: the two of them and I, locked, three beings from the former death camp. One of them—the highest authority—and I, gray ash and dust, *Häftling* [prisoner], together on one level, equal in the face of death though so different in guilt.
>
> Suddenly I noticed that both German women were walking towards me. Mandl walked first, Brandl followed her. The old fear filled me completely. I was standing there terrified and helpless, and they kept walking toward me surrounded by steam as thick as fog and streams of water from the showers, naked and wet. The moment seemed like a century. "Oh God," I whispered helplessly. "What else do they want from me?" And ex-*Oberaufseherin* Mandl from Brzezinka stood two steps from me, wet, humble, and from her eyes tears, streams of tears were flowing.
>
> Slowly, with great difficulty gasping for breath, but clearly, she said, "I ask, beg for forgiveness." All of my old Oświęcim dreams came back, beating, revenge, vanished in the twinkling of an eye... A feeling of great mercy, sorrow and forgiveness took over my soul. I was crying together with them over this mysterious human heart, which through the loss of the entire humanity had entered the path of penance and understanding. I took the

outreached, begging hand and said, "I forgive on behalf of the prisoners." In response they both fell to their knees and kissed my hands.

The guard then returned and we were taken back to our cells. Mandl was let into her cell first and at the last moment turned, smiled warmly and gratefully and said aloud, clearly, in Polish, one word; "Dziękuję" [thank you].

I did not see them anymore. After a few days they were executed and I know that Mandl was the last one.

Anna, Rachwałowa's daughter, later noted that "after three years in Auschwitz and ten years in prison they finally let my mother go. That was in 1956 when Stalin died." It was around this time that Stanisława wrote an account of the encounter with Mandl in the showers.

Rachwałowa returned to her family and, ultimately, died in Rzeszów in October of 1984. With the approval of her daughter, Rachwałowa's account was published in the Polish journal *Przegląd Lekarski*. Immediately Rachwałowa's credibility was challenged. Many survivors questioned the sincerity of Mandl's repentance, Rachwałowa's right to forgive Mandl in any way, and *especially*, her right to forgive Mandl on behalf of *all* the prisoners.

Some former inmates believed that Rachwałowa had fabricated this account, as she had made up so many stories in the camp to distract them from their daily life. One survivor remembers that Rachwałowa was "a very nice person, but that she liked to add 'color.'"

Rachwałowa's daughter contests this belief. Anna states that for many years after the war her mother refused to speak *at all* of her experiences at Auschwitz, much less to glorify or embellish them in any way. "She tried to avoid the topic of Auschwitz and the prison after the war, and she always made it half-jokingly: no martyrology!"

She emphasizes that her mother had a very firm grasp on reality and that, while in the camp, Rachwałowa believed she had a responsibility as a mature and stable figure to act as a source of strength for the younger women. She asserts that the fact her mother made up stories to entertain and distract the younger prisoners in their darkest days in no way implicates her in the possible fabrication of this story.

"I just wanted to tell you that when my mom was in Montelupich she was incarcerated with probably six other women, and she was very liked by them because she read a lot and she would tell them films and books. And those stories were always very positive, and they always ended very well. That's the truth." Hanna Wysocka concurred that "it was good to have such a person in the cell, because there were women from all walks of life; the young ones, especially, would despair. Someone like Rachwalowa could tell beautiful stories and keep them occupied and distracted."

Rachwałowa's daughter claims that, for the rest of her life, her mother was convinced she had done the right thing in forgiving Mandl.

CHAPTER 99

Si non è vero

Si non è vero, è ben trovato (Even if it isn't true, it's a good story)
—GIORDANO BRUNO, 1585, AS QUOTED BY
DANUTA WOJNAR-GÓRECKA

Is THE ACCOUNT OF RACHWAŁOWA's encounter with Maria in the
prison shower possible? In theory, it was against regulations to
allow German and Polish prisoners to co-mingle in the showers, and
Pani Jadzia, the Montelpich guard, later stated that this could not
have happened.

However, in practice, this *is* something that happened occasionally.

Hanna Wysocka remembers an earlier incident in which she and
some fellow inmates were taken to the baths in the basement. As
they entered the shower room, some German prisoners were already there. "An older woman, Janka Oszas, who was gray-haired
and very handsome started to shout 'We are leaving from here, let's
turn our backs and we are not going to shower!' And the guard was
surprised, she was stupefied and didn't expect that, so she hurriedly
took the [German] women out of there, and then we took a shower.
That was the first time."

Danuta Wojnar-Górecka, a close friend of both Maria Zabianka
and Rachwałowa, believes that the prison rules concerning prisoners
sentenced to death were rigid; that they did not allow them to have

any contact with other prisoners. "That order was strictly enforced, under harsh penalties. So, theoretically, it was totally impossible that Mandl and Rachwałowa could shower together."

However, as Danuta later noted, "their case was extraordinarily exciting for the prison's personnel, especially for Kunda, the chief female guardian, that one cannot exclude any dis-subordination to this rule on her part. It would be for her a 'once in a lifetime' unforgettable spectacle. So, she might take that forward, be [at] risk of violating this rule, and let them shower together. But that is a supposition."

Corroborating testimony has emerged in the years since Rachwałowa's account was published. Various other people remember hearing about the incident at the time, thus precluding the assumption that Rachwałowa made the story up in her later years.

Hanna Wysocka overheard a group of friends, which included Rachwałowa and Zaba, talking about the incident in early 1948. In 2004, when she told this story, Hanna's voice became more tense and stressed. "I heard she forgave them—in any case, I was very upset about it. I think she forgave them and I was very surprised. So she [Rachwałowa] was talking about it in the cell, with the pack of women, right after it happened."

It makes sense that Mandl would identify Rachwałowa as a person to whom she would want to apologize. Rachwałowa was one of the most recognizable ex-prisoners from Auschwitz, and she had many interactions with Mandl in the prison; from encounters in the hall, to insults spoken through the door every time Rachwałowa passed Mandl's cell.

Danuta Mosiewicz-Mikusowa, the young woman who had been aided by Rachwałowa in Birkenau, also ended up in Montelupich. She remembers an incident, after both Rachwałowa and Mandl had been sentenced to death, in which one of the young female guards came to Rachwałowa and said, "Look Rachwałowa, you know German and there are German women and I cannot communicate with them." So Rachwałowa was taken to their cell, and when she saw Mandl, she greeted her with the same words that Mandl had used to the women in the camp: "You shit," "You dirty Slavic pig," and "You dirty commode!"

Danuta related that when Rachwałowa came back to their cell she started crying because she was so ashamed of her own behavior. She said, "I am sentenced to death. She is sentenced to death, so in the face of death I shouldn't have behaved like this because I am a practicing Catholic."

Danuta also remembered that shortly thereafter a guard came to Rachwałowa and said that Mandl would soon be executed and that she was requesting Rachwałowa, *especially* Rachwałowa, to go and meet with her. So he took her to the bath. Afterward, Stanisława told her friends that Mandl spoke these words: "Ma'am, I am sentenced to death. And just today I realize that I deserve it—that I deserve to die. Can you forgive me all the evil that I have done?" And Rachwałowa said, "I forgive on behalf of all women prisoners."

Afterward, as they were talking, Rachwałowa asked Danuta if she would have forgiven Mandl. When Danuta replied that she *did* forgive Mandl, Rachwałowa said, "So you do forgive me because I forgave her on behalf of everybody?" Danuta responded, "Absolutely. What kind of faith would you have if you didn't forgive?" And Rachwałowa said, "Well, because some other women held it against me that I forgave her on behalf of everyone. Someone said, you can forgive in your own name but not on my behalf."

When asked in 2005 if she trusted Rachwałowa's story and found her a credible witness, Danuta responded with an emphatic "YES!"

CHAPTER 100

Remorse

THE QUESTION THAT LIES AT the center of the shower room incident is whether Mandl truly felt remorse for her crimes and accepted responsibility for her actions. In her first year at Montelupich, she certainly did not.

However, after the death sentence and denial of the pardon, Maria cried, prayed in her cell, and withdrew into herself. Sixty years later Zofia Cykowiak, the survivor of the women's orchestra who attended Mandl's trial, still struggles to understand her behavior. On one hand she cites Mandl's cruelty, and on the other—her sensitivity towards Alma Rosé. "Her behavior makes me think that she had to experience very deeply that period, to think it over and draw some deep conclusions. The fact that she stayed in the courtroom on the break when the others left made a deep impression on me. I don't know how deep but some reflection on summing up her life towards herself and towards God [must have taken place]."

Raised from birth as a Catholic, regardless of the ebbs and flows of commitment to her faith during the Nazi years, Maria would have been taught certain theologies. As paraphrased many years later by Sister Ortrudis, the head of the convent where Maria attended school, the tenets of the faith Maria was taught are that mankind was not created as an existentially evil creature but that everyone is born with original sin. Therefore, all are vulnerable and susceptible to evil.

However, all sinners can be redeemed through Christ, and there is nothing that cannot be forgiven if the person asks for it and properly repents the evil that they have done. The scope of forgiveness is in accordance with the scope of remorse and love, not according to the magnitude of the crime.

Ortrudis believes that when Maria realized how severely she had sinned she saw her execution as penance, as an earned punishment, although there was not much time for penance left to her. "God alone knows the background and heart of man down to its root; however, he also has the power to free people—Maria would have been able to experience that in prison. For that reason, she was once again able to pray, to show remorse."

In less mystical terms, psychologists John Grotgen and Fay Altman believe that during Maria's life and her time in the camps she "doubled." Doubling, in psychological terms, is extreme compartmentalization used for survival. "This is not the same as a sociopath—it is a created self; you become that character—like an actor. But when doubling wears off, what then? The re-coming together would be a tough process."

CHAPTER 101

Hanging, by
Rope, Until Dead

*The Camp's Oberaufseherin Maria Mandl cynically and with
delight watched the deadly processions as thousands of people
walked towards the gas chambers... I remember her always
well-combed blond head, set on a shapely though short neck.
Could she know that soon, on this well-groomed neck, in nearby
Krakow, they would put the rope?*
—Kazimierz Piechowski, Bylem Numerem
(I Was a Number)

It is an odd thing to watch a hanging... Even with the comforting
buffer of time and old-style black-and-white photography, even
knowing that in these cases the punishment is well deserved, the act
of watching someone's life come to an end while you're comfortably
seated in a theater viewing room seems both wrong and a little absurd.

We settle ourselves into a dark and cool hall at the film archive
in Warsaw. The facility has footage of several executions of Nazi
criminals. Later research has revealed that these hanging videos, labeled as coming from Montelupich, were in fact filmed at Mokotow
Prison in Warsaw. Nonetheless, the hanged men were also perpetrators of the Holocaust, and although no video or photographs have
yet surfaced of Maria's execution, it seems a safe assumption the process was similar at Montelupich.

The Warsaw executions took place in a brick courtyard. There is a single gallows, with five steps leading to the top. The smallish structure, essentially a wooden box with a trapdoor, is supported by a large sawhorse on each end. Gallows in postwar Poland were often portable like this, stored and then reassembled as needed.

The executioner is a burly man in uniform. He holds a rope and wears a disconcerting black mask that looks like a harlequin. All the executioners and their assistants are wearing masks. There is some snow on the grounds and the building eaves; it looks cold. The witnesses wear heavy overcoats, and guards wear heavy uniforms with black belts and prominent buckles. A person reading the sentences stands to the left of the gallows with a sheaf of papers and addresses the accused, who stands facing it. The people around him salute.

The prisoner has his arms tied behind his back and is directed up onto the gallows. The noose is coarse rope, narrow. There are two executioners—one to put the noose around his neck, one to pull the cord. Despite the cold neither man is wearing gloves. There is a kind of a grate behind the gallows which they kick a few times to release the catch. The man falls quickly and it appears death is almost instantaneous. His hands flex a little as he dies. Strangely, there doesn't seem to be obvious trauma as his life is taken. The executioner continues holding the rope. From the background three men come up. As the body is released, they catch the dead weight. Five soldiers gather around and throw the man facedown onto a stretcher without ceremony.

The line of condemned prisoners continues and the men appear calm, almost drugged.

These executioners are good at their job; the process is very fast, very efficient. Perfunctory. More bodies are thrown onto the collection stretchers, some faceup, some facedown, like garbage.

Clinical descriptions of hangings provide distance, and detail. When a person is hanged, their weight causes strangulation, cutting off oxygen. The face goes blue, the tongue sticks out, many people lose control of bladder and bowels, men can ejaculate.

During the Nuremberg executions it was noted that although hanging does not immediately kill a person, if done properly the person loses consciousness when the rope snaps his or her neck. "Complete cessation of his heartbeat, and the official determination of death, occurs within 8–12 minutes after he drops. During that time he does not gasp or choke; he may have bitten off his tongue and lost control of his bowels when his neck snapped, but he would not be aware of either."

Any extra suffering was considered just in the case of the SS prisoners, and the hangman would often deliberately prolong the process by regulating the height and placement of the rope. With a longer drop, which happens faster, the neck breaks and the person dies almost immediately.

CHAPTER 102

Site of Execution

*We never cared to get some more information where the execu-
tion took place. As a matter of fact, we did not care; we had our
own colleagues sentenced for death; our own interrogations and
horrors to contemplate.*

—DANUTA WOJNAR-GÓRECKA

IN THE YEARS AFTER THE Auschwitz staff was hanged, there has
been dialogue and disagreement about where the executions
took place. Undoubtedly, planning and carrying out the hanging of
twenty-one people, and then dealing with multiple bodies, was a logistical challenge.

The most logical site, of course, would have been on the grounds
of Montelupich Prison. However, as late as 2005, prison officials
shared a clearly doctored document stating that Maria Mandl's execution had taken place at another prison, on Senacka Street, across
town from Montelupich.

After the war, with feelings running so high in Poland, there was
a great deal of interest in punishing the Nazi perpetrators and, for
some, in doing it publicly. Before the war the death sentence was
often executed simply, with just a few people in a closed setting.
After the war there was a decree set up by the Supreme National
Tribunal which allowed such executions to be done in public. The

underlying principle was to give survivors satisfaction by watching the death of the people who had wronged them.

In the Krakow area the only public execution was that of Auschwitz *Kommandant* Rudolf Höss, which took place on the grounds of the camp. However, a large trial of staff from the Stutthof camp in 1946 resulted in a mass execution in Gdańsk on July 4 of that year.

This very public set of hangings was, in a way, a collective catharsis. People had seen so much during the Occupation and war. Every family had had someone killed, murdered, who fought on the war front, was detained in a concentration camp; if not their family, then friends and neighbors. To go and watch the Nazis being punished was the thing to do, even with your children. Additionally, the country was in ruins, housing was scarce, people didn't know whom to trust. There was no television, and even if someone had a radio, hearing an execution would not be the same.

Different sources speculate that the number of attendees was approximately 250,000 for the Gdańsk executions. The crowd roared, mostly women who were screaming "For our husbands! For our children!"

There were some unfortunate side effects to this very public spectacle of revenge. Children started hanging their toys, and there were cases where one child hanged another after seeing a public hanging. Also, the crowd swarmed the bodies after the hangings and began trying to pull those bodies apart—"pulled from the legs and tackle them to pieces. So [the officials] took down the bodies, put them on a car, and drove away."

As a result, authorities decided to stop public executions, and by 1947–48 such violent feelings had subsided somewhat. Perhaps this is why it is so difficult to determine today where the hangings of Maria and her colleagues took place, and why there is still obfuscation.

Logically, it does not make sense that the large number of people to be executed that day were transported to Senacka Street. As Danuta Wojnar-Górecka points out, "It would be an enormous expedition—over twenty Germans and lots of prison officials who were present at the execution out of curiosity."

Political prisoner Franciszek Oremus believed that the executions did indeed take place at Montelupich and notes that "discrepancies in the accounts of the execution location [were] common in the Communist period. The Communist authorities would keep the public informed of one thing, and then do something else and keep it secret to cover their tracks."

Polish historian Stanisław Kobiela, who has undertaken extensive research on the Nazi prisoners held in Poland, feels certain that the hangings of the Auschwitz staff took place in a small building in the courtyard of Montelupich.

As the day of execution approached, preparations ramped up. The planned executions were to follow a set schedule and protocol. Executioners were hired and brought to Montelupich. Several accounts note that one of the executioners was a dwarf. "He had crossed eyes and because of his low self-esteem, he was doing the job—as executioner." Hannah Wysocka remembered him well. "And there was a dwarf, a very disproportionate body, the head, the legs, you know, he was said to be for the removal of the stool from below the feet, so when he appeared there, it was known, not when, but that there will be a hanging."

Another of the executioners brought in for the hangings was called "French," as he came from France. Other people working at the executions were guards from the prison. "They never looked into people's eyes."

CHAPTER 103

EGZEKUCJA

FATHER MARIAN STARK WOKE WITH a start on the cold morning of January 24, 1948, dread enshrouding his spirit even as a cold fog was enveloping a deserted street in the nearby Auschwitz death camp. The temperature that day registered twenty-six degrees Fahrenheit, with a mild wind and cloudy sky.

That same Saturday a local newspaper noted that a theater was performing the operetta *Modest Susanna*, Winston Churchill was weighing in on the politics of the African Republic of Benin, the Krakow Philharmonic was performing Brahms's First Symphony, and practical advice was being offered on how to cure syphilis.

Stark's personal calendar entry for the day notes simply, "Execution Auschwitz Perpetrators, 5:45-10:00 A.M., (7 Catholics)."

Although the sentenced prisoners were not told the exact day of the executions, they were certainly aware it was imminent. Maria had already asked the guard, *Pani* Jadzia, to be the one to search her for contraband before she was taken to be hanged. *Pani* Jadzia later noted sadly that she was off work that day and believes that Mandl was kept alone by herself the night before the executions. "Not with Brandl. Alone in her cell." Other sources state that Mandl and Brandl were still sharing a cell and that "Mandl was silent and paced, Brandl was terrified and cried."

Danuta Wojnar-Górecka remembered the day of the hangings vividly.

It was a cold, dark and inconspicuous morning. The bucket, full after a night's use, stood already at the door awaiting pick-up by the corridor cleaners. The emptying of the buckets always followed roll call immediately. (Roll call had been hurried that morning but no one noticed—that was not unusual.) No one picked up the bucket.

Only then did the women notice the deep silence on the corridor. No one shouted the usual morning orders while opening and closing the doors. No corridor cleaners were running back and forth between the cells and the bathroom with the buckets.

The rectangle of sky as seen through the top of the blinds on the windows grew paler. In recent days the deep blue of the sky was seen only well after breakfast.

The sky turned grey already and daylight began to penetrate the cell. Suddenly footsteps were heard below the windows. Through the little holes in the bottom of the iron blinds, pierced to allow rainwater out, the women saw a large group of people in military uniforms passing by. They didn't march, they just walked in pairs in complete silence. The hush which followed after they disappeared was even stiller than before. It seemed to permeate the prison walls.

No one talked. The women sat on the floor, leaning against the walls and bunks, some dozing, some praying, others just waiting passively with their eyes closed. The condemned prisoners in their cells must have been hyper-aware of this hush. Surely most suspected that their time had come.

CHAPTER 104

It Begins

Prison officials had been ordered to begin the hangings at 7:00 A.M. in small groups of five to six. Each condemned prisoner was assigned to a group according to the order of names put on the sentence. The first group consisted of Artur Liebehenschel, Maximilian Grabner, Hans Aumeier, Karl Möckel, and Maria Mandl.

As the guards collected the first group, Liebehenschel and Möckel were distressed but calm. Like Mandl, both men had spent the preceding weeks praying in their cells. All of the prisoner's hands were tied. Grabner, who had once enjoyed killing people for sport, kneeled before the officers trying to kiss their boots and begging for mercy. Maria Mandl was collected from her cell while Therese Brandl remained for the moment, paralyzed with fear.

The group was led down the stairs, along the side of the prison, and then across the courtyard to a small building where the gallows had been set up.

The executions were attended by the prosecutor, the prison warden, a court clerk, an interpreter, the prison doctor, various guards as "spectators," a Protestant minister, and Father Stark. The names of the executioners and their assistants, by custom, were known only to the governor of the prison.

At 7:09 the process began. The prisoners were guided to the gallows and placed underneath the noose. If they wished, they were then allowed a very brief conversation with either Father Stark or

338

the minister. The prosecutor read the verdicts and the rejection of the appeals which the interpreter translated into German. Nooses were placed around the necks of the condemned, the trapdoor was released, and the convicts were hanged. As they died, Father Stark and his colleague prayed for their souls.

Official procedures required that the condemned remain in the noose for fifteen minutes, after which Dr. Dormicki certified their death. Once that had happened, the bodies were removed.

CHAPTER 105

The Death of Maria

Maria Mandl was the last in her group to be hanged. Although we do not know the exact number of gallows utilized, we do know that between 7:08 and 9:08 a.m. all twenty-one condemned prisoners were executed and that a subsequent group of five to six prisoners was brought in about every thirty minutes. Since the bodies had to remain hanging for fifteen minutes, it is likely there were multiple gallows.

Maria probably witnessed the first executions. Jan Brandys, who spoke with the supervising prosecutor, stated that Liebehenschel yelled "Long live Poland," as the trapdoor was released. Brandys also noted that Grabner died badly and behaved like a coward, struggling, sobbing, screaming, and begging for his life. Nevertheless, he was forced to the gallows and hanged. At that point it is likely Möckel and Mandl were still living.

We do not know what transpired in the final exchange between Father Stark and Maria. Sister Ortrudis conjectures he may have used words Maria heard every time during confession in her youth. "Maria, Jesus waits for you, have faith that he redeemed you. In the name of all-mighty God, I proclaim that you are free from your sins."

The guard Hania shared an explicit account of the hanging with Hanna Wysocka. They had become friends, of sorts, and Hanna noted that Hania "was the one that I trusted the most. She didn't gossip." There was a tradition in Montelupich that every guard had to, at least once, observe an execution. Hania had been chosen to attend this hanging and stated that it was Maria Mandl who showed the most resistance.

> They had the biggest trouble with Mandl because they had to drag her through the courtyard. And all of those were drunk—the prosecutor was drunk as a skunk, and the guards, and the director too… Mandl had to be dragged, and the section guards who escorted them were laughing and ridiculing—they poked fun at her then, and they also had trouble during the hanging because she was struggling.

Hania described Mandl throwing her head around, but not her body, as the guards teased and taunted her. "Although the words were abusive and nudging and pushing a little, they were all drunk, [and] she just closed her eyes, didn't acknowledge it. And her last words were '*Polska żyje*' ['Poland lives'], not Long live Poland, but Poland lives. And then they hanged her."

We can only begin to conjecture what prompted Maria to end her life with the words "Poland lives." Perhaps it was a statement of sarcasm. Perhaps this cry was an expression of remorse for all the suffering Mandl had caused to the Polish people. Zaba always stated that in the last weeks of her life Maria did only two things: "She prayed a lot and tried to learn Polish." In the stress of the moment, Maria may have echoed what she'd heard Liebehenschel yell only moments before.

Perhaps, on a subconscious level, Maria repeated a cry that was heard many times at the black execution wall of death in Auschwitz I. There, the courtyard was located next to the administrative offices of Maria's early days in the camp. In addition, Mandl certainly overheard the Polish political prisoners sent to execution in Ravensbrück, who, "without exception, died shouting, 'Long Live Poland!'"

Whatever their inspiration, Maria's last words were just that and her execution by hanging was completed at 7:32 A.M. Maria Mandl was dead at the age of thirty-six.

CHAPTER 106

Sentence Complete

B Y 9:00 A.M. ON JANUARY 26 all of the Auschwitz criminals had been hanged. Prison officials signed reports certifying the deaths while news of the completed executions spread quickly through the prison grapevine.

Danuta Wojnar-Górecka remembered the aftermath.

> The glow of the day mixed unpleasantly with the electric light when it was turned on. Finally approaching steps broke the silence. Everyone rushed to the windows. The uniformed people passed by once again from the opposite direction, only the line was much shorter than before.
>
> In a few minutes life returned to the prison. "Anna" [the wardress] opened the cell, face pale grey, terror in her eyes. "The Germans were hanged. I saw it." Her statement was met with silence.
>
> "It got so cold. If I knew I wouldn't have gone. It was awful." She stood there uneasily...Someone asked "It took a long time?" "Oh yeah, 22 of them. It took a long time. Oh God, I'm sick of it." That's all she said.
>
> Breakfast wasn't served that day.

CHAPTER 107

Aftermath

I was not interested in the trial and did not attend. [After-ward] I did not go to look at her body which was, after the execution, brought to the anatomical laboratory at our Medical Academy. In spite of the fact that my colleagues tried to per-suade me to go and did go themselves.

—WANDA POŁTAWSKA, RAVENSBRÜCK LAB RABBIT

IN THE IMMEDIATE AFTERMATH OF the executions prison officials were left with twenty-one bodies. Protocol dictated notification to the registrar in Krakow that the sentences had been carried out. In addition, the registrar recorded their most recently known address. Maria's read simply "Village Münzkirchen, Upper Austria."

A decision was made to donate the bodies to the medical institute of Jagiellonian University for use by students in anatomy and dissection classes. Dr. Jerzy Ludwikowski, then a medical student, was at school when he heard that bodies of the war criminals had been delivered. "The truck which delivered the bodies was just a normal city truck and the corpses were thrown into it in a disorderly manner, unloaded with no ceremony and no respect. [The only proviso was] the number of bodies had to tally with the paperwork." Most camp survivors would have enjoyed the parallel between the treatment of

bodies at Auschwitz and the hanged bodies of their murderers care-
lessly dumped at the medical institute.

The common procedure for donated bodies was to preserve
them in formalin for several months to "harden them up." Afterward,
the bodies could last for years, discarded only when they had been
"used up," or dissected beyond repair. Ludwikowski noted, "At that
time, after the war, there was no shortage of corpses. They were
stored in a special room where they had tubs, containers, where they
kept the bodies in formalin."

Several medical students remember working on the corpses of
the Auschwitz staff. Mandl's body, especially, made a great impact.
The future director of the Forensic Medicine Institute, Professor
Zdislaw Marek, took his anatomy exam on Maria's corpse and em-
balmed the right leg. In addition to the medical students at
Jagiellonian, art students from the Krakow Academy of Fine Arts
were taken to see the bodies. Budding sculptor Wojciech Plewiński
commented that when they entered a large hall full of tables he

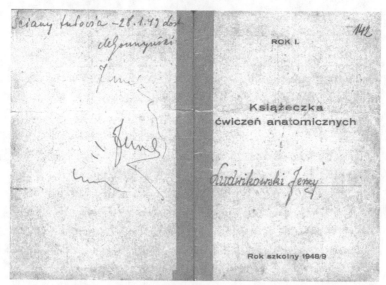

*Academic Report of Dr. Jerzy Ludwikowski, who, as a medical student, dissected Maria
Mandl's abdominal cavity after her hanging.* COURTESY OF DR. JERZY LUDWIKOWSKI..

noticed "the bull's neck of an SS man and a young, pretty woman, it was probably Maria Mandel [*sic*] who was the harlot from Brzezinka."

In June of 1949 Jerzy Ludwikowski took an anatomy exam on the well-preserved body and has vivid memories of his personal encounter with the dead Maria Mandl.

> I was very nervous, as was usual during exams. On the table was a corpse of a well-built woman of fantastic musculature. The examiner gave me the task of making an oval opening in the abdominal cavity of the femoral artery. I focused on the task and obviously didn't look at the deceased. I would have failed the exam if not for the examiner who said, "Here you can cut deeper, you certainly can see what thick fatty tissue she has?" So I went that direction and I succeeded ideally. I passed the exam with the mark "B."
>
> As I was leaving the room Staszek entered it. Dr. G, who was a friend of his and a social acquaintance of mine, asked me if I knew on whom I had taken the exam? I was surprised by the question and looked at him in astonishment. Then he said, "You cut the commanding officer of the Oświęcim camp."
>
> I can't remember if he mentioned her name or just the function. I was still stupefied by the exam and his answer surprised me, even shocked me, because I could remember from the Auschwitz trial this awful although very pretty woman—Mandl—whose criminal acts froze blood in the courtroom. In the fall of 1947 [I] had gone several times to see the trial and knew someone who got us free passes. I was there during the announcement of the death sentences and Dr. G knew that, so perhaps that is why he asked me such a question.
>
> The door to the dissecting room was not closed, or perhaps Dr. G had not closed it on purpose. I took a more careful look at the body. Krupa was doing something to it

but I could see the whole body. Yes! It was the same Maria Mandl! I had no doubts.

Despite postmortem changes and the fact that the body had to be kept in formalin, she was not ugly. She had long hair, much longer than what I remembered from the trial. She even had eyebrows and eyelashes. Her neck was uncovered so I saw how she died because on her neck there was a deep, clear trace of the crease after the hanging.

Maria Mandl's body remained in one piece and despite the effects of the formalin, each muscle of the body could be well seen. From that point of view, she was a fantastic didactic exhibit for the medical students.

After the exam I talked to Staszek Krupa, who used some terse epithet to express his recognition for the anatomical build of the deceased.

In later years, scholars questioned whether students like Ludwikowski could really have worked on Mandl's body as late as 1949, well over a year after her execution. A forensic physician confirms this was indeed possible. "It's normal practice that before a student can work on a body, it has to stay in formalin for a few months and only then can you work on it. That confirms that the doctor who said he did the exam on Mandl could indeed have done so!"

This doctor's manner is forthright; he seems bemused by our quest for information. He is enthusiastic about his specialty, and knowledgeable.

We meet on a gray and rainy morning, which seems appropriate given that the topic of our conversation is hanging. He remarks at the outset, commenting as an aside, that one of the notable manifestations of a hanged body is a slight odor of breath and that it was long a common practice at the medical institutes to use bodies not claimed by families or other people as material for students and other people to develop their dissection skills and extend their knowledge of the human body. During and after the war, that was naturally extended to the surfeit of bodies that were "created" from executions.

He notes that the Forensic Institute didn't need bodies from executions since their students already had access to a wide variety of bodies from accidents, murders, natural deaths, etc. However, the anatomy institutes needed large numbers of bodies. "Nowadays we don't use corpses anymore, we have computer programs, models, but in those days that was the only way we could teach future doctors anatomy."

Corpses were kept in coolers, and then, for the next two to three years, were used for anatomy classes. "Bodies were dissected to such an extent that sometimes they would cut off an arm, so that was just an arm separately, so it also could have happened that one corpse had four different people with four different parts of the body. After a year or two such bodies were not fit for further dissections. And then they were buried in the cemetery."

As we speak, sirens wail continually in the street, providing a suitable backdrop for our conversation.

The author mentions that when we watched the hanging videos from the Warsaw film archive, the prisoners seemed dazed, almost unaware; also that two guards from the prison believe the condemned prisoners were given sedatives before execution. The doctor adamantly states that tranquilizers were *never* given to the condemned prisoners.

"On the contrary! The heart of the matter pertaining to the executions for those sentenced to death, was that the sentenced person had to be *fully* aware that he was going to die. To such an extent that, for instance, if the sentenced person got sick then they would heal him first [before execution] so that he was fully aware of what was going to happen."

We view some archival photos of hanged prisoners. The rope creases in the necks are brutal and uncompromising. Concluding our interview, we thank the doctor and emerge into a rainy day, filled with thoughts of the Nazi perpetrators and the final retribution taken against them.

CHAPTER 108

Certificate of Death

IN AUSTRIA, AT THE END of the war, Maria Mandl was listed as missing. At the request of the public prosecutor's office in the Ried am Inn district, she was officially declared dead by the district court in 1975, with an arbitrarily assigned death date of December 31, 1944.

The court, after consultation with the International Tracing Service in Arolsen, announced "that Maria Mandl was admitted to a German concentration camp in 1939 and since then there has been no sign of life. The circumstances under which Maria Mandl went missing result in ... a high probability of her death."

To the outrage of survivors who discovered this document some years later Maria Mandl, the perpetrator, had now in the eyes of this court become a victim of the National Socialist regime.

The mayor of Münzkirchen defended the initial death certificate, stating that the local office had released that document after consultation with the Arolsen center. "I hope that I have helped you better understand the history of this death certificate."

After action by the Austrian Mauthausen Committee (MKÖ) in 2017, the record has now been corrected. "It is unacceptable that the justice system would support the falsification of history with this record" said Robert Eiter, a committee board member. "Real victims of concentration camps, many of whom are still alive, feel humiliated by the fact that the Nazi executioner is depicted as one of them."

Part Eight

CHAPTER 109

The Accounting

May the general public simply go on seeing me as the blood-thirsty beast, the cruel sadist, the murderer of millions, because the broad masses cannot conceive the Kommandant of Ausch-witz in any other way. They would never be able to understand that he also had a heart and that he was not evil.

—Rudolf Höss, *Kommandant* of Auschwitz,
WRITTEN SHORTLY BEFORE HIS EXECUTION

War makes murderers out of otherwise decent people. All wars. And all decent people.

—Ben Ferencz, prosecutor, Nuremberg Trials

Nils Christie was a longtime scholar of the perpetrator mindset. Beginning in 1960 Christie engaged in ongoing discussions with Polish criminologist Stanisław Batawia, who had spoken to several Nazi perpetrators before their executions. The two men soon realized they had several common experiences. "First, neither of us had met any monsters from the camps. Bad news for those hoping to find beasts behind the atrocities, by and large they are not there." On the hangings of many of these perpetrators, Christie commented simply "With closeness to the atrocities, it was revenge that was asked for, not analysis."

James Waller and Christopher Browning, two of our foremost contemporary scholars on the nature of evil, note that there is still a prevailing assumption that evil people are somehow "different" or flawed. They rightfully ask why extraordinary evil is considered aberrant or abnormal, when it has been a constant presence within our species throughout time.

The Münzkirchen community had long suspected what Maria was doing during the war. Maria herself flaunted those choices when she returned home for visits in full uniform, accompanied by SS officers in a fancy black car. At the same time, people were afraid to speculate too openly. "During the war nobody dared to say a SINGLE word! Because, if you talked too much, off you went!"

After the war, townspeople learned of Maria's arrest through the local grapevine. In subsequent months, as she was detained first in Germany and then in Poland, more news filtered back into the insular community.

Like most small towns Münzkirchen had a designated "movie theater," or rather, a dimly lit small hall with chairs in it. Irmgard Hunt, who lived in a similar small town, remembers that "Preceding every show was *Die Deutsche Wochenschau*, a weekly newsreel, which always began with a short, punctuated melody, that I remember today and that brings up—though much faded—images of soldiers and ravaged battlefields." Hunt notes that these newsreels were often followed by a lighthearted, fluffy feature film with a happy ending.

A *Wochenschau* featuring Maria's capture and extradition by the Allied Forces was shown repeatedly in Münzkirchen. "It ran for four weeks! Lasted three to four minutes and was shown before every film. After the *Wochenschau* then people began to talk, but no one really knew anything."

While some people in the community struggled to understand, many others concentrated on building a new life, free of the past. "After the war there was so much depression and so much pain in every family. Nobody wanted to talk about it. Everybody was working for a new life and leaving [the past] behind."

Several families felt a great sense of loyalty to Franz Mandl, who was known for his kindness and philanthropy toward the local poor. During the war Franz had always helped large families who could not afford shoes for all of their children, by scraping up some extra leather and making them shoes. Leather was strictly regulated so this was officially forbidden. "During the war years, he really helped families get through by making these shoes."

Neighbors remember that Maria's father suffered greatly over what had happened. "He really had it very hard. He couldn't get over it … Everybody kept kind of quiet because the family—and the sisters and the brother—were very decent, honored, and respected people; good people and good Catholics."

When Franz Mandl died in 1967, some twenty years after Maria's execution, over a thousand people attended his funeral—a very visible sign of the great respect with which he was viewed in the small community.

CHAPTER 110

The Family

I never told my relatives anything about Auschwitz, it was too awful. For 25 years I received three letters from my old father, one from my sister at the end of August 1946, sent to the camp at Ludwigsburg. I tried to write here, no answer up to now. My life consisted only of worrying and sorrow.
　　　　　—MARIA MANDL, IN MONTELUPICH

There are only empty envelopes. She was a Geheimnistrager—a person with secrets . . .
　　　　　—MÜNZKIRCHEN CITIZENS

A SOCIOPATH CAN BE DEFINED as someone who has a lack of conscience, empathy, or remorse. Maria Mandl, although guilty of terrible acts, also showed empathy and compassion toward her family, especially her father and sisters, and to her friend Margit. This is the difficult crux of trying to understand her life and actions. Maria was not a monster, although she committed monstrous acts. Her very humanity complicates our understanding.

Maria's relatives too struggled to comprehend. "The entire family does not understand how Maria followed such a path. They were down to earth, they were Catholic, the father was a Christian man. The family would like to know themselves how it all happened."

Before Maria's mother died in 1944, "she went to Mass every day…
This was unusual because you went to church on Sunday but not
every day. Her mother went to Mass EVERY day!" Already frail
from her nervous condition, "she really suffered by her daughter
being a part of the Nazi Party."

Maria had placed her sister in an incredibly difficult situation
when she appeared after the war asking for sanctuary. But Anna
loved Maria and felt she had to help.

When the children of Maria's brother and sisters were growing
up, their grandfather, Maria's father, never spoke of their aunt. He
simply taught them through his example, and when he believed in
something, he stood up for it. He did not gossip. "At that time men
were very hard and they had to work such a hard life. They did not
openly show kindness, love, and affection; and yet—all the grand-
children felt that anyway. When we spoke to other people in the
village, people told us that Maria was very sensitive and had feelings for other people—no one could understand how she had
gotten into this."

Although Franz was notified that Maria had received the death
sentence, he was not advised of when or if the sentence was carried
out. Seeking to protect his other daughters as much as possible,
Franz traveled to Anna's farm and told her about the notification.
Anna was told to never say a single word to Maria's other sister, Aloisia (Loisi), about the specifics of Maria's probable death. They were
able to protect her somewhat since Loisi lived in Switzerland, and
at that time, the Swiss were very strict about letting letters in and
out. In his lifetime Maria's father never received definite confirmation of Maria's death.

In 1973 Maria's brother Georg died, and finally, on September 9,
1975, the death certificate for Maria was sent to Münzkirchen.

CHAPTER 111

The Father

*Franz Mandl was strict, open, fair, treated everybody equally,
and was receptive to new ideas. He was an honorable man.*
—MANDL EMPLOYEE

*Maria was very sad that her father still had to worry so much
about her in his older years. If it had been possible, she would
have undone everything for her father's sake.*
—MARGIT BURDA

MARIA'S FRIEND MARGIT TRAVELED BACK to Germany after her release from prison. The economy of the postwar years was bleak,
and she had no other option but to move back to her family home in
a tiny village. "I couldn't find work and found myself living with my
old, sick mother, miserably and pathetically." When Margit and Maria
had met for the last time in the prison, Maria had asked Margit to
travel to Münzkirchen and explain to her father her "*Leidenweg*—her
Path of Suffering." Due to her lack of resources Margit could not do
this in person, so in 1948 she wrote a letter to Franz Mandl.

Since Margit had left Krakow before the verdicts in the trial, she
did not know of the death sentence. She asked Franz if he had any
news of Maria and of how she was doing. Neither knew that Maria
had now been dead over eleven months. Margit told Franz that she

prayed for Maria and her family and sent greetings to all her relatives, especially her sisters.

> I was with Maria for two years, we shared our greatest sorrows and only a little joy, and only in such hours does one really get to know a person. I must state that Maria in EVERY way was a good comrade.
>
> I can maintain that everything that was said about her were lies and deceit.

Poignantly she concludes, "I am sending you a lock [of hair] which I cut from Maria with lots of loving greetings and kisses to her loving, little father."

Franz responded to Margit in the new year of 1949, in a letter dated January 10, Maria's birthday. Obviously suffering, he refers to Maria by the diminutive Mari. He has still not received official notification of her death. Franz asks Margit for information, cites his great grief and sorrow, and laments the fact that his child had to go through such a tragedy. He concludes that this state of fate has been a very severe burden and test for a father.

Margit remembers, perhaps, a few more letters but these and their content have been lost to history and memory.

Franz suffered Maria's death until the end of his own life. It is in her father's anguish, and loss, that we see most clearly Maria's humanity. The loss of what she could have been and the life she could have had.

His letter to Margit, in its entirety, is reprinted in translation below.

January 10, 1949

Dear Fräulein Burda,

For your letter from December 8, 1948, thank you so much. I am enclosing in this letter a few stamps so that you can sell them to a stamp collector and receive a little

something for your expenses, because at the current time
it is not possible for me to send money.

And now dear Miss Margit, I must tell you that the
only thing we know about Mari is what people tell us.
From the Urteil [judgment/sentence] I know that she was
sentenced to death. We know about this sentence but then
later heard that the people involved in the Auschwitz
Trial were not sentenced to death but to a long life in jail,
that the penalty was changed to life in prison.

Upon hearing this I wrote a letter to the Red Cross in
Berlin and to Mari, using her former address, but have received no answer. Do you have any information? I'm
asking you to inform me of what happened, if possible.
Even though I can see in advance that it would hurt if the
news is bad and would bring me great grief and sorrow—
that one of my children has to go through such a tragedy.
I would never have believed it. Our family goes back 250
years and up to the present day not a single person has
been on record for a crime or brought shame upon the
family. This state of fate is a very severe test and burden
for a Father...

Dear Fräulein, please send a description with the
truth and nothing but the truth. I am prepared to hear the
worst. If the news is bad, because she would suffer too
much [if she heard the truth], please send a letter to my
daughter who is married and lives near us saying that our
beloved Mari died a natural death and was not executed.
Please write in the same manner to my other daughter in
Switzerland, who is prepared to help her [Mari] in the future get back on her feet should she still be alive and have
a future.

This war has brought a lot of tragedy upon us and we
don't know how much more will come. There are about
800 refugees from Romania in our village—very, very decent people who have lost their home country. They are

in the Gemeinde [community]. They have lost all their possessions which they have built up over several hundred years. We also have five people living in our house, very good people, who are now hoping to immigrate to France.

I was just called to the telephone because I have to be ready to travel within 15 minutes and will not be back for a few days, therefore I am ending this letter. I will try to send you a package, if I receive permission for that, and am hoping and looking forward to receiving an answer from you.

I remain,

[Franz] Mandl

[P.S.] Please excuse the typewritten letter, but my hands are so shaky I am not capable of writing with the fountain pen anymore. And again, please accept my greetings and thanks.

CHAPTER 112

What Might Have Been

IN 1938, A YOUNG JEWISH girl was sent alone to America in a desperate attempt by her parents—who were killed shortly thereafter—to save her life. Although she did survive, the scars from that abrupt severing of home and family were profound. Decades later, she traveled with her adult daughter back to Germany to reckon with the past and see what her life would have been like had she stayed. To her astonishment, most of her classmates had never traveled outside of their town and most didn't have professions or jobs. Certainly, in contrast, she now had a better life, but it had come at a terrible cost.

Maria Mandl also paid a heavy price for a better life, although, totally unlike the young girl, her choices were voluntary. In 2005, when Margit looked back on her friendship with Maria, she stated: "I believe that Maria wanted a marriage and children if she were to come out of imprisonment. I don't think that she would have settled in Münzkirchen. Maybe she would have settled in a big city. I didn't allow myself to begin that kind of conversation with her. We knew that a terrible, tragic ending could be in both of our futures."

Maria Mandl's life journey and descent into depravity mirrors that of many perpetrators in the Nazi period. Maria, as she progressed through camp service, fully embraced this new life until it was simply too late, and she had done too much, for there to be any other way forward.

In prison, when reflecting on her past, Mandl stated that "my life led me on such a path of trial, tribulation and misfortune that I lost all my belief in the Almighty God. Since [the beautiful days of my childhood] I have been dogged by misfortune. There are few days where I can be happy."

And yet Maria persisted until the end of the war, to freely and willingly continue on the path she had chosen, seemingly without concern for the great suffering she was causing others. Orchestra member Anita Lasker-Wallfisch says simply, "She was a nobody. Suddenly she was a somebody. That explains it."

In Auschwitz, at the height of her power, Maria loved to ride a horse at twilight from the front gate at Birkenau to the crematorium. Galloping like a Valkyrie, sitting erect, head held high, she was confident in her authority and in the image she presented. Yet this was also the woman who came to the orchestra for comfort, for music to soothe her conscience, and to escape—on some level—the current reality of her life. Zofia Cykowiak later observed, "I was amazed and I would stand there and watch. And then I would ask, how is it possible? [softer] How is it possible?"

Who was the real Maria Mandl? On some level, both were.

Oskar Gröning, a bookkeeper at Auschwitz and one of Maria's colleagues, served three years in a British POW camp after the war. In 1985, after reading an account by a historical revisionist who claimed the Holocaust never happened, he was moved to speak out about the things he had seen. Gröning spent the next three decades of his life helping educate the next generations. In 2017 he was once again arrested, now presented as a kind of figurehead for all perpetrators of the Holocaust in a widely publicized trial, and was convicted for his camp service at Auschwitz. Before he died in 2018, Gröning shared his *Lebenslauf* (*Life's Journey*) with the author. This document is an unflinching account of his descent into the madness of National Socialism.

Gröning vividly describes his internal struggle once he realized and began to witness firsthand what was happening at Auschwitz/Birkenau. Raised and indoctrinated from childhood in the Nazi state,

Gröning felt trapped between the ideologies he was taught, and which were reinforced daily, and the physical evidence of atrocity appearing before his eyes. In later correspondence he stated that it was not as simple as being brave or being cowardly. "There was no starting point to be able to show courage from."

For Oskar Gröning, indoctrinated in that system, there was not. How many among us in similar circumstances, would have the strength, knowledge, and ability to initiate such a starting point?

And yet some people did find that starting point, that courage. When asked if it was possible for an *Aufseherin* to retain her job without brutality, Ravensbrück survivor Zofia Ciszek said, "Yes. Because not all of them were so cruel."

Maria, unlike many others, also had a normal upbringing and the additional example of her father, an upright, honest, and compassionate man.

Wanda Półtawska, one of the Ravensbrück Lab Rabbits, believes that "there is some good in every human being, no matter how bad he or she appears, and one must search for that good seed, however small, cherish it and help it to grow. We should never divide people into categories of good and bad. The dividing line between good and evil lies within ourselves, within each and every one of us."

Slavenka Drakulić, in her book *They Would Never Hurt a Fly: War Criminals on Trial in The Hague,* summarizes that "the more you realize that war criminals might be ordinary people, the more afraid you become. Of course, this is because the consequences are more serious than if they were monsters. If ordinary people committed war crimes, it means that any of us can commit them."

She was a nice girl from a good family.

Coda

BIRKENAU, TODAY. WIND BLOWING THROUGH the trees, leaves singing their own unique song in the wind. Birds trilling, chirping, constant. Green striped frogs, alert and watchful.

Auschwitz is alive as no place of death should be.

The orchestra block where music sounded is silent and crumbling. Only the footprint of the floor is visible, and the ochre-colored remnants of the brick stove. Dull green lichens cover the ground, not quite barren.

Maria's office is also gone, overgrown with just the faintest borders to show it ever existed. In winter the cold of the roll calls echoes still, marrow-deep, fathomless. Block 25 remains, haunted with ghosts of the women who suffered there.

Restless spirits stalk these grounds, forever in motion.

Eternal witness to a time when hate led the world, and the world followed.

Acknowledgments

ANY PROJECT THAT HAS SPANNED over two decades could not have
come to fruition without the help of many kind and sharing individ-
uals. It has truly taken a village.

For nurturing and supporting my early interest in music and the
Holocaust, I thank Dr. Benny Kraut. He was a kind and wise mentor
until his untimely death in 2008.

I am thankful for my dear friend and adopted family member,
Kurt Michaelis, an oboist in the Berlin Kulturbund Orchestra who
entered my life at the age of ninety-two. Kurt patiently answered
many questions about what it was like to work as an artist under the
Nazi regime and about his harrowing escape in the nick of time.
Born only a year after Maria Mandl, he was invaluable to me in deci-
phering her old-style German penmanship and aided with many
German translations. Kurt's oboe, which first brought us together, is
now on display at the United States Holocaust Memorial Museum,
where it has been viewed by over 47 million visitors.

John K. Roth has been a valuable mentor and constant supporter
of my work, as has Daniel Patrick Brown. I thank you both. I am honored to know Sara Lambert Bloom and grateful for her long-term
musical and personal mentorship.

For tirelessly sharing their insights, talents, and support, I thank
Gina Roitman, Jerry Eischeid, Michael Spremulli, and Luis Baerga.

Elizabeth Goode and Kenneth Kirk—I have cherished their dec-
ades-long friendship and am very grateful for their encouragement
and for their discerning and critical proofreading skills. I thank Karla
Ekholm, valued sounding board and unfailing aesthetic eye who,

despite being an exacting grammarian, continues to indulge my fondness for the Oxford comma.

I am grateful to my agent, Scott Mendel, who first saw the potential in this book and helped move it forward. I value his counsel and expertise. To my editor, Michaela Hamilton, I can only express voluminous thanks for her unwavering support and encouragement, her sage insights and advice, and her patience with the many details of what has often been an unwieldy project. Michaela, working with you has been a joy.

The completion of this book has required processing materials and interviews in at least eight different languages, and I could not have navigated these complexities without the help of several linguists. Thank you, Elana Keppel Levy, Anja Strnad, Daniel Richwien, and many others. Special thanks to Eva Kalousova for her help in the Czech Republic, and to Gabriele Stellmacher, who always aided me in finding just the right shade of meaning in German and who unsparingly gave of her time and expertise, often at very short notice. Gabriele—thank you.

I remain inspired, and humbled, by the extraordinary survivors who shared their stories. From them I learned about true courage and resilience. Special thanks must be given to Zofia Cykowiak, luminous spirit and compassionate soul, who bravely shared her memories—often at great personal cost. I am grateful for Helena Dunicz Niwińska and her fierce quest for truth, who held me to a high standard and eventually shared the softness underneath; Hanna Wysocka awed me with her courage, grace, and strength; and I was honored to know Danuta Wojnar-Górecka, who allowed me to accompany her on a difficult journey of remembrance.

Special thanks must also go to the surviving members of the Auschwitz-Birkenau women's orchestra who spoke of their direct experiences with Mandl. I am also most grateful to the sons of three of those musicians—Philippe Kahn, Olivier Jacquet, and Arie Olewski—for sharing memories of their mothers and for their continued support.

For all the others who shared, I am beyond grateful and will do everything in my power to make sure your stories are remembered and honored.

For the citizens of Maria's hometown, Münzkirchen, thank you for welcoming me into your community and sharing your memories. You have added an important dimension to Maria's story.

Stanisław Kobiela was an important influence during my early forays into Poland, generously and selflessly sharing information, contacts, and advice. He became a friend and I truly miss his presence in this world.

Oskar Gröning was a valuable link in my understanding of the nature of evil and the perpetrator mindset. From the beginning of our acquaintance, Herr Gröning fully accepted responsibility for what he had done during the war and unflinchingly answered even the most invasive of questions. Entering into the last years of his life, he did everything in his power to educate younger generations about his experiences and to counteract the Holocaust deniers. "I saw everything," he later wrote. "The gas chambers, the cremations, the selection process. One and a half million Jews were murdered in Auschwitz. I was there."

I could not have told the second half of Maria's story without the immense contributions of Margit Burda, Maria's friend. She never knew the "Auschwitz Maria" and, from her experiences, loved Maria as a warm and kind soulmate. Her testimony, more than anything, illustrates the dichotomy between good and evil present in all of us.

I have immense respect for and appreciation of members of the Mandl family, who graciously invited me into their homes and unstintingly shared memories of their childhood and of Maria. They vividly remember the anguish of Maria's parents and siblings when her personality transformed and have showed great courage and commitment in allowing me to tell her story fully. I thank them from the bottom of my heart.

For my liaison in Austria, Eva Riedler, I owe an immense debt of gratitude. Eva worked tirelessly over several years to help investigate every possible angle of Maria's early life. She was indefatigable and always there when I needed her most. Thank you, my friend.

I could not have told this story without the constant help and support of my "Polish sister," Lidia Jurek. Who could have envisioned when I started this journey that I would find such a wonderful friend and colleague? Lidia's brilliant mind, curiosity, tenaciousness in helping me explore every lead in Poland, and constant good humor sustained me during challenging times. She is truly a kindred spirit and I am so very thankful for her presence in my life and for her help with this project.

My faithful furry writing companions, especially my heart-dog Wolfie, provided many hours of support and kept my head in a good place when I became overwhelmed with the darkness of Maria's story.

Finally, for my husband Charles, I can only express the greatest of thanks. Charles has been steadfast in his support, tolerating many years of a distracted wife who exceeded by far any normal stereotype of an absentminded professor. As my brain filled with the many aspects of Maria's story, I often missed most normal modes of communication. I couldn't have done this without him.

Notes

ABBREVIATIONS

AMSL	Museum Schloss Lichtenburg
APMO	Archivum Państwowego Muzeum w Oświęcimiu
ARa	Archiv Mahn und Gedenkstätte Ravensbrück
BAB	Bundesarchiv Berlin-Lichterfelde
BADH	Bundesarchiv-Zwischenarchiv Dahlwitz-Hoppegarten
IPN G	Instytut Pamieci Narodowej, Gdańsk, Poland
IPN W	Instytut Pamieci Narodowej (IPN), Warszawa, Poland
IPN Wi	Instytut Pamieci Narodowej, Wieliczka, Poland
IWM	Imperial War Museum, London, England
LUD	Zentrale Stelle der Landesjustizverwaltungen, Bundesarchiv, Ludwigsburg, Germany
MONTE	Montelupich Prison archives, Krakow, Poland
MÜNZ	Gemeindeamt Archiv, Münzkirchen, Austria
NARA	National Archives and Records Administration, Washington, DC
NAC	Narodowe Archivum Cyfrowe, Warszawa, Poland
ÖNB	Österreichische Nationalbibliothek, Wien, Austria
ÖST-WIEN	Dokumentationsarchiv des Österreichischen Widerstandes, Archiv, Wien, Austria
SNT	Supreme National Tribunal
USHMM	United States Holocaust Memorial Museum
YV	Yad Vashem, Israel
ZE-ZB	Ze Zbiorów Archivum, Państwowe w Krakowie
ZKM	Zgromadzenia Księży Misjonarzy, Krakow, Poland

PREFACE

his own heart, xiii: Aleksandr Solzhenitsyn, *The Gulag Archipelago 1918–1956* (New York: Harper & Row Publishers, 1973), 168.

PART ONE

Author's Note

The chapters about life in Münzkirchen during Maria's lifetime are an amalgam of multiple interviews undertaken with community members between 2004 and 2007. When several sources shared the same information, the citation will be credited as "Münzkirchen Community." For specific quotes, the individual person will be credited in normal format. A special thank-you to community members Alois Bauer, Kreszenzia Edelmann, Cäcilia Schmid Gaderbauer, Roland Habermann, Maria Höller, August Grundinger, Martha Leithner, Helmut Pfaffenbauer, Inge Reidinger, Franz Ruhmanseder, Alois Schiller, Father Friedrich Traunweiser, and Martin Zauner.

Chapter 1: Hometown

a good family, 3: Münzkirchen Community.

village of Münzkirchen, 3: Münzkirchen, Austria, Gemeindeamt. Archiv, church and baptismal records, May 2005.

"[time] of my [life]" 4: Maria Mandl statement, Archivum Państwowego Muzeum w Oświęcimiu (APMO); Proces Zalogi, t. 56a; ss. 96-139. Dpr-ZOd/56a; 98.

In 1947, while Mandl was being detained in the Polish prison Montelupich and at the urging of the investigating attorney, she wrote an account of her history and activities in the concentration camp system. Much of the account is an attempt at exculpation in view of her upcoming war crimes trial. Nonetheless, it provides valuable insights into her perspective at the time. This document will be referred to as "Mandl statement" in future citations. The original document is on file in Warsaw at the Institute of National Remembrance (Instytut Pamięci Narodowej), IPN.

There is an additional deposition which was taken on May 19 and 20, 1947, by the Committee for the Investigation of German Crimes on Polish Soil. This document will be referred to as "Mandl deposition" in future citations. Translations by Kurt Michaelis.

a nice scent, 5: Members of the Mandl Family, interview with Susan Eischeid, Schardenberg, Austria, May 17, 2006.

hamlet of Freundorf, 5: Pfarrkirche Maria Himmelfahrt church records, Münzkirchen, Austria, May 2005.

responsibilities of her life, 5: Alois Bauer and Roland Habermann, interview with Susan Eischeid, Münzkirchen, Austria, May 21, 2005.

Vervensach (nerve disease), 5: Mandl deposition, 19 May 1947.

"best on earth", 6: Mandl statement, APMO, 98.

with his neighbors, 6: Franz Ruhmanseder, interview with Susan Eischeid, Münzkirchen, Austria, May 21, 2005, and May 25, 2006.

"salted animal hides", 6: Helmut Pfaffenbauer, interview with Susan Eischeid, Münzkirchen, Austria, May 23, 2005.

"An honorable man", 6: Richard Högl, telephone interview, St. Florian/Schärding, Austria, May 17, 2006.

town band rehearsing, 7: Ruhmanseder interview, 2005.

Chapter 2: Childhood

during Maria's childhood, 9: Roland Haberman, "25 Jahre Hauptschule Münzkirchen." Institut für Ostbarische Heimatforschung (OÖ: Landesverlag Ried, 1975), 32.

than in his teaching, 9: Münzkirchen Community.

"hit the pupils!", 9: Ibid.

"'must be order!'", 10: Irmgard Hunt, *On Hitler's Mountain* (New York: Harper Collins, 2005), 122.

was still evident, 10: Mandl statement, APMO.

do chores, 10: Cäcilia Schmid Gaderbauer, interview with Susan Eischeid, Ficht, Austria, May 23, 2005.

"red-faced blond", 10: Ibid.

pig was slaughtered, 10: Ibid.

variety of subjects, 10: Münzkirchen Community.

sewing, crocheting, 10: Gaderbauer interview.

green paper cover, 10: Schulnachrichtenbuch für Schmid, Cäcilia. Schuljahr 1920, Münzkirchen, Austria.

sixty-six absences, 11: Gaderbauer interview.

to play with, 11: Ibid.

"never missed church!", 11: Ibid.

up the aisle, 11: Ibid.

shared communally, 11: Ibid.

who the spanker was, 11: Ibid.

"no games just exercises", 12: Ibid.

"**immodest clothing**", 12: "100 Jahre Festchrift Allg. Turnverein Münzkirchen 1881–
    1981," Dr. Josef Ratzenböck and Erich Slupetzky, Münzkirchen, Austria.
girls wore skirts, 12: Inge Reidinger, interview with Susan Eischeid, Münz-
    kirchen, Austria, May 25, 2005.
with a sailor collar, 12: "100 Jahre Festscrift," *Der Verein in Jahre 1929*, 29.
exit certificate, 12: Roland Habermann, Maetrikel Book, telephone interview
    via Eva Riedler, Münzkirchen, Austria, May 2005.
school for girls, 12: "Vom Wasserschloss zum Inselkloster," via Schwester Obe-
    rin Ortrudis Maier, Kloster der-Maria-Ward-Schwestern, Neuhaus
    am Inn, Germany, May 18, 2006.
privileged existence, 13: Oberin Ortrudis Maier, interview with Susan Eis-
    cheid, Neuhaus am Inn, Germany, May 18, 2006.

Chapter 3: Coming of Age

"**always a struggle**", 14: Kreszenzia Edelmann, interview with Susan Eischeid,
    Münzkirchen, Austria, May 25, 2005.
"**strength to work**", 14: Gaderbauer interview.
and children, 14: Gaderbauer interview.
"**it doesn't matter**", 15: Margit Burda, interview with Susan Eischeid, Munich,
    Germany, May 20, 2008.
"**preferable to none**", 15: Alison Owings, *Frauen* (New Brunswick, NJ, Rutgers
    University Press, 1999), xxix–xxx.
in Brig, 15: Mandl statement, APMO, 98.
otherwise simple town, 15: Brig / Switzerland Tourism, https://www.myswit-
    zerland.com/en/brig/html.
home until 1934, 16: Mandl statement, APMO, 98.
worked until 1936, 16: Deposition, Questioning of Maria Mandl, 19 May 1947. Mon-
    telupich Prison, Krakow. Recording Clerk: Krystyna Szymańska,
    Regional Investigating Judge: Jan Sehn, Prosecutor: Helena Turowicz.
yellow pus, 16: Members of the Mandl Family, May 2006.
filled with fluid, 17: Dr. Eugene LeBauer, interview with Susan Eischeid,
    Greensboro, NC, July 2007.
"**of a big ocean**", 17: Mandl statement, APMO, 99.

Chapter 4: Anschluss

torches and flags, 18: Martin Pollack, *The Dead Man in the Bunker*, trans. Will
    Hobson, (London: Faber & Faber, 2004), 84.
Hitler's expectations , 18: Franz Wallner, *Der Österreich-Anschluß 1938* (Öster-
    reich: Arndt), 22–23.

"Ein Führer!", 18: Pollack, 84. See also Wallner, 17–32.

gone to school, 18: 90 Jahre OÖ—Vocklabruck. *Rundschau,* 47 a / Sonntag, 23 November 2008, 8. Ed. Josef Ertl.

easterly direction, 19: "Schärding anno dazumel." Schärdinger-Zeitung, Nr. 122, Seite 22. Wirkl. Amstrat Franz Jäger (85), langjähriges Mitglied des OÖKB—Stadtverband Schärding.

I had forbidden, 19: Ibid.

surrender of Austria, 19: Ibid.

a few Communists, 19: The consensus in the town is that there were two major political parties, Nazi (variously described as Browns or Reds) and not Nazi (ÖVP). There were also a few members of the Communist party. Münzkirchen Community.

"Music from hell", 19: Habermann/Bauer.

Black, ÖVP, 19: Members of the Mandl family, 2005.

NOT Nazis!, 19: August Gründinger, interview with Susan Eischeid, Münzkirchen, Austria, May 25, 2005. See also Münzkirchen Community.

after the war, 19: Members of the Mandl family, 2005.

"coming into Austria", 20: Mandl family, 2005; Maria Krenn, Münzkirchen, meeting with Mandl family, 19 November 2006.

of the Nazi Party, 20: Bezirk Schärding 1945 "Ende und Neubeginn." Unterrichtspraktischen Veröffentlichung, Nr. 62. Des Pädagogisches Institut des Bundes in OberÖsterreich, Eigenvervielfältigung Linz, 1986. Roland Habermann, Johann Höller, and others.

in her success, 20: Münzkirchen Community.

was thrown out, 20: Mandl statement, APMO, 99.

sort of post, 20: Evan Bukey, email correspondence, August 5, 2003.

to the ÖVP, 20: Münzkirchen Community.

damage his future, 21: Mandl statement, APMO, 99.

was unrequited, 21: Münzkirchen Community.

was a policeman, 21: Ibid.

before the Anschluss, 21: Martin Zauner, email correspondence to Susan Eischeid, November 4, 2022.

trouble continued, 21: Mandl statement, APMO, 99.

PART TWO

Chapter 5: Aufseherin

no way out, 25: Hans Münch, statement, witnessed by Auschwitz survivor Eva

Mozes-Kor, "Documenting the Gas Chambers at Auschwitz, 27 January 1995," http://Samilhistory.com/tag/hans-munch/.

become a nurse, 25: Mandl deposition, 19 May 1947.

for these positions, 26: Aleksander Lasik, "The Auschwitz Garrison, I.Women in the SS," Auschwitz 1940-1945, Volume I (Oświęcim: Auschwitz-Birkenau State Museum, 2000) 281.

difficult women, 26: Werner Dietrich, *Konzentrationslager Lichtenburg* (Leipzig: MEDIEN PROFIS, Förderkreis Schloss Lichtenburg, Prettin/Elbe, 2002), 64.

light physical work, 26: Irmtraud Heike, "*... da es sich ja lediglich um die Bewachung der Häftlinge handelt...,*" *Frauen in Konzentationslagern: Bergen-Belsen und Ravensbrück*, eds. Claus Füllberg-Stolberg et al. (Bremen: Edition Temmen, 1994), 232.

erected for prostitutes, 26: Monika Müller, *Die Oberaufseherinnen des Frauenkonzentrationslagers Ravensbrück, Magisterarbeit* (Brandenburg: Brandenburgische Ravensbrück, Gedenkstätten Sachsenhausen, Sammlungen, 2002), 48–49.

prostitute or "antisocial", 26: Klaus Drobisch, *Konzentrationslager Im Schloss Lichtenburg* (Cottbus: Kommission zur Erforschung der Geschichte der örtlichen Arbeiter—bewegung der Bezirksleitung Cottbus der SED, 1987), 68. See also Dietrich, 64.

criminal convictions, 26: Daniel Patrick Brown, *The Camp Women* (Atglen: Schiffer Military History, 2002), 16.

forty-five years old, 26: Simone Erpel, "Einführung," in *Gefolge der SS: Aufseherinnen des Frauen-KZ Ravensbrück* (Berlin: Metropol Verlag, 2007), 31.

overseer was 25, 26: Ibid.

or skilled, 26: Brown, 16.

the middle class, 27: Lina Haag, *Eine Handvoll Staub* (Frankfurt am Main: Fischer Taschenbuch Verlag, 1995), 149.

as the men, 27: Brown, 14.

lower-ranked female overseers, 27: Elissa Mailänder, *Female SS Guards and Workaday Violence* (East Lansing: Michigan State University Press, 2015), 3.

authority over prisoners, 27: Ibid, xiv.

"*streng aber gerecht*", 27: Mandl statement, APMO, 105.

Chapter 6: KZ Lichtenburg

"small gift items", 28: Barbara U. Cherish, *The Auschwitz Kommandant* (Gloucestershire: The History Press, 2009), 27.

trendy films, 28: Oskar Gröning, *Ein Lebenslauf: Dreißig Lebens-und Erlebensjahre Von 1921 bis 1951* (Schnerverdingen: 1996), 30.

"ideal concentration camp", 28: Lina Haag, *"Ankunft im KZ Lichtenberg,"* in Barbara Bromberger, Hanna Elling, Jutta von Freyberg, Ursula Krause-Schmitt, *Schwestern vergeßt uns nicht* (Frankfurt: VAS, Verl. Akad. Schriften, 1988), 40.

and putrefaction, 29: Dietrich, 70.

eight hundred inmates, 29: Drobisch, 65.

race and worldview, 29: Brown, 235.

and field caps, 29: Lasik, 283.

new environment, 29: Mailänder, 82.

may have had, 29: Ibid.

in the camp, 29: Mandl, deposition.

"I'm staying", 29: Karin Berger and Elisabeth Holzinger, Lotte Podgornik, Lisbeth Trallori (Hersg.), *Ich geb Dir einen Mantel, daß Du ihn noch in Freiheit tragen kannst. Widerstehen im KZ Österreichische Frauen erzählen* (Wien: ProMedia Edition Spuren, 1987), 136.

Chapter 7: A Good, Orderly Life

Good, Orderly Life, 30: Mandl statement, APMO, and Mandl deposition, 19 May 1947.

tubs for excrement, 31: Hans Hesse and Jürgen Harder, "Und wenn ich lebenslang in einem KZ bleiben müßte…," *Die Zeuginnen Jehovas in den Frauenkonzentrationslagern Moringen, Lichtenburg und Ravensbrück* (Germany: Klartext-Verlagsges, 2001), 92.

an extended period, 31: Ibid.

irrigation ditches, 31: Dietrich, 68.

hysterical broads, 31: Dietrich, 78. See also Drobisch, 83.

in the camp, 31: Dietrich, 67.

Chapter 8: Rein kommt Ihr alle

"wieder lebend raus", 32: Dietrich, 65.

and their dogs, 32: Lina Haag, *How Long the Night* (London: Victor Gallancz Ltd., 1948), 129–130.

Johanna Langefeld, 32: Mandl deposition, 19 May 1947.

"terrible things", 32: Dietrich, 64; Brown.

"come out alive!", 32: Dietrich, 65.

in and surrendered, 33: Michel Reynaud and Sylvie Graffard, *The Jehovah's Witnesses and the Nazis* (New York: Cooper Square Press, 2001), 76.

"dole out punishment", 33: Margit Burda, interview with Susan Eischeid, Munich, Germany, May 2007.
its nightly harvest, 33: Haag, "Spießbürger-Karrieren," in Bromberger, et al., *Schwestern vergeßt uns nicht*, 41.
sign of mistreatment, 33: Dietrich, 71.
desirable living quarters, 33: Ibid.
on no longer, 34: Haag, *How Long the Night*, 135.
handful of dust, 34: Dietrich, 71. See also Lina Haag, *Eine Handvoll Staub*.

Chapter 9: The Transformation

"us from killing?", 35: Karl Ove Knausgaard, "The Inexplicable; Inside the Mind of a Mass Killer," Letter from Norway, *New Yorker*, May 25, 2015 issue, https://www.newyorker.com/magazine/2015/05/25/the-inexplicable.
were rewarded, 35: Germain Tillion, *Frauenkonzentrationslager Ravensbrück* (deutsche Ausgabe Frankfurt, 2001; französische Originalausgabe Paris, 1973), 140.
of that training, 35: Brown, 18.
"to beat people", 36: Loretta Walz, *"Und dann kommst du dahin an einem schönen Sommertag," Die Frauen von Ravensbrück*, in Emilie Neu, *Zu Gott kann man Heil! Sagen, aber nicht zu Hitler* (Germany: Verlag Kunstmann Antje, 2005), 114.
the cells were, 36: Statement of Klara S (probably Schnippering although not clarified on the statement) from June 11, 1948, BADH, ZM 1636, A-3, Sheet 45.
given to sit, 36: Drobisch, 71.
durchgepeitscht, 36: Dietrich, 70.
mass of the others, 37: Oskar Gröning, email to Susan Eischeid, August 28, 2006.
presented to us, 37: Oskar Gröning, email to Susan Eischeid, April 21, 2006.
tendencies of a person, 37: James Waller, *Becoming Evil.* (New York: Oxford University Press, 2002), 29.
"culture of cruelty", 37: Ibid., 203.
her activities, 37: Ibid., 211.
may say so, 38: Hatzfeld, 22.
pleasantly easy, 38: Ibid, 25.
over the mind, 38: Ibid, 47.
squashing an ant, 38: Andrew Tilghman, "Encountering Steven Green," Outlook, *Washington Post*, July 30, 2006, B1. Green, the serviceman, was later charged with rape and brutal killings in Iraq.

PART THREE
Chapter 10: Ravensbrück

wondering, fearing, 41: Edgar Allan Poe, "The Raven," *Complete Tales and Poems* (New Jersey: Castle Books, 1985), 773.

by the lakebed, 41: Sarah Helm, *Ravensbrück* (New York: Doubleday, 2014), 3.

around the shore, 42: Ibid., 4

their business, 42: Corrie Ten Boom, *The Hiding Place* (New Jersey: Bantam Books, 1971), 189.

the location, 42: Ten Boom, 189.

in their kennels, 42: Gemma LaGuardia Gluck, *My Story* (New York: David McKay Company, Inc., 1961), 27.

camp street, 42: Helm, 4.

rabbits, 42: Helm, 5.

throughout the camp, 42: Ibid.

squawking parrot, 42: Helm, 75.

various birds, 43: Mandl statement, APMO, 101.

be moved into, 43: Ibid.

the male housing, 43: Mailänder, 84.

112 overseers, 43: Mailänder, 87.

laundry room, 43: Ibid.

with a child, 43: Simone Erpel (Hrsg.), in *Gefolge der SS: Aufseherinnen des Frauen-KZ Ravensbrück*; Jeanette Toussaint, *Nach Dienstschluss* (Berlin: Metropol Verlag, 2007), 97.

ironing, and mending, 43: Mailänder, 91–92.

live and work, 44: Erpel, Toussaint, *Nach Dienstschluss*, 89.

Chapter 11: Daily Life

in the sun, 45: Oskar Gröning, *Lebenslauf*, 81.

pistols, and whips, 45: Claudia Taake, *Angeklagt: SS Frauen vor Gericht* (Oldenburg: BIS: Bibliotheks-und Informationssystem der Universität Oldenburg, 1998), 32.

weapon, to kick, 45: Mailänder, 100.

initial work assignment, 45: Helm, 5.

brutal sadist, 000: Jane Bernigau, statement, witness questioning, 1 December 1968. LUD; Band II, Bl. 97 bis 245; 158.

"especially tortured", 45: Minnie Artner, statement, ÖST-Wien, 50.752, 541, Blatt 1.

affair with Kögl, 46: Armanda Larsch, statement, Frankfurt am Main 12 November 1973. LUD, 918/72, 385-392, seite 5, 388.

penalties increased, 46: Aleksandra Steuer, Deposition, Krakow, Poland, 20 August 1947. APMO, Proces zalogi, +57d, ss. 259-262 (432-435). D-Zod/57.1, nr. 20; 434/261.

resentments and conflicts, 46: Lasik, 283–284.

"not 100% SS", 46: Helm, 179

"disastrous confusion", 46: Helm, 179. See also Margarete Buber-Neumann, *Die erloschene Flamme* (Frankfurt: Langen Mueller, 1991).

a local school, 46: Helm, 179.

"well with Mandl", 47: Klara Pförtsch, statement, Frankfurt am Main, 5 September 1974. LUD, Band IV, Bl. 568; 4.

leather briefcase, 47: Eugenie Emma von Skene, Deposition No. 2, English translation, Ref. WO309/692, sheet 81961. Hamburg. See also Helm, 26. See also Hamburg, 8.7. 1948, TNA/WO 235-528, Bi. 91. First Ravensbrück trial, Hamburg, Germany, December, 1946-1947.

"No such love", 47: Zofia Kawińska Ciszek, interview with Susan Eischeid, Gdańsk, Poland, May 2005.

trial period, 47: Mailänder, 71. See also document from Ravensbrück concentration camp, regarding application of female camp guards, BA, NS/4/Ra.1

worked at Ravensbrück, 47: Erpel, *Im Gefolge der SS*; Toussaint, *Nach Dienstschluss*, 99.

"hit the prisoners", 47: Mailänder, 79. See also Statement by Hermine Ryan Braunsteiner, 20 August 1973; Düsseldorf, HStA Düsseldorf, Ger. Rep. 432 No. 193, p.54.

Chapter 12: The Visit

twenty below zero, 48: Helm, 64.

where she lay, 48: Ibid, 66.

caps, and boots, 48: Assembled Aufseherinnen at FKL Ravensbrück, January 1940 (ARa 1622); Himmler's inspection of the Aufseherinnen (ARa 1624).

Jehovah's Witnesses, 49: Helm, 69.

for these jobs, 49: Brown, 16

nearby estate, 49: Helm, 68.

"request to him", 49: Mandl statement, APMO, 138/105

by 4 months, 50: Helm, 69.

Chapter 13: "To work!"

The prisoner died, 51: Erika Buchmann, statement, 2 January 1965. ÖST-Wien 50-280, 119. Bericht 668, "Schwerin"

changed daily, 51: Irmtraud Heike, *Frauen in Konzentrationslager*, "... *da es sich ja lediglich um die Bewachung der Häftling*," 227.

"camp business", 51: Buchmann, 1.

"sand desert", 51: Minnie Artner statement, ÖST-Wien, 50.752, 541, Blatt 1.

extra overseer, 51: Heike, 227.

"the mare", 52: Ibid., 228.

Himmler promoted, 52: Ibid, 226.

necessary human guards, 52: Mailänder, 263. See also Höss, in Martin Broszat, ed., Kommandant in *Auschwitz. Autobiographische Aufzeichnungen des Rudolf Höss*, 17th ed. (Munich, 2000), 180ff.

with a dog, 52: Eugenie Emma von Skene, Deposition No. 2, English translation, Ref. WO309/692, sheet 81961. See also Nanda Herbermann, statement, Frankfurt am Main, 29 January 1974, LUD 4 Js918/72, 453-460, Seite 7/659. See also Johanna Baumann, statement, Frankfurt am Main, 5 March 1974, LUD 4 Js 918/72, 538-539, Seite 4/541.

on the throat, 52: Adele Obermayr, statement, Innsbruck, 30 April 1966, ÖST-Wien, Seite 1.

dog bites, 52: Katharina Zeh, statement, Frankfurt am Main, 7 June 1974, LUD 4 Js 918/72, 708-711, Seite 3/710.

something had happened, 52: Mandl statement, 108.

"anything, anymore", 52: Mailänder, 264. See also Hildegard Lächert, in Eberhard Fechner, *Norddeutscher Rundfunk: Der Prozess: Eine Darstellung des Majdanek-Verfahrens in Düsseldorf*, videotape (1984), part 2.

"sand digging", 53: Mandl, deposition, 19 May 1947.

"burying us alive", 53: Wanda Półtawska, And I Am Afraid of My Dreams, trans. Mary Crai. (New York: Hippocrene Books, 1964), 44.

from the lakeside, 53: Rochelle G. Saidel, *The Jewish Women of Ravensbrück Concentration Camp* (Madison: University of Wisconsin Press, 2004), 13.

and a jacket, 53: Minnie Artner, statement, ÖST-Wien, 50.752, 541, Blatt 1.

"feverish as well", 53: Loretta Walz, "*Und dann kommst du dahin an einem schönen Sommertag*," Die Frauen von Ravensbrück, 121., quoting prisoner Hanna Burdówna.

"'often works wonders!'", 53: Luise Mauer testimony; Jutta von Freyberg and Ursula Krause-Schmitt, *Moringen-Lichtenburg-Ravensbrück, Frauen im Konzentrationslager 1933–1945* (Frankfurt: VAS, 1997); Seite, 107.

"beat me then!", 54: Ciszek interview.

"for this work", 54: Minnie Artner, statement, Blatt 1, Blatt 3.

shoe factory, 54: Taake, *Angeklagt: SS Frauen vor Gericht*, 25–26. See also Minnie Artner, statement, Blatt 2.

Chapter 14: Leisure Time

their new jobs, 55: Jeanette Toussaint, *Nach Dienstschluss* (Erpel: Im Gefolge), 93.

local fairs, 55: Ibid., 91–92.

of the town, 56: Helm, 194.

from the crown, 56: Helm, 180. Interview with Edith Sparmann by Sarah Helm.

and a library, 56: Toussaint/Erpel, 92.

city life, 56: Mailänder, 90.

of the moment, 56: Wanda Półtawska, email correspondence with Susan Eischeid, June 18, 2004.

"few days earlier", 56: Helm, 196. Testimony of Maria Bielicka.

Chapter 15: Christmas in Ravensbrück

Christmas carols, 57: Ciszek interview.

winter solstice holiday, 57: Erin Blakemore, "The Nazis' War on Christmas," *HISTORY*, https://www.history.com/News/The-nazis-war-on-christmas, accessed 14 June 2020.

their families, 57: Helm, 135.

"our duties", 57: Półtawska, 51.

the camp, 57: Ibid., 49.

"noisy surroundings", 57: Ibid., 50.

"could not continue", 58: Ibid., 50.

beaten and killed, 58: Półtawska, email correspondence, 2004.

Christmas tree, 58: Erna Krafft, statement, Aurich, 4 March 1974, LUD, LKPA. Niedersachsen, Sonderkommission Z, 34-37, Blatt 4.

Chapter 16: The Prisoners

"no guilt!", 59: Ciszek interview.

a deterrent, 59: Helm, 89.

wild animals, 59: Ibid., 88. Testimony of Grete Buber-Neumann.

aggressive lesbianism, 000: Ibid., 89.

after curfew, 60: Lagerordnung Ravensbrück, in National Archives and Records Administration (NARA), RG 549, 000-50-11 Box 522, Folder no. 3, pp. 39-41.

"open air", 60: Mandl statement, APMO, 101–102.

exchange gossip, 60: Morrison, 116.

jangled our nerves, 60: Półtawska, *And I Am Afraid of My Dreams*, 83.

we were placed, 61: Jane Bernigau, LUD, 2 December 1968, Band II, g7-
245,409AR-Z3g/5g SH2; 155.
were eight thousand, 61: Mandl statement, 109

Chapter 17: The Bunker

behaving insolently, 62: Mandl statement, 19 May 1947, 4.
of the camp, 62: Mandl statement, 103.
Johanna Langefeld, 62: Helm, 66.
"the garden", 63: Countess Karolina Lanckorońska, Michelangelo in Ravensbrück,
    trans. Noel Clark (Cambridge MA: Da Capo Press, 2007), 216.
airy cells, 63: Mandl statement, 103
"bad bed-making", 63: Klub Ravensbrück, Statement, Warszawa 23 June 1947.
    APMO, Proces zalogi, t. 57, ss. 17-18/26-29, D-Zod / 57.
black and blue, 63: Ibid.
frostbite was common, 63: Irmtraud Heike and Andreas Pflock, "Geregelte
    Strafen, willkürliche Gewalt und Massensterben," Füllberg-Stollberg,
    Frauen in Konzentrationslagern Bergen-Belsen—Ravensbrück, 243–244.
floors of the cells, 63: Ibid. See also: Emmi Thoma-Handke, RA Erlebnis. Bd.
    17, No. 42, ARa.
from starvation, 63: Margarete Buber-Neumann, Under Two Dictators (Great
    Britain: Random House Group Ltd., 2008), 182.
stripped naked, 63: Rochelle Saidel, 13–14.
in this way, 63: Helm, 171.
in the camp, 64: Mandl statement, 103-104.
Himmler approved it, 64: Ibid.
naked backside, 64: Ibid, 77. See also Heike/Pflock, "Geregelte Strafen," 242.
death sentence, 64: Silke Schäfer, 77.
in the Bunker, 64: Armanda Larsch, statement, Frankfurt am Main 12 No-
    vember 1973. LUD, 918/72, 385-392, seite 5, 388.
"would be killed", 64: Armanda Larsch, 388–389.
leaving the barracks, 65: Elisabeth Lynhard, RA Erlebnis. Bd. 17, No. 55. Ara.
her uncovered flesh, 65: Helm, 70
death often followed, 65: Larsch, LUD, 388.
to muffle screams, 65: Mailänder, 217.
complete darkness, 65: Johanna Baumann, statement, Frankfurt am Main, 5
    March 1974, LUD 4 Js 918/72, 538-554; 548.
"and without exception", 65: Konzentrationslager Buchenwald, Der Komman-
    dant, 20 April 1940, IPN W, 137-138.
radiant and happy, 65: Klub Ravensbrück, statement, Warszawa 23 June 1947.
    APMO, Proces zalogi, t. 57, ss. 17-18/26-29, D-ZOd / 57; 18.

abused by Mandl, 65: Klara Schnippering, statement, 30 August 1974 Frank-
    furt/Main. LUD, 4 Js 918/72; 786-787.
"swell with hunger!", 65: Aleksandra Steuer, deposition, 20 August 1947, Krakow,
    Poland. APMO Proces zalogi, t. 57d, ss. 259-262 (432-435), D-ZOd /
    57d; 259-260.
"did I survive", 66: Nelia Epker, deposition, Den Haag, Netherlands, 23 June
    1947. APMO, 394-395/225-226, Proces zalogi, t. 57c, s.225 (394-395), D-
    ZOd/57c; 394.

Chapter 18: In Charge

sadistic beast, 67: Margarete Buber-Neumann, *Under Two Dictators*, 213.
seasoned guards, 67: Helm, 182.
with the prisoners, 67: Mandl statement, APMO, 104-105
"anger her", 68: Brown, *The Camp Women*, 240.
problem in Ravensbrück, 68: Mandl, 109–110.
"trouble about it", 68: Mandl, 109
because of it, 68: Mandl, 110

Chapter 19: "The Mistress of Life and Death"

Blut geleckt, 70: https://www.openthesaurus.de/synonyme/Blut+geleckt+haben.
flushed with power, 70: Miklaszewskie, APMO.
closest available barrack, 70: Wozniakowna, 51.
was accounted for, 71: Morrison, 110–111.
caw unpleasantly, 71: Grete Stabej, ÖST-Wien, Vienna, Austria, "Ein erschüt-
    ternder ZÄHLAPPELL-Abschluss! Seite 1.
on the bike, 71: Stanisław Kobiela, *Maria Mandel—part IV*, "*Więzienie Zbrodni
    Wojennych w Dachau*" (Bochnia, Poland, August 2003). See also Mel-
    chior Wańkowicz, Vol. II, *Karafka La Fontaine'a* (Krakow:
    Wydawnictwo Literackie, 1981), 94–95.
work assignments, 71: Morrison, 111.
"stand in open air", 72: Maria Liwo, deposition, 21 August 1947, Rzeszów, Poland.
    APMO, Proces zalogi, t. 57, ss. 446-448 (270-272), D-ZOd / 57.
multiple prisoners, 72: Michalina Wozniakowna, Obóz Koncentracyjny Dla
    Kobiet Ravensbrück. (Poznan: Nakładem Zwiazku B. Wiezniow Po-
    litycznych w Poznaniu, 1946, 51-52.
"more pretty", 72: Helena Julia Miklaszewskie, deposition, 28 June 1947, Krakow,
    Poland. APMO Proces zalogi, t. 57, ss.24-29 (37-42), D-ZOd / 57.
"Life and Death", 72: Wozniakowna, 51–53.
kaleidoscope of colors, 72: Półtawska, 42.

horror movie, 72: Półtawska, 46–47.
"the Tigress", 72: Miklaszewskie, APMO. See also Aleksandra Rybska, deposition, 12 September 1947, APMO. Proces zalogi, t. 57, ss.278-279 (458-459), D-ZOd / 57d.
tremendous suffering, 72: Kamila Kanicka, deposition, 14 August 1947, Bydgoszczy, Poland. IPN W; NTN, 140,u. 267; 442-443. See also: Józefina Węglarska (Ziuta), deposition, 20 June 1947, Krakow, Poland. APMO Proces zalogi, t. 57, ss. 14-17 (21-24), D-ZOd / 57d; 22.
of proper treatment, 72: Dr. Zofia Mączka, deposition, 1947 Krakow, Poland. APMO Proces zalogi, t. 57, ss.254-257 (425-431), D-ZOdl57d; 254-255.
anyone's feet, 72: Aleksandra Steuer, deposition, 20 August 1947, Krakow, Poland. APMO, Proces zalogi, +57d, ss. 259-262 (432-435). D-Zod/57.1.
"triumph on her face", 73: Maria Mandl, 4-5., *Wspomnienia i myśli związane z oberaufseherin Maria Mandl* [Memories of Maria Mandl] by Urszula Wińska, obtained directly by Stanisław Kobiela, Sopot, Poland. Wińska died in 2003. Wińska also published her general memories of Ravensbrück under the title *Zwyciężyły wartości: wspomnienia z Ravensbrück* (Gdansk: Wydawn Morskie: 1985). See also Maria Buslówa, deposition, 1947 Krakow, Poland. APMO Proces zalogi, t. 57, ss.254-257 (425-431), D-ZOd / 57d; 431. See also *Urszula Wińska*, by Stanisław Kobiela, *Wiadomości Bocheńskie*, ROK XIII, nr. 4 (60), jesień 2003, 32-35.
"by her power!", 73: Urszula Wińska, *wspomnienia i myśli związane z oberaufseherin Maria Mandl*, 16.
"victims couldn't walk", 73: Miklaszewskie, APMO.
on both occasions, 73: Dr. Zofia Mączka, deposition, 1947 Krakow, Poland. APMO Proces zalogi, t. 57, ss.254-257 (425-431), D-ZOd /57d; 254-255.
"the toughest ones", 73: Ciszek interview.

Chapter 20: The Hunt of the Curly-Heads

when we were beaten, 74: Vivien Spitz, *Doctors from Hell* (Boulder, CO: Sentient Publications, 2005), 147.
"every SS woman", 74: Ibid.
"her own importance", 74: Ursula Wińska.
"then beat her", 74: Maria Wiedmeyer, deposition, 9 May 1947, Berlin, Germany, BAB VgM, 1025 A. 1.
"shot of poison", 75: Aleksandra Rybska, deposition, 12 September 1947, Warsaw, Poland. APMO Proces zalogi, t. 57d, ss. 278-279 (458-459), D-ZOd / 57d.

constantly punished, 75: Heike/Pflock, 243. See also Lucia Schmidt-Fels, *Deportiert nach Ravensbrück—Bericht einer Zeugin 1943–1945* (Düsseldorf 1981), S. 70f.

"months of Strafblock", 75: Maria Liwo, deposition, 21 August 1947, Rzeszów, Poland. APMO, Proces zalogi, t. 57, ss. 446-448 (270-272), D-ZOd /57.

"fasting/starvation", 75: Aleksandra Steuer, deposition, 20 August 1947, Krakow, Poland. APMO Proces zalogi, ss. 259-262 (432-435), D-ZOd/ 57d

"on the face", 75: Minnie Artner, deposition, 25 June 1946, ÖST-Wien 50.752, 541; Blatt 4.

extra beatings, 75: Statement, APMO Proces zalogi, t. 57d, s (473), D-ZOd / 57d.

"persecute us", 75: Maria Liberak, deposition, 17 June 1947, APMO Proces zalogi, t. 57, s 11 (17-18), D-ZOd / 57.

into a bun, 75: Working Rules of the Ravensbrück Concentration Camp, page 16, 38, BAB, Film 41303.

locks of hair, 76: Margarete Buber-Neumann, *Als Gefangene bei Stalin und Hitler* (Stuttgart: Deutsche Verlags-Anstalt, 1958), 277–278.

shooting started, 76: Józefina Węglarska (Ziuta), deposition. 20 June 1947, Krakow, Poland. APMO Proces zalogi, t. 57, ss. 14-17 (21-24), D-ZOd / 57d; 22.

of every week, 76: Statement, APMO Proces zalogi, t. 57d, s (473), D-ZOd / 57d.

evening roll call, 76: Wanda Urbańska, deposition, September 13 1947, APMO. Proces zalogi, t. 57, ss. 286-287 (467-468), D-ZOd / 57d.

"crossed off the list", 76: Wanda Urbańska, deposition, September 13 1947, APMO. Proces zalogi, t. 57, ss. 286-287 (467-468), D-ZOd / 57d. See also Stanisław Kobiela, Maria Mandel, Part IV.

bruised faces, 76: Józefina Węglarska (Ziuta), statement, 22.

"thousands of people", 77: Półtawska, 107.

Chapter 21: *The Biggest Cruelty*

with one punch, 78: Maria Wiedmeier, deposition, 9 May 1947, Berlin, Germany, BAB VgM, 1025 A. 1.

such a big offense, 78: Mandl, deposition, 19 May 1947, SNT, APMO, p.4.

dozen or so times, 78: Józefina Węglarska, deposition, 15-16 (22-23).

plank of wood, 78: Statement, APMO Proces zalogi, t. 57d, s (473), D-ZOdl57d. See also Anne Szyller, deposition n, 11 March 1947, Grodzkiej, Poland. IPN W, NTN 139, u. 83-86; 84.

or no provocation, 78: Stanisława Marchwicka, deposition, 5 August 1947, Krakow, Poland. APMO Proces zalogi, t. 57d, ss. 254-257 (425-431), D-ZOd / 57d; 255. See also Regina Morawska, deposition, 30 September 1947, APMO Proces zalogi, t. 57d, ss. 305-327 (491-495), D-ZOd / 57d; 493-494.

high falsetto, 79: Testimonies consisting of letters and documents, placed into the official court record by Jan Sehn on June 28, 1947, Krakow, Poland, including Helena Miklasweska, Krystyna Czyzówna, Janine Marciniek, Jadwiga Bielska, Wanda Wojtasik, Maria Kusmierczuk, Heleny Tyrankiewicz, and Maria Swiadek. APMO Proces zalogi, t. 57d, ss. 24-29 (37-42), D-ZOd / 57.

"we were young", 79: Półtawska interview.

"to hit me!", 79: Urszula Wińska, 13–14, told by Nelia Epker.

"I can beat you!", 79: Ibid.

"they knew her", 80: Karin Berger and Elisabeth Holzinger, Lotte Podgornik, Lisbeth Trallori (Hersg.), *Ich geb Dir einen Mantel, daß Du ihn noch in Freiheit tragen kannst. Widerstehen im KZ Österriechische Frauen erzählen* (Wien: ProMedia Edition Spuren), 1987, 136.

Sturm's account may be suspect. She goes on to incorrectly state that Mandl's father was a teacher in Braunau and that Mandl's parents came to her after the war asking about their daughter. Maria's mother was dead by then and her father largely stayed in Münzkirchen, with an occasional visit to Switzerland to visit another daughter.

"punished them", 80: Elisabeth Thury, statement, 18 June 1946, Vienna, Austria. ÖST-Wien, 50.307, 145; Blatt 3.

kidney damage, 80: Aleksandra Rybska, deposition, 12 September 1947, Warsaw, Poland. APMO Proces zalogi, t. 57d, ss. 278-279 (458-459), D-ZOd / 57d.

"biggest cruelty", 80: Testimonies consisting of letters and documents, placed into the official court record by Jan Sehn on June 28, 1947, Krakow, Poland, including Helena Miklasweska, Krystyna Czyzówna, Janine Marciniek, Jadwiga Bielska, Wanda Wojtasik, Maria Kusmierczuk, Heleny Tyrankiewicz, and Maria Swiadek. APMO Proces zalogi, t. 57d, ss. 24-29 (37-42), D-ZOd / 57.

any harm to them, 80: Mandl statement, 106.

such a big offense, 80: Mandl, deposition, 19 May 1947, SNT, APMO, p.4.

Chapter 22: Lab Rabbits

rotting corpses, 81: Helm, 221. Zofia Kawińska, interviewed by Sarah Helm.

"belong to the party", 81: Mandl, deposition,19 May 1947. Recording Clerk: Krystyna Szymańska, Regional Investigating Judge: Jan Sehn, Prosecutor: Helena Turowicz. P. 4.

brutal treatment, 82: Helm, 210–211.

men in battle, 82: Ibid, 211–212.

September of, 82: Roger Goodman, *The First German War Crimes Trial, Volume I. Chief Judge Walter B. Beals' Desk Notebook of The Doctor's Trial, held in Nuremberg, Germany, December 1946 to August 1947* (Salisbury, NC: Documentary Publications), 142.

gangrene, and tetanus, 82: Goodman, 142−143.

to the Appellplatz, 82: Helm, 214.

of their papers, 82: Morrison, 246.

for the night, 83: Półtawska, 81−82.

permanent disability, 83: Ibid, 142−143.

German soldiers, 83: Morrison, 247.

killed by injection, 83: Ibid.

had no insight, 83: SPN Urteil, p. 117; Act. Nr NTN 5/47; LUD Trial IV 409, AR-Z 39/59; 77-92.

in Ravensbrück, 83: Supreme National Tribunal, 22 December 1947, Judgement (118), "Testimonies of witnesses Maczka and Marchwicka prove incontrovertibly that for medical experiments performed in Ravensbrück the defendant personally chose and assigned more than 80 prisoners." APMO Aktu procesu zalogi KL Auschwitz. See also testimony of Zofia Czerwinska, SNT files, Vol. 56.

summoned again, 83: Spitz, *Doctors from Hell*, 124. Testimony of Vladislava Karolewska, 37, victim of sulphanimide and bone/muscle/nerve regeneration experiments, operated on six times by Dr. Fischer.

for these operations, 84: Zofia Mączka (APMO), Marta Baranowska (APMO), (A)neja Zarzecka (IPN W).

about the experiments, 84: Marta Baranowska, deposition, 18 June 1947, Bydgoszcz, Poland. APMO.

"some couldn't walk", 84: Zofia Mączka statement.

"describe the pain", 84: Zofia Ciszek, interview with Susan Eischeid, Gdańsk Poland, 2005.

"couldn't continue", 85: Ibid.

body and soul, 85: Wacława Gnatowska, letter to Susan Eischeid, January 15, 2005.

Chapter 23: The Transfer

like an animal, 86: Maria Wiedmeier, deposition, 9 May 1947, Berlin, Germany, BAB VgM, 1025 A. I.

out of it quickly, 86: Mandl statement, 113.

treatment of prisoners, 86: Michalina Wozniakowna, *Obóz Koncentracyjny Dla Kobiet Ravensbrück* (Poznan: Nakładem Związku B. Więzniow Politycznych w Poznaniu, 1946), 51−53.

fullfill their duties, 87: *Rudolph Höss, Death Dealer; The Memoirs of the SS Kommandant at Auschwitz*, ed. Steven Paskuly, trans. Andrew Pollinger
(Buffalo New York: Prometheus Books, 1992), 147.
"flustered hens", 87: Ibid.
a male prisoner, 87: Ibid, 149. See also Helm, 188.
exponential increase, 87: Ibid.
"dared to breathe", 87: Johanna Langefeld, Sworn Declaration, 26 December
1945. NARA, RG 338-000-50-11; Sheet 4.
the SS hierarchy, 87: Helm, 237238.
"refused to go to the East", 87: Mandl statement, 107.
conditions were awful, 88: Mandl, deposition, 20 May 1947.

PART FOUR

Chapter 24: Anteroom to Hell

"order in the camp", 91: Regina Morawska, deposition, 30 September 1947, Krakow, Poland. APMO Proces zalogi, t. 57d, ss. 305-309 (491-495),
D-ZOd / 57; 493-495.
by camp personnel, 91: Oskar Gröning, *Lebenslauf*, 53.
for that purpose, 91: Lore Shelley, *Auschwitz—The Nazi Civilization* (University
Press of America, 1992), 64.
few industrial plants, 92: Gröning, *Lebenslauf*, 53.

Chapter 25: Hell

lack of water, 93: Mandl, deposition, 20 May 1947. APMO; p. 5.
kind of home, 93: Seweryna Szmaglewska, *Smoke Over Birkenau*, trans. Jadwiga
Rynas (Warsaw: Książka I Wiedza, 2001), 15.
manic and unrelenting, 93: Szmaglewska, 29.
to walk normally, 93: Teresa Świebocka, compiler and editor, *Auschwitz: A History in Photographs* (Bloomington: Indiana University Press, 1993), 111.
See also Pery Broad, *KL Auschwitz Seen by the SS: Rudolf Höss, Pery
Broad, Johann Paul Kramer* (Oświęcim: Auschwitz-Birkenau State Museum, trans. Krystyna Michalik, 1972), 141.
entered one's mouth, 93: Szmaglewska, 30
unprecedented circus, 93: Margot Větrovcová, ČTYŘI ROKY, an excerpt
adapted by the author, shared with Susan Eischeid May 2006. Also
excerpted in a collection of articles *"Bojovali jsme a zvítězili 1938–1945"*
(Praha: Svoboda Publishing House, 1979), 129–137.

a "camp officer", 94: Ibid.
"discarded black mess", 94: Antonina Kozubek, deposition, 15 September 1946, Oświęcim, Poland. APMO Oświadczenia, + 45, s. 29, Ośw / Kozubek / 935.
"in the barrack", 94: Antonina Kozubek, statement, 17 September 1947, Oświęcim, Poland. APMO Oświadczenia, + 33, ss. 105-107, Ośw / 809.
were lying around, 94: Mandl deposition, Record of Questioning, SNT, 20 May 1947. APMO; p. 5.
"next to them", 94: Hermann Langbein, *Der Auschwitz-Prozeß, Eine Dokumentation, Band 1* (Frankfurt/Main: Verlag Neue Kritik KG, 1995), 55. Testimony of Ella Lingens.
help them instead, 95: Mandl statement addendum, 123.
no floorboards, 95: Monika Müller, 55.
macabre tableau, 95: Janina Lenc, letter to Susan Eischeid, February 7, 2006, Warszawa, Poland. Also included her early testimony after liberation.
SS man or woman, 95: Anna Palarczyk statement; Hermann Langbein, *Der Auschwitz-Prozeß, Eine Dokumentation, Band 1* (Frankfurt/Main: Verlag Neue Kritik KG, 1995), 55.
of sanitation, 95: Höss, *Death Dealer*, 146–147.
quietly died, 96: Ibid., 145.
further downhill, 96: Mandl statement, APMO, 111-112.
to be impossible, 96: Mandl statement, APMO, 123.

Chapter 26: Order and Discipline

order and discipline, 97: Mandl statement, APMO, 121.
Latrine Block, 97: Antonina Kozubek, statement, 17 September 1947, Oświęcim, Poland. APMO Oświadczenia, t. 33, ss. 105-107, Ośw / 809.
relaxed slightly, 98: Mandl statement, APMO, 115
transmitting diseases, 98: Ibid, 115
Tauber was helpful, 98: Ibid, 116
camp population, 98: Ibid, 116
It was awful, 99: Ibid, 116–117
epidemics were reduced, 99: Ibid.

Chapter 27: "Appell was Torture"

numb, bestial suffering, 100: Gisella Perl, *I Was a Doctor in Auschwitz* (London: Lexington Books, 2019), 49.
at roll calls, 100: Aleksandr Kinsky, statement, 13 August 1947, IPN W, NTN 139 u. 158-160 (205-207); 158-159.

due to exhaustion, 101: Mandl deposition, 20 May 1947. APMO; p. 5.

female guards floundered, 101: Jürgen Matthäus, *Approaching an Auschwitz Survivor* (Oxford University Press, 2009), 134.

counting roll call, 101: Mandl statement, APMO, 113-114.

as a result, 101: Gerda Schneider, deposition, 19 September 1947, Oświęcim, Poland. APMO Proces zalogi, t. 57d, ss. 180-182 (230-232), D-ZOd / 57b4; 181-182.

anyone could remember, 101: Ibid.

prisoners were separated, 101: Mandl statement, 113.

for the duration, 101: Elisabeth Volkenrath, statement, Bergen-Belsen Prozess, Lüneburg, Germany. APMO. Oświadczenia, + 12, s. 150. Ośw / Volkenrath/ 330; 150.

some were beaten, 102: Richard Newman with Karen Kirtley, *Alma Rosé: Vienna to Auschwitz* (Portland: Amadeus Press, 2000), 240. See also Helena Dunicz-Niwińska, *One of the Girls in the Band* (Oświęcim: Auschwitz Birkenau State Museum, 2014), 57–58.

completely terrorized, 102: Helena Dunicz Niwińska, *One of the Girls*, 56.

our misery was, 102: Anita Lasker-Wallfisch, *Inherit the Truth* (New York: St. Martin's Press, 1996), 73.

for the gas, 102: Izabella Sosnowska, deposition, 29 September 1947, IPN W, NTN, 141, u.50; (33-35); 34-35.

the following day, 102: Janina Frankiewicz, testimony, 11th day of the trial, IPN W, NTN, 16u, k. 167-168.

Chapter 28: A Normal Life

the other things, 103: Oskar Gröning, *Lebenslauf,* 83.

German town, 103: Ibid.

more or less, separate, 103: Matthias Geyer, "The Bookkeeper from Auschwitz (2)—An SS Officer Remembers," *SPIEGEL* Online 19 / 2005, 4, http://service.spiegel.de/cache/international/spiegel/0,1518,355188-2,00.html.

tended lawns, 103: Yehuda Koren and Eilat Negev, *In Our Hearts We Were Giants* (New York: Carroll & Graf Publishers, 2004), 135.

"[like] princesses", 103: Trial testimony, SNT, December 1947. IPN W; 218. NTN, 15u.k. 212.

alcohol ration, 103: Oskar Gröning, email to Susan Eischeid, September 6, 2006.

vanilla ice cream, 104: Koren/Negev, 99.

checkered quilts, 104: Matthias Geyer, 2.

movie area, 104: Oskar Gröning, email to Susan Eischeid, September 6, 2006.

did not know, 104: Mandl statement, APMO, 119.

watch zone, Tag, 104: Oskar Gröning, letter to Susan Eischeid, March 23, 2006.

soup bones, 104: Geyer, 4.

"a spa city", 104: Oskar Gröning, email to Susan Eischeid, July 4, 2006.

departments and sections, 104: Barbara Cherish, *The Auschwitz Kommandant* (United Kingdom: The History Press, 2009), 73–74.

"restaurant in town", 104: Ibid., 105.

"only at Christmas", 104: Helga Schneider, *Let Me Go* (New York: Walker & Company, 2001), 83.

"interesting to read", 105: Ibid.

in the region, 105: Michel Gordey, "Echoes from Auschwitz," New Republic, December 22, 1947.

the other SS, 105: Helen Tichauer, telephone interview with Susan Eischeid, January 28, 2003.

to make jam, 105: Koren/Negev, 128.

"it and left", 105: Alois Schiller, interview with Susan Eischeid, Münzkirchen, Austria, May 25, 2005.

"time to time", 105: Tichauer interview 2003.

"absolutely believable", 105: Oskar Gröning, email to Susan Eischeid, August 14, 2006.

from a sickness, 105: Gröning, *Lebenslauf*, 73.

playing an accordion, 105: USHMM, Photo Archives, Photograph # 34586. "Nazi officers and female auxiliaries (Helferinnen) run down a wooden bridge in Solahuette. The man on the right carries an accordion."

back on with joy, 105: Oskar Gröning, BBC, *Auschwitz: Inside the Nazi State*, Episode 4, "Corruption," https://www.pbs.org/auschwitz/about/tran scripts_4.html.

Chapter 29: Oberaufseherin

a small whip, 106: Stanislawa Rzepka-Palka, interview with Susan Eischeid, Bielsko-Biała, Poland, May 2004.

"knees there", 106: Zofia Cykowiak, interview with Susan Eischeid, Krakow, Poland, June 10, 2003.

Oberaufseherin Mandl, 106: Newman, 226.

"ride perfectly", 106: Zofia Cykowiak, interview with Susan Eischeid, 1May 10, 2004, Krakow, Poland.

"and a motorcycle", 106: Stanisława Rachwałowa, court testimony, Rudolf Höss trial files, Vol. 3, page 127.

utilized bicycles, 106: Anna Palarczyk, interview with Susan Eischeid, Krakow, Poland, June 11, 2003.

heady stuff indeed, 107: USHMM, Photo Archives, Photograph # 34804, "Nazi officers watch Commandant Richard Baer shake hands with Karl Bischoff during the dedication of the new SS hospital in Auschwitz."

Franz Hössler, 107: Lasik, Vol. I, 285.

with one another, 107: Concentration Camp Auschwitz II, Order by the Kommandantur No. 1/43, 24 November 1943. APMO Kommandturbefehl, t. u, s. 308; D-Aus-1 /56.

was competition, 107: Anna Palarczyk, interview with Susan Eischeid, June 11, 2003.

stood a chance!, 108: Stanisława Rzepka-Palka, interview with Susan Eischeid, Bielsko-Biała, Poland, May 2005. See also: Zofia Czerwińska, deposition, 31 March 1947, Gdańsk, Poland. APMO Proces zalogi, t. 5b, ss. 61-62 (89-91), D-Zod/56; 62.

women's camp, 108: Lasik, Volume I, 285.

Chapter 30: The Lover

to impress him, 109: Helen Tichauer, interview with Susan Eischeid, January 28, 2003.

Bischoff, 109: Lasik, Vol. I, 80.

wife beater, 109: Maria Pawela, statement, 26 April 1974, Oświęcim, Poland. APMO, Oświadczenia, t. 82, ss. 163-166. Ośw /Buch/1852.

After the war Bischoff was sometimes incorrectly identified as Maria's lover. However, the majority of prisoners agree that Mandl's lover was indeed Janisch. See Anna Palarczyk, interview, 2003. Ms. Palarczyk stated at this time that another survivor, Wanda Marosanyi, also confirmed that Janisch was Mandl's lover.

law and order, 109: Tichauer interview, January 28, 2003.

procured by Janisch, 110: Ibid.

"just building things", 110: Palarczyk interview, 2003.

sexual intercourse, 110: Ibid.

resumed her practice, 111: Ella Lingens-Reiner, Prisoners of Fear (London: Victor Gollancz Ltd., 1948), 145.

before Appell, 111: Tichauer interview.

"beautiful horses", 111: Helen Tichauer, interview with Susan Eischeid, February 5, 2003.

"in the order", 111: Oskar Gröning, Lebenslauf, 62.

wailing and pleading, 111: Ibid.

There is no record of Maria and Josef having any contact after they left Auschwitz. Janisch survived the war and died in 1964. He never married Maria and was never prosecuted for any crimes of war. Gerhard Faul, Eckart Dietzfelbinger: Slave workers for the final victory. Hersbruck concentration camp and the Dogger armaments project. Documentation center concentration camp Hersbruck e. V., Hersbruck 2003, ISBN 3-00-011024-0, pp. 37, 159.

Chapter 31: The "Ladies"

as a wardress, 112: Lingens-Reiner, 131.

mistress in the camp, 112: Krystyna Zywulska, trial testimony, Tom. V, karta 129. See also Rzepka-Palka interview, 2005.

average age of twenty-eight, 112: Lasik, Volume 1, 333.

were unmarried, 112: Mailänder, 68.

or Austrian, 112: Lasik, Volume I, 334.

"came after them", 112: Höss, Death Dealer, 147–148.

household of their own, 113: Lingens-Reiner, 131–132.

scolded for that, 113: Mandl, deposition, 19 May 1947, APMO, 6.

unattractive, vulgar, 113: Szmaglewska, 23. See also Heather Dune Macadam, *999—The Extraordinary Young Women of the First Official Jewish Transport to Auschwit,* (New York: Citadel Press, 2020), 262.

she resented, 113: Niwińska, *One of the Girls in the Band,* 123.

"eardrum was destroyed", 113: Klara Pförtsch, statement, February 18, 1972, Frankfurt/Main, Germany. LUD Band IV, Bl. 568; 3.

"friends with Drexler", 113: Antonina Piatkowska, deposition, 20 May 1946, Krakow, Poland. APMO, Proces zalogi, t. 56, ss. 7-8 (10-12), D-ZOd / 56; 11-12.

"tried to accumulate", 113: Gerda Schneider, deposition, 10 September 1947, Oświęcim, Poland. APMO, Proces zalogi, t. 56q, ss. 180-182 (230-232), D-ZOd / 5ba; 181-182.

"Die Kuh", 114: Ingrid Müller-Münch, *Die Frauen von Majdanek* (Hamburg: Rowohlt Taschenbuch Verlag, 1982), 117.

from Vienna, 114: Olga Lengyel, *Five Chimneys* (New York: Howard Fertig, 1983), 147–148.

horded substance, 114: Daniel Patrick Brown, *The Beautiful Beast* (Ventura, CA: Golden West Historical Publications, 1996), 36.

"underwear and clothing", 114: Trial testimony, 24/Therese Brandl, APMO Proces zalogi (stenogram), t. I, ss. 30-31 (16), D-ZOd / 1.

SS lovers, 114: Germaine Tillion, *Ravensbrück*, trans. Gerald Satterwaite (Garden City, NJ: Doubleday, 1975), 62.

"or the hallways", 115: Kosciuszkowa testimony, 9th day of trial, Vol. III, p. 255; 6 December 1947.

dissolute atmosphere, 115: Szmaglewska, *Smoke Over Birkenau*, 270–271.

"Hurren (whores)", 115: Lechosław Cebo, *Więźniarki w obozie hitlerowskim w Oświęcimiu Brzezince* (Katowice: Uniwersylei Slqski, 1984), 47–48.

"their deaths", 115: Michel Gordey, "Echoes from Auschwitz," *New Republic*, December 22, 1947.

recreation room, 115: Cherish, *The Auschwitz Kommandant*, 74. Memo from Arthur Liebehenschel regarding the living quarters of the SS Women, December 7, 1943.

"different Sturmbannführer", 115: Gerda Schneider, 182.

Chapter 32: *"Mandelka"*

"Mandelka", 116: Derisive nickname coined by the prisoners for Mandl. Janina Unkiewicz, deposition, 25 January 1947, APMO. Proces zalogi, t. 56, ss. 31-36 (45-53), D-ZO / 56; 31.

very last one, 116: Jean Hatzfeld, *Machete Season: The Killers in Rwanda Speak* (United Kingdom: Picador Press, 2006), 226.

Blockführerstube, 116: Genowefa Ułan, deposition, 3 June 1947, Krakow Poland. APMO Proces zalogi, t. 56, ss. 131- 133 (166-168), D-ZOd / 5ba; 131.

administering the camp, 116: Aleksandr Kinsky, deposition, 13 August 1947. APMO Proces zalogi, t. 56a, ss. 146-161 (188-208), D-ZOd / 5ba; 158-160.

See also regarding location of Mandl's office: Genowefa Ułan, deposition, 3 June 1947, Krakow Poland. APMO Proces zalogi, t. 56, ss. 131- 133 (166-168), D-ZOd / 5ba; 131.

In Mandl's trial she specifically rebutted testimony that her office was located mid-camp, across from the selection ramp. "There Drechsel had HER office!" See: Mandl, deposition, 20 May 1947. p. 7.

to pass by, 116: Lore Shelley, *Auschwitz—The Nazi Civilization* (University Press of America, 1992), 251–252.

tall stone wall, 116: Janina Frankiewicz, testimony, 11th day of the trial. IPN W: NTN 16u, k. 167- 184; 172. See also Szmaglewska, 42-43.

for her approval, 116: Aleksandr Kinsky, deposition, 13 August 1947. APMO Proces zalogi, t. 56a, ss. 146-161 (188-208), D-ZOd / 5ba; 158-160.

next to the wall, 117: Helena Niwińska, *One of the Girls*, 54.

with the mud, 117: Szmaglewska, *Smoke over Birkenau*, 42.

"barred windows", 117: Adam Bujak, *Auschwitz: The Residence of Death* (Bialy Kruk, 2007), 104. From memoirs written during the war by Polish political prisoner Zofia Kossak-Szczucka.

were common, 117: Aleksandr Kinsky, deposition, 13 August 1947. APMO Proces
zalogi, t. 56a, ss. 146-161 (188-208), D-ZOd / 5ba; 158-160.

gas chamber, 117: Janina Frankiewicz, testimony, 11th day of the trial. IPN W:
NTN 16u, k. 167- 184; 172. See also Aleksandr Kinsky, APMO.

"Block 25 was empty", 117: Lore Shelley, *Secretaries of Death* (New York: Shengold Publishers, 1986), 14.

Chapter 33: The Embodiment of Satan

"unleash" her anger, 118: Maria Gatkiewicz, deposition, 5 August 1947, Krakow,
Poland. APMO Proces zalogi, t. 56a, ss. 146-161 (188-208), D-ZOd /
5ba; 155-156.

"embodiment of Satan", 118: Stanisława Gempert (?- illegible name), deposition,
19 September 1947, IPN W; NTN 141, u 39-42; 42.

"just for fun", 118: Margot Větrovcová, interview with Susan Eischeid, May 2006,
Karlovy Vary, Czech Republic.

"and drive away", 118: SNT, 17th day of the trial; IPN W - NTN 166, u. 129; 14/1.

in the face, 119: Anna Palarczyk, interview with Susan Eischeid, Krakow, Poland. June 11, 2003.

kicking them, 119: Hermine Jursa, deposition, 22 June 1946. WIEN: 50:695 /
484. See also: Helena Przetocka, deposition, 5 August 1947, Krakow,
Poland. APMO Proces zalogi, t. 56a, ss. 146-161 (188-208), D-ZOd /
5ba; 157.

"boiling soup", 119: Genowefa Ułan, deposition, 3 June 1947, Krakow Poland.
APMO Proces zalogi, t. 56, ss. 131- 133 (166-168), D-ZOd / 5ba; 132.

"breaking jaws", 119: Anna Szyller, deposition, 11 March 1947, Krakow, Poland.
IPN W: NTN 139, u. 83-84; 83. See also Dr. Janina Kościuszkowa, tes-
timony, SNT, 6 December 1947 (Vol. III, p. 225); APMO
Oświadczenia, t. 82, ss. 117-122. Ośw; 121.

be washed off, 119: Wanda Marossanyi, deposition, 7 March 1947, Krakow, Poland. APMO, Proces zalogi, t. 56, ss. 81-82 (56-57), D-ZOd; 82.

"mercy or pardon", 119: Anna Szyller, deposition, 11 March 1947, Krakow, Poland.
IPN W: NTN 139, u. 83-84; 84.

life and death, 119: SNT, testimony of Seweryna Szmaglewska, IPN W: NTN
165, u. 116-124.

"until the blood runs", 119: Szmaglewska, 274. See also Stanisława Gempert, 41.

and watched, 120: Maria Budziaszek, deposition, 21 June 1947, Krakow, Poland.
APMO Proces zalogi, t. 56a, ss. 135-136 (172-175), D-ZOd / 5ba; 135.5.

continued her activity, 120: Luba Reis, deposition, 4 August 1947, Krakow, Poland.
APMO Proces zalogi, t. 56a, ss. 146-161 (188-208), D-ZOd / 5ba; 151-154.

Chapter 34: "We ALLOW you to work for us!"

"ALLOW you to work for us!", 121: SNT, trial testimony, 17th day of the trial. IPN W; NTN 166, 6.124 – 135; 12/1-12/2.

guards were unstoppable, 121: Nic Dunlop, *The Lost Executioner: A Journey to the Heart of the Killing Fields* (New York: Walker & Company, 2005), 148.

visible pleasure, 121: Władysława Janik, deposition, 11 June 1947, Krakow, Poland. APMO Proces zalogi, t. 56a, ss. 146-161 (188-208), D-ZOd / 5ba; 161.

curly hair, 121: Rzepka-Palka, interview with Susan Eischeid.

"afterwards and died", 121: Teresa Wicińska, deposition, 16 June 1947, Krakow, Poland. APMO Proces zalogi, t. 56a, ss. 134-134A (163-164), D-ZOd / 134-134.5.

"work for us!", 122: SNT, testimony; IPN W: NTN 166.6, 124-125, 129, 132,135.

"will be hanged", 122: SNT, testimony; IPN W: NTN 166.6, 124-125, 129, 132, 135.

serious consequences, 122: Barbara Iboja Pozimska, deposition, 28 August 1947, Oświęcim, Poland. IPN W. NTN, 139, u. 221-225; 222.

savage beating, 122: Stanisława Gempert(?), deposition, 19 September 1947, IPN W. NTN, 141, u. 39-42; 41.

of us all, 122: Wanda Tarasiewicz, testimony read into the record, 15th day of the trial. IPN W. NTN 166, u. 66-67.

such a burning, 122: Antonina Pietkowska, deposition, 20 May 1947, Krakow, Poland. APMO. Proces zalogi, t. 56, ss. 7-8 (10-12), D-ZOd / 56; 11.

until the end, 122: Elżbieta Wondraczek, deposition, 28 October 1947, Nowy Targ, Poland. IPN W. NTN, 151, u. 95, 95v, 96; 95-96.

holding bricks, 122: Władysława Janik, letter, 16 July 1947. APMO Proces zalogi, t. 56a, ss. 146-161 (188-208), D-ZOd / 56a; 161.

around the elbows, 122: Romualda Cieślik-Cieśielska, statement, 10-12 October 1961, Warsaw, Poland. APMO. Oświadczenia, t. 22, s. 123, s.127. Ośw / Cieślik-Cieśielska / 65b; 5 (127).

them with sticks, 123: SNT. Trial testimony. IPN W. NTN, 16U, k. 212-213 (29/2-29/2), 212.

not show off, 123: Ibid., 213.

Chapter 35: Humiliated, Appalled, and Helpless

right to do it, 124: Mandl statement, 163-164.

her profanity, 124: Zofia Cykowiak, interview with Susan Eischeid, Krakow, 2003.

to insult the prisoners, 124: Lore Shelley, Secretaries of Death, 133. Testimony of Regina Steinberg.

"kleine Mistbiene!", 124: Ibid.

"Hurweiber", 124: Luba Reiss, deposition, 4 August 1947, Krakow, Poalnd. APMO, Proces zalogi, t. 56a, ss. 146-161 (188-208), D-ZOd / 56a, 151-154; 154.

"loathesome pig Jews!", 124: Genowefa Ułan, deposition, 3 June 1947, Krakow, Poland. APMO Proces zalogi, t. 56, ss. 166-169 (131-133), D-ZOd / 5b; 133.

"she would curse", 124: Zofia Cykowiak, interview with Susan Eischeid, Krakow, 2004.

"German system", 124: Genowefa Ułan, deposition, 3 June 1947.

women disrobe, 124: Stanisława Gempert, deposition, 19 September 1947, IPN W; NTN 141, k. 39-42; 39/25. See also Władysława Chudobowa, deposition, 28 October 1947, Nowy Targ, Poland. IPN W: NTN 151, u. 45.

women's body hair, 125: SNT, witness statements Pozimski & Piatkowska, APMO Oświadczenia, t. 82, ss. 117-122. Ośw ; 122.

"women ANY more!", 125: Margot Větrovcová, interview with Susan Eischeid, May 2006, Karlovy Vary, Czech Republic.

"Jewish chief doctor", 125: Ella Lingens-Reiner, *Prisoners of Fear* (London: Victor Gollancz Ltd., 1948), 147.

with prostitutes, 125: Testimony of Maria B., and Michalina J., SNT sentence, p. 64. Urteil Krakauer Auschwitz-Prozess, Bl. 64.

did so voluntarily, 125: Herman Langbein, People in Auschwitz (Vienna: 1995), 406.

"German women", 125: Helen Tichauer, interview with Susan Eischeid, January 28, 2003. See also Karolina Wilinska, deposition, 12 March 1947, Krakow, Poland. IPN W: NTN 139, u. 85-86; 86.

"away from prostitution", 125: Helen Tichauer, interview, 2003.

Chapter 36: A Pause, to Acknowledge Courage

define my life, 126: Zofia Cykowiak, interviews with Susan Eischeid, Krakow, Poland; June 10, 2003, and May 10, 2004.

effects of evil, 126: Helga Schneider, *Let Me Go*, trans. Shaun Whiteside (New York: Walker Publishing Company, 2004), 21.

"a long time", 128: Alina Dabrowka, Warsaw, Poland, telephone interview, May 2006, Lidia Jurek, translator.

broke my nose, 128: Zofia Cykowiak, interviews with Susan Eischeid, Krakow, Poland, June 10 2003, and May 10, 2004.

and ourselves, 129: James Waller, *Becoming Evil* (Oxford University Press, 2002), xiii–xiv.

Chapter 37: The Whip

carried a small whip!, 130: Stanisława Rzepka-Palka, interview with Susan Eischeid.

on many occasions, 130: Danuta Mosiewicz-Mikusowa, interview with Susan Eischeid.

pieces of their bodies, 130: Barbara Iboja Pozimska, Deposition, IPN, Sygn. 139, 221-225.

and with sticks, 130: Dr. Szaynoka, Deposition, IPN, Sygn. 222, u. 387.

no apparent reason, 130: Wanda Mysłakowska, deposition, 29 September 1947. IPN W: NTN 141, u. 48-49.

in the camps, 130: Maria Mandl, SNT testimony. APMO: Proces zalogi, t. VIII, ss. 192-195. Dpr – 20/8; 194.

State Museum, 131: APMO, Photograph. PMO-5; E14/.

Chapter 38: Selections

go by themselves!, 132: Zofia Czerwińska, deposition, 31 March 1947, Gdańsk, Poland. APMO Proces zalogi, t. 5b, ss. 61-62 (89-91), D-ZOd / 5b; 61-61.5.

selection process, 132: APMO Oświadczenia, t. 82, ss. 117-122. Ośw; 117.

Tauber and Drexler, 132: Helena Przetocka, deposition, 5 August 1947, Krakow, Poland. APMO Proces zalogi, t. 5a, ss. 146-161 (188-208), D-ZOd / 5ba; 157b.

was being built, 132: Mandl deposition, 20 May 1947, 6.

and not her, 132: Ibid, 3.

sentence of death, 134: Frauenlager Birkenau, 21 August 1943, Betr.: G.U.v.21.9.43; death list of 298 Greek women signed by Mandl. APMO Materiały Ruchu Oporu, t. IV, ss. 262-266. D-RO/87.

their contacts, 134: Henryk Świebocki, *Auschwitz 1940–1945*, Vol. IV, "Gathering and Disseminating Evidence of the Crimes" (Auschwitz-Birkenau State Museum, Oświęcim, 2000), 279.

through the camp, 134: Koren/Negev, *In Our Hearts We Were Giants*, 77.

"with 'verstorben' (dead)", 134: Maria Żumańska, statement, 17 August 1957, Krakow, Poland. APMO Oświadczenia, t. 4, ss. 412, 416-418, 421. Ośw/ Żumańska / 84 ; 416.

Chapter 39: All Begging Was in Vain

it is dead, 135: Virgil, as quoted by Dante Alghieri, *The Divine Comedy*, 1320, Inferno Canto XX, "The Eighth Circle" (New York: The Heritage Press, 1944), 77.

and cowardice, 135: Fradel Kiwetz, "*An eine gewisse Aufseherin!*," poem written in 1944 about SS overseer Luise Danz, IPN W: NTN 141, k. III.

along the ground, 135: Maria Budziaszek, deposition, 21 June 1947, Krakow, Poland. APMO. Proces zalogi, t. 56, ss. 135-136 (172-175), D-ZOd / 56; 135b.

of the truck, 136: Maria Zumańska, statement, 17 August 1957, Krakow, Poland. APMO Oświadczenia, t. 4, ss. 412, 416-418, 421. Ośw/Żumańska/84; 417.

"prisoner stinks!", 136: Budziaszek deposition, 136.

"'They deserved it'", 136: Zofia Czerwińska, deposition, 31 March 1947, Gdańsk, Poland. APMO Proces zalogi, t. 5b, ss. 61-62 (89-91), D-ZOd / 5b; 90-91.

"begging or pleading", 136: Wanda Marossanyi, deposition, 7 March 1947, Krakow, Poland. APMO. Proces zalogi, t.56, (81-82), D-ZOd156 inw 49747. See also Janina Frankiewicz, testimony, 11th day of the trial. IPN W; NTN, 16u, k. 167-184; 168-169.xc

stand a chance, 136: Antonina Pietkowska, deposition, 20 May 1947, Krakow, Poland. APMO. Proces zalogi, t. 56, ss. 7-8 (10-12), D-ZOd / 56; 10. See also Anna Szyller deposition.

"selected 3,000 women", 136: Zofia Czerwińska, deposition, 31 March 1947, Gdańsk, Poland. APMO Proces zalogi, t. 5b, ss. 61-62 (89-91), D-ZOd / 5b; 61.5.

with a dog, 136: Barbara Iboja Pozimska, deposition, 28 August 1947, Oświęcim, Poland. IPN W. NTN, 139, u. 221-225; 222.

"in that block", 137: Ibid.

to the gas chambers, 137: Ibid., 222–223.

transport from Paris , 137: Maria Stromberger, testimony about Mandl at trial

of Rudolf Höss, 137: March 1947. Chronicles of Terror: Witold Pilecki Center for Totalitarian Studies. https://www.zapisyterroru.pl/content/3766/Stromberger Maria en.pdf. See also: Files in the criminal case of the former members of the SS crew at Auschwitz-Birkenau concentration camp. IPN GK 196/III. pp. 55-78.

was transferred, 137: Ibid.

Chapter 40: "I often cried"

women supervisors, 138: Mandl statement, APMO, 110.

force in Auschwitz, 138: Ibid., 124.

time of my life, 138: Ibid., 119–120.

women supervisors, 138: Ibid., 109–110

prisoner's belongings, 138: Lasik, *Auschwitz 1940–1945*, Vol. I, "The Auschwitz SS Garrison," 290.

a huge issue, 139: Daniel Patrick Brown, *The Camp Women*, 17.

just one example, 139: Ibid.

"concentration camps", 139: Lasik, 290. SS-*Gruppenführer* Richard Glücks letter to all camp commandants, November 1944.

"the other way", 139: Oskar Gröning, *Lebenslauf*, 68.

"and were arrested", 140: Ibid., 68–69.

"without saying anything", 140: Gerda Schneider, deposition, 9 October 1947, APMO. Proces zalogi, t. 56q, ss. 180-182 (230-232), D-ZOd / 56a; 182.

"of her salary", 140: Ibid.

"at her command", 140: Aleksandra Steuer, deposition, 20 August 1947, Krakow, Poland. IPN W: NTN 140, u. 259-262; 261-262.

were delivered, 140: August Grundinger, interview with Susan Eischeid, Münzkirchen, Austria, May 25, 2005. See also Alois Schiller, interview with Susan Eischeid, Münzkirchen, Austria, May 25, 2005.

"station in Schärding", 140: Martin Zauner, interview with Susan Eischeid, Münzkirchen, Austria, May 2005.

the service station, 140: Der SS-Standertälteste, Auschwitz-Birkenau, Standortbefehl Nr. 30/43; 28 July 1943. APMO Standortbefehl, t. 1, ss. 143-146. D-AuJ – 1/31; 144.

and onto us, 141: Oskar Gröning, email to Susan Eischeid, July 4, 2006.

to help them, 141: Mandl statement, 123–124.

SS medical records, 141: Report Oberaufseherin Maria Mandl, Hygiene and Bacteriology of the Combat Branch of the SS Southeast 03, on 5/5/43. APMO Akta SS-Hygiene Institut, seg. 17, 11a, 43, 58, 59; ss. 1132, 127, 575, 178, 1125; D. Hyg. Inst / 15, 21, 64, 179, 180.

string beans, 141: https://www.cdc.gov/parasites/ascariasis/gen_info/faqs.html.

with this activity, 142: Abschrift, 27 March 1944, Sondervergütung für die Oberaufseherin des F.K.L. Auschwitz Frl. Mandel. B.Arch/Wienhold. NS3/405.

Oberstürmbannführer, 142: Ibid.

Chapter 41: The Orchestra

latter opinion, 143: Szymon Laks, *Music of Another World* (Evanston, IL: Northwestern University Press, 1989), 5.

which was hope, 143: Janina Lenc, letter to Susan Eischeid, January 1, 2006.

marched to work, 144: Gabriele Knapp, "Befohlene Music, Musik und Musikmißbrauch im Frauenlager von Auschwitz-Birkenau," *Acta Musicological*, vol. 68, no. 2, July–December 1996, 154.

musicians for advice, 144: Newman, 230–231. Helen Tichauer testimony.

women's camp, 144: Helena Dunicz Niwińska, *One of the Girls in the Band*, 65.

"with a capital H", 144: Ibid., 67.

"to an organ grinder", 145: Newman, 234.

"was terrible", 145: Margot Větrovcová, interview with Susan Eischeid, May 2006.

Chapter 42: Hope

medical experiments, 146: Newman, 218.

to Maria Mandl, 146: Ibid., 219.

"one last time", 146: Regina Kupferberg Bacia, letters to Richard Newman, 1985–1995.

transferred to Birkenau, 147: Newman, 225.

maiden name, Rosé, 147: Ibid., 235.

Chapter 43: Alma

formidable task, 148: Newman, 235.

and six singers, 148: Zofia Cykowiak, "Wspomnienie o Alma Rosé." September 1985. APMO Wspomnienie, t. 190, ii. 1-19. Wsp./Cykowiak/ 1021; 2.

could keep clean, 148: Niwińska, One of the Girls, 80.

"was a luxury!", 149: Zofia Cykowiak, interviews with Susan Eischeid, June 3, 2003, and May 15, 2004, Krakow, Poland.

"capable of doing", 149: Margot Větrovcová, interview with Susan Eischeid, May 2006.

"complete sensation", 149: Cykowiak, Wspomnienie, p. 2

a gentle smile, 149: Cykowiak interview.

of such class, 149: Cykowiak, Wspomnienie, 1.

liver sausage, 149: Cykowiak interview.

the whole orchestra, 150: Ibid.

inside the building, 150: Newman, 264.

grow their hair, 150: Newman, 251.

women prisoners stood, 150: Knapp, 160.

had forbidden this, 150: Ibid., 160–161.

to the concerts, 150: Katarina Grünsteinova, Hodonin, Czech Republic, letter and statement to Susan Eischeid via Zuzana Prudilová, June 20, 2006.

"off on command!", 151: Ibid.

"social event", 151: Knapp, 159–162.

civilized, 151: Ibid.

"reality was bitter", 151: Cykowiak interview.

Chapter 44: At the Gate

number was right, 152: Walentyna Nikodem, Katowice, Poland, letter to Susan Eischeid, January 5, 2006.

"zwei-drei-vier", 152: Katarina Grünsteinova, Hodonin, Czech Republic, letter and statement to Susan Eischeid via Zuzana Prudilová, June 20, 2006.

marches repeatedly, 152: Niwińska, *One of the Girls*, 85.

official on charge, 152: Knapp, 154.

"was often laughing", 152: Krystyna Zywulska, testimony, SNT, 14th day of trial. IPN W: NTN, 165, u. 129.

supervise them, 153: Niwińska, *One of the Girls*, 64.

"ten hours a day", 153: Větrovcová, ČTYŘI ROKY, p. 6.

"horrible sight", 153: Schulamith Khalef, born Sylvia Wagenberg, *Memories, 2003*, published in Inge Franken, Gegen das Vergessen (Berlin: Text Verlag, 2005), 126–127.

"moving an eyelash", 153: Szmaglewska, 23.

"when released", 153: Szmaglewska, 23–24.

"streaks of dawn", 153: Szmaglewska, 23–24.

"I was terrified", 153: Cykowiak, interview with Susan Eischeid, 2003.

"out of control", 154: Ibid.

were really doing, 154: Knapp, 164.

"many others", 154: Niwińska, *One of the Girls*, 81. See also Niwińska interview.

bloodies its wings, 154: Langbein, *People in Auschwitz*, 128. Quoting Manca Svalbova.

all-day rehearsals, 154: Niwińska, 80.

by these issues, 154: Niwińska, 84.

an inhuman way, 155: Cykowiak, *Wspomnienie*, 3.

Chapter 45: "Music, transported..."

"Would Look Beautiful", 156: Michael Daëron, Bach in Auschwitz (film documentary), Zofia Cykowiak testimony (New York: Winstar TV and Video, 2000).

angel-like, 156: Janina Lenc, letter to Susan Eischeid, 2006.

came to us, 156: Cykowiak interview, 2003.

upon the music, 156: Cykowiak, Niwińska interviews 2003; Grünsteinova interview 2006.

"Ober's coming!", 156: Niwińska interview, 2003.

"form of therapy", 156: Cykowiak interview, 2003.

"the orchestra play?", 156: Ibid.

"**girl's ineptitude**", 157: Niwińska interview, 2003.
"**connoisseur she was!**", 157: Cykowiak interview, 2003.
off a shift, 157: Ibid.
"**some place else**", 157: Niwińska interview, 2003.
"**to go away**", 157: Cykowiak interview, 2003.
"**absolutely intelligent**", 157: Niwińska interview, 2003.
"**always elegant**", 157: Cykowiak interview, 2003
"**up to scratch**", 158: Ibid.
herself with pride, 158: Ibid.
I achieved that, 158: Ibid.

Chapter 46: The Men

as an equal, 159: Niwińska interview.
ranking SS officials, 159: Niwińska, *One of the Girls*, 64.
as his subordinate, 159: Niwińska interview, 2003.

> This is interesting to note because later, at her war crimes trial, Mandl attempted to take refuge in and bolster her defense by emphasizing her lower status at Auschwitz. She stated that the female *Aufseherinnen* were definitely not equal, not members of the SS, and that they were simply state workers or "clerks."
>
> Indeed, she was correct in this statement, as the female guards were only ever classified as an auxiliary group to assist the SS in the running of the camps and were never intended to play a direct role in any aspect of administration.

always in competition, 159: Anna Palarczyk, interview with Susan Eischeid, June 11, 2003.
of February , 159: Newman, 295.
of the orchestra, 160: Ibid.
"**Fantastic...**", 160: Niwińska interview, 2003.
"**were lying flat!**", 160: Cykowiak interview, 2003.

Chapter 47: "The Orchestra Means Life!"

we'll go to the gas, 161: Hilde Grünbaum Simche, interview, March 16, 2007, Tel Aviv, Israel, quoting Alma Rosé.
"**demanded respect**", 161: Niwińska interview, 2003.
UNBELIEVABLE!, 161: Newman, 287–288.
a gas chamber, 162: Ibid.
was so good, 162: Cykowiak interview, 2003.

"from deceased people!", 162: Hélène Scheps, letter to Susan Eischeid, November 22, 2005.
"Orchestra Means Life", 162: Niwińska, *One of the Girls*, 77.
Eichmann's visit, 162: Cykowiak, Niwińska interviews, 2003.
"have it distributed", 162: Newman, 275.
the orchestra continued, 163: Cykowiak interview, 2003.
"a unique position", 163: Anita Lasker-Wallfisch, in Newman, 251.
"Jewish orchestra", 163: Cykowiak interview, 2003.
non-Jewish performers, 163: Cykowiak, *Wspomnienie*, 13; Cykowiak interview, 2003.
the crematorium, 163: Hilde Grünbaum Simche, interview, March 16, 2007, Tel Aviv, Israel.

Chapter 48: Christmas in Auschwitz

Christmas candles, 165: Erminie Schulung, "Christmas in the KZ Auschwitz," November 13, 1973, Velden, Austria, ÖST-WIEN.
"Wir Deutsche!", 165: Szmaglewska, 232.
to the gas, 166: Michael Daëron, *Bach in Auschwitz*.
a roll call, 166: Szmaglewska, 232.
"to the song", 166: Szmaglewska, 232–233
to fall outside, 166: Ibid.
are going home, 166: Větrovcová, interview with Susan Eischeid, 2006.
"ruined the orchestra!", 166: Rachela Zelmanowicz Olewski, *Crying Is Forbidden Here!* (Tel-Aviv: Olewski family, 2009), 35.
enemy of Alma, 166: Newman, 284–285.
turnips and water, 166: Erminie Schulung.
heartrending sobbing, 167: Ibid.

Chapter 49: The Paradox

good and evil, 168: Herman Langbein, *People in Auschwitz*, 329.
true of them, 168: Ella Lingens-Reiner, *Prisoner of Fear*, 137.
in the choice, 168: John Grotgen and Faye Altman, interview with Susan Eischeid, June 25, 2003, Valdosta, GA.
in every way, 168: Mandl statement, 121. See also "Tchórzliwe kłamstwa morderczyni," Głos ludu, December 4, 1947.
very ladylike, 169: Helen Tichauer, interview with Susan Eischeid, 2003.
stay in bed, 169: Ibid.
Block , 169: Newman, 227
"well-being!", 169: Tichauer, 2003.

"she gave advice", 169: Ibid.

"in a selection!", 169: Ibid.

"life and death", 170: Anita Lasker-Wallfisch, *Inherit the Truth*, 80–81. See also Lasker-Wallfisch, interview with Susan Eischeid, 2003.

any punishment, 170: Aleksander Kinsky, deposition 1947, APMO; 158.

as a favor, 170: Hilde Simche interview, 2007.

"an office job", 171: Lore Shelley, *Secretaries of Death*, 117. Testimony of Hermine Markovits.

girl's release, 171: Anna Palarczyk, interview with Susan Eischeid, 2003.

When contacted to see if the identity of the young girl could be confirmed, the Siemens Corporation responded that although inquiries had been made regarding her identity, there was now no way to confirm her identity. She could possibly have been a sister of Ernst, Peter, or Hermann von Siemens. But there is no one alive now who knows. Martin Groß, Chief Executive's Office Siemens Corporation, Munich, Germany, letter to Susan Eischeid, October 15, 2003.

"among the prisoners", 171: Lingens-Reiner, 143.

for a time, 171: Ibid., 149.

"nice parcel", 172: Ibid., 146.

"the Krätzenblock", 172: Stanisława Rachwałowa, "Spotkanie z Maria Mandel," *Przegląd Lekarski*, Nr. I, 1990, Tom. XLVTT, 188.

many to survive, 172: Heather Dune Macadam, *999—The Extraordinary Young Women of the First Official Jewish Transport to Auschwitz* (New York: Citadel Press, 2020), 237.

towards her personnel, 173: Cykowiak interview, 2003.

Chapter 50: The Children

there for me, 174: Lucyna Filip, *Auschwitz Information* 61, Ausgabe, Juni 2003, Institut für Sozial und Wirtschaftsgeschichte, Johannes Kepler Universität Linz, www.kz-auschwitz.de/PDF_Audio/Opfer_und_Taeterinnen.pdf.

cheerful commotion, 175: Stanisława Rachwałowa, "Spotkanie z Marią Mandel," *Przegląd Lekarski*, Tom XLVII, Nr. 1, 1990, 185–189.

"be more careful", 175: Romualda Cieślik-Ciesielska, statement, 12 October 1961, Warsaw, Poland. APMO Oświadczenia, t. 22-23, ss. 123, 127, 129. Ośw/ Cieślik-Ciesielska / 656 ; 129.

"like my own", 175: Langbein, *People in Auschwitz*, 396.

was burned too, 175: Zofia Ulewicz, statement, APMO Wspomnienia / godło "Wincka," tom. 88; 192.

the gas chambers, 175: Cykowiak, Niwińska interviews, 2003; Yvette Assael-Lennon, *Bach in Auschwitz.*
"'How is it possible?'", 176: Cykowiak interview, 2003.

Chapter 51: The Child Was Eaten by Rats

repellant adult Jews, 177: Schneider, *Let Me Go*, 159.
"too was Mandl", 177: Stanisława Rachwałowa, "*Spotkanie z Marią Mandel*," *Przegląd Lekarski*, Tom XLVII, Nr. 1, 1990, 185–189.
"and child care", 177: Mandl deposition, 20 May 1946.
"remain alive", 178: Anna Palarczyk, witness testimony, Frankfurcki process załogi Auschwitz, 100/101. Verhandlungstag, 15-16 October 1964, http://www.aushwitz-prozess-frankfurt.ed.
mothers and killed, 178: Dr. Kosciuszk, testimony, SNT, APMO Aktu procesu zalogi KL Auschwitz, Dpr-20 / la; p. 120.
child to death, 178: Aleksander Kinsky deposition.
eaten by rats, 178: Antonina Piatkowska, testimony, SNT, Aktu procesu zalogi KL Auschwitz, Dpr-20 / la; p. 120
"phenol shots", 178: Antonina Piatkowska deposition.
there to die, 178: Dr. Kosciuszkowa, testimony, SNT, Aktu procesu zalogi KL Auschwitz, Dpr-20 / la; p. 120
gas chambers, 178: Ibid. 119
"to the gas", 178: Luba Reiss deposition.
"need for power", 179: Grotgen interview, 2003.

Chapter 52: An Untimely Death

alas, herself, 180: Niwińska, *One of the Girls*, 78.
conducting motions, 180: Newman, 299.
with bedding, 180: Ibid.
said goodbye, 181: Cykowiak interview, 2003; Lasker-Wallfisch, *Inherit the Truth*, 85.
SS seemed upset, 181: Anita Lasker-Wallfisch, *Inherit the Truth*, 85.
been the orchestra, 181: Ibid.

Chapter 53: Mala

punished with death, 182: Mandl statement 125-126.
improve their conditions, 183: Herman Langbein, *Der Auschwitz-Prozess*, Band 1, "Testimony of Raya Kagan" (Frankfurt/Main: Verlag Neue Kritik, 1995), 129.

in the camp, 183: Anna Palarczyk, interview with Anna Kazimierowicz, March 11, 2000, Krakow, Poland. See also: Lore Shelley, *Secretaries of Death*, 252.

were incredulous, 183: Jacek Bławut, "*Tödliche Romanze," An Auschwitz Love Story*, film documentary, 1989; testimony of Wiktor Sawik. See also "The Story of Mala Zimetbaum and Edek Galiński," The Chronical Reportage,   http://www.en.reporter.edu.pl/layout/set/print/content/view/full/67. See also testimony of Alicja Jakubowic-Roth.

"she had escaped!", 183: Anna Palarczyk interview, 2000.

up the pursuit, 183: Herman Langbein, *Der Auschwitz-Prozess*, Band 1, "Testimony of Raya Kagan" (Frankfurt/Main: Verlag Neue Kritik, 1995), 129. See also Josef Kramer telegrams, APMO Microfilm 88-157/158.

"I'm doing well", 184: Herman Langbein, *Der Auschwitz-Prozess*, Band 1 "Testimony of Raya Kagan" (Frankfurt/Main: Verlag Neue Kritik, 1995), 129.

"weather was good", 184: Anna Palarczyk interview, 2000.

other officials, 184: Jacek Bławut, *"Tödliche Romanze"* (film); testimony of Wanda Kaprowska.

paper in her hand, 184: Palarczyk interview, 2000.

"must be hanged", 184: Donald L. Niewyk, ed., *Fresh Wounds: Early Narratives of Holocaust Survival* (Chapel Hill: University of North Carolina Press, 1998), 318.

"raised her hand!", 184: Alicja Jakubowic, *zrodło relacji sprawdzić*, Tom 49, s.84.

"hours are numbered", 184: Lorenz Sichelschmidt, *Mala* (Bremen: Donat Verlag, 1995), 149–150.

"her own hand", 184: Palarczyk interview, 2000.

"lump, a mess", 184: Jacek Bławut, *"Tödliche Romanze"* (film); testimony of Aniela Turecka-Wajd.

beating and kicking, 184: Janina Frankiewicz, SNT, 11thd ay of the trial, testimony; IPN W: NTN 16u, k. 171.

"chimney alive!", 185: SNT, 11th day of the trial, testimony; IPN W: NTN 16u, k. 171. See also Lorenz Sichelschmidt, *Mala* (Bremen: Donat Verlag, 1995), 149–150.

on a carriage, 185: Frankiewicz, 171.

"at the crematorium", 185: Mandl rebuttal, SNT, 11th day of the trial; IPN W: NTN 16u, k. 176-177.

Chapter 54: Summer of '44 / Homecoming

beautiful long boots, 186: August Gründinger, interview with Susan Eischeid, Münzkirchen, Austria, May 25, 2005. See also Münzkirchen community.

full dress uniform, 186: Münzkirchen community. See also Alois Bauer and
Roland Habermann, interview with Susan Eischeid, May 2005,
Münzkirchen, Austria.
"the Nazi Party", 187: Members of the Mandl family, May 2005, Schardenberg,
Austria.
her daughter's soul, 187: Martin Zauner, interview with Susan Eischeid, May
2005, Münzkirchen, Austria. See also Münzkirchen community.
"her feel good", 187: Habermann/Bauer interviews, 2005.
officers with her, 187: Ibid.
"your friend can't", 187: Ibid.
"Teller-Mutze" hat, 187: Martha Leithner, interview with Susan Eischeid, May
2005, Münzkirchen, Austria.
"VERY proud!", 187: Alois Schiller, interview with Susan Eischeid, May 2005,
Münzkirchen, Austria.
"plate-like hats", 187: Zauner interview, 2005.
"NOBODY knew that!", 187: Ibid.
concentration camp, 188: Maria Höller, telephone interview, May 2005.
"say one word!", 188: Zauner interview, 2005.
"have been deported!", 189: Ibid.
"distant and rigorous", 189: Paula Bauer, *Pechmarie*, Christian Strasser and
David Neumayr, 2014 (Austria: Nemada Film Production).
"Americans were coming", 189: Zauner, *Pechmarie*.
"come to that", 189: Ibid.

Chapter 55: The Living Hell

masses of people, 190: Gröning, *Lebenslauf*, 76.
the living hell, 190: Matthäus, *Approaching an Auschwitz Survivor* (Helen Tichauer, 2000), 112.
in the war, 191: Mandl deposition, 20 May 1947, p. 6
Kommandant Kramer, 191: Ibid.
"work positively", 191: APMO, Proces zalogy (stenogram), st. 1, ss. 63-66. Dpr-
Zod / 1; 65b.
August 2, , 191: Danuta Czech, *Auschwitz Chronicle 1939–1945* (London: I.B. Tauris
& Co., Ltd Publishers, 1990), 663 and 677.
"them than ever", 191: Gröning, *Lebenslauf*, citing Höss.
"summer of 1944", 191: Rudolf Höss, deposition, Nuremberg War Crimes Trial,
https://www.jewishvirtuallibrary.org/rudolf-h-ouml-ss.
"Auschwitz train station", 191: Gröning, *Lebenslauf*, 58–59.
in Oświęcim, 192: Gröning, email to Susan Eischeid, September 6, 2006.
about the procedures, 192: Ibid., 76.

"repertoire—everyone", 192: Hélène Scheps, Flora Schrijver-Jacobs, Hilde
    Simche; Daëron, *Bach in Auschwitz.*
burned there, 193: Inge Franken, GEGEN DAS VERGESSEN, Erinnerungen
    an das Jüdische Kinderheim Fehrbelliner Straße 92, Berlin-Prenz-
    lauer Berg. Testimony of Schulamith Khalef (Sylvia Wagenberg)
    (Berlin: TEXTPUNKT Verlag, 2005), 126–127.
whole life thereafter, 193: Ibid.
and died there, 193: Ibid.
pyres was reinitiated, 192: Gröning, *Lebenslauf,* 62.
"the living hell", 193: Matthäus, *Approaching an Auschwitz Survivor* (Helen Ti-
    chauer, 2000), 112.
"on the ramp", 193: SNT, 11th day of the trial, witness testimony. IPN W: NTN,
    16u, k.175.
to the gas, 193: Stanisław Kobiela, *Proces—rozprawa glowna, Marii Mandl* (Boch-
    nia: 2003), Part 9.

Chapter 56: Dissolution

attack planes, 194: Gröning, *Lebenslauf,* 80.
fires of the war, 194: Ibid.
mid-September, 194: Czech, *Auschwitz Chronicle,* 692 and 708.
"far spread out", 194: Gröning, *Lebenslauf,* 80.
"to the bunker!", 195: Anna Palarczyk, interview with Susan Eischeid, 2003.
few more months, 195: Mandl statement, 119-120.
longer go on, 195: Mandl family, 2006.
Hössler's absences, 195: Cykowiak interview 2003.
"a new orchestra", 195: Palarczyk interview, 2003.
"with Hössler", 195: Cykowiak interview, 2003.
"ceased to exist", 196: Niwińska, 122–123.
"idyllic period", 196: Helm, 483.
"won her over", 196: Tichauer, interview with Eischeid, 2003.
"imagined the world", 197: Lingens-Reiner, *Prisoners of Fear,* 146–147.

PART FIVE

Chapter 57: Mühldorf

emotionally breaking down, 201: Mandl statement, 119-120.
super Aryan chickens, 201: Bill Gluck, interviews with Susan Eischeid, No-
    vember 21, 2003, and March 18, 2004.

of its existence, 202: Müller, *Die Oberaufseherinnen*, 57–58.

eight hundred women, 202: Ibid., 57. See also Gabriele Hammerman, Die Dachauer Außenlager um Mühldorf, Dachauer Hefte, 15. Jahrgang 1999, Heft 15 (Nov. 1999), 77-98.

lost their lives, 202: Ibid. See also Edith Raim, *Die Dachauer KZ-Aussenkommandos Kaufering und Mühldorf* (Landsberg a Lech: 1992).

quicker than flies, 202: Gluck interviews 2003, 2004.

for her brutality, 202: NARA, Bernard Greenstein, testimony, Report on Work Lagers in Mühldorf Area, War Crimes Investigating Team #6827, Volume 1. 2 June 1945. NARA. RG 549, M1093, Records of U.S. Army, Europe.

lost in a daydream, 202: Ibid.

ourselves in a trap, 203: Mandl statement 119-120.

by these bombings, 203: I.A. Hr. Hamberger, The Air Attack on Mühldorf am Inn; 19 March 1945 & 20 April 1945; 20 December 1999, Stadtarchiv Muhldorf, http://www.angelfire.com/wv/liberator/franz.html.

"some pray", 203: Bill Neutzling's B-24 Liberator Site: Recollections of German Citizens Muhldorf, http://www.angelfire.com/wv/liberator/franz.html.

"if nothing happened", 203: Gluck interview.

"Germans defeated", 203: Kate Bernath, interview with Linda Kuzmack—USHMM, 22 March 1990; videotaped USHMM Archives, RG-50.030*0023.

"sight it was!", 204: Gluck interview.

Maria fled, 204: Mandl statement, 120.

"them at all", 204: Aaron A. Eiferman, affidavit, 8 November 1986. U.S. soldier who liberated camp. Raim, p. 276.

preparation for reburial, 204: USHMM Photo Archives, # 1945–1946. Taken by Ivo Sciarra, U.S. army officer.

Chapter 58: Escape and Capture

became the victim, 205: Mandl statement, 120

"from tanks", 205: Mandl statement, 120.

"for what you have done", 205: Münzkirchen community. See also Alois Schiller, interview with Susan Eischeid, Münzkirchen, Austria, May 25, 2005.

"my own name", 206: Mandl statement, 120.

piercing eyes, 206: Bernard Greenstein, testimony, Report on Work Lagers in Muhldorf Area, War Crimes Investigating Team #6827, Volume

1. 2 June 1945. NARA. RG 549, M1093, Records of U.S. Army, Europe.

displaced civilians, 206: Walter Lauer, *Battle Babies, the Story of the 99th Infantry Division in World War II* (Battery Press: 1985), 324–325. See also: Joseph Halow, *Innocent at Dachau* (CA: Institute for Historical Review: 1993), 31–33.

him by others, 207: Mandl statement, 120.

Chapter 59: Dachau

it's cleaned up, 208: Lavan Robinson, interview with Susan Eischeid, 8 November 2005, Valdosta, GA.

mandatory arrestees, 208: Joshua M. Greene, *Justice at Dachau* (New York: Broadway Books, 2003), 31.

had at liberation, 208: Ibid., 22.

was still strong, 208: Ibid.

next three years, 208: Ibid., 1.

women and men, 209: Harold Marcuse, *Legacies of Dachau* (United Kingdom: Cambridge University Press, 2001), 69.

#29-1277, 209: Wanted Report; Mandl, Maria; War Crimes Branch—US Army, status update 3 April 1946, M. Muszkat. APMO ZABRONIONE. War Crimes Enclosure, 6.

electric light, 209: Lord Russell of Liverpool, *Scourge of the Swastika* (Cornwall: Greenhill Books, 2002), 251.

if not tasty, 209: Robinson interview, 2005.

"you could stand!", 209: Margit Burda, interview with Susan Eischeid, May 2006, Munich, Germany.

barracks for exercise, 209: Robinson interview, 2005.

father and sister, 209: Mandl statement, 122.

"faithful about that", 209: Robinson interview, 2005.

relationship with him, 209: Mandl statement, 163-164.

wrote about Mandl, 210: Melchior Wańkowicz, *Karafki La Fontaine'a*, Vol. 2 (Krakow: Wydawnictwo Literackie, 1981), 94–95.

refused to cooperate, 210: Hanno Loewy, "*Die Mutter aller Holocaust-Filme?*," in Erpel, *Im Gefolge der SS*, 281.

visibly swallowing, 210: Steven Spielberg Film & Video Archive, USHMM. "In Prison for Defendants; Landsberg Hangings." Accession # 1994.119.1; RG-60.2336; Film ID 896.

"know Maria there", 210: Margit Burda, interview with Susan Eischeid, May 2006, Munich, Germany.

Chapter 60: Margit

Personification of Evil, 211: Elsa Berkomiczowa, deposition, 31 July 1947, Katowice, Poland. APMO Proces zalogi, t. 56a, ss. 146-161 (188-208); ZOd / 56a; 147.

good and kind friend, 211: Burda interview, 2006.

in occupied Poland, 211: Wendy Lower, *Hitler's Furies; German Women in the Nazi Killing Fields* (Boston: Houghton Mifflin Harcourt, 2013), 5-7.

"come to an end", 211: Burda interview, 2006.

was wearing gloves, 213: Margit Burda, letter to Susan Eischeid, February 15, 2007.

"and her relatives", 213: Burda interview, 2006.

"had to punish them", 213: Ibid.

she did 100%, 213: Margit Burda, letter to Susan Eischeid, May 20, 2008.

"laugh about anything", 213: Margit Burda, letter to Susan Eischeid, December 11, 2006.

"hurt her father", 213: Burda interview, 2006.

lies and deceit, 214: Margit Burda, letter to Franz Mandl, December 12, 1948.

Chapter 61: Treated with Respect

lovely it was!, 215: Margit Burda, letter to Susan Eischeid, August 21, 2007.

"have been treated", 215: Robinson interview, 2005.

I can still hear that…, 216: Burda interview, 2006.

the green blankets, 216: Ibid.

were very nice, 216: Margit Burda, letter to Susan Eischeid, August 21, 2007.

proud of it, 216: Ibid.

clothing collection, 217: Ibid.

camp more visceral, 217: Greene, *Justice at Dachau*, 35.

of that trial, 217: Stanisław Kobiela, Śledztwo, "Oględziny rzeczy Marii Mandel." (Examination of Mandl's belongings at Montelupich), 10 May 1947. See also IPN W: 139, h. 104-105.

five of us, 217: Burda interview, 2006.

"until I recovered!", 218: Ibid.

"and messed around", 218: Burda interview, 2006.

Chapter 62: Extradition

Germany to Poland, 219: Mandl statement, 97.

men to Poland, 219: Polish War Crimes Liaison Detachment, Report of Extradition, 7 September 1946. IPN W. PMW-B2W, 587, k.67.

and was dreadful, 219: Margit Burda, letter to Franz Mandl, December 12, 1948.
"Polish authorities", 219: Chester Bednarczyk, Report on Prisoner Escape, Dziedzice, Poland, 7 September 1946. IPN W. PMW-B2W; 587, k.66.
man to suicide, 219: Report of Extradition, 1946.
Johanna Langefeld, 219: Ibid.
"told us anything", 220: Burda interview, 2006.

Chapter 63: Selbstmord

Kill them!, 221: Burda interviews, 2006; May 20, 2008.
"famous pilot", 221: In press coverage Mandl was often confused with Hanna Reitsch (1912–1979), one of the world's first female test pilots and an experienced aviatrix for the Third Reich. Reitsch was a fervent admirer of Adolf Hitler. http://www.ctie.monash.edu.au/hargrave/reitsch.html.
"work in KZs", 221: *Dziennik Bałtycki*, December 22, 1946.
throw us to them!, 222: Burda interviews, 2006; May 20, 2008.
"in Polish hands", 222: Stanisław Kobiela, *Maria Mandel—Part V*, "*Ekstradycja do Polski,*" January 17, 2004.
"Commit suicide!", 222: Margit Burda, letter to Susan Eischeid, August 21 2007; Burda interview, 2008.
underway for 7 days, 222: Margit Burda, letter to Susan Eischeid, August 21, 2007; Burda interviews, 2006, 2008.

Chapter 64: The Beater Becomes the Beaten

"mauled or petted", 223: Cykowiak interview, 2003.
nose and mouth, 224: Mandl statement, 97-98.
"hearing is impaired", 224: Ibid.
"was very sick", 224: Ibid.

Chapter 65: Cieszyn

not heal completely, 225: Mandl statement, 97-98.
in right eye, 225: Karta Ambulatoryjna, 390-H6, Mandel, Maria; Cieszyn. ZE-ZB; Monte 223.
traveling to Poland, 226: Mandl statement, 98.
"together in the evenings", 226: Margit Burda, letter to Franz Mandl, December 12, 1948.
"could stand it", 226: Ibid.

Chapter 66: Montelupich

years of service, 227: Mandl statement, 163-164 (129b).
"emotional stresses", 227: Hans Münch, *The Meeting*, ed. Bernhard Frankfurter (Syracuse: Syracuse University Press, 2000), 71–72.

Chapter 67: Arrival in Prison

regardless of rank, 230: Prosecutor Jan Brandys, interviewed by Stan Kobieła, January 1985, Tarnów, Poland.
her right hand, 231: Intake document, Maria Mandl, Montelupich Prison. ZE-ZB; Monte-223.

Chapter 68: Harsh, but Better

nobody starved, 232: Bernhard Frankfurter, ed., *The Meeting* (New York: Syracuse University Press, 2000), 127.
former political prisoners, 232: Meeting of former political prisoners, Montelupich Prison, December 6, 2004, Krakow, Poland.
"or carve with", 232: Captain Franciszek Oremus, interview with Susan Eischeid via Lidia Jurek, December 7, 2004, Poland. See also Zofia Moskała, interview with Susan Eischeid via Lidia Jurek, December 7, 2004, Poland.
inside as outside, 232: Stanisław Potoczny, interview with Susan Eischeid, June 2003.
made of rutabaga, 233: Meeting of former political prisoners, 2004.
"12 or so days", 233: Hanna Wysocka, interviews with Susan Eischeid, May 2005 and 2006, Krakow, Poland.
"it was horrible", 233: Moskała interview, 2004.
do that today, 233: Potoczny interview, 2003.
"good for the trial", 233: Wiezienie Montelupich w Krakowie, orders from Kpt. Klitenika to Director of the Prison, 13 June 1947. Nr. G.I.2185/2160/47. See also "Top Secret" concessions toward the Nazi war criminals, Lt. A.M. Kozłowski. 21 November 1946, Krakow. ZE-ZB: WW u8.
"in any way", 234: "*Pani* Jadzia," interview with Susan Eischeid, Krakow, Poland, May 2005.
"stretched to capacity", 234: Margit Burda, letter to Susan Eischeid, December 11, 2006. See also Burda interview, 2006.

Chapter 69: The Escape

"and for Germankind", 235: Burda interview, 2006.

was unusually lucky, 235: Margit Burda, letter to Franz Mandl, December 12, 1948.

It was freezing, 235: Burda interview, 2006

winter in our cells, 235: Burda, letter to Franz Mandl.

into hiding, 236: Müller, *Die Oberaufseherinnen*, 41ü–42.

always consoled her, 236: Burda, letter to Franz Mandl.

"asked for me!", 236: Margit Burda, letter to Susan Eischeid, August 21, 2007.

how to help, 236: Margit Burda, letter to Susan Eischeid, August 21, 2007.

Chapter 70: Time Passed Slowly

on her head, 237: Burda interview, 2008

day or night, 237: Ibid.

one by one, 237: Oremus/Moskała interviews, 2004

salted herring, 237: Burda interview, 2006.

white blouse, 238: Margit Burda to Susan Eischeid, November 12, 2006.

out of luck, 238: Burda interview, 2006.

quite as bad, 238: Ibid.

"in our hair", 238: Moskała interview, 2004.

"of the water", 238: Burda interview, 2008.

"remember for sure", 238: Moskała interview, 2004.

"executions took place", 238: Wysocka interview, 2006.

"Kamienna Street", 238: Danuta Wojnar Górecka, *Klementyna: Więzienne wspomnienia z procesu WiN-u* (Krakow: Księgarnia Akademicka, 1997). See also correspondence with Susan Eischeid, June 2006–May 2007.

> *Klementyna* is a book that Górecka wrote about her experiences in Montelupich during the same period as Mandl's incarceration. Ultimately, she was released from prison and emigrated to the United States, where she translated much of her original book into English as part of her language classes. During subsequent correspondence with Susan Eischeid she shared the enclosed passages as they appear here.

for how long?, 239: Ibid.

Chapter 71: Cellmates

"are in prison", 240: Górecka interview.

style as Maria, 241: APMO No. 1662.

her forehead, 241: Detention Report, Therese Brandl, IC #77 #3546. IPN W: NTN 141, u. 16-17, 30.

"she was crazy!", 241: Burda 2006

"prayed to the shoes", 241: Ibid.

Chapter 72: "Pani Jadzia"

wear a uniform!, 242: "*Pani* Jadzia," interview with Susan Eischeid, May 2005, Krakow, Poland.

> *Pani* Jadzia's real name and identity are on record in the author's files, confirmed by Ms. Wysocka and witnessed by translator Lidia Jurek.

Polish Communists, 242: The acronym WiN (Zrzeszenie I Niezawisto ŚĆ) stood for "Freedom and Independence." The main activity of WiN was to avoid Soviet domination over Poland and to fight Communism. Dr. Janusz Marek Kurtyka, Ph.D., *WiN | Freedom and Independence—A Historical Brief* (Instytut Pamięci Narodowej IPN, Poland).

for the disabled, 242: Barbara Otwinowska and Teresa Drzal, *Zawołać Po Imienu*, Tom. II (Pruszków: Oficyna Wydawniczo-Reklamowa VIPART, 2003), 386.

"I'm from nobility", 244: "Pani Jadzia," interview with Susan Eischeid, May 2005, Krakow, Poland. This and all subsequent quotes from Pani Jadzia are taken from this interview, witnessed by Hannah Wysocka and translator Lidia Jurek.

into her cell, 244: This does seem contradicted by other sources, including testimony from a former Auschwitz prisoner, who was given the opportunity. "When it was suggested that they would let me into the cell of Oberaufseherin Mandl so that I could pay her back for everything, teaching me how to beat so as not to leave traces on her body, I refused. I couldn't force myself to do it." Zenon Jagoda, Stanisław Kłodinski, Jan Masłowski; Stosunek ofiar Oświęcimia-Brzezinki do Prześladowców. Przegląd Lekarski "Oświęcim nr. 1 1981 r.," str. 50.

Chapter 73: Always Full of Ideas

and going crazy, 246: Burda interview, 2008.

"standing and sitting!", 246: Burda interview, 2006.

"clean, clean, clean!", 246: Ibid.

"we cooked", 247: Margit Burda, letters to Susan Eischeid, June 20, 2006, and September 26, 2006.

"beautifully yellow", 247: *Kochbuch für Anny Mandl*, Mandl family, 2006.

"wife and mother", 247: Burda interview, 2008.

"anything good", 247: Margit Burda, letter to Susan Eischeid, June 20, 2006.

Chapter 74: Personal Encounters

busy and occupied!, 248: Margit Burda, letter to Franz Mandl, December 12, 1948.
"chest really well", 248: Wysocka interview, 2005, quoting Stanisława Rachwałowa.
"Auschwitz Duchess!", 248: Górecka, *Klementyna*.
"remain human", 250: Ibid.

Chapter 75: "The Dirties"

claims or resentment, 251: Wysocka interview, 2005.
"playing on her", 251: Ibid.
related to work, 252: Examination of Mandl's belongings at Montelupich. IPN
    W (NTN): 139, h. 104-105.
"played the game", 252: Eryk Dormicki file; biographical data. IPN Wi: Wie-
    liczka, Poland, 2006.
"few from him", 252: Bernhard Frankfurter, ed., *The Meeting*, (New York: Syr-
    acuse University Press, 2000), 127.
"he would leave", 252: Wysocka interview.
sew perfectly, 252: Karta Ambulatoryjna "Mandel, Maria," Montelupich
    Prison; ZE-ZB: Monte 223.
typhoid inoculation, 252: Ibid.

Chapter 76: "Virgin mother of my God, let me be fully your own"

in my heart, 253: Virgil, The Aeneid, 323, https://www.loebclassics.com/
    view/virgil-aeneid/1916/pb_LCL063.323.xml.
"'Mandelka' is gray", 253: Piękność Oświęcimia jest dziś szara. Tylko ręce sie
    nie zmieniły – ręce morderczyni. Dobry Wieczór nr 326 – 27.XI.47
    (21 November 1947).
time in prison, 253: Moskała interview, 2004.
"fully your own"', 253: Margit Burda, letter to Susan Eischeid, November 12, 2006.
not a bad person, 254: Burda interview, 2008.

PART SIX

Chapter 77: The Tribunal

was dealing with, 257: Margit Burda, letter to Franz Mandl, December 12, 1948.
"quickly punish him", 257: Jan Brandys, interview with Stanisław Kobiela. Tar-
    nowski Magazyn Informacyjny. 27 stycznia 1985 r. Nr 4 (255), 1 & 5.

See also Israel Gutman, ed., *Encyclopedia of the Holocaust* (New York: Macmillan Publishers, 1990), 1514.

Auschwitz defendants, 258: Andrew Nagorski, *The Nazi Hunters* (New York: Simon & Schuster, 2016), 63–64, 74–75.

"staffer in need", 258: Ibid.

"volumes of materials", 259: Ryszard Kotarba, interview with Susan Eischeid, May 19, 2004, Wielizcka, Poland.

in the courtroom, 259: Nagorski, 123.

recording clerk, 259: Jan Brandys interview with Kobiela

any other defendant, 259: SNT, prosecution statement. IPN W: NTN, 166, u. 249.

Chapter 78: The Lawyers

wits and wisdom, 260: Władysław Bartoscewski, interview with Susan Eischeid, Warsaw, Poland, May 18, 2004.

had to take it, 260: Jacek Kanski, interview with Susan Eischeid, May 19, 2004, Krakow, Poland.

"a high standard", 261: Jan Brandys, interview with Stanisław Kobiela, "To Był Rzetelny Proces." Tarnowski Magazyn Informacyjny. 27 stycznia 1985 r. Nr 4 (255), 1 & 5.

"from this duty", 261: Jolanta Ostrawska-Jaźiecka, interview, March 17, 2004, Krakow, Poland.

"was not common", 261: Wallisch recusal SNT. IPN W: NTN 159, u. 50.

"not even considered!", 261: Brandys, interview with Kobiela.

"a similar dilemma", 261: Ostrawska interview.

Chapter 79: Rymar

for understanding him, 262: Stanisław Rymar, Jr., interviews with Susan Eischeid, November 2003, May 2004, Warsaw, Poland.

"with a client", 263: Ibid.

"about those issues", 263: Ibid.

"a defense lawyer", 263: Ibid.

"intelligence and knowledge", 263: Ibid.

"yielded to anyone", 264: Wojciech Dudek, letter to Susan Eischeid, February 21, 2004.

"not 'politically correct'", 264: Wojciech Dudek, interview with Susan Eischeid, May 19, 2004, Krakow, Poland.

"way he wanted", 264: Ibid.

brought up too, 264: Rymar, Jr., interview.

Chapter 80: Deposition

But how?, 266: Margit Burda, letter to Susan Eischeid, November 12, 2006.

Krystyna Szymanska, 266: Maria Mandl, deposition SNT, 19 May 1947, Krakow, Poland.

administrative offices, 266: Oremus interview, 2004.

"questioning in another", 266: Wspomnienia p. Krystyny Szymańskiej, sekretarki Okręgowej Komisji Badenia Zbrodni Niemieckich w Krakowie. See also IPN Kr, 1/106, Wspomnienia Krystyna Szymańskiej, (1980 r.), k. 57-60.

noted in the report, 267: Krystyna Szymańska, interviewed by Stanisław Kobiela, 1985. See also Wspomnienia p. Krystyna Szymańska.

KZ system, 267: These accounts were written with chemical pencils, which were goldish-orange with a round and thick shaft and soft lead. They contained a chemical that caused the lead to change color when written, from a soft blackish hue to blue.

my future fate, 267: Mandl statement, 121-122.

report or *Protokol*, 268: Kanski interview, 2004.

Chapter 81: The Trial

believe in justice, 269: Mandl statement, 122.

she was scared, 269: Burda interviews, 2006 and 2007.

against the light, 270: Dr. Jerzy Ludwikowski, interview with Susan Eischeid, May 2004, Nowy Wisnicz, Poland.

amount of interest, 270: Jan Brandys, interview with Stanisław Kobiela. Tarnowski Magazyn Informacyjny. 27 stycznia 1985 r. Nr 4 (255), 1 & 5.

and correspondents, 271: Ibid.

7:00 or 8:00 P.M., 271: Najwyższy Trybunał Narodowy, 11 listopada 1947, Krakow; Nr. NTN.5/47. ZE-ZB: WW u. 8.

"very hostile", 271: Ludwikowski interview, 2004.

"weren't jail clothes", 271: Burda interview, 2008.

prisoners unloading, 271: *March of Time*—outtakes—Krakow scenes; War Crimes Trial: "Butchers of Auschwitz," Steven Spielberg Film & Video Archive, USHMM, Accession # 1994:119:1; RG-60.0983; Film ID 917.

Chapter 82: In Session

waiting for a bus, 273: Ben Ferencz, "The Last Living Nuremberg Prosecutor Turns 100," *60 Minutes*, March 11, 2020.

"primitive and vulgar", 273: Jan Brandys, interview with Stanisław Kobiela. Tarnowski Magazyn Informacyjny. 27 stycznia 1985 r. Nr 4 (255), 1 & 5.

the main judge, 274: The trial was presided over by Dr. Alfred Eimer. Judges were Dr. Witold Kutzner, Dr. Jozef Zembaty, and Judge Henryk Ciesluk, while the jury consisted of members of parliament.

even more vivid, 274: *March of Time*—outtakes—Krakow scenes; War Crimes Trial: "Butchers of Auschwitz," Steven Spielberg Film & Video Archive, USHMM, Accession # 1994:119:1; RG-60.0983; Film ID 917.

behaved dishonorably!, 274: Brandys interview with Kobiela.

Chapter 83: Opening

"following orders" defense, 275: *Słowo Powszechne*, No. 244, November 26, 1947.

in the courtroom, 275: Stanisław Kobiela, "*Proces—rozprawa główna*, Bochnia: 2003, Part 9."

filming the trial, 275: This film was originally produced as a newsreel by *TIME* magazine, then distributed as a multipart documentary, part of the newsreel series called *The March of Time.*

the gas chambers, 276: APMO, Actu procesu zalogi KL Auschwitz, Dpr – 20/1a; 13.

inhuman punishments, 276: Tadeusz Cyprian and Jerzy Sawicki, *Sledem Procesów, Przed Najywyższym Trybunałem Narodowym* (Poznan: Instytut Zachodni, 1962), 149.

"thousands of people", 276: APMO, Proces zalogi (stenogram), st. I, ss. 63-66. Dpr-ZoD /4; 40/0.

Polish vodka, 277: Tadeusz Cyprian, letter, December 3, 1947. See also Stanisław Kobiela, "Opinia Tadeusza Cypriana," Przemówienia oskarżyciela, obrońców I ostatnie słowo Marii Mandl, Part X, Bochnia, Poland; 2004.

"torn to pieces", 277: Ibid.

collective experiences, 277: Ibid.

irritated the audience, 277: Ibid.

Chapter 84: The Case Against Mandl

of moral conduct, 278: Stanisław Rymar in his opening statement for the defense of Maria Mandl, IPN W: NTN 167IPN W: NTN 167, k.u. 85.

abusing human dignity, 278: IPN W: NTN 166, u. 247-248.

"no human feelings", 279: Ibid.

"rest of the line", 279: Ibid., 249.

"courage to proceed", 279: IPN W: NTN 167, u. 82-84.

cruelties and atrocities, 279: IPN W: NTN 167, u. 82-84.
"afraid of me", 279: Ibid., 84.
"of moral conduct", 279: Ibid., 85.
people/government, 280: Ibid., 87.
"human life", 280: Ibid. 85.

Chapter 85: The Evidence

evil people in check, 281: Margit Burda, letter to Susan Eischeid, September 26, 2006.
beat and kicked her, 281: Janina Frankiewicz, testimony, IPN W. NTN 16u, k. 167-178; 167-168.
seen again (died), 282: Ibid., 172.
on the road, 282: Ibid., 170.
"cut her wrists", 282: Ibid., 171–172.
"to the gas chambers", 282: Ibid., 172–173
less and coffee, 282: Ibid., 167–168.
even in the dark, 283: Ibid., 175–176.
gave prisoners shots, 283: Ibid., 176
come from Berlin, 283: Ibid., 176–177
Hungarian transports, 284: Ibid., 178.
"Yes!", 284: Ibid., 178
"and her order", 284: Felicja Pleszowska, testimony, IPN W. NTN 16u, k. 182.
such a burning, 284: Antonina Piatkowska, APMO: Proces zalogi, t. 56, ss. 7-8 (10-12). D-ZOd / 56.
"system for annihilation", 284: Seweryna Szmagelwska, testimony, IPN W: NTN 165, u 116-123.
"so many died", 284: Ibid., 117.
"continue to spread", 285: Ibid., 117–118.
to "stay alive", 285: Ibid.
this for death, 285: Janina Unkiewicz, deposition, 25 January 1947, APMO. Proces zalogi, t. 56, ss. 31-36 (45-53), D-ZO / 56; 31.
"with a whip", 285: Elżbieta Wondraczek, statement, IPN W: NTN 151, h 95v. Quoting Rozalia Huber.
out of step, 285: Krystyna Zywulska, IPN W: NTN 165, u. 129.
one thousand women prisoners, 285: Maria Zumańska, APMO Oświadczenia, t. 4, ss. 412; 416-418; 421. Ośw / Zumańska / 84.
be washed off, 285: Wanda Marossanyi, APMO, Proces zalogi, t.56, s. 56 (81-82). D-ZOd / 56. Quoting Karolina Wilinska.
"her shoes helped", 285: IPN W: NTN, 139, u. 83-84.

"in the stomach", 286: APMO; Proces zalogi, t. 57, ss. 14-15 (21-24), D-ZOd / 57.
"hunger in Ravensbrück", 286: IPN W: NTN, 167, k 193-196; 195.
"cooked to perfection", 286: Mandl statement, 129.
"the pan proper", 286: Burda interview, 2006.

Chapter 86: Defense

was awfully hard, 287: Mandl, IPN W: NTN 167, k. 194.
"names for the list", 287: APMO: Aktu procesu zalogi KL Auschwitz, Dpr –
    200 / 1a; 117.
"day and night", 287: IPN W: NTN 166, u. 249.
"over other guards", 288: IPN W: NTN 166, u. 141-142.
"Defendant Liebenschel", 288: IPN W: NTN 167, k. 193
"place under Höss", 288: Ibid. 194.
"his exclusive power", 288: IPN W: NTN 164, k. 157.
give any punishments, 288: IPN W: NTN 167, k. , 000
"some other guard", 288: , 000: Ibid., 193.
"or a revolver", 289: IPN W: NTN 165, u. 55-56.
"deaths in Auschwitz", 289: IPN W: NTN 165, u. 116-124.
away from herself, 289: Müller, Die Oberaufseherinnen, 63–68.
"to his conscience", 289: Whitney R. Harris, Tyranny on Trial (Dallas: South-
    ern Methodist University Press, 1999), 176.
responded "No", 289: Trial Files, Vol. 1, p. 185. See also Trybuna Dolnośląska,
    No. 303, 30 November 1947.
"'would come of it'", 289: Wspomnienia p. Krystyna Szymańskiej sekretari
    Okręgowej Komisji Badania Zbrodni Niemieckich w Krakowie.
    See also interview with Stanisław Kobiela, 1985. See also See also
    Filip Gańczak, Jan Sehn (Wołowiec: Wydawnictwo Zarne, 2020),
    104.

Chapter 87: The Game Is Lost (Final Innings)

"of his contempt", 290: Langbein, People in Auschwitz, 505.
brought on by stress, 291: Karta Ambulatoryjna, Mandel-Maria, ZE-ZB 223.

Chapter 88: The Press

does he want?, 292: Krystyna Żywulska, "Z Naszej Perspektywy," Wolni Ludzi,
    Nr. 17, Str. 5, December 1947.
after the war, 292: Brown, The Camp Women, 22.

"love with her", 292: Andrzej Wydroynski, *"O zmroku na Sali rozpraw,"* Trud/ *Try-buna Ludu*, December 24, 1947.

nickname, "Mandelka", 292: "The Beauty of Auschwitz Is Gray Today," *Wieczór*, No. 326, November 27, 1947. See also "Before the Auschwitz Trial," *Wolnych ludzi*, November 15, 1947.

"second rate Bierstube", 292: *Trybuna Dolnósląska*, No. 303, November 30, 1947. See also *Głos Robotnicky*, No. 338, December 10, 1947.

"Human Bodies", 292: "Monsters in Human Bodies," *Wolność*, No. 280/983, December 14, 1947.

"carefree" and "cheerful", 293: *Echo Krakowa*, November 29, 1947.

during recesses, 293: *Echo Krakowa*, December 1 and 3, 1947.

"frozen in terror", 293: *"Dramatczny moment konfrontacji Świadka z oskarżonymi,"* *Słowo Powszechne*, November 30, 1947.

extensive the coverage, 293: Michel Gordey "Echoes from Auschwitz," *New Republic*, December 22, 1947.

"world for us!", 294: Trial Proceedings, Vol. IV, 185. See also Kobiela, *Prozes roz-prawa głowna*.

"by the witnesses", 294: *Trybuna Dolnósląska*, No. 303, November 30, 1947. See also *Głos Robotnicky*, No. 338, December 10, 1947.

"No", 294: *Echo Krakowa*, December 5, 1947.

Maria's demeanor, 294: *"Tchórzliwe kłamstwa morderczyni,"* *Głos Ludu*, December 4, 1947.

voice is shaking, 294: *Kurier Codzienny*, December 7, 1947.

"pure formality", 294: "The Beauty of Auschwitz Is Gray Today," *Wieczór*, No. 326, November 27, 1947.

"with loud laughter", 294: *Trybuna Dolnósląska*, No. 303, November 30, 1947. See also *Głos Robotnicky*, No. 338, December 10, 1947.

signed the list, 294: *"Wiedźma Oświęcimia"* ("Witch of Auschwitz"), *Robotnik*, No. 331, December 1947. See also *Kurier Codzienny*, December 4, 1947.

"does he want?", 295: Krystyna Żywulska, *"Z Naszej Perspektywy,"* *Wolni Ludzi*, Nr. 17, Str. 5, December 1947.

Chapter 89: Challenge of the Orchestra Women

Can't see, 296: Karta Ambulatoryjna "Mandel, Maria," Montelupich Prison; ZE-ZB: Monte 223.

inner turmoil, 296: Cykowiak, interview, 2003.

"it was my duty", 296: Ibid.

encounter with Mandl, 296: Ibid.

Chapter 90: Closing Arguments

a very sick person?, 299: Rymar, closing statement, IPN W: NTN 167, 90-94.
"to defend her", 299: Ibid.
"[for her crimes]", 299: Ibid.
the gas chamber, 300: Ibid.
"normal and necessary", 300: Ibid.
to oppose orders, 300: Ibid.

Chapter 91: Guilty

insane women deaths, 302: APMO Judgement. Aktu procesu zalogi KL Auschwitz, Dpr – 20 / 1a ; 117-122.

Chapter 92: Sentence

but Justice, 303: *Echo Krakowa*, December 24, 1947.
"the accused guilty", 303: *Wolni Ludzie*, No. 18, December 23, 1947.
only person acquitted, 304: Ibid.
whole face, 304: *Echo Krakowa*, December 24, 1947.
"'Heil Hitler!'", 304: Jerzy Luwikowski, interviews with Stanisław Kobiela, Nowy Wisnicz, Poland, 1955 and 2003.
was all purple!, 304: Cykowiak interview, 2004.

PART SEVEN

Chapter 93: The Waiting

death of millions, 307: Tim Townsend, *Mission at Nuremberg* (New York: William Morrow Publishers, 2014), 245.
is my future fate, 307: Mandl statement, 127 (160).
previous trial, 307: The sentence was later commuted.
"very, very difficult", 307: Wysocka interview, 2005.
"That's all", 308: Ibid.
"carved their names", 308: Moskała, interview, 2004.
"terrible sadists", 308: Ibid.
"had enough", 308: Ibid., describing testimony of Helena Jedrzejowska.
above-mentioned convicts, 308: Mandl, Request for Pardon to President Bierut, 27 December 1947, Krakow, Poland. IPN W: SNT files.
"civilian employee", 308: Ibid.
"to have mercy", 309: Ibid.

Chapter 94: Christmas Eve 1947

magic of Christmas?, 310: Cherish, *The Auschwitz Kommandant*, 214.

a few days before, 311: Danuta Wojnar Górecka, *Klementyna; Więzienne wspomnienia z procesu WiN-u* (Krakow: Księgarnia Akademicka, 1997). See also correspondence with Susan Eischeid, June 2006–May 2007.

Chapter 95: Zaba

treated you unfairly, 312: Uwe Timm, *In My Brother's Shadow: A Life and Death in the SS* (New York: Farrar, Straus and Giroux, 2003), 82.

before execution, 312: Wysocka interview, 2005.

"Come quickly", 312: Gorecka interview.

"these two women", 313: Ibid., quoting Maria Żabianka.

"sympathy for the SS", 313: Wysocka interview.

WiN organization, 313: Barbara Otwinowska and Teresa Drzal, *Zawołać Po Imienu*, Tom. II (Pruszków: Oficyna Wydawniczo-Reklamowa VIPART, 2003), 388.

"cleaned for them", 313: Wysocka interview.

sentence for sure, 313: Ibid.

"even studied Polish", 313: Ibid., quoting Żabianka.

Chapter 96: Father Stark

God than himself, 314: Father Władysław Piotrowski, interview with Susan Eischeid, Tarnów, Poland, May 6, 2004.

and intelligent, 314: Father Marian Stark, photograph, ZKM, Krakow, Poland, May 2004.

"of being a priest", 314: Piotrowski interview.

"for God himself", 315: Ibid.

loss of faith, 315: Luis Baerga, letter to Susan Eischeid, Goshen, NY, June 29, 2004.

"the Almighty God", 315: Mandl statement, 98.

"and the like", 315: Mandl deposition, 20 May 1947, p. 7.

"contrition is true", 315: Baerga interview.

"of the gallows", 316: Townsend, *Mission at Nuremberg*, 8.

Chapter 97: Final Goodbye

bad, very sad, 317: Burda interviews.

"and I was gone", 317: Ibid.

including Mandl, 317: Montelupich records, ZE-ZB: 223.

"Will Be Hanged", 317: "23 Criminals from the Auschwitz Camp Will Be Hanged," *Trybuna Robotnicza,* January 17, 1947.

at 7:00 A.M., 317: Montelupich records, ZE-ZB: 223.

the death cells, 317: Oremus, interview, 2004.

Chapter 98: Rachwałowa and the Shower Room

in the death camps, 318: Laurence Thomas, "Forgiving the Unforgiveable?," in Eve Garrard and Geoffrey Scarre, *Moral Philosophy and the Holocaust* (England: Ashgate Publishing Company, 2003), 202.

"very tough", 318: Anna Wicentowicz, interview with Susan Eischeid, Gmina Wieliczka, Poland, May 2006.

"and we laughed", 319: Ibid.

Auschwitz-Birkenau, 319: Barbara Otwinowska and Teresa Drzal, Zawołać Po Imienu, Tom. II (Pruszków: Oficyna Wydawniczo-Reklamowa VI-PART, 2003),179–181.

sitting awake, 319: Lucyna Filip, "auschwitz information," 61 Ausgabe, Juni 2003, Institut für Sozial und Wirtschaftsgeschichte, Johannes Kepler Universität Linz.

"place you somewhere", 320: Danuta Mosiewicz-Mikusowa, interview with Susan Eischeid, Zabrzeg, Poland, May 2005.

"EXCEPTIONALLY brave!", 320: Ibid.

underground movement, 320: Otwinowska/Drzal, *Zawołać Po Imienu,* 179–180.

"'you very much'", 320: Wicentowicz interview.

liberated in May, 320: Otwinowska/Drzal.

underground contacts, 320: IPN Wi; Schema Kontaktów, Rachwał Stanisława, ps."Zygmunt."

and degraded, 321: Stanisława Rachwałowa, "*Spotkanie z Marią Mandel,*" *Przegląd Lekarski,* Tom XLVII, Nr. 1, 1990, 187.

on any occasion, 321: Ibid.

looked at me, 321: Rachwałowa, 188.

common waiting, 321: Rachwałowa, 189

the last one, 323: Ibid.

when Stalin died, 323: Wicentowicz interview.

"to add 'color'", 323: Mosiewicz-Mikusowa interview.

"no martyrology!", 323: Wicentowicz interview.

fabrication of this story, 324: Ibid.

"That's the truth!", 324: Ibid.

"occupied and distracted", 324: Wysocka interview.

Chapter 99: Si non è vero

good story, 325: Górecka, letter to Susan Eischeid, January 18, 2007.
not have happened, 325: *Pani* Jadzia interview, 2005.
the "first time", 325: Wysocka interview.
"could shower together", 326: Danuta Wojnar Górecka, correspondence with Susan Eischeid, June 2006–May 2007.
"that is a supposition", 326: Ibid.
at the time, 326: Wysocka interview. See also Mieczyslaw Zajac, statement, "auschwitz information," 2003.
after it happened, 326: Wysocka interview, 2004.
passed Mandl's cell, 326: Górecka interview.
"You dirty commode!", 327: Mosiewicz-Mikusowa interview.
"a practicing Catholic", 327: Ibid.
"all women prisoners", 327: Ibid.
"on my behalf", 327: Ibid.
"YES!", 327: Ibid.

Chapter 100: Remorse

withdrew into herself, 328: Wysocka interview.
"[must have taken place]", 328: Cykowiak interview.
magnitude of the crime, 329: Sister Oberin Ortrudis Maier, letter to Susan Eischeid, August 19, 2006; interview with Susan Eischeid, May 2006, Kloster der Maria-Ward-Schwestern, Neuhaus am Inn, Germany.
"show remorse", 329: Ibid.
a "tough process", 329: Grotgen/Altman interview, June 25, 2003.

Chapter 101: Hanging, by Rope, Until Dead

would put the rope, 330: Kazimierz Piechowski, *Byłem Numerem* (*I Was a Number*) (Warsaw: 2004), 136.
in Warsaw, 330: IPN: Egzekujce zbrodniarzy hitlerowskich, Ludwig Fischer, Mokotów Prison, Warsaw, Poland. See also https://www.youtube.com/watch?v=k-oKNPaNMWI. See also Stanisław Kobiela, email to Susan Eischeid, May 14, 2018.
reassembled as needed, 331: Stanisław Kostka, interview with Susan Eischeid, Krakow, Poland, May 2004.
men can ejaculate, 331: Dr. Eugene LeBauer, MD, interview with Susan Eischeid, Greensboro, NC, July 2007.

"aware of either", 332: Townsend, *Mission at Nuremberg*, 256. Testimony of Lt. Stanley Tilles.

of the rope, 332: Mailänder, 198.

dies almost immediately, 332: LeBauer interview.

Chapter 102: Site of Execution

horrors to contemplate, 333: Górecka correspondence.

town from Montelupich, 333: "*Więzienie Krakow, ul. Senacka* 3," Montelupich "document" shared with Susan Eischeid, 2003.

had wronged them, 334: Dr. Tomasz Konopka, interview with Susan Eischeid, Krakow, Poland, May 2006.

not be the same, 334: Lidia Jurek, correspondence with Susan Eischeid, 2006–2007.

"For our children!", 334: Waldemar Kowalski, *Dwie Strony Krat* (Gdańsk, 2003), 130.

a public hanging, 334: Ibid., 131.

"and drove away", 334: Piotr Szubarczyk, Powróz na Szczęście..., Bulletyn IPN; 07.07.2003, 41-45; "Nowe informacje po latach," 44-45.

stop public executions, 334: Kowalski interview.

had subsided somewhat, 334: Szubarczyk interview.

"out of curiosity", 334: Górecka interview.

"cover their tracks", 335: Oremus interview.

courtyard of Montelupich, 335: Stanisław Kobiela, *Tajemnice Historii*, "The Trial and Execution of KL Auschwitz-Birkenau Crew in Cracow in 1947/1948" (/index.php/artykuly/Auschwitz/92-auschwitz9). See also email, Kobiela to Eischeid, May 14, 2018.

as "executioner", 335: Kostka interview, 2004.

"be a hanging", 335: Wysocka interview.

into people's eyes, 335: Oremus, Potoczny interviews.

Chapter 103: EGZEKUCJA

and cloudy sky, 336: Jagiellonian University Observatory, January 24, 1948, IMGW-PIB Krakow.

"7 Catholics", 336: Datebook, Father Marian Stark, Sobotá 24, Tymoteusza, Styczen, 1948. ZKM, Krakow, Poland, 20 May 2004.

"Alone in her cell", 336: *Pani* Jadzia interview.

"terrified and cried", 336: Stanisław Kobiela, *Tajemnice Historii*, "The Trial and Execution of KL Auschwitz-Birkenau Crew in Cracow in 1947/1948"

(/index.php/artykuly/Auschwitz/92-auschwitz9). See also interview with Susan Eischeid, Bochnia, Poland, 2004.
time had come, 337: Górecka, *Klementyna.*

Chapter 104: It Begins

and Maria Mandl, 338: Kobieła, *Tajemnice Historii.*
paralyzed with fear, 339: Kobieła, *Tajemnice Historii,* see also interview, 2004.
Father Stark, 339: ZE-ZB; Monte 223.
bodies were removed, 339: Ibid.

Chapter 105: The Death of Maria

to be hanged, 340: ZE-ZB: Monte 223.
multiple gallows, 340: Kobieła, *Tajemnice Historii.*
trapdoor was released, 340: Ibid.
"from your sins", 340: Ortrudis interview, 2006.
didn't gossip, 340: Wysocka interview.
she was struggling, 341: Ibid, quoting Hania the guard.
"didn't acknowledge it", 341: Ibid.
"hanged her", 341: Ibid.
"to learn Polish", 341: Górecka, correspondence.
in Auschwitz I, 341: Świebocka, *Auschwitz: A History in Photographs* (Bloomington: Indiana University Press, 1993), 127.
"'Long Live Poland!'", 341: Countess Carolina Lanckorońska, *Michelangelo in
Ravensbrück* (Cambridge: DaCapo Press, 2001), 207.

Chapter 106: Sentence Complete

served that day, 342: Górecka, *Klementyna.*

Chapter 107: Aftermath

did go themselves, 343: Wanda Półtawska, correspondence with Susan Eischeid, 2004.
Upper Austria, 343: ZE-ZB; Monte 223.
"with the paperwork", 343: Dr. Jerzy Ludwikowski, interview with Susan Eischeid, May 2004, Nowy Wisnicz, Poland.
bodies in formalin, 344: Ibid.
right leg, 344: Katarzyna Siwiec, Miczysław Czuma, Leszek Mazan, *Madame,
wkładamy dziecko z powrotem!* (Krakow: Anabasis, 2009), 445–446.

harlot from Brzezinka, 345: Kobieła, *Tajemnice Historii*. See also Katarzyna Ko-siorowska, "*Kociaki to masa roboty,*" *Gazeta Wyborca* (internet edition) June 17, 2012, http://www.wyborca.pl/duzyformat.

of the deceased, 346: Jerzy Ludwikowski, interview with Stanisław Kobiela, Nowy Wisnicz, Poland, May 3, 1955. See also Kobieła, *Tajemnice Historii* lekarza; *Wiadomości Bocheńskie* no. 4 (31) 1996; 11-13, 21-25.

have done so!, 346: Dr. Tomasz Konopka, interview with Susan Eischeid, Krakow, Poland, May 2006.

future doctors anatomy, 347: Ibid.

in the cemetery, 347: Ibid.

before execution, 347: *Pani* Jadzia interview.

"going to happen", 347: Konopka interview.

Chapter 108: Certificate of Death

December 31, , 348: Declaration of Death for Maria Mandl, District Court of Ried am Inn, 10 September 1975.

"of her death", 348: Ibid.

this death certificate, 348: "Aufregung um falsch Todesklärung für brutale Mörder in des SS," OÖNachrichten, March 10, 2017, http://www .nachrichten.at/.../Aufregung-um-falsch-Todesverklarung.

one of them, 348: *"Justiz hob Todeskla̋rung auf: Innviertlerin was kein Nazi-Opfer,"* *Salzburger Nachtrichten*, April 25, 2017, http://www.pressreader.com/ austria/salzburger.../Z8179280891508.

PART EIGHT

Chapter 109: The Accounting

was not evil, 351: Rudolf Höss, *Death Dealer: The Memoirs of the SS Kommandant at Auschwitz*, ed. Steven Paskuly, trans. Andrew Pollinger (New York: Prometheus, 1992), 186.

all decent people, 351: Ben Ferencz, "The Last Living Nuremberg Prosecutor Turns 100," *60 Minutes*, March 11, 2020.

not analysis, 351: Nils Christie, "Answers to Atrocities," paper presented at the 35th Biannual Congress of the International Institute of Sociology, Krakow, Poland, July 11−16 July 2001, 5.

throughout time, 352: James Waller, *Becoming Evil* (Oxford: Oxford University Press, 2002), vii and xii−xiii.

"off you went!", 352: Franz Ruhmanseder, interview with Susan Eischeid, Münz-
     kirchen, Austria, May 21, 2005.
with a happy ending, 352: Irmgard Hunt, *On Hitler's Mountain* (New York: Wil-
     liam Morrow, 2005), 185.
knew anything, 352: Alois Bauer and Roland Habermann, interview with Susan
     Eischeid, Münzkirchen, Austria, May 21, 2005.
"[the past] behind", 352: Mandl family, 2005.
"making these shoes", 353: Mandl family, 2006.
"and good Catholics", 353: Martin Zauner, interview with Susan Eischeid,
     Münzkirchen, Austria, May 25, 2005.
attended his funeral, 353: Mandl family, 2005.

Chapter 110: The Family

worrying and sorrow, 354: Mandl statement, 122.
empty envelopes, 354: Mandl family, 2005.
"person with secrets…", 354: Ruhmanseder interview, 2005.
how it all happened, 354: Mandl family.
"of the Nazi Party", 355: Zauner interview, 2005.
"gotten into this", 355: Mandl family.
about the notification, 355: Ibid.
Maria's death, 355: Ibid.

Chapter 111: The Father

an honorable man, 356: Richard Högl, telephone interview via Eva Riedler,
     St. Florian/Schärding, Austria, May 17, 2006.
her father's sake, 356: Burda interview, 2006.
letter to Franz Mandl, 356: Margit Burda, letter to Franz Mandl, December
     12, 1948.
loving, little father, 357: Ibid.
Maria's birthday, 357: Franz Mandl, letter to Margit Burda, January 10, 1949.
     (Translation by Eva Riedler and Elana Keppel Levy.)
severe test for a father, 357: Ibid.

Chapter 112: What Might Have Been

a terrible cost , 360: Fern Schumer Chapman, *Motherland* (New York: Viking
     Press, 2000), 157.
"both of our futures", 360: Margit Burda, letter to Susan Eischeid, March 26,
     2007.

"I can be happy", 361: Mandl statement, 98.

"That explains it", 361: Anita Lasker-Wallfisch, interview with Susan Eischeid, September 9, 2003.

"is it possible?", 361: Cykowiak interview, 2003.

"show courage from", 362: Gröning, *Lebenslauf,* 56.

"were so cruel", 362: Zofia Ciszek, interview with Susan Eischeid, Gdánsk, Poland, May 2005.

"every one of us", 362: Wanda Połtawska, letter to Susan Eischeid, June 18, 2004.

"can commit them", 362: Slavenka Drakulic, *They Would Never Hurt a Fly: War Criminals in The Hague* (New York: Penguin Books, 2005), 190–191.

Bibliography

ARCHIVES

Austria

Dokumentationsarchiv des Österreichischen Widerstandes, Wien
Gemeindeamt Münzkirchen
Österreichische Nationalbibliotek, Wien

England

Imperial War Museum, London

Germany

Archiv Gedenstätte, Buchenwald
Archiv Mahn-und Gedenkstätte Ravensbrück
Archiv Museum Schloss Lichtenburg, Prettin
Bundesarchiv Berlin, Bundesarchiv Berlin—Lichterfelde
Kloster der Maria Ward Schwestern, Archiv, Neuhaus am Inn
Siemens AG, company archives, München
Zentralle Stelle der Landesjustizverwaltungen, Ludwigsburg

Israel

Yad Vashem

Poland

Archivum Państwowego Muzeum w Oświęcimiu
Instytut Ekspertyz Sądowych, im Prof. Jana Sehna w Krakowie
Instytut Pamieci Narodowej, Gdańsk

Instytut Pamieci Narodowej, Warszawa
Instytut Pamieci Narodowej, Wieliczka
Kancelaria Adwokacka Archive, Krakow, Szczecin
Katedra Kryminologii—Uniwersytet Jagielloński Kraków
Montelupich Prison archives, Krakow
Narodowe Archivum Cyfrowe, Warszawa
Państowy Instytut Sztuki Filmowej, Warszawa
Państwowe Muzeum Stutthof w Sztutowie, Sztutowo
Polskie Towarzystwo Kryminologiczne im. Prof. Stanisława Batawii, Warszawa
Rakowicki Cemetery records, Krakow
Ze Zbiorów Archivum, Państwowe w Krakowie
Zgromadzenia Księży Misjonarzy, Krakow

United States

National Archives and Records Administration
National Personnel Records, Center Archive, U.S. Military, St. Louis
The Shoah Foundation, USC
United States Holocaust Memorial Museum
U.S. Department of Justice, Office of Special Investigations, Criminal Division, Washington, DC

SOURCES

Adlington, Lucy. *The Dressmakers of Auschwitz*. New York: Harper, 2021.

Amesberger, Helga, and Brigitte Halbmayr. *Vom Leben und Überleben—Wege nach Ravensbrück*. Band I & II. Wien: Promedia, 2001.

Arendt, Hannah. *Eichmann in Jerusalem—A Report on the Banality of Evil*. New York: Penguin Classics, 1976.

Berger, Karin, and Elisabeth Holzinger, Lotte Podgornik, Lisbeth Trallori (Hersg.). *Ich geb Dir einen Mantel, daß Du ihn noch in Freiheit tragen kannst. Widerstehen im KZ Österreichische Frauen erzählen*. Wien: ProMedia Edition Spuren, 1987.

Bławut, Jacek. *"Tödliche Romanze": An Auschwitz Love Story*. Film documentary, 1989.

Broad, Pery. *KL Auschwitz Seen by the SS: Rudolf Höss, Pery Broad, Johann Paul Kramer*. (Krystyna Michalik, trans.) Oświęcim: Auschwitz-Birkenau State Museum, 1972.

Bromberger, Barbara, Hanna Elling, Jutta von Freyberg, Ursula Krause-Schmitt. *Schwestern vergeßt uns nicht*. Frankfurt: VAS Verl. Akad. Schriften, 1988.

Brown, Daniel Patrick. *The Beautiful Beast.* Ventura: Golden West Historical Publications, 1996.

Brown, Daniel Patrick. *The Camp Women.* Atglen: Schiffer Military History, 2002.

Browning, Christopher. *Ordinary Men: Reserve Police Battalion 101 and the Final Solution in Poland.* New York: Harper Collins, 1998.

Buber-Neumann, Margarete. *Die erloschene Flamme.* Frankfurt: Langen Müller, 1991.

Buber-Neumann, Margarete. *Under Two Dictators: Prisoner of Stalin and Hitler.* Great Britain: Random House Group Ltd., 2008.

Bujak, Adam. *Auschwitz: The Residence of Death.* Bialy Kruk: Auschwitz-Birkenau State Museum, 2007.

Bukey, Evan Burr. *Hitler's Austria.* Chapel Hill: University of North Carolina Press, 2000.

Busch, Christophe, and Stefan Hördler, Robert Jan Van Pelt. *Das Höcker-Album: Auschwitz durch die Linse der SS.* Darmstadt, Germany: Philipp von Zabern Verlag, 2013.

Cebo, Lechosław. *Więźniarki w obozie hitlerowskim w Oświęcimiu Brzezince.* Katowice: Uniwersylei Slqski, 1984.

Central Commission for the Investigation of German Crimes in Poland 1946–1947. *German Crimes in Poland.* Vols. 1–3. New York: Howard Fertig, 1982.

Chapman, Fern Schumer. *Motherland.* New York: Viking Press, 2000.

Cherish, Barbara. *The Auschwitz Kommandant.* Gloucestershire: The History Press, 2009.

Christie, Nils. "Answers to Atrocities." Paper presented at the 35th Biannual Congress of the International Institute of Sociology, Krakow, Poland, July 11–16, 2001.

Cyprien, Tadeusz. *Nazi Rule in Poland, 1939–1945.* Warsaw: Polonia, 1961.

Cyprien, Tadeusz, and Jerzy Sawicki. *Sledem Procesów, Przed Najwyższym Trybunałem Narodowym.* Poznan: Instytut Zachodni, 1962.

Czech, Danuta. *Auschwitz Chronicle 1939–1945.* London: I.B. Tauris & Co., Ltd., 1990.

Daëron, Michael. *Bach in Auschwitz* (film documentary). New York: Winstar TV and Video, 2000.

Dietrich, Werner. *Konzentrationslager Lichtenburg.* Leipzig: MEDIEN PROFIS, 2002.

Drakulic, Slavenka. *They Would Never Hurt a Fly: War Criminals on Trial in The Hague.* New York: Penguin Books, 2005.

Drobisch, Karl. *Konzentrationslager Im Schloss Lichtenburg.* Cottbus: Kommission zur Erforschung der Geschichte de örtlichen Arbeiter, 1987.

Dunlop, Nic. *The Lost Executioner: A Journey to the Heart of the Killing Fields.* New York: Walker & Company, 2005.

Egger, Günther, and Elke. *Der Landkreis Mühldorf a. Inn in Nationalsozialismus.* Berlin: Rhombos Verlag, 2001.

Eischeid, Susan. *The Truth About Fania Fénelon and the Women's Orchestra of Auschwitz-Birkenau.* Switzerland: Springer Publishing, Palgrave MacMillan, 2016.

Elshtain, Jean Bethke. *Women and War.* New York: Basic Books, Inc., 1987.

Erpel, Simone. *"Einführung."* Im Gefolge der SS: Aufseherinnen des Frauen-Konzentrationslager Ravensbrück. Berlin: Metropol Verlag, 2007.

Fechner, Eberhard. *Der Prozess: Eine Darstellung des Majdanek-Verfahrens in Düsseldorf.* Norddeutscher Rundfunk: videotape (1984), part 2.

Filip, Lucyna. "auschwitz information," 61 Ausgabe, Juni 2003. Institut für Sozial und Wirtschaftsgeschichte, Johannes Kepler Universität Linz.

Finder, Gabriel, and Alexander Prusin. *Justice Behind the Iron Curtain—Nazis on Trial in Communist Poland.* Toronto: University of Toronto Press, 2018.

Franken, Inge. *Gegen das Vergessen.* "Memories, 2003" by Schulamith Khalef. Berlin: Text Verlag, 2005.

Frankfurter, Bernhard, ed. *The Meeting.* New York: Syracuse University Press, 2000.

Freyberg, Jutta von, and Ursula Krause-Schmitt. *Moringen-Lichtenburg-Ravensbrück, Frauen im Konzentrationslager 1933–1945.* Frankfurt: VAS, 1997.

Füllberg-Stolberg et al., eds. *Frauen in Konzentrationslagern: Bergen-Belsen und Ravensbrück.*—Bremen: Edition Temmen, 1994.

Gańczak, Filip. *Jan Sehn.* Wołowiec: wydawnictwo zarne, 2020.

Geyer, Matthias. "The Bookkeeper from Auschwitz: An SS Officer Remembers (2)." *SPIEGEL* Online 19 / 2005, 4. http://service.spiegel.de/cache/international/spiegel/0,1518,355188-2,000.html

Gluck, Gemma LaGuardia. *My Story.* New York: David McKay Company Inc., 1961.

Goodman, Roger. *The First German War Crimes Trial, Vol. 1.* Salisbury, NC: Documentary Publications, 1947.

Gordey, Michael. "Echoes From Auschwitz." *New Republic,* December 22, 1947.

Górecka, Danuta Wojnar. *Klementyna: Więzienne wspomnienia z procesu WiN-u.* Krakow: Księgarnia Akademicka, 1997.

Greene, Joshua M. *Justice at Dachau.* New York: Broadway Books, 2003.

Gröning, Oskar. *Ein Lebenslauf. Dreißig Lebens-und Erlebensjahre Von 1921 bis 1951.* Schnerverdingen, Germany: October 31, 1996.

Gröning, Oskar. "Corruption." *Auschwitz: Inside the Nazi State,* Episode 4, BBC. https://www.pbs.org/auschwitz/about/transcripts_4.html

Gutman, Israel, ed. *Encyclopedia of the Holocaust.* New York: Macmillan Publishers, 1990.

Haag, Lina. *Ein Handvoll Staub.* Frankfurt am Main: Fischer Taschenbuch Verlag, 1995.

Haag, Lina. *How Long the Night.* London: Victor Gallancz Ltd., 1948.

Halow, Joseph. *Innocent at Dachau.* CA: Institute for Historical Review, 1993.

Hammermann, Gabriele. "*Die Dachauer Außenlager um Mühldorf.*" *Dachauer Hefte*, Jahrgang 1999, Heft 15 (November 1999).

Harris, Whitney R. *Tyranny on Trial.* Dallas: Southern Methodist University Press, 1999.

Haste, Cate. *Nazi Women.* London: Macmillan Chanel 4 Books, 2001.

Hatzfeld, Jean. *Machete Season: The Killers in Rwanda Speak.* United Kingdom: Picador Press, 2006.

Heberer, Patricia, and Jürgen Matthäus. *Atrocities on Trial: Historical Perspectives on the Politics of Prosecuting War Crimes.* University of Nebraska Press, 2008.

Heike, Irmtraud, and Andreas Pflock. "*Geregelte Strafen, willkürliche Gewalt und Massensterben.*" *Frauen in Konzentrationslagern: Bergen-Belsen und Ravensbrück.* Füllberg-Stolberg et al, eds. Bremen: Edition Temmen, 1994.

Heineman, Elizabeth D. *What Difference Does a Husband Make?* Berkeley: University of California Press, 1999.

Helm, Sarah. *Ravensbrück.* New York: Doubleday, 2014.

Hesse, Hans, and Jürgen Harder. "*Und wenn ich lebenslang in einem KZ bleiben Müßte…*" *Die Zeuginnen Jehovas in den Frauenknozentrationslagern Moringen, Lichtenburg und Ravensbrück.* Germany: Klartext-Verlagsges, 2001.

Heubner, Christoph, Alwin Meyer, Jürgen Pieplow. *Gesehen in Auschwitz.* West Berlin: Lebenszeichen, 1987.

Hilberg, Raul. *The Destruction of the European Jews.* Vol. 3. New York: Holmes & Meier, 1985.

Höss, Rainer. *Das Erbe des Kommandanton.* Germany: Belleville Press, 2013.

Höss, Rudolf. *Death Dealer, The Memoirs of the SS Kommandant at Auschwitz.* Steven Paskuly, ed. (Andrew Pollinger, trans.) Buffalo: Prometheus Books, 1992. See also 17th edition, in German, Munich, 2000.

Hunt, Irmgard. *On Hitler's Mountain.* New York: Harper Collins, 2005.

Knapp, Gabriele. "*Befohlene Musik,*" *Musik und Musikmißbrauch im Frauenlager von Auschwitz-Birkenau. Acta musicological*, Vol. 68, No. 2, July-December 1996.

Knausgaard, Karl Ove. "The Inexplicable. Inside the Mind of a Mass Killer." May 25, 2015, Letter from Norway, *New Yorker.* https://www.newyorker.com/magazine/2015/05/25/the-inexplicabl

Kobiela, Stanisław. "Egzekucja." Marii Mandel—Part XIII. Bochnia, Poland; 2004.

Kobiela, Stanisław. "*Ekstradycja do Polski.*" *Marii Mandel –Part V.* Bochnia, Poland: 2004.

Kobiela, Stanisław. "*Irma Grese i Maria Mandel.*" *WSTĘP, IV.* Bochnia, Poland: 2004.

Kobiela, Stanisław. "*Oględziny rzeczy Marii Mandel.*" *Śledztwo.* Bochnia, Poland: 2004.

Kobiela, Stanisław. "Przemówienia oskarżyciela, obrońców i ostatnie słowo Marii Mandl." Part X. Bochnia, Poland; 2004.

Kobiela, Stanisław. "The Trial and Execution of KL Auschwitz-Birkenau Crew in Cracow in 1947/1948." *Tajemnice Historii.* http://index.php/artykuly/Auschwitz/92-auschwitz9

Kobiela, Stanisław. "*Więzienie Zbrodni Wojennych w Dachau.*" *WSTĘP, IV.* Bochnia, Poland: 2004.

Koren, Yehuda, and Eilat Negev. *In Our Hearts We Were Giants.* New York: Carroll & Graff Publishers, 2004.

Kotarba, Ryszard. "*Okręgowa Komisja Badania Zbrodni Hitlerowskich w Krakowie 1945–1953.*" *Studia Historyczne / Polska Akademia.* Nauk, 2003, s. 66–74.

Kowalski, Waldemar. *Dwie Strony Krat.* Gdańsk, 2003.

Laks, Szymon. *Music of Another World.* Evanston: Northwestern University Press, 1989.

Lanckorońska, Countess Karolina. *Michelangelo in Ravensbrück.* (Noel Clark, trans.) Cambridge: DaCapo Press, 2007.

Langbein, Hermann. *Der Auschwitz-Prozeß, Eine Dokumentation, Band 1.* Frankfurt/Main: Verlag Neue Kritik KG, 1995.

Langbein, Hermann. *People in Auschwitz.* (Harry Zohn, trans.) Chapel Hill: University of North Carolina Press, 2004.

Lasik, Aleksander. "The Auschwitz Garrison; Women in the SS." *Auschwitz 1940–1945,* Vol. 1. Oświęcim: Auschwitz-Birkenau State Museum, 2000.

Lasker-Wallfisch, Anita. *Inherit the Truth.* New York: St. Martin's Press, 1996.

Lauer, Walter. *Battle Babies, the Story of the 99th Infantry Division in World War II.* Battery Press, 1985.

Lengyel, Olga. *Five Chimneys.* New York: Howard Fertig, 1983.

Lingens-Reiner, Ella. *Prisoners of Fear.* London: Victor Gollancz Ltd., 1948.

Loewy, Hanno. "*Die Mutter aller Holocaust-Filme?*" Erpel, Simone. *Im Gefolge der SS: Aufseherinnen des Frauen-Konzentrationslager Ravensbrück.* Berlin: Metropol Verlag, 2007.

Lord Russell of Liverpool. *Scourge of the Swastika.* Cornwall: Greenhill Books, 2002.

Lower, Wendy. *Hitler's Furies: German Women in the Nazi Killing Fields.* Boston: Houghton Mifflin Harcourt, 2013.

Lukowski, Jerzy. *Bibliografia obozu Koncentracyjuego Oświęcim-Brzezinka 1945–1965. Część II: Procesy Zbrodniarzy Hitlerowskien-czionków administracji I zalogi: zbrojnej obozu.* Warszawa: 1968.

Macadam, Heather Dune. *999—The Extraordinary Young Women of the First Official Jewish Transport to Auschwitz.* New York: Citadel Press, 2020.

Mailänder, Elissa. *Female SS Guards and Workaday Violence.* East Lansing: Michigan State University Press, 2015.

Marcuse, Harold. *Legacies of Dachau.* United Kingdom: Cambridge University Press, 2001.

Marwell, David G. *Mengele. Unmasking the Angel of Death*. New York: W.W. Norton & Company, 2020.

Matthäus, Jürgen. *Approaching an Auschwitz Survivor*. Oxford: Oxford University Press, 2009.

McFarland-Icke, Bronwyn Rebekah. *Nurses in Nazi Germany—Moral Choices in History*. New Jersey: Princeton University Press, 1999.

McLean, French. *The Camp Men*. Atglen, PA: Schiffer Pub. Ltd., 1999.

Morrison, Jack G. *Ravensbrück*. Princeton: Markus Wiener Publishers, 2000.

Müller, Monika. *"Die Oberaufseherinnen des Frauen Konzentrationslagers Ravensbrück." Magisterarbeit*. Brandenburg: Brandenburgische Ravensbrück, Gedenkstätten Sachsenhausen, Sammlungen, 2002.

Müller-Münch, Ingrid. *Die Frauen von Majdanek*. Hamburg: Rowohlt Taschenbuch Verlag, 1982.

Nagorski, Andrew. *The Nazi Hunters*. New York: Simon & Schuster, 2016.

Naumann, Bernd. *Auschwitz*. New York: Frederick A. Praeger, 1966.

Neu, Emilie. *"Zu Gott kann man Heil! Sagen, aber nicht zu Hitler." Die Frauen von Ravensbrück*. Germany: Verlag Kunstmann Antje, 2005.

Newman, Richard, with Karen Kirtley. *Alma Rosé: Vienna to Auschwitz*. Portland: Amadeus Press, 2000.

Niewyk, Donald. *Fresh Wounds: Early Narratives of Holocaust Survival*. Chapel Hill: University of North Carolina Press, 1998.

Niwińska, Helena Dunicz. *One of the Girls in the Band*. Oświęcim: Auschwitz-Birkenau State Museum, 2014.

Olewski, Rachela Zelmanowicz. *Crying Is Forbidden Here*. Tel-Aviv: Olewski Family, 2009.

Otwinowska, Barbara, and Teresa Drzal. *Zawołać Po Imienu*. Tom. II. Pruszków: Oficyna Wydawniczo-Reklamowa VIPART, 2003.

Owings, Alison. *Frauen: German Women Recall the Third Reich*. New Brunswick: Rutgers University Press, 1999.

Perl, Gisella. *I Was a Doctor in Auschwitz*. New Hampshire: Ayer Co., Publishers Inc., 1948.

Piechowski, Kazimierz. *Byłem numerem*. Warsaw, 2004.

Plewe, Reinhard, and Köhler, Jan Thomas. *Baugeschichte Frauen-Konzentrationslager Ravensbrück*. Berlin: Edition Hentrich, 2000.

Poe, Edgar Allan. "The Raven." *Complete Tales and Poems*. New Jersey: Castle Books, 1985.

Pollack, Martin. *The Dead Man in the Bunker*. (Will Hobson, trans.) London: Faber & Faber, 2004.

Półtawska, Wanda. *And I Am Afraid of My Dreams*. (Mary Craig, trans.) New York: Hippocrene Books, 1964.

Rachwałowa, Stanisława. "*Spotkanie z MariąMandel.*" *Przegląd Lekarski.* Tom. XLVII, Nr. 1 (1990).

Raim, Edith. *Die Dachauer KZ-Aussenkommandos Kaufering und Mühldorf.* Landsberg a Lech: 1992.

"Ravensbrück." United States Holocaust Memorial Museum. https://encyclopedia.ushmm.org/content/en/article/ravensbrueck.html (accessed May 15, 2019)

Reynaud, Michel, and Graffard, Sylvie. *The Jehovah's Witnesses and the Nazis.* New York: Cooper Square Press, 2001.

Roth, Paul A. "Hearts of Darkness: 'Perpetrator History' and Why There Is No Why." *History of the Human Sciences,* Vol. 17, Nos. 2/3. London: SAGE Publications, 2004.

Rückerl, Adalbert. *The Investigation of Nazi Crimes 1945–1978.* Karlsruhe: C.F. Müller, 1979.

Saidel, Rochelle. *The Jewish Women of Ravensbrück Concentration Camp.* Madison: University of Wisconsin Press, 2004.

Schäfer, Silke. "*Zum Selbstverständis von Frauen im Konzentrationslager: Das Lager Ravensbrück.*" Dissertation D83. Berlin: Technischen Universität, 2002.

Schneider, Helga. *Let Me Go.* New York: Walker and Company, 2001.

Shelley, Lore. *Auschwitz—The Nazi Civilization.* University Press of America, 1992.

Shelley, Lore. *Secretaries of Death.* New York: Shengold Publishers, 1986.

Sichelschmidt, Lorenz. *Mala.* Bremen: Donat Verlag, 1995.

Siwiec, Katarzyna, Miczysław Czuma, and Leszek Mazan. *Madame, wkładamy dziecko z powrotem!* Krakow: Anabasis, 2009.

Solzhenitsyn, Aleksandr. *The Gulag Archipelago 1918–1956.* New York: Harper & Row Publishers, 1973.

Spielberg, Steven. Film & Video Archive, USHMM. "In Prison for Defendants: Landsberg Hangings." Accession #1994.119.1; RG-60.2336; Film ID 896.

Spitz, Vivien. *Doctors from Hell.* Boulder: Sentient Publications, 147.

Stoppelman, Nettie. Testimony. *Law Reports of Trials of War Criminals, Vol. II. The Belsen Trial.* London: The United Nations War Crimes Commission, 1947.

Strasser, Christian, and David Neumayr. *Pechmarie* (film documentary). Austria: Nemada Film Production, 2014.

Sturm, Hanna. *Die Lebensgeschichte einer Arbeiterin: Vom Burgenland nach Ravensbrück.* Vienna: Verlag für Gesellschaftskritik, 1982.

Świebocki, Henryk. "Gathering and Disseminating Evidence of the Crimes." *Auschwitz 1940–1945, Vol. IV.* Oświęcim: Auschwitz-Birkenau State Museum, 2000.

Świebocka, Teresa, comp. and ed. *Auschwitz: A History in Photographs*. Bloomington: Indiana University Press, 1993.

Szmaglewska, Seweryna. *Smoke Over Birkenau*. (trans. Jadwiga Rynas) Warszawa: Ksiązka I Wiedza, 2001.

Taake, Claudia. *Angeklagt: SS Frauen vor Gericht*. Oldenburg: BIS Bibliotheks-und Informationssystem der Universität Oldenburg, 1998.

Ten Boom, Corrie. *The Hiding Place*. New Jersey: Bantam Books, 1971.

Thomas, Laurence. "Forgiving the Unforgiveable," in *Moral Philosophy and the Holocaust*, ed. Eve Garrard and Geoffrey Scarre. England: Ashgate Publishing Company, 2003, 201–230.

Tilghman, Andrew. "Encountering Steven Green." Outlook, *Washington Post*, July 30, 2006, B1.

Tillion, Germain. *Frauenkonzentrationslager Ravensbrück*. Frankfurt: Deutsche Ausgabe, 2001, French original edition, Paris: 1973 and 1988.

Tillion, Germaine. *Ravensbrück*. (trans. Gerald Satterwaite) Garden City: Doubleday, 1975.

Timm, Uwe. *In My Brother's Shadow: a Life and Death in the SS*. New York: Farrar, Straus & Giroux, 2003.

Toussaint, Jeanette. *"Nach Dienstschluss." Im Gefolge der SS: Aufseherinnen des Frauen-Konzentrationslager Ravensbrück*. (Hrsg. Simone Erpel) Berlin: Metropol Verlag, 2007.

Toussaint, Jeanette. *"Tradierung von Entlastungslegenden."* (Hrsg. Simone Erpel) Berlin: Metropol Verlag, 2007.

Townsend, Tim. *Mission at Nuremberg*. New York: William Morrow Publishers, 2014.

Tutorow, Norman E. *War Crimes, War Criminals, and War Crime Trials*. New York: Greenwood Press, 1986.

Větrovcová, Margot. *ČTYŘI ROKY. "Bojovali jsme a zvitězili 1938–1945."* Praha: Svoboda Publishing House, 1979.

Waller, James. *Becoming Evil*. Oxford: Oxford University Press, 2002.

Walz, Loretta. *"Und dann kommst du dahin an einem schönen Sommertag." Die Frauen von Ravensbrück*. Germany: Verlag Kunstmann Antje, 2005.

Wańkowicz, Melchior. *Karafka La Fontaine'a, Vol. II*. Krakow: Wydawnictwo Literackie, 1981.

Wińska, Urszula. *"Wspomnienia i myśli związane z oberaufseherin Maria Mandl."* Sopot, Poland.

Wińska, Urszula. *Zwyciężyły wartości: wspomnienia z Ravensbrück*. Gdańsk: Wydawn Morskie: 1985.

Wozniakowna, Michalina. *Obóz Koncentracyjny Dla Kobiet Ravensbück*. Poznan: Nakładem Zwiazku B. Wiezniow Politycznych w Poznaniu, 1946.

Index